The British Moralists on Human Nature
and the Birth of Secular Ethics

MICHAEL B. GILL

University of Arizona

CAMBRIDGE UNIVERSITY PRESS
Cambridge, New York, Melbourne, Madrid, Cape Town, Singapore, São Paulo

Cambridge University Press
32 Avenue of the Americas, New York, NY 10013-2473, USA

www.cambridge.org
Information on this title: www.cambridge.org/9780521852463

First published 2006

Printed in the United States of America

A catalog record for this publication is available from the British Library.

Library of Congress Cataloging in Publication Data
Gill, Michael B.
The British moralists on human nature and the birth of secular ethics /
Michael B. Gill.
    p.   cm.
Includes bibliographical references and index.
ISBN 0-521-85246-3 (hardback)
1. Ethics, Modern – 17th century.   2. Ethics – Great Britian – History –
17th century.   3. Ethics, Modern – 18th century.   4. Ethics – Great Britian –
History – 18th century.   I. Title.
        BJ602.G55   2006
    170.941 – dc22   2005031228

ISBN-13 978-0-521-85246-3 hardback
ISBN-10 0-521-85246-3 hardback

For Sarah Louise Megan Griffiths
With love, admiration, and gratitude

Contents

vii

Contents

Introduction

Are human beings naturally good or evil? Are we naturally drawn to virtue or to vice? Is it natural for us to do the right thing, or must we resist something in our nature in order to do what is right? Call this the Human Nature Question.

Most of us have asked the Human Nature Question at one time or another. Sometimes it's other people's behavior that prompts us to ask it. Sometimes it's our own.

We may ask the Question when we hear of monstrous acts – of torture, genocide, slaughter. How could people do such things to each other? Is such behavior rooted in something natural to human beings, or is it a perversion of what we naturally are? We may ask the Question when we hear of acts of great generosity and self-sacrifice. Are people who do such things shining examples of the basic goodness of human beings, or can their acts be explained by factors less flattering to humanity? We may ask the Question when we scrutinize our own relatively normal conduct and motivation. What leads us to act in the ways we do? Is it something we should be proud of or something that is not at all to our credit?

Our answer to the Question will greatly influence our view of ourselves and others, and it can play a leading role in our conception of morality, of what it means to live as we ought. It should come as no surprise, therefore, to find that responses to the Question have been central to accounts of morality and human nature throughout the ages, from ancient Greek moral philosophy to medieval Christian theology to modern European political theory to contemporary sociobiology.

In this study, I examine how the Human Nature Question shaped moral thought in Great Britain in the seventeenth and eighteenth centuries. In Part One, I describe the Negative Answer (i.e., human nature is basically evil) of the English Calvinists and the Positive Answer (i.e., human nature is basically good) of the Cambridge Platonists. In Part Two, I explore the Positive Answer of the third Earl of Shaftesbury. In Part Three, I explore the

Positive Answer of Francis Hutcheson. And in Part Four, I explain how David
Hume undermined the Question and thus cleared the way for a "science"
of morality and human nature "built on a foundation almost entirely new"
(THN Introduction 6).

By focusing on the Human Nature Question, I believe, we will gain a particularly clear view of some of the most important features of the changing
philosophical landscape of the early modern period. Such a focus will elucidate the rise of religious liberty and the increased use of empirical observation in accounts of morality and human nature. It will reveal a Copernican
Revolution in moral philosophy, a shift from thinking of morality as a standard against which human nature as a whole can be measured to thinking
of morality as itself a part of human nature.

And, perhaps most significantly, it will help explain the birth of modern
secular ethics – of ethical thought that is entirely independent of religious
and theological commitment. In 1600, almost all English-speaking moral
philosophy was completely embedded in a Christian framework. But by
1700, some philosophers had begun to develop moral positions that, while
still fundamentally theistic, lacked any distinctively Christian elements. And
by 1750, still other philosophers had begun to advance accounts of morality
that were disengaged not only from Christianity but also from belief in God.
This transition was one of the most momentous in the history of European
ideas, and an explanation of how it occurred will uncover the roots of contemporary secular positions on the origins of morality as well as the roots of
some of the deepest worries about those positions.

I should make it clear, however, that this study does not constitute anything like a comprehensive map of the entire territory of early modern moral
philosophy. My goal is to chart a path that allows for a detailed examination
of some of the most significant landmarks of ethical thought in the seventeenth and eighteenth centuries. But there are other landmarks, equally
significant, that this path does not offer a close view of. So while I say a lot
about the Cambridge Platonists, Shaftesbury, Hutcheson, and Hume, I say
relatively little about other philosophers – Hobbes, Locke, Clarke, Bayle,
Toland, Butler (the list is very incomplete) – who were just as important.[1]
I have done this because I think the works I do discuss form an illustratively
coherent story line, and I did not think I could do an adequate job of also
handling those other works within the confines of a single book.[2]

Discussion of primary, historical sources occupies almost all of my main
text. There are many valuable secondary sources on this material, but I have
placed my discussion of them in the endnotes. I followed this procedure not
because I think the recent scholarship unworthwhile but because I found
it difficult to include discussion of it in the main text and still present a
readable version of the philosophical story I was trying to tell.

Some of the chapters are descendants of previously published articles of
mine. Parts of Chapters 1 and 5 derive from "The Religious Rationalism of

Benjamin Whichcote," *Journal of the History of Philosophy* 27 (1999): 271–300. Parts of Chapter 4 derive from "Rationalism, Sentimentalism, and Ralph Cudworth," *Hume Studies* 30 (2004): 149–82. Parts of Chapter 9 derive from "Shaftesbury's Two Accounts of the Reason to Be Virtuous," *Journal of the History of Philosophy* 38 (2000): 529–48. Parts of Chapter 14 derive from "Nature and Association in the Moral Theory of Francis Hutcheson," *History of Philosophy Quarterly* 12 (1995): 281–301. Parts of Chapter 15 derive from "A Philosopher in His Closet: Reflexivity and Justification in Hume's Moral Theory," *Canadian Journal of Philosophy* 26 (1996): 231–56. Parts of Chapter 17 derive from "Fantastick Associations and Addictive General Rules: A Fundamental Difference between Hume and Hutcheson," *Hume Studies* 22 (1996): 23–48. And parts of chapter 18 derive from "Hume's Progressive View of Human Nature," *Hume Studies* 26 (2000): 529–48.

A great many people have helped me in the course of writing this book. While I was at the University of North Carolina I received invaluable help from Simon Blackburn, Thomas Hill, Gerald Postema, and Geoffrey Sayre-McCord. While I was at Purdue University: Jan Cover and Manfred Kuehn. While I was at the College of Charleston: Deborah Boyle and Shaun Nichols. And while I was at the University of Arizona: Julia Annas, David Chalmers, Tom Christiano, Jenann Ismael, David Owen, David Schmidtz, and Houston Smit. I have also greatly benefited from the comments of: Kate Abramson, Donald Ainslie, Charlotte Brown, Rachel Cohon, David Como, John Corvino, Stephen Darwall, Cliff Doerksen, Don Garrett, Sandeep Kaushik, Chris Lydgate, David Fate Norton, Elizabeth Radcliffe, Marty Smith, Jacqueline Taylor, Doremy Tong, and Kenneth Winkler. Annette Baier, Stephen Darwall, Manfred Kuehn, and Shaun Nichols read earlier versions of the manuscript, and I am profoundly grateful for the time and energy they so generously bestowed on my work.

The thanks I owe to my wife Sarah, my daughter Hannah, and my son Jesse are more than I know how to express. You all have my deepest love.

PART ONE

WHICHCOTE AND CUDWORTH

1

The Negative Answer of English Calvinism

Ralph Cudworth was born in 1617 in Somerset, England. His father, also named Ralph, was "a man of genius and learning" who was rector of the parish and chaplain to the king (Birch vii). Most importantly for our purposes, the elder Cudworth was a devout Calvinist. Describing the Calvinism of Cudworth's father is the goal of this chapter.[1]

A defining feature of the English Calvinism the elder Cudworth preached and practiced was an ardent belief in the sinfulness of all humans. According to this Calvinist view, humans had originally been created pure and good but through original sin had fallen to the depths of degradation. As a result, each and every human is now corrupt through and through. The corruption of the Fall, moreover, was so complete, afflicting as it did all of our faculties, that we now lack even the ability to do anything to improve our degenerate state. Human sinfulness is inherent and ineradicable. All people deserve eternal damnation in hell. And when the elder Cudworth spoke of hell, he would have done so in vivid and horrifying terms – as an actual place of the most extreme, never-ending torment.

The English Calvinists did not believe that everyone would go to hell. They thought that God had predetermined that some few people – the elect – would be saved. But the vast majority would be damned. And, crucially, even the elect did not *deserve* salvation. They just happened to be lucky enough to win, as though in a lottery, God's undeserved grace. Sin suffused the soul of the elect and reprobate alike.

The elder Cudworth's belief in the inherent and ineradicable sinfulness of humanity constitutes a perfectly clear Negative Answer to the Human Nature Question. All human beings, on this Calvinist view, are ineluctably drawn toward evil, wickedness, and vice. So to the question of whether humans are basically good, the elder Cudworth and his Calvinist fellows would have responded with a resounding No.

To grasp fully the depth and intensity of this Negative Answer, we need to go beyond a bare statement of its propositional content. We need to

7

appreciate how the belief in inherent and ineradicable sin would have saturated the daily lives of English Calvinist families, creating in children such
as young Ralph Cudworth an intimate and constant awareness of their own
corruption.

We can sketch a picture of how the Negative Answer would have colored
Cudworth's upbringing by looking to the writings of William Perkins, the
most influential Calvinist thinker in England at the beginning of the seventeenth century. Cudworth's father was a close follower of Perkins, editing
a number of his works and publishing a supplement to one of his biblical
commentaries, and Perkins handpicked the elder Cudworth to be his suc-
cessor as minister of St. Andrews' Church in Cambridge. It seems safe to
assume, therefore, that young Ralph Cudworth would have grown up in a
household governed by the principles Perkins espoused.

A work of Perkins that offers a clear view of how Calvinist principles
would have been instilled in a seventeenth-century English household is his
catechism, "Foundation of Christian Religion Gathered into Six Principles,"
which young children such as Ralph would have been made to memorize and
recite. The catechism begins with the question "What doest thou believe concerning God?", to which the child responds, innocuously enough, "There is
one God, creator and governor of all things, distinguished into the Father,
the Son and the Holy Ghost" (Perkins 146). Immediately after that innocuous exchange, however, the Negative Answer, in full Calvinist armor, comes
charging onto the scene. For the second question is "What doest thou believe
concerning man and concerning thine own self?" And to this the child must
answer, "All men are wholly corrupted with sin through Adam's fall and
so are become slaves of Satan and guilty of eternal damnation" (Perkins
146). The child is then made to elaborate on the complete corruption of
his soul, explaining that he "is by nature dead in sin as a loathsome carrion,
or as a dead corpse [that] lieth rotting and stinking in the grave, having
in him the seed of all sins" (Perkins 150). Corruption and sin, the child
must continue, is in "every part of both body and soul, like as a leprosy
that runneth from the crown of the head to the sole of the foot" (Perkins
151). And just in case the message has still not gotten through, the child is
then made to show "how every part is corrupted with sin" by repeating the
following:

First, in the mind there is nothing but ignorance and blindness concerning heavenly
matters. Secondly, the conscience is defiled, being always either benumbed with sin,
or else turmoiled with inward accusations and terrors. Thirdly, the will of man only
willeth and lusteth after evil. Fourthly, the affections of the heart, as love, joy, hope,
desire, etc., are moved and stirred to that which is evil to embrace it, and they are
never stirred unto that which is good unless it be to eschew it. Lastly, the members of
the body are the instruments and tools of the mind for the execution of sin. (Perkins
151)

But the catechism doesn't leave matters there. It goes on to ask the child, "What hurt comes to man by his sin?" And the child must respond by reciting the various parts of the "curse of God" to which all humans are "continually subject" because of their sinfulness (Perkins 151–2). The curse of God the child is made to describe consists of pains in this life and damnation in the next. The pains of this life include all the unpleasant, unfortunate, and tragic events that can afflict a person – disaster, disease, and the death of loved ones. The catechism thus impresses on the child the idea that everything bad that happens to him is warranted punishment for his sin. The catechism also impresses on the child the horrors of "eternal perdition and destruction in hell-fire." Indeed, the final part of the catechism – the last bit the child must recite, the bit that will echo in his mind when the lesson is complete – is the following description of the three things that await all reprobates:

[F]irst, a perpetual separation from God's presence; secondly, fellowship with the devil and his angels; thirdly, an horrible pang and torment both of body and soul arising of the feeling of the whole wrath of God, poured forth on the wicked for ever, world without end; and if the pain of one tooth for one day be so great, endless shall be the pain of the whole man, body and soul for ever. (Perkins 167)

The catechism does also explain that some people will reach heaven. These heaven-bound people will, of course, accept Jesus Christ as their savior. But even acceptance of Christ is inextricably linked to an intimate and constant awareness of corruption. For the catechism teaches the child that he can have real faith in Christ only after he has fully embraced the sharp sorrow of his own sin. Only if the child's inner being becomes so "touched with a lively feeling of God's displeasure" that he "utterly despairs of salvation in regard of anything in himself" and acknowledges that what he actually deserves is "shame and confusion eternally" – only then can he truly appreciate the nature of Christ's sacrifice (Perkins 157).

So the English Calvinists emphasized the importance of an internal sense of sin. They insisted that the essence of Christianity – the essence of true acceptance of Christ – involved not merely agreement with statements of Calvinist doctrine, but also a vital and fulsome *feeling* of one's own corruption. This emphasis on an internal sense or feeling will be highly significant in our later discussion. For we will see that while Whichcote and Cudworth eventually repudiated the Calvinist belief in inherent and ineradicable sinfulness, they always remained firmly committed to the notion that what is most important to religion and morality is an individual's internal state of mind.

Unfortunately, most people (according to the English Calvinists) do not cultivate in themselves the proper internal state. They perform the requisite external actions, going to church, reciting their prayers, taking the sacraments, and refraining from "gross and palpable sins" (Perkins 286).

And they think that these activities are sufficient to put themselves in "God's favor." But they are actually dreadfully mistaken. For true repentance involves something much more difficult than simply going through the proper outward motions. It involves taking to heart the full nature of one's own sinfulness.

The very fact that most people are sanguine about the state of their soul is (according to the English Calvinists) conclusive evidence of the superficiality of their own self-survey. For the soul of each of us is a "sea of corruption," and if someone doesn't see his own sin, that merely means he isn't looking hard enough. But how can we find all the sin within ourselves? How can we be sure that we have adequately condemned all the myriad things within ourselves for which condemnation is so justly warranted? It isn't easy. In fact, Perkins tells us, it's the "hardest thing in the world." And those who think it is easy – those who think they've managed to find all the sin within themselves without too much trouble – have undoubtedly failed to do so.

What one must do is search within one's soul for every single spot of sin. And one must find and claim it all – every grand evil and small infraction, as well as every sinful thought, even if it did not issue in an external act. One must

search narrowly, as a man would do for a piece of gold or a precious jewel which is lost in a great house, or as a man may search for gold in a mine of the earth and but very little gold ore. Hence we may learn that in true repentance and conversion we must not search so only as only to find gross and palpable sins of our lives, but so as we may find those sins which the world accounts lesser sins and espy our secret faults and privy corruptions. Some corruptions seem more near akin to our nature and therein men hope to be excused when they forsake many other greater sins. But a true penitent sinner must search for such so as a good magistrate searcheth for a lurking traitor which is conveyed into some close and secret corner: and he must ransack his heart for such corruption as wherein his heart takes special delight and must think that no sin can be so small but it is too great to be spared and that every sin great or little must be searched for, as being all traitors to God's majesty. (Perkins 286–7)

Perkins is instructing us to view all our motives with suspicion, if not outright hostility. For he takes it as an undeniable given that sin lurks within our soul. And the sin within our soul is crafty. It uses camouflage and misdirection to trick us into thinking we have found it all when in fact some still remains concealed. But we must find it all, for he who "breaks but one of the commandments of God, though it be but once in all his lifetime, and that only in one thought, is subject to and in danger of eternal damnation thereby" (Perkins 157). Indeed, our good works themselves may be tools used by Satan to lull us into a false sense of security. Thus, since God "will find in the best works we do more matter of damnation than salvation," we "must rather condemn ourselves for our good works than look to be justified before God thereby" (Perkins 159).

The Negative Answer of English Calvinism   11

So we must engage in constant self-examination, continually "ransacking" our heart. This obsessive internal scrutiny will never succeed in locating all the sin in our soul, let alone rooting it all out. But if we perform this self-inquisition with proper zeal, and if we are lucky, we may find within ourselves elements of God's grace (Perkins 159).

Now no one can ever merit salvation; Perkins is clear about that. Everyone's soul is a "sea of corruption." But God decided to bestow His grace on some people anyway. Why did God elect the people He did and damn the rest? It is impossible for us to know. God's reasons are not for us to understand. We do know, however, that whatever God decided, He decided before the moment of Creation. For we know that every event that ever takes place has been predetermined by God.

The religion of Cudworth's father thus consisted of two central notions: a Negative Answer that proclaimed that everyone is fundamentally evil, corrupt, and sinful, and a fatalism that proclaimed that everyone's eternal fate has been forever sealed. Coupled to those two notions was a vividly literal conception of hell and a never-ending exhortation to engage in obsessive fault-finding self-scrutiny. It must all have loomed over the heads of young children like the sword of Damocles.

2

Whichcote and Cudworth's Positive Answer

The elder Cudworth died in 1624, when Ralph was seven. His mother remarried to a man named John Stoughton, who was also a committed Calvinist. Dr. Stoughton took charge of young Ralph's education, and did so with "great care," making sure that by the time Ralph was thirteen "he was as well grounded in school learning as any boy of his age that went to University" (Birch viii). When he was fifteen, Cudworth was sent to Emmanuel College in Cambridge, where Stoughton himself had gone and was well connected.

This choice of college is significant. Emmanuel had been founded in 1584 by an early English Calvinist named Walter Mildmay with the express intention of preparing young men for the ministry. And by the time Cudworth arrived in 1632, the college had earned a reputation as the prime training ground for Calvinist preachers. Clearly, Stoughton's idea was to groom Cudworth to don the mantle that Perkins had worn and then passed to Cudworth's father. Ralph was a brilliant young man of impeccable background – just the person to carry forward the godly message of English Calvinism.

But it didn't happen. Although Cudworth remained politically and socially associated with the Calvinists for years to come, he quickly became one of the leading lights of a philosophical movement that was diametrically opposed to Calvinism's fundamental tenets. It was a movement based on a firm and abiding belief in the natural goodness of human beings – in an unabashedly Positive Answer to the Human Nature Question, one that would have had William Perkins and the elder Ralph Cudworth spinning in their graves. Describing the origins and shape of this Positive Answer is the goal of the present chapter.

A. "Govern Thyself from *Within*"

In addition to Cudworth, the anti-Calvinist movement at Cambridge included Henry More, who was three years older than Cudworth, and

John Smith, who was a year younger. But the leader of the movement was Benjamin Whichcote, who was in his mid-twenties and already a Fellow of Emmanuel when More, Cudworth, and Smith arrived at Cambridge as teenagers.[1] This Whichcote was an exceptional person, and an understanding of his life and thought will help us to create a full picture of the development of the Positive Answer in seventeenth-century England.

Whichcote's early education was dominated by the writings of Perkins, and he was sent to Emmanuel when he was seventeen, clear indications that he, like Cudworth, had had a Calvinist upbringing. His primary tutor at Emmanuel was Anthony Tuckney, a prominent Calvinist who would have been the perfect choice to guide Whichcote to a career as a Calvinist preacher. But Whichcote rejected Tuckney's Negative Answer, and that inevitably led to his rejecting other defining features of Calvinism as well.[2]

Whichcote believed that human nature was basically good. This belief was not without antecedents in seventeenth-century England. Dissident and radical religious groups had for decades been advancing various versions of the Positive Answer, and a number of independent thinkers of the 1630s (dubbed the "Great Tew Circle") proposed ideas somewhat similar to Whichcote's.[3] It is possible, as well, that when he had been a student in the 1620s Whichcote had encountered tutors at Cambridge who were inclining away from the Calvinist emphasis on the sinfulness of man.[4] But the nature of Whichcote's belief in the goodness of human nature was new. And it seems likely that Whichcote's answer grew to a large extent out of his own temperament.

Whichcote was consistently portrayed as extraordinarily calm and kind, "a man of rare temper; very mild and obliging," who "was hardly ever seen to be transported with anger" (Aphorisms xxxi and xxix). He was also portrayed as being an exceedingly considerate and respectful conversationalist and interlocutor, one who would always listen carefully to what others had to say, no matter how contrary to his own views their statements may have seemed. "Never passionate, never peremptory: so far from imposing upon others, that he was rather apt to yield: And though he had a most profound and well-poised judgment; yet was he, of all men I ever knew, the most patient to hear others differ from him; and the most easy to be convinced, when good reason was offered; and, which is seldom seen, more apt to be favourable to another man's reason, than to his own" (Aphorisms xxviii–xxix). It seems that almost everyone who knew Whichcote liked and respected him. And Whichcote seems to have sincerely liked and respected almost everyone he knew.

At least as important, Whichcote seemed to have sincerely liked and respected himself. In one of his aphorisms, he says, "To Enjoy a man's *self*, is the greatest Good in the world; the Serenity and Composure of the mind is *Happiness* within" (Aphorisms 576), and all the evidence suggests that Whichcote was happy with himself, that he knew firsthand the importance of "Self-Enjoyment" (Aphorisms 278 and 280). Whichcote is also consistently portrayed as possessing real self-confidence. "Patient to hear others differ from him" he might have been, but he wasn't wishy-washy or a pushover (Aphorisms xxviii). When he thought he was right, he would remain true to his principles in the face of even the most powerful opposition, showing a willingness to defend his position "against the whole world." He was secure enough both to question his own beliefs whenever anyone raised reasonable doubts about them, and, when he was satisfied with his own reasoning, to stand up for his beliefs no matter who questioned them.

Now as we've already noted, Whichcote was raised on the Calvinism of William Perkins. So he would have been instructed to scrutinize his heart and soul to find the sinfulness that lay therein. It seems likely, however, that when Whichcote looked within himself, he did not find the wickedness Perkins insisted would be there. What he likely found instead was a self that was fundamentally decent – a self that simply did not resemble the corrupt picture of human beings that was the core of Perkins's Negative Answer – and he was not willing to accede to the Perkinsian claim that his favorable self-impression was actually born of self-deceptive sinfulness. All the biographical descriptions we have, in any event, suggest that Whichcote refused to adopt a Perkinsian self-assessment, and his aphorisms explicitly maintain that it is possible for a person to be justifiably satisfied with his own survey. To appreciate the significance of this feature of Whichcote's thought, it will be helpful to situate it within the broader arc of larger developments in the history of moral philosophy.

In the first part of the eighteenth century, a number of philosophers began to place at the center of their moral views the importance of being able to "bear one's own survey." Their idea was that persons should conduct themselves so that when they look at their own reasons for action, they are content with what they see. The Third Earl of Shaftesbury (as we will see in Chapter 9) said that we ought to be virtuous because only a person of virtue can possess "a Mind or Reason well compos'd, quiet, easy within it-self, and such as can freely bear its own Inspection and Review" (Virtue or Merit 66). Francis Hutcheson (as we will see in Chapter 14) argued that a virtuous person will be in perfect internal harmony. Joseph Butler believed that virtue enables us to attain "sincere self-enjoyment and home satisfaction" (Butler 180). And David Hume maintained that honesty is what produces "inward peace of mind, consciousness of integrity [and] a satisfactory review of our own conduct" (Second Enquiry 156). This idea of being able to bear one's own survey continued to exert a powerful influence on moral theory throughout the eighteenth, nineteenth, and twentieth centuries, and it continues to have great resonance with many people today. Many people continue to believe that one of the most important reasons to do what is right is that it will enable one to look oneself in the eye, to live with oneself, to respect oneself.

But while the importance of being able to bear one's own survey is an idea with a long forward stretch, its backward reach is even longer. Socrates expressed the idea through the *Apology*, and his life and death are an object lesson in how to embody it. And in the *Republic* Plato drew a clear link between morality and being able to bear one's own survey, contending that the just person is the one who "harmonizes" with himself and "is his own friend," while the unjust person is the one who suffers "turmoil" and has "a kind of civil war" within himself (Plato 119–21).

The idea that a good person will be satisfied with his own character was, however, conspicuously absent in the period leading up to Whichcote. There was no talk among seventeenth-century English Calvinists of seeking to have all one's parts "harmonize" with each other, or of one's mind being "easy with itself," or of being one's "own friend." The line of thought that placed great importance on self-respect and being able to bear one's own survey – found in Socrates, Plato, Shaftesbury, Butler, Hume, and numerous contemporary thinkers – suffered a break.

What broke it was the belief that humanity is inherently and ineluctably sinful – a belief vivified by the Christian doctrine of the Fall of Man in general, and the Calvinists' extreme interpretation of this doctrine in particular. This belief, which is what I am calling the Negative Answer, implies that our soul will always harbor corruption and sin. Those people who are completely pleased with their own characters must, therefore, be profoundly misguided, either unaware of their own sinfulness or (what is worse) so far gone that awareness of their own sin no longer upsets them. We should not, consequently, seek to be in complete harmony with ourselves nor to be friends with all of our aspects. Our goal, rather, should be to gain a full awareness of the sinfulness of our nature and to feel a real hatred of it. It is not internal harmony the Calvinists extol, but a kind of constant internal warfare between our higher and lower aspects.

Whichcote was a turning point – back toward Plato and forward toward Shaftesbury and other modern champions of self-respect. It's not that Whichcote was unaware of the inward turmoil of the sinner. He speaks often of the great misery and "perpetual Disquiet" of "self-condemnation" (Aphorisms 391 and 394). But Whichcote, like Plato and Shaftesbury, believed that people who were constantly condemning themselves were doing something wrong. We condemn ourselves when we do things that "we cannot own," when we "cannot approve [our] own actions" (Aphorisms 391). It is, however, possible for us to live in a way that does allow us to "own" and "approve" our own actions. Such a way of life, one that includes enjoyment of our own character, is what religion truly consists of. "Religion doth lay the Foundation of mental Peace, Satisfaction, and Content" (Aphorisms 949). It gives us "*Serenity* of *Mind*, and Calmness of Thought" (Aphorisms 280) and makes our life "all of a piece" (Aphorisms 1113). The Calvinist goal of constant self-condemnation is terribly misguided. You can live a life of "innocency," "truth of conscience," and "self-justification" (Aphorisms 391 and 202); you can be happy with yourself. And it is just such a life that you ought to lead. As Whichcote rhetorically asks, "Why should one deal roughly with his Bosom-Friend, the Sense of his Mind; which, if in Peace, is his Solace in all Solitaries?" (Aphorisms 1092).

"Govern thyself from *within*," Whichcote tells us (Aphorisms 178). And he continually insists on being "true to" oneself, on respecting one's own "integrity," on conducting oneself in a manner that will allow one to maintain "reverence" for oneself. He insists on such things because he thinks that humans are basically good, and that if we would just follow our true nature we would live as we should. "For such a nature as the nature of man is, intellectual nature, it gives a law to itself, and carries a law with it, and is made with the law, and the law is in its own bowels, and is never extirpated while it continues in being: the law of reason is inherent to human nature" (Whichcote iv.434; cf. iii.21). All humans have and always will have within themselves the law of how to live, and they need only follow the principles of their own soul to achieve righteousness. This is as clear a statement of an anti-Calvinist Positive Answer that one could ever hope to find. And in making this statement, Whichcote both revived the Platonic idea that one's goal ought to be to live in harmony with oneself and launched a self-respect and integrity-based view of morality that is still in full sail today.

But although Whichcote's Positive Answer is clearly anti-Calvinist, his Calvinist upbringing undoubtedly helped set him on the path to his view of human nature. For the English Calvinists elevated to central importance the activity of self-scrutiny. As we saw in our discussion of Perkins, the Calvinists exhorted everyone to search his soul "narrowly, as a man would do for a piece of gold or a precious jewel which is lost in a great house, or as a man may search for gold in a mine of the earth." Whichcote learned well this Calvinist lesson of looking within. Throughout his life, he never strayed from the idea that the essence of religion and morality lay within each individual – that true religion and morality grow out of inward examination. But when Whichcote looked within himself, he found not the intractable sin the Calvinists claimed must be there but the possibility of real goodness. Whichcote obeyed the Calvinist demand to examine his own soul, but what he encountered looked less like the fallen Adam and more like God's original creation – less like Perkins and more like Socrates.

All the biographical accounts also suggest that Whichcote's view of others mirrored his sanguine view of himself. (Whichcote himself said that one's opinion of others, and of God, inevitably reflects one's view of oneself [Aphorisms 163, 388, and 716].) He thought almost everyone had good intentions and the potential for wisdom. So he listened thoughtfully to what others had to say, seeming really to believe that there was just as much chance that he could learn from someone else as there was that someone else could learn from him. This willingness to listen and learn from others is well expressed in a number of Whichcote's aphorisms, as for instance when he says, "Man, as a *sociable* Creature, is made for Converse with those that are his Equals; to Receive *from* them, and to Communicate *to* them; to *Be* the Better for them, and to *Make* them the Better for him" (Aphorisms 678).

Whichcote's speaking style attests to this respectful attitude toward others' intellectual ability. His sermonizing was relatively plain and unshowy, lacking the flowery similes and thunderous attacks common to other preachers of his day. He said things straightforwardly, and his tone was conversational, giving people the impression that he was speaking *with* them, not *at* them. All of this fits well with Whichcote's optimistic view of human nature. Everyone, Whichcote believed, is able to understand everything of moral and religious importance. So clear, calm, and respectful discussion is the appropriate method for instruction. One does not need to browbeat people to get them to do what's right or scare them out of their wits. Indeed, if people acquiesce to one's message only because of the bombastic force of one's rhetoric, then one has done little more than engage in spiritual bribery, blackmail, or bullying. One has not brought about real understanding. And (as we will see in the rest of this chapter) real understanding – not mere acquiescence – is the core of true religion and morality.

Whichcote's clear and straightforward delivery made his preaching much beloved at Cambridge, where he delivered the Sunday sermons at Trinity Church for nearly twenty years, and his effectiveness as a public speaker must have been greatly enhanced by his uncanny ability to express his ideas in a simple, concise, memorable manner (Roberts 1968, 2). One indication of this talent is the fact that posthumously published collections of aphorisms culled from Whichcote's sermons remained enormously popular in England for over 100 years.

All of these qualities – his psychological astuteness and intellectual generosity, his strength of conviction and confidence in the intentions and abilities of others, his willingness to consider others' ideas, his pleasant conversation, his knack for coining the quotable phrase, his friendliness and sincerity – must have made Whichcote a spectacularly effective teacher. It's unsurprising, therefore, that he developed such a devoted following among his students at Cambridge in the 1630s, Ralph Cudworth among them. At the time, moreover, a Cambridge tutor was charged not only with academic instruction but also with the moral and religious edification of his tutees, many of whom were expected to become ministers themselves and thus eventually to bring to future congregations moral and religious edification of their own. Formation of character was as much a tutor's job as improvement of intellect. We should also keep in mind that Cudworth and his other friends were in their mid-teens when they arrived at Cambridge. They were not independent adults who had come simply to attend classes, but adolescents for whom college was an all-around formative experience.

Whichcote would thus have been more than just a professor to them. He would have been mentor, advisor, minister, and father figure all at once.

B. "The Spirit of a Man Is the Candle of the Lord"

Under Whichcote's influence, Cudworth and his friends came to reject the Negative Answer that had been at the center of their Calvinist upbringing. They became convinced that human beings were basically good – that if a person followed the principles of his nature he would live in accord with true morality and religion. And they all set out together, guided by their shared commitment to the Positive Answer, to forge a new moral and religious path.

It must have been an exhilarating time for Cudworth and the others. All of them had been brought up in strict households dominated by Calvinist ideas of sin and corruption, and it's easy to imagine that they had all chafed under the ponderous Calvinist discipline. Now they were away from home for the first time, and who should they encounter but Benjamin Whichcote, a charismatic and encouraging teacher who had himself shrugged off the heavy Calvinist baggage of his upbringing. The young men were also becoming friends with each other, and the touchstone for their friendship was their mutual engagement with the issues Whichcote raised. Their friendship thus animated their religious and moral thinking, while at the same time their thoughts animated their friendship. In such heady circumstances, ideas can intoxicate. The fact that the other students at Emmanuel and the older tutors stuck to Calvinist dogma probably only added to the thrill of their joint intellectual enterprise. They were a special group, united by belief in the Positive Answer and rejection of the dour surrounding orthodoxy. Let me outline some of their most distinctive ideas now.[5]

One of the most fundamental beliefs to which Whichcote, Cudworth, More, and Smith were committed was a deeply theistic conception of the Positive Answer. Every human being is basically good, they believed, because every human soul is God-like. As Whichcote put it, "Reverence God in *thyself*: for God is *more* in the *Mind* of Man, than in any part of this world besides; for we (and we *only* here) are made after the image of God" (Aphorisms 798). Or as Whichcote put it elsewhere, "He that hath no Reverence for *himself,* and his own Nature hath no Reverence for God" (Aphorisms 255). This theistic conception of the Positive Answer is best summed up by the claim, explicit in the work of Whichcote, Cudworth, and their friends, that human nature is *deiform,* or God-like.[6]

Whichcote and Cudworth's deiformity claim reveals plainly their rejection of English Calvinism. For while the Calvinists insisted on the difference between God and man, Whichcote and Cudworth insisted on the similarity.[7] While the essence of the Calvinists' religion was an awareness of one's sinfulness, the essence of the religion of Whichcote and Cudworth was an awareness of one's capacity to be God-like.

Their rejection of Calvinism is clearly evident in the use Whichcote and Cudworth made of Psalms 20:27: "The spirit of a man is the candle of the Lord." Cassirer calls this verse "the motto of the Cambridge movement" (Cassirer 1953, 40), and with good reason: they quoted it throughout their writings and sermons, and their interpretation of it captures well the spirit of their Positive Answer. To appreciate the novelty and boldness of their interpretation of Psalms 20:27, we need only to set it against the backdrop of the mainstream Protestant reading.

On the mainstream Protestant reading, "The spirit of a man is the candle of the Lord" was intended to focus our attention on the *difference* between humans and God. We are, on this understanding, supposed to compare a candle's weak and flickering, uncertain flame to the brilliance of the sun, source of all light. In making this comparison, we come to realize how profoundly inadequate a candle really is – how insufficient its dim light would be in guiding us through a world of darkness. And just as a candle suffers in comparison to the sun, so too does our "spirit" suffer in comparison to God. Imagine yourself completely lost in the dead of a pitch black night, and consider how ill-equipped you would be to find your way home if you had only a candle to help you navigate. You are, according to the mainstream Protestant interpretation of Psalms 20:27, just as ill-equipped to find the path of righteousness when you rely only on the resources within your own soul.

This emphasis on the *difference* between God and humans is well exemplified by Nathanael Culverwell's exposition of the verse.[8] Culverwell, who was also at Emmanuel in the 1630s, maintained that the candle is "but a brief and compendious flame, shut up, and imprison'd in a narrow compasse. How farre distant is it from the beauty of a Starre? How farre from the brightnesse of a Sun? . . . God never intended that a creature should rest satisfied with its own candle-light, but that it should run to the fountain of light, and sunne it self in the presence of its God" (Patrides 1970, 11). The point was put even more sharply by Francis Quarles, a popular Puritan writer of the period, who wrote, "Let Phylosophy not be asham'd to be confuted, nor Logick blush to be confounded; What thou canst not comprehend, beleeve; and what thou canst beleeve, admire; So shall thy Ignorance be satisfied in thy Faith, and thy doubts swallowed up with wonders; The best way to see day-light is to put out thy Candle" (Patrides 1970, 11). To Quarles's mind, looking to one's own soul for guidance was irreligious and counterproductive. Real guidance must come from without, from the external light of God.

Whichcote and Cudworth, in contrast, insisted that we can and must look to our souls for real guidance. ("Govern thyself from *within*.") And John Smith, another of Whichcote's students and one of Cudworth's good friends, maintained that true religion is "an *inward Nature* that conteins all the laws and measures of its motion within it self. A Good man finds not his Religion *without* him, but as a living Principle *within* him" (Patrides 1970, 159). But such confidence in the guidance of each person's own soul requires an interpretation of Psalms 20:27 very different from that of Culverwell and Quarles. It requires that we read the verse as intending to focus our attention on the *similarity* between God and humans.

The deiformity claim thus turns the traditional Protestant reading of the candle metaphor on its head. Instead of emphasizing the dimness of a candle, Whichcote and the others focused attention on the fact that the light of a candle is the very same stuff as the light of the sun. There is, of course, a great *quantitative* difference between a candle and the sun (the sun is a lot bigger). *Qualitatively*, however, the two are the same: they both emit the light that enables us to see (see Aphorisms 262). Thus, according to this reading, Psalms 20:27 is telling us that just as the flame of a candle is essentially identical to the fire of the sun, so too the spirit of each of us is fundamentally God-like. Also crucial to the imagery of the verse is the idea that a candle has to be lit by someone. But whose candle is our spirit? The Lord's. The Lord, then, is the one who has ignited our spirit, and in so doing He has placed in us the very same light-giving stuff of which He Himself is constituted.

So as the four Cambridge friends saw it, the lesson of Psalms 20:27 is that each of us has within himself a spark of the divine, something that is literally a piece of God. And to ignore that divine spark within is to disrespect both oneself and one's Creator. For it is God who has placed inside each of us a divine guide, and it is just as wrong to reject that internal guidance of His as it is to reject the guidance of the scriptures He has given us. As Whichcote put it in what could have been a direct rebuttal of Quarles's injunction "to put out thy candle," "God hath set up two lights to enlighten us in our way: the light of reason which is the light of his creation; and the light of Scripture, which is after-revelation from him. Let us make use of these two lights and suffer neither to be put out" (Aphorisms 109).

C. "I Was Not Able to Ascribe to God Those Dreadful Decrees"

Each of us, then, is deiform or God-like. But what is God like? What is His nature? What are His attributes? Whichcote notes that one's answer to this question will depend on one's own character. "Every one attributes to *God*, what he finds in *Himself*," he tells us (Aphorisms 388). As we might have expected, consequently, Whichcote's God was kinder, gentler, and calmer than the God of his Calvinist forbears. Indeed, Whichcote and Cudworth thought that almost all the errors of the Calvinists were rooted in one particular belief they held about God – namely, that God arbitrarily decided before the moment of creation that certain humans would eventually suffer eternal damnation.

That God determined before the moment of creation every event that would ever take place is the doctrine of predestination, which is central to Calvinist thinkers. And the belief that God decided before creation who would eventually be damned – which is known as "supralapsarianism" – is a consequence the Calvinists explicitly drew from predestination. We have, however, not yet explained why Whichcote and Cudworth attributed to the Calvinists the idea that God's decision to damn certain people was *arbitrary*. Let us address this point now.

The arbitrariness of God's decision follows in part from a Calvinist idea that is closely related to predestinarianism and supralapsarianism: namely, a voluntarist conception of God. According to voluntarism, prior to God's act of creation nothing existed. There was no material world, no numbers, no geometric entities – and no morality. Then (according to voluntarism) God willed everything into existence, creating through that act of will the material world, numbers, geometry, morality, and everything else.

Voluntarism is closely related to predestinarianism and supralapsarianism in that they all grow directly out of an emphasis on the omnipotent will of God. Just as the Calvinists believed that God's omnipotence implied that it was He who determined the occurrence of every event, so too they believed that His omnipotence implied that He created morality. To hold that there were standards of right and wrong that existed prior to God's creations – that is, that there were standards of morality that God did not create – was as repugnant to the Calvinist conception of God's omnipotence as it was to hold that there were events that God did not control or material things He could not alter.

The combination of voluntarism and supralapsarianism implies the arbitrariness of God's decision to damn certain humans because it implies that that decision was unguided by any sort of moral consideration. According to this view, morality – and all the considerations we think of as moral reasons – did not exist before God made His decision, for God created morality at the same time that He determined that certain people should suffer eternal torment. So the determination that certain people should suffer was made by His will alone, by a will completely unfettered by any prior constraints or moral requirements, by a will that was arbitrary in an etymologically strict sense.

Whichcote and Cudworth contested this view of God in two different ways.[9] They argued, first, that voluntarism hollowed out the goodness of God. This point can be put in strictly logical terms. In order for God's will to be good in a significant or non-tautological sense, there must be some independent standard of goodness against which God's will can be measured. It is substantially meaningful to say that God does what is good only if the standard of goodness has an existence independent of God's will. But on the voluntarist view, God's actions create goodness. His will brings the moral standard into existence. So on the voluntarist view, before God acted there was no moral standard at all. It thus becomes tautological – or empty – to say that God's will is good, in that goodness is determined entirely by God's will itself.

But that logical point was not Whichcote and Cudworth's only objection to the Calvinist conception of God. They also claimed that it would have been *wrong* for God to condemn people to eternal torment before they had ever been born. Whichcote and Cudworth held that it would have been *immoral* for God to have created a world in which people were predestined to sin and damnation. As Cudworth explained in a letter he wrote late in life describing the development of his thought in the 1630s, "I was not able to ascribe to God those dreadful decrees, which he inevitably condemned innocent men out of arbitrariousness to guilt and sin, for which they are to atone by everlasting torture. . . . And from that time on a very large number of men at our university, influenced by the evidence of this one truth, have gone over to the camp of the Remonstrants" (Cassirer 1953, 79; cf. 122–3). Whichcote made the same point when he claimed that it was "Blasphemy" to say that God had "determined" humans "to Sin or Misery" before they came "into Being" (Aphorisms 811).

Whichcote and Cudworth based their claim that it would be "blasphemous" and "dreadful" to attribute the predetermination of damnation to God on a moral principle, sometimes called the "*ought-implies-can*" principle, that tells us that all the things one *ought* to do also have to be things that one *can* do. Their idea was that it would be *wrong* for God to predetermine damnation of His creatures because it would constitute His punishing people for things outside of their control. As Whichcote explained, "If Sin were *Necessary*, it could not be Avoided; if Duty were *Impossible*, it could not be done: This would be an *Answer* to God Himself; an Answer to the Indictment, that might be brought against us at the Last day" (Aphorisms 532).

There are several notable features of Whichcote and Cudworth's ought-implies-can objection to Calvinism. First of all, this objection is distinct from the strictly logical objection to voluntarism. The logical objection, which holds that voluntarism hollows out God's goodness, doesn't tell us that the Calvinists are wrong to say that their conception of God implies that He is good; it tells us, rather, that on the Calvinist conception, God's goodness is merely tautological. But the ought-implies-can objection holds that the Calvinist conception of God is *inconsistent* with moral goodness. It implies that the Calvinist conception of God must be *false*, since that conception implies the absurdity that God, who is perfectly moral, has acted immorally.

Secondly, the ought-implies-can objection reveals Whichcote and Cudworth's willingness to limit God's power in order to affirm a particular view of morality. Not even the power of God, according to this objection, can alter the eternal and immutable standards of morality, for those standards are prior even to God's act of creation. Morality is a necessary feature of reality, and so God's will must "Answer" to morality, not the other way around.

Thirdly, the ought-implies-can objection shows that Whichcote and Cudworth placed their own moral convictions at the origin of (or prior to) their conception of religion. Theology, as they saw it, had to conform to their idea of morality, not the other way around. For it seemed to them absolutely clear that it was wrong to condemn people for things they could not have avoided. And they therefore concluded that God could never have decreed such a condemnation. The fact that this conclusion flew in the face of the central doctrines of Calvinism did not seem to bother them at all. When faced with the choice between their own moral judgment and the religion of their parents, tutors, and fellow students, they chose their own moral judgment seemingly without hesitation. Finally, then, the ought-implies-can objection reveals Whichcote and Cudworth's breath-taking self-confidence. (I'm not sure whether their being in their teens and twenties when they first developed this line of thought makes their self-confidence more startling or less so.)

The Calvinists of the day surely would have told Whichcote and Cudworth not to place so much trust in their own moral judgment. Just because something seems immoral to you, the Calvinists would have counseled, does not mean it really is so. For the human mind is wholly corrupt and will thus inevitably produce a distorted picture of reality. Moreover, the Calvinists would have continued, to maintain that God Himself must be restrained by one's own idea of morality is to denigrate Him by denying His omnipotence and to arrogate to oneself God-like knowledge of good and evil. It is to commit the original sin of pride, for which Adam was expelled from Paradise and Satan condemned to Hell.

But Whichcote and Cudworth brushed off the accusation that they lowered God by elevating themselves. It seemed clear to them that predestined damnation was wrong, and that for them was sufficient ground on which to build a new theology. Far from denigrating God, such confidence in their own moral judgment, as Whichcote and Cudworth saw it, was positively reverential, as the mind of man is a candle of the Lord. What was denigrating to God, from Whichcote and Cudworth's point of view, was to contradict one's own moral judgment. For that moral judgment, coming as it does from within one's deiform mind, is none other than the voice of God Himself.

The root idea of Calvinism was the Fall of Man. So for Calvinists, the sin of pride always loomed large, a constant danger. But the thought of Whichcote and Cudworth grew out of a radically different idea, namely, that all humans are deiform, made by God in the image of God. For Whichcote and Cudworth, self-respect merged with respect for God, and worries about the sin of pride withered and fell away.

D. Cambridge Platonism

So opposition to the voluntarist views of the Calvinists was a cornerstone of Whichcote and Cudworth's philosophy, a building block they laid very early in their intellectual lives. They did not claim, however, that these anti-voluntarist ideas were original to them. They claimed, rather, that these ideas came right out of Plato's *Euthyphro* (see Cudworth, Commons 384). And it wasn't just their anti-voluntarism that Whichcote and Cudworth attributed to Plato. They traced almost all of their philosophical positions to one Platonic text or another. Cudworth, in particular, would at times have you believe that virtually every element of his philosophy is simply an explication of something that can be found in Plato's dialogues. Indeed, the influence of Plato on Whichcote, Cudworth, More, and Smith was so conspicuous and profound that the four friends eventually came to be known collectively as the Cambridge Platonists.

Plato was the perfect ally in the battle against the Calvinists, for his philosophy was a wonderful representation of the Positive Answer. Of course, Plato did not think that every human being is virtuous; there are plenty of dishonorable characters in his dialogues. He did believe, however, that a human being can achieve real knowledge and goodness, that human nature is not ineluctably benighted but capable of finding its way to full sunlight.

We have already mentioned two aspects of Plato's thought that are in line with the anti-Calvinist Positive Answer: the anti-voluntarism of the *Euthyphro* and the claim in the *Republic* that it is possible for a human to "harmonize" with himself, to be "his own friend" or bear his own survey. Later in the *Republic*, Plato draws this second claim out more fully, developing a metaphysically elevated view of the human ability to grasp the Form of the Good. The *Meno*, with its story of the slave boy and its doctrine of recollection, is another example of Plato's confidence in the human ability to get things right. And the *Symposium*'s speeches, at least as the Cambridge Platonists interpreted them, reveal the heights of true spiritual love to which human beings can aspire.

But nothing in Plato's works made a bigger impression on the Cambridge Platonists than the character of Socrates himself. For the Socrates of the *Apology*, the *Crito*, and the *Phaedo* is a person of complete virtue and happiness, someone who does what's right and does it cheerfully. There is no conflict within the soul of Socrates. He is self-content. And that is not because he is ignorant of his true nature but rather because he knows himself fully. He also has confidence in the human ability to think things through, which shapes his entire life's project of speaking plainly with people about how they should live. Socrates is the embodiment of the Positive Answer. When you consider, as well, that it was Whichcote who introduced Socrates – Whichcote, whose character resemblance to Socrates his three students must have noted – it's not too difficult to imagine the attraction for Cudworth, More, and Smith.

That attraction might have been enhanced by the attitude of the other tutors and students. For while Whichcote and Cudworth were avidly embracing Plato, most of the rest of Emmanuel was keeping him at arm's length. It would be overstating matters to say that Plato was forbidden reading at Emmanuel, but he was certainly thought of as having no business at the core of one's thought. The Cambridge Platonists' overt allegiance to Plato thus helped them forge their philosophical identity not only in the positive sense of defining their own positions but also in the negative sense of distinguishing them from others. So to appreciate fully the "Platonist" part of the Cambridge Platonist label, we need to understand why a close connection to Plato was something the others at Emmanuel resisted.

The Cambridge Platonists' penchant for tracing their views back to earlier thinkers did not on its own set them apart from their contemporaries. It was common practice in seventeenth-century England to attribute one's ideas to the writings of past masters. Intellectual heritage was generally taken to be more important than originality of thought. Indeed, many of the religious and political battles of the day can be cast as disputes over the legitimacy of conflicting claims on the legacy of a common religious or political ancestor.

Most of the English intellectuals of the 1630s claimed as their antecedents the pillars of Christianity in general and Protestantism in particular. They were thus keen to establish an unbroken line between their ideas and the thought of Augustine, Aquinas, Luther, Calvin, Perkins, and the like. There was no place for Plato in this hall of saints. For Plato, writing in Athens in the fifth century B.C., did not know of Christ and did not have God's scriptures. He was, as one Cambridge tutor of the time put it, one of the "Wretched Heathens" consigned to Hell (Patrides 1970, 96). And such a person could offer no guidance for Christians.

This dim view of Plato and the other pre-Christian philosophers follows directly from the mainstream Protestant version of the Negative Answer. If human nature is wholly corrupt, then we must not trust advice that comes solely from the human mind. We need instead to look to the scriptures, which have been given to us precisely because we are ill-equipped to find the right path on our own. But because he did not have the benefit of Christ or scripture, Plato did have to rely entirely on his own mind. We should be wary, consequently, of placing our confidence in his philosophy. And we should certainly keep his views in their place, which is decidedly below that of the Christian fathers.

Conversely, the Cambridge Platonists' embrace of Plato fits perfectly with their Positive Answer. The human mind, on the Cambridge Platonist view, is God-like, the Candle of the Lord – and that means every human mind, Christian or heathen. We are, therefore, just as likely to learn something from a heathen as from a Christian. All humans come equipped to discover real and important truths, whether they have had the benefit of scripture or not.

With this context in mind, we can now see that the Cambridge Platonists' habit of quoting Plato was controversial, even distinct from the content of any of those quotations. The act of Plato quotation in and of itself – not to speak of the conspicuous absence of quotations from Calvin and Perkins – implied a rejection of the Calvinist view that human nature is wholly corrupt.

This anti-Calvinist message wasn't lost on the other students and tutors at Emmanuel. In an exchange of letters, Anthony Tuckney, Whichcote's former tutor, expressed concern about Whichcote's study of the heathen philosophers and downright alarm at their presence in Whichcote's sermons. He urged Whichcote to abandon "philosophy" (a term for the non-Christian thought of Plato and the other Greeks) and concentrate exclusively on scripture instead. Whichcote's response indicates clearly his belief that a lack of scriptural knowledge does not disqualify one from providing real and important guidance. He wrote:

> The time I have spent in philosophers I have no cause to repent of, and the use I have made of them I dare not disown. I heartily thank God for what I have found in them; neither have I, upon this occasion, one jot less loved the Scriptures. I find the philosophers that I have read good, so far as they go; and it makes me secretly blush before God when I find either my head, heart or life challenged by them, which I must confess I have often found. I have sometimes publicly declared what points of religion I have found excellently held forth by them; and I have never found them enemies to the faith of the Gospel. (Cragg 1968, 44)

E. Heaven and Hell

Whichcote and Cudworth's theology and conception of human nature also led them to develop a new understanding of heaven and hell. In opposition to the prevailing Calvinist approach, Whichcote and Cudworth argued that ministers ought not to describe heaven as "a place of rest and content" and hell as "a place of *fire and brimstone, weeping and wailing, and gnashing of teeth*" (Whichcote II 196–7). Indeed, ministers ought not to emphasize the idea that heaven and hell are *places* at all. For what is most important about heaven and hell is that they are *states of mind* that follow necessarily from our awareness of the rightness or wrongness of our own conduct. The essential feature of heaven is not any externally bestowed benefit but rather the consciousness of having lived in a God-like fashion. And the essential feature of hell is not the external torment of being placed in a lake of fire but the internal torment of knowing that one has done wrong – not the "misery and harm" that "proceed from *abroad*," but the bite of self-condemnation that "arise[s] from *within*."

The internal mental states that follow from one's awareness of one's own conduct are so important to Whichcote and Cudworth that they even go so far as to suggest that God Himself cannot bring unhappiness to a person who is aware of his own goodness nor bring happiness to a person who is aware of his own evil. Thus Whichcote says that even if "omnipotence itself should load me with all burdens, if I am innocent within, I shall be able to bear it," while an "unregenerate" person "cannot be happy" even if (*per impossible*) he is "in heaven" (Whichcote III 86). And Cudworth maintains that "nothing without us can make us either happy or miserable; nothing can either defile us, or hurt us, but goeth out from us, what springeth and bubbleth up out of our own hearts" (Commons 403).

So real happiness and unhappiness, for Whichcote and Cudworth, arise from one's own view of oneself – whether or not one can bear one's own survey – and that cannot be altered by any external force, no matter how powerful. This idea, which is rooted in the Socratic dictum that "a good man cannot be harmed either in life or in death," receives full expression in the following passage from one of Whichcote's sermons:

All misery arises out of ourselves. It is a most gross mistake; and men are of dull and stupid spirits, who think that that state which we call *hell* is *an incommodious place* only, and that God by his sovereignty throws men therein: for hell arises *out of a man's self*; and hell's fewel is *the guilt of a man's conscience*. And it is impossible that any should be *so* miserable as hell makes a man, and as there a man is miserable; but by his own condemning himself: and on the other side, when they think that heaven arises from any *place*, or any nearness to God or angels; this is not principally so: but it lies in a *refined temper*, in an *internal reconciliation to the nature of God, and to the rule of righteousness*. So that both hell and heaven have their foundation *within* men. (Whichcote II 139–40)[10]

Each person has within himself all the resources necessary to achieve salvation. Indeed, salvation is not a reward for good behavior but rather the state of mind we possess when we conduct ourselves as we ought.

Whichcote and Cudworth make it clear, moreover, that we can experience the states of mind that constitute heaven and hell in this world, not merely in the afterlife. They are, as Whichcote explains, states that are "present" to us here and now, "things that we are well acquainted with in this world."[11] Or as Cudworth puts it when criticizing the concentration on painted pictures of a paradisiacal heaven:

Nay, we do but deceive ourselves with names. Hell is nothing but the orb of sin and wickedness, or else that hemisphere of darkness in which all evil moves; and Heaven is the opposite hemisphere of light, or else, if you please, the bright orb of truth, holiness and goodness; and we do actually in this life instate ourselves in the possession of one or other of them. (Commons 394)

So while the Calvinists thundered on about blissful and tormented afterlives, Whichcote and Cudworth spoke of developing a righteous character here and now. Whichcote and Cudworth believed, moreover, that every person can successfully develop a righteous character, that every person can become truly God-like. As a result, according to Whichcote and Cudworth, every person has the wherewithal to free himself entirely from the fear of hell. The most important aspect of heaven is, moreover, within each person's power to achieve, within each person's immediate grasp. This conception of heaven and hell could not be further – in letter or spirit – from the Calvinists' Negative Answer.

Whichcote and Cudworth's conception of heaven and hell as present states of mind also constitutes a significant moment in the history of modern moral philosophy. For it lays the groundwork for a view of morality according to which the *reason* certain conduct is right (or the conduct's moral *justification*) and one's *motivation* for conducting oneself in that way are essentially connected to each other. This point can be obscured if we describe Whichcote and Cudworth's view as one according to which we experience a heavenly mental state when we act righteously, for that locution can give the impression that the heavenly mental state is distinct from the righteous conduct itself; it can give the impression that the mental state is something that flows in only after the righteous conduct has been completed and done with. But the real point Whichcote and Cudworth are trying to make is that righteousness consists of a particular kind of "temper" or state of mind and that to possess that temper or state of mind is to be as happy as one can possibly be. For Whichcote and Cudworth, no substantive distinction can be drawn between righteousness and a heavenly state of mind: they are two ways of describing a single thing.

The connection Whichcote and Cudworth drew between justification and motivation stands out clearly when contrasted with the Calvinist picture of heaven and hell. If we repent fully, according to the Calvinists, we may go to heaven after our death. And the hope of heaven, plus the fear of hell, are strong motivations to repent. Indeed, the Calvinists' great emphasis on vivid descriptions of heavenly bliss and hellish torments indicates their belief that the prospects of heaven and hell are the primary motivators of religion. But the reason repentance is warranted – the justification of the demand that each of us repent – is our sinfulness. And our sinfulness is something that cannot be equated to heaven. The difference between the repentance Calvinism requires and the heavenly reward that motivates the Calvinists to repent becomes obvious when we realize that those in the Calvinist heaven must not be spending eternity engaging in obsessive self-scrutiny of their own sinfulness.

In drawing tightly together the justification of and motivation for righteousness, Whichcote and Cudworth helped pave the way for what came to be known in the twentieth century as an "internalist" conception of morality.[12] Because the term has been subjected to so much intense philosophical debate, it's difficult to say precisely what "internalism" is. It is, however, easy enough to see the ways in which Whichcote and Cudworth's thought is much more internally oriented than the Calvinist views against which they set themselves.

First of all, Whichcote and Cudworth believed that all persons have within their own souls sufficient motivation to conduct themselves righteously, whereas Calvinism implied that the prospect of externally imposed reward and punishment (i.e., heaven and hell as *places*) was a necessary motivating tool. Secondly, Whichcote and Cudworth believed that all persons have within their own souls the ability to discern right from wrong, whereas Calvinism implied that people need the externally bestowed scriptures to determine what they ought to do. And thirdly, Whichcote and Cudworth believed that all persons have within their own souls the wherewithal to become truly righteous and thus achieve salvation, whereas Calvinism implied that one could never make oneself truly deserving of salvation and was thus always dependent on externally administered grace.

We should be careful, however, not to equate Whichcote and Cudworth too closely to twentieth-century moral internalists. For Whichcote and Cudworth gave God a role that distinguishes them from most twentieth-century internalists in a crucial way.

The Calvinists had drawn an ironclad distinction between wretched humanity and perfect God. God could not be found within the human soul because the human soul was wholly corrupt. God, therefore, had to come from without; He had to be external to the sinful human soul. Whichcote and Cudworth, in contrast, brought God into every human soul. They believed that there was a sense in which God is present within each of us, a sense in which a reconciliation with God is equivalent to a reconciliation with oneself. That is why we should look within – because within each of us is present God Himself.

This understanding of the relationship between God and humans is fundamental to the internal orientation of Whichcote and Cudworth's philosophy. But it also makes it difficult to place their philosophy into the internalist–externalist taxonomy of recent philosophical debate. For while Whichcote and Cudworth wanted to locate God within each human mind, they also had to hold on to the idea of God as an external entity. Even for Whichcote and Cudworth, God could not be identical to the human mind; it had to be possible for God to exist while humans did not. How Cudworth developed this view – in which God is both internal to and independent of the human mind – is something we will examine in Chapter 4. The point I want to make here is that such a view (however the details are worked out) is not going to fit easily into either the internalist or externalist camp. For central to Whichcote and Cudworth's overall philosophy is a conception of God that bridges the internal and the external, and it's difficult to find room for such an entity within recent meta-ethical debates.

3

Whichcote and Cudworth on Religious Liberty

In the preceding chapter, I cast the thought of Whichcote and Cudworth as a reaction against the Calvinism of their families and fellow students and tutors at Emmanuel. But the goal of this chapter is to explain Whichcote and Cudworth's crucial role in the development of religious liberty. And to do this, we need to situate them in a broader context, amid the political and religious upheavals of mid-seventeenth-century England as a whole. In Section A, I fill in some of this background. In B, I sketch the main points of Whichcote and Cudworth's views on religious liberty and how Whichcote embodied those views during the civil war in the 1650s. And in C, I look at arguments for religious liberty Cudworth gave in 1647.

A. Religion and State in Mid-Seventeenth-Century England

In the 1630s and early 1640s, there were numerous disputes between the king and Parliament that erupted into civil war in 1642. The English Calvinists were squarely on the Parliamentary side of this conflict, and Whichcote and Cudworth were generally associated with the Parliamentary cause as well. Part of the reason for this association was social. Whichcote and Cudworth came from Calvinist families and they attended a Calvinist college. And while they were certainly opposed to the Calvinists' religious doctrines, there is no indication of personal hostility between them and their families and colleagues. The evidence suggests, rather, that Whichcote and Cudworth remained very close to the people with whom they grew up and studied. As profound as Whichcote and Cudworth's disagreement with Calvinism was, it remained a disagreement among friends. And in determining associations during the civil war, such cultural factors could be as influential as ideology.

From a certain perspective, moreover, Whichcote and Cudworth were intellectually closer to the Calvinists' endorsement of the Parliamentary side than to the ideology of the Royalists. The key similarity between Which-cote and Cudworth and the Calvinists was an emphasis on the individual.

Whichcote and Cudworth had, of course, a very different conception of human nature, but they agreed with the Calvinists that all matters of ultimate religious importance originated within each person – whether that involved awareness of sin and repentance, as the Calvinists maintained, or self-respect and internal harmony, as Whichcote and Cudworth argued. In line with this emphasis on the individual, they all also credited conscience, which allowed for personal judgment in a manner that could be used to justify resistance to the king.

Whichcote and Cudworth were never partisans, however. Though associated with members of the Parliamentary cause, they never explicitly advocated for one side or the other of the civil war. Instead, they argued for tolerance and liberty, a position at odds not only with the Royalists but also with many within the Parliamentarian camp.

Because the ideals of religious freedom are so entrenched in our own society, it's easy for us to overlook the boldness and significance of Whichcote and Cudworth's call for religious liberty. There can be no question, however, that theirs was very much a minority position in the 1640s. Religious disagreements were roiling the country, but most people on all sides agreed that there had to be a single enforceable state religion for all Englishmen. The battles were over which form the state religion should take. Most people did not seriously consider the idea that the state should allow individuals the latitude to make their own religious decisions. As Conrad Russell has pointed out, "The word 'religion,' both by common usage and by prevailing etymology, meant first and foremost rules which were to be enforced" (Russell 1990, 63). So while "religion" tends to call to our minds something private and personal, most seventeenth-century Englishmen would have taken the word to refer to something that was essentially a public duty. Seventeenth-century England, as Russell explains, was "a society with a code of values and a political system which were only designed to be workable with one" religion (Russell 1990, 63).

B. Whichcote and Cudworth's "Spirit of Religion"

The belief in the necessity of a single enforceable state religion fueled fierce disputes in the 1640s about the particulars of churchly procedure. People battled over questions such as: How much of the Sunday service should be devoted to sermonizing and how much to worship and prayer? Should there be an altar, and if so, should it be raised? Should organ music be allowed in church? Should there be images in the stained glass? Where should the communion table be placed, at the east end of the church or in the middle? Should the sacrament be given with wafers or "common bread"?

Whichcote and Cudworth thought this was all tragically much ado about next to nothing. The forms of Sunday service, they thought, were not essential to "*the state of religion*" itself, but merely dispensable tools that were useful for some people at some times and not useful for other people at other times. Each individual, Whichcote and Cudworth argued, should be given the freedom to decide for him- or herself whether or not to use any of these tools. If one person's religious spirit is roused by organ music, stained glass representations of Christ's travails, and an ornate altar with rails, then that person should be allowed to attend a church with those features. If another person finds such things distracting or offensive, then he or she should be allowed to attend a bare wooden church free of ornamentation and organ.

The one course of action that was wrong, according to Whichcote and Cudworth, was to force people to practice religion in ways they would not freely have chosen. It was intolerance of different forms of religion that was contrary to religion, not any of the forms themselves. For the essence or ultimate end of religion is peaceful love of one's neighbor. Intolerant divisiveness about forms of service thus amounted to a sacrifice of the end of religion for the sake of that which was merely instrumental. As Whichcote put it, "Religion, which is a Bond of *Union*, ought not to be a Ground of Division: but is in an unnatural use, when it doth disunite. Men cannot *differ*, by *true* Religion; because it is true Religion to *agree*. The Spirit of Religion is a Reconciling Spirit" (Aphorisms 712). Or as he explained elsewhere, "The more *False* any one is in his Religion, the more *Fierce* and furious in Maintaining it; the more Mistaken, the more Imposing.... The longest Sword, the strongest Lungs, the most Voices, are false measures of *Truth*" (Aphorisms 499–500).

This call for liberty of worship – it is worth emphasizing again – was the furthest thing from a bromide in the 1640s. Most Englishmen at the time thought it an exceedingly dangerous idea, one that would lead to moral turpitude, social chaos, and eternal damnation. But Whichcote and Cudworth stuck to their guns, continuing to insist on tolerance even as the forces of intolerance grew more and more belligerent.

We can gain a sense of Whichcote's personal commitment to religious liberty by looking at how he conducted himself in 1644, when the parliamentary commissioners offered him the provostship of King's College, Cambridge.[1] The previous provost had been Samuel Collins, but Collins was associated with the Royalists, and so when the civil war began, the parliamentary commissioners had him dismissed. Whichcote respected Collins and was disturbed that university positions were being determined by partisanship. As a result, Whichcote seriously considered turning down the commissioners, despite the prestige and importance of the provostship. In the end, he accepted the position, mainly because he believed his duty to the university required him to work for its betterment. But he said he would take the job only if a certain condition was met: His stipend as provost had to be paid in full to the ousted Collins. Moreover, Whichcote took the position while still refusing to sign the Parliamentary Covenant, a document pledging allegiance to the Parliamentary cause. Now according to the law Parliament passed in 1644, anyone failing to sign the covenant would be barred from holding any governmental or university position. But Whichcote was made provost nonetheless, and his stipend was duly paid to Collins. Parliament's willingness to allow Whichcote this latitude must have been due in part to his stature as a teacher, administrator, and minister. And it must also have been due to his well-earned reputation for nonpartisanship. Whichcote's advocacy for Collins and his refusal to sign the covenant must have been interpreted, that is, as further evidence of his being above the fray, and not as evidence of his harboring any secret partisan sympathies.

C. Cudworth's 1647 Sermons

Cudworth's commitment to religious tolerance was just as manifest as Whichcote's. This commitment became especially clear in 1647, when Cudworth delivered two electrifyingly brilliant sermons, one to the House of Commons and the other to the Society of Lincolnes Inn. These sermons were truly remarkable performances – rhetorically, politically, philosophically – and must be counted among the greatest neglected masterpieces of seventeenth-century English thought.

According to Cudworth's 1647 sermons, the biggest problem of the age was confusion about what was essential to religion, with many people concentrating all their energies on what wasn't essential and neglecting the things that were. Crucially, Cudworth's sermons supported neither the Parliamentary nor the Royalist side. His overriding message was that both sides were missing the point. Each had been fighting to instate its own conception of religion and eradicate the other, but the things that separated the different conceptions were all inessential, religiously peripheral at best, while the hostility of each side to the other violated the essence of religion.

At the very beginning of the dedication of his sermon to the House of Commons, Cudworth made clear his intention to criticize those who believed that the religious differences of the day were worth fighting over. The purpose of his sermon, he started out by saying, "was not to contend for this or that opinion, but only to persuade men to the life of Christ," without which "those many opinions about religion, that are everywhere so eagerly contended for on all sides...are but so many shadows fighting with one another" (Commons 370). Cudworth went on to caution those who would

please themselves only in the violent opposing of other men's superstitions, according to the genius of the present times, without substituting in the room of them an inward principle of sport and life in their own souls. For I fear many of us that pull down idols in churches may set them up in our hearts; and whilst we quarrel with painted glass, make no scruple at all of entertaining many foul lusts in our souls, and committing continual idolatry with them. (Commons 371)

This was a remarkable thing for Cudworth to say. For within Commons at the time there were many people who *had* contended for this or that opinion – people who *had* pulled down idols in churches and quarreled with painted glass. Now Cudworth did leave open the possibility that some members of the contending parties had within their hearts the inward principle of Christ. But he just barely left that possibility open. He came very close, that is, to asserting that all those actively engaged on one side or the other of the conflict were guilty of idolatry in their soul. And he made this statement to the House of Commons itself – in a lion's den of religious contention.

In his sermon at Lincolnes, Cudworth was equally clear in his criticisms of both sides of the raging religious disputes. There were some, he said, who contended that particular kinds of observance of the Sabbath and the Sacrament were essential to religion, and they were willing to fight for the cause of requiring them. And there were others who contended that such observances were superstitious, and they were willing to fight for the cause of eradicating them. But the fact was that it was essential neither to require such observances nor to eradicate them. One person could be truly religious while practicing them, while another person could be truly religious while not practicing them. Such things were indifferent, neither bad nor good. The one wrong reaction to such things was to take either their requirement or their eradication to be essential to religion (see Lincolnes 59–60).

The philosophical basis of Cudworth's call for religious liberty will stand out more clearly when placed against the justification many seventeenth-century Englishmen would have given for the enforcement of a single state religion. A large part of this justification would have rested on the widely accepted idea that creating properly religious citizens was an essential role of government. Rulers had as their charge the welfare of their subjects. And nothing was more important to the subjects' welfare than the state of their souls, which determined their eternal fate. Rulers were obligated, therefore, to do everything in their power to put their subjects on the right spiritual track – which meant that rulers were obligated to enforce religion. According to this way of thinking, a ruler who did not try to promote the spiritual welfare of his subjects by enforcing religion would be as remiss in his duties as a ruler who did nothing to defend his country against foreign invasion or as a parent who neglected to care for the safety of his child.

Underlying this justification for the enforcement of religion were two assumptions. The first assumption was that enforcement was necessary to ensure that people did the right thing. The second assumption was that people's spiritual welfare was well served when they were forced to do the right thing. The belief that religion had to be enforced involved, in other words, the idea that people would not perform the actions required by religion if the magistrate did not threaten them with punishment for nonperformance and the idea that people who performed certain actions in order to avoid the magistrate's punishment were doing what religion required. Cudworth thought both of these ideas were profoundly mistaken.

He thought the first idea was mistaken because it was grounded in the belief that human nature is basically corrupt. It implies that people do not have within themselves proper motivation to do what is right and that the external threats of the magistrate are therefore necessary. Take away the threat of punishment, according to this way of thinking, and people's natural tendency to sin will inevitably lead them to all manner of transgressions. But Cudworth believed that human beings are naturally drawn toward the good, and that all of us do have within ourselves proper motivation to do what is right. That is not to say that everyone *will* always do the right thing – the Positive Answer doesn't have to be *that* positive – but rather that everyone has the internal resources to do it. And the best way to get people to use their internal resources is by reasonable discussion and calm persuasion, not by the threat of punishment.

Cudworth thought the second idea underlying the enforcement of religion – that people who performed certain actions in order to avoid the magistrate's punishment were doing what religion required – was mistaken because it was grounded in the belief that religion consists of external actions, regardless of the motivation behind them. It implies that someone who performs certain actions because he fears punishment if he does not is doing what religion requires. But religion, Cudworth maintained, essentially consists of an internal state of mind, and that state of mind is something that the fear of punishment can never produce.

Another way of putting the problem with the second idea is this: if things are as bad as the Negative Answer says they are, then external enforcement isn't really going to do any good. For all external enforcement can do is make people perform certain acts rather than others. It cannot change a person's character or disposition. The fear of punishment may, for instance, make some people attend church on a Sunday instead of carousing. But so long as they are attending church only because they fear punishment if they do not, they are still motivated by narrow, irreligious "self-will." And people with such motivation are just as far from being truly religious when they are in a church as when they are outside of it.

Cudworth's basic point is that religion consists of one's internal state – of the kind of person one is – and forcing someone to perform external acts won't change this internal state. That which is essential to religion is inside each person and thus out of the magistrate's reach. As Cudworth put it in his Lincolnes sermon, "For the true Gospel-Righteousness, which Christ came to set up in the world, doth not consist merely in outward Works, whether Ceremonial or Moral, done by our own Natural power in our Unregenerate state, but in an inward Life and Spirit wrought by God" (Lincolnes 31). Or as he put it in his sermon to the House of Commons, "The *Law of the Letter* without us sets us in a condition of a little more liberty, by restraining us from many outward acts of sin; but yet it doth not disenthral us from the power of sin in our hearts" (Commons 405).

Cudworth's conception of heaven and hell underscores the futility of trying to enforce religion. As we have seen, Cudworth believed that heaven and hell are not primarily places at which one arrives after death but states of mind that arise from one's character. Now a person with a narrow, irreligious character can be forced to perform certain actions. But if he performs those actions only because he fears punishment, his character will still be irreligious, and hell-bound he will remain. The magistrate cannot save your soul any more than he can make you fall in love. As Cudworth explains,

I do not therefore mean by holiness, the mere performance of outward duties of religion, coldly acted over as a task; nor our habitual prayings, hearings, fastings, multiplied one upon another (though these be all good, as subservient to an higher end); but I mean an inward soul and principle of divine life, that spiriteth all these; that enliveneth and quickeneth, the dead carcass of all our outward performances whatsoever.... [I urge] an inward self-moving principle living in our Hearts. (Commons 403)

In his 1647 sermons, then, Cudworth argued that the essence of religion consists of a certain kind of internal spirit, disposition, temper, or character. And he also maintained that a person with this spirit or character will not necessarily perform any particular rituals nor necessarily refrain from any particular rituals. Rituals in general, because they are outward acts that can be aligned to virtually any character, are religiously indifferent. There's nothing intrinsically right or wrong about them. If some people find that rituals help them cultivate a truly religious spirit, they should go ahead and engage in them. If other people find that rituals are a hindrance, they should refrain. Whatever works. The only wrong position to take is that either ritual or non-ritual is religiously essential. Because while having a righteous character is consistent with both ritual and non-ritual, having an unrighteous character is consistent with both of those things as well. It is, moreover, certainly unrighteous to enforce either ritual or non-ritual when that involves violating what *is* essential to religion, which is God's commandment of love (Commons 371). So Cudworth argued. And so he argued in the middle of a civil war fueled by disagreement over religious ritual.

Religious tolerance has won a decisive enough victory in Britain and the United States that it might require some effort for us to imagine living in a society governed by the principles of a one-religion state. Whichcote and Cudworth are as responsible for that victory as anyone. We've looked at how Cudworth's public sermons worked to win people over to a conception of religion that allowed for – indeed, required – individual liberty of worship. But Whichcote and Cudworth exerted just as much influence through their teaching at Cambridge, where they had as colleagues and students a number of the men who would spearhead the Latitudinarian movement (i.e., the movement to give individuals latitude to decide for themselves how to worship) that helped effect real change in the Church of England in the late seventeenth and early eighteenth centuries.[2] There is, as well, a direct line of intellectual descent from Whichcote and Cudworth to John Locke, whose calls for tolerance and liberty helped pave the way for the Toleration Act of 1690 and influenced greatly the U.S. Constitution.[3]

4

Rationalism, Sentimentalism, and Ralph Cudworth

Whichcote and Cudworth's role in the development of religious liberty was pivotal to Enlightenment thought. But Cudworth (and, to a lesser extent, Whichcote) was instrumental to the development of another highly influential line of thought as well: moral rationalism.

Moral rationalism is the view that morality originates in reason alone.[1] It is often contrasted with moral sentimentalism, which is the view that the origin of morality lies at least partly in (non-rational) sentiment. The eighteenth century saw pitched philosophical battles between rationalists and sentimentalists, and the issue continues to fuel debates among philosophers today.

The eighteenth-century rationalists took Cudworth to be one of their champions and the sentimentalists of the period agreed, placing Cudworth squarely in the opposing camp (see Price 20 and Hume's Second Enquiry 93). This view of Cudworth was further solidified in 1897, when Selby-Bigge published an influential two-volume collection of the writings of the British moralists. In his preface, Selby-Bigge explained that the first volume contained the writings of moral sentimentalists and the second volume the writings of moral rationalists. Cudworth appeared in the second – the rationalist – volume (see Selby-Bigge 1897/1964, xxxii). Since many twentieth-century philosophers knew Cudworth and numerous other British moralists primarily through Selby-Bigge's collection, it is understandable that they came to think both that the most important distinction in early modern British moral philosophy was between rationalism and sentimentalism and that Cudworth was one of the rationalists.

Selby-Bigge's characterization is not entirely off-base. Eighteenth-century thinkers such as Hutcheson, Balguy, Hume, and Price did devote a great deal of philosophical energy to the question of whether morality originates in reason alone or at least partly in sentiment. And the work of Cudworth's that was most familiar to both eighteenth- and twentieth-century philosophers was the *Treatise concerning Eternal and Immutable Morality*, which is, as we will see, a thoroughly rationalist text.

But the sermons Cudworth gave in 1647 paint a different picture, one that offers at least as much succor to sentimentalists as to rationalists. For in the sermons, Cudworth exalted an aspect of the soul that seems to share at least as much with what eighteenth- and twentieth-century philosophers thought of as sentiment as with what they thought of as reason.[2]

Part of the explanation for Cudworth's not fitting squarely into the rationalist or sentimentalist camp is that at the time he was writing the distinction had not yet been sharply formulated. But Cudworth also vacillated. In certain works, he seemed to want to emphasize the role passion must play in the righteous life and to suggest that rationality is less important. In other works, he insisted that rationality is essential and seemed to imply that passion is dispensable. But however that may be, I think it is clear that Cudworth anticipated some of the most crucial aspects of both sentimentalism and rationalism, and an examination of his views can shed valuable light on that later debate.

Perhaps most importantly, we can look to Cudworth to find the deepest common ground between the later rationalists and sentimentalists. For while Cudworth might have vacillated between proto-sentimentalist and rationalist positions, he always remained firmly and clearly committed to the idea that to live righteously is to act in accord with principles internal to one's own constitution. He always remained firmly and clearly opposed to the idea that to live righteously one had to depend on the assistance of some external force. And with Cudworth's goal of showing that morality originates in principles internal to each individual – with his goal of affirming the Positive Answer – the later rationalists and sentimentalists would all agree. An examination of Cudworth can thus help us to see that the dispute between rationalists and sentimentalists was a relatively mild disagreement among thinkers allied on the same side of the Human Nature Question.

In Section A of this chapter, I describe the conception of morality implied by the two sermons Cudworth gave in 1647. In B, I describe the conception of morality implied by Cudworth's posthumously published *Eternal and Immutable Morality* and how it differs – at least in emphasis, if not in substance – from that of the sermons. And in C, I explain why Cudworth expounded these two positions and what lies in common beneath them.

A. The Proto-Sentimentalism of the 1647 Sermons

In his sermons, as we've seen, Cudworth was concerned to distinguish between what is essential to religion and what is inessential. What is crucial for our purposes in this chapter is that he said in the sermons that the essence of religion lies in the "heart" and not in the "head" (Commons 378).

This heart-based religion Cudworth argues for in the sermons consists entirely of the "law of love" (Commons 404). This "law" is not an external command but an internal spirit of action, a "kindling" and "warming" principle of the heart (Commons 387) that "enliveneth and quickeneth . . . all our outward performances" (Commons 403). To be truly religious, Cudworth tells us, is not to be in mere "outward conformity to God's commandments" (Commons 404) but to have a certain kind of motivation or character, a certain kind of "temper and constitution of the soul" (Commons 380). It is not simply to perform particular actions but for one's heart to be in the right place.

Throughout the sermons, Cudworth repeatedly contrasts the essential "inward" spirit of religion with relatively unimportant "outward" observances (Commons 378). In the category of religiously peripheral outward things, Cudworth places specific churchly procedures and modes of worship, such as "habitual prayings, hearings, fastings" (Commons 403) and all other "*Rites* and *Ceremonies*" (Lincolnes 59). As we saw in Chapter 3, Cudworth acknowledges that these "external observances" (Lincolnes 60) may help influence the hearts of some people and thus may "be good, as subservient to a higher end" (Commons 403). But he believes that in themselves they are "*Indifferent*" (Lincolnes 59), there being "no intrinsecal Goodness at all in them" (Lincolnes 42).

In the category of peripheral outward things Cudworth also places theologically sophisticated doctrinal matters, such as the "infinite problems" concerning Christ's "divinity, humanity, union of both together, and what not" (Commons 373). Such "systems and bodies of divinity" may be "useful in a subordinate way," but on their own they cannot make one into a "true Christian" (Commons 374). They concern only "dry speculations" and the "dead skeleton of opinions" (Commons 380), while true Christianity consists of character, motivation, a spirit of action.

> [T]he knowledge of Christ doth not consist merely in a few barren notions, in a form of certain dry and sapless opinions. . . . Christ came not to possess our brains only with some cold opinions that send down nothing but a freezing and benumbing influence upon our hearts. Christ was vitae magister, not scholae; and he is the best Christian whose heart beats with the truest pulse towards heaven, not he whose head spinneth out the finest cobwebs. (Commons 378)

Here Cudworth is attacking scholasticism, and this is not the only place in the sermons where he does so.[3] In another passage he says, "Many of the more learned, if they can but wrangle and dispute about Christ, imagine themselves to be grown great proficients in the School of Christ" (Commons 374). And elsewhere he ridicules those who believe one needs "many school distinctions, to come to a right understanding" of Christ (Commons 379). The scholastics, Cudworth argues, made skill at syllogistic reasoning the "*alpha* and *omega* of their religion" (Commons 380). But one person can be an outstanding practitioner of the forms of scholastic disputation and yet lack all love for his fellow man, while another person can be ignorant of all the rules of Aristotelian logic and yet possess a truly Christian spirit. What scholasticism places great value on is neither necessary nor sufficient for true religion (Commons 375, 379).

So Cudworth claims that "rites and ceremonies," doctrinal "beliefs," and scholastic "speculations" are religiously inessential, and he justifies this claim by pointing out that such things have no necessary connection to the motivating spirit of one's actions.[4] Such things occupy the head and not the heart, but it is only the heart that is essential to true religion.[5] Attention to such things is, in fact, likely to be counterproductive, producing "*a bitter Zeal*" (Lincolnes 61) that draws one away from the true spirit of religion. Cudworth thus attacks "the distemper of our times," which works "to scare and frighten men only with opinions and make them only solicitous about the entertaining of this and that speculation, which will not render them anything the better in their lives, or the liker unto God" (Commons 379). Or as he puts it in another gibe at scholasticism, "Christ came not into the world to fill our heads with mere speculations; to kindle a fire of wrangling and contentious dispute amongst us and to warm our spirits against one another with nothing but angry and peevish debates, whilst in the meantime our hearts remain all ice within towards God and have not the least spark of true heavenly fire to melt and thaw them" (Commons 378).

Cudworth's rebuke to those battling over "*Ceremonial Observations*" and "systems and bodies of divinity" goes hand in hand with his conspicuous ecumenicalism. What is both necessary and sufficient for true religion, according to Cudworth, is an "inward principle" that is compatible with virtually any interpretation of Christianity. At times, Cudworth even suggests the Pelagian view that possession of this inward principle is compatible with a complete lack of distinctly Christian beliefs, as for instance when he claims that one who "endeavors really . . . to comply with that truth in his life which his conscience is convinced of, is nearer a Christian, though he never heard of Christ, than he that believes all the vulgar articles of the Christian faith and plainly denieth Christ in his life" (Commons 378).[6]

Now what is particularly relevant to the purpose of asking about Cudworth's relationship to the later dispute between rationalists and sentimentalists is that the sermons' emphasis on the internal motivational aspect of religion also leads him to dismiss the religious importance of propositional knowledge in general. Over and over again, he says that it is wrong to focus our religious energies on "speculations," "beliefs," "notions," "knowledge," "understanding," and other denizens of the "brain" and "head." For none of these things "kindles," "warms," "enlivens," or "quickens" the "heart," and within the heart lies the essence of religion. Propositional knowledge – knowledge that can be gained through discursive rational thought – is neither necessary nor sufficient for the "divine temper and constitution of the soul" that is the heart of true religion (Commons 380; cf. 403–4, 406–7).

[T]here is a soul and spirit of divine truths that could never yet be congealed into ink, that could never be blotted upon paper; which [is] able to dwell or lodge nowhere but in a spiritual being, in a living thing, because itself is nothing but a life and spirit. Neither can it, where indeed it is, express itself sufficiently in words and sounds, but it will best declare and speak itself in actions.... Words are nothing but the dead resemblances and pictures of those truths which live and breathe in actions; and "the kingdom of God (as the apostle speaketh) consisteth not in word," but in life and power. (Commons, 389–90)

The essence of religion is "a living principle in us" that cannot be captured by language (Commons 374). It is something that lies beyond the reach of discursive rational thought. "[W]ords and syllables, which are but dead things, cannot possibly convey the living notions of heavenly truths to us. The secret mysteries of a divine life . . . cannot be written or spoken, language and expressions cannot reach them" (Commons 374–5).

In the sermons, then, Cudworth elevates "heart" over "head" in a manner that leads him to marginalize propositional knowledge and discursive thought, claiming that in matters of religion such knowledge and thought can play a merely peripheral, nonessential role at best.[7] Indeed, the sermons at times come close to an outright condemnation of those whose primary focus is on rational thought, contending that such people are liable to lose touch with the essence of religion by concentrating on matters that are neither necessary nor sufficient. But this is hardly what we would expect from a philosopher known as a rationalist. The sermons seem to be, rather, the work of someone who wants to insulate the essence of religion from the workings of the rational faculty.

Cudworth's embrace of *mystery* in the sermon before the House of Commons also suggests a desire to keep rationality at arm's length. In that sermon, Cudworth repeatedly contends that the essence of religion is a "great mystery" and that all true Christians are "so many mystical Christs" (Commons 387, 390; cf. 375, 380). Cudworth also places mystery at the heart of religion in his 1642 sermon "The Union of Christ and the Church; in a Shadow," where he endorses the view (which he attributes to Plato) that there is contained "some Mysticall meaning concerning the Nature of Divine Love," by which a man might "recover himselfe, and so by degrees work up himself again unto God, and be made perfectly one with him" (Union 23). The incompatibility between these endorsements of mystery and a robust confidence in the faculty of rationality stands out clearly when we attend to the word "mystery" itself. The original Greek meaning of "mystery" – of which Cudworth would have been aware – is a secret religious ceremony, closed to the public, open only to initiates.[8] And while that sense of the word was not what Cudworth intended, he must have had in mind the sense that evolved from it, which is (according to the *Oxford English Dictionary*) "a doctrine of faith involving difficulties which human reason is incapable of solving" or "a matter unexplained or inexplicable; something beyond human knowledge or comprehension." By ushering mystery into religion's essential inner sanctum, Cudworth seems to be showing discursive rational thought the door.

B. The Rationalism of *Eternal and Immutable Morality*

In contrast to the 1647 sermons, *Eternal and Immutable Morality*, which Cudworth probably wrote in the early to middle 1660s, demands to be interpreted as a rationalist tract. This is not simply because EIM elevates to supreme importance something that is labeled "reason," but because of the way that EIM conceives of both what is labeled "reason" and the concept of morality.

Cudworth tells us in the first chapter of EIM that its goal is to show that if morality exists at all, it must exist *necessarily* (16). EIM seeks to establish that morality will be real if and only if the moral categories – of good and evil, just and unjust, virtuous and vicious – are as "eternal and immutable" as the categories of logic and mathematics. So if what we think of as morality turns out to be based on merely contingent facts, then (according to EIM) we will have to conclude that morality doesn't exist. We will have to conclude that our moral terms don't refer to anything real at all, that everything we think of as morally significant is actually an illusion, a sham. Let us call this the "necessity of morals thesis."[9]

The necessity of morals thesis is a metaphysical claim. But Cudworth draws from it the epistemological implication that wc will have reason to trust our moral ideas (we will have reason to think our moral ideas track moral reality) only if those ideas originate in reason alone. For it is reason and reason alone that comprehends necessary truth (EIM 134, 137). Reason is that which discerns what is "necessary, firm, immutable, and adamantine" (EIM 137). It is the "power in the soul" that comprehends "that which absolutely IS and IS NOT" (EIM 134). If, in contrast, our moral ideas turn out to originate in something other than reason alone, then we will lack grounds for thinking that they accurately depict reality.

Cudworth's belief that our moral ideas can be trustworthy only if they originate in reason alone is part of a general epistemological position he holds. The general position is that something constitutes knowledge or science if and only if it is known to be necessarily true. This is an all-or-nothing epistemology in that it tells us that any belief that falls short of necessary understanding does not qualify as knowledge at all. All knowledge consists of necessary understanding, while beliefs we cannot be sure are necessarily true are all equally "whiffling," on an epistemic par with the most sottish of superstitions.

This is a very high epistemological standard – too high, most contemporary philosophers would say. Our understanding of mathematics and logic may be of the type EIM longs for, but that doesn't mean (most contemporary philosophers would say) that anything that falls short of that understanding is fit for the epistemological scrap heap. There are other standards that may also be perfectly acceptable, even if they aren't as high as mathematical and logical understanding. Most of what is now called science, in fact – physics, chemistry, biology – we do not understand in the way we understand math and logic. But we do not feel compelled to say that because we cannot grasp the logical necessity of the principles of, say, biology, the study of biology is a complete sham. Indeed, most contemporary meta-ethicists think they would completely vindicate moral realism if they could show that our moral judgments can achieve the epistemological status of physics, chemistry, and biology. Very few, if any, contemporary moral realists are still pining for a moral theory that looks like math and logic. But what typically passes for moral realism today would not have been good enough for the Cudworth of EIM. To constitute knowledge, according to EIM, our grasp of morality has to be of the same type as our understanding of math and logic. Nothing less will do.

Cudworth was not alone in subscribing to this high epistemological standard. Many other seventeenth-century philosophers also held that beliefs truly deserving the status of knowledge had to involve an understanding of the necessity of what was believed. Many other seventeenth-century philosophers held that our understanding of the natural world – if that understanding was ever to be worthy of the name of "science" – would eventually be based on laws that we would see are necessary in the same way math and logic are. A putative science that lacked such laws would be incomplete at best. So from the perspective of this seventeenth-century conception of knowledge, to show that morality is on an epistemic par with systems of logically non-necessary inductive generalizations would not be to do morality any favors, as non-necessary inductive generalizations would not have qualified as science at all.

The epistemological implication Cudworth draws from the necessity of morals thesis is central to EIM's argument against his two greatest foes: Hobbes and the English Calvinist voluntarists. As Cudworth construes them, Hobbes and the voluntarists both maintain that our moral duties originate in the commands of a being with great power – in the case of Hobbes it is the sovereign, in the case of the voluntarists it is God.[10] But this powerful being does not issue the commands he does for reasons we can fully understand. We could not, through the use of reason alone, have predicted what the commander would command. We require the commander's dicta, either in the form of proclamations and decrees or in the form of scripture. More-over, our reasons for obeying the commands are not the same as the commander's reasons for issuing them. The normative force of the commands depends on their being commands and does not issue entirely from their being things we understand to be necessarily true. Indeed, as Cudworth construes them, the Hobbesian and the voluntarist imply that our ultimate reason for obeying the commands necessarily involves our thinking that we will be punished by the commander if we do not. But such fearful obedience bears no resemblance to the purely rational understanding that must undergird what Cudworth takes to be a real and justified commitment to morality.

The epistemological implication Cudworth draws from the necessity of morals thesis is also central to his rejection of the view (which he associated with Protagoras) that morality originates in sensation. One's own sensations are not the same as the commands of another. In EIM, however, Cudworth argues that one's sensations are crucially like voluntarist and Hobbesian commands in that they defy understanding. Just as it is impossible for us to discover fully intelligible reasons for the commands the voluntarist God or the Hobbesian sovereign issues (at least insofar as Cudworth interprets voluntarism and Hobbesianism), so too is it impossible for us to discover fully intelligible reasons for the sensations we experience. Our sensations are things that just happen to us. We experience them as mere occurrences, brute facts. We might be able to correlate some of these experiences with others of them, but we cannot understand *why* they occur. Our awareness of them always remains on the same plane, as it were, on the surface (EIM 58).

Of course, Cudworth did not know of the sentimentalist moral theories that would later be expounded by Hutcheson and Hume. I believe it's pretty clear, though, that the arguments of EIM imply that moral sentiments, or the deliverances of a moral sense, are just as impenetrable to our understanding as mere sensations and arbitrary commands. EIM implies that sentiments are things we experience as just happening to us, brute facts, not ideas we can understand. According to EIM, therefore, sentiments cannot ground the reality of morals, nor can they be the source of moral distinctions that we can have adequate reason to accept.

So Cudworth uses the necessity of morals thesis and its epistemological implication as a battering ram against voluntarism, Hobbesianism, and the view that morality and moral judgment depend on sensation. But Cudworth also explores the positive or constructive side of the thesis and its epistemological implication, explaining what would have to be true in order for us to have knowledge of morality, as well as explaining what a science of morals would look like. Let us look at those positive aspects now.

As we've seen, Cudworth believes that to have knowledge of something is to understand that it is necessarily so. And to have such an understanding, we must comprehend the essential nature of a thing (EIM 62). Cudworth also maintains that we can never comprehend the essential nature of things that exist outside of our minds, for we can only experience such external things' effect on us, not how they are in and of themselves (EIM 57–60).

That is why sensation can never produce knowledge – because "sense itself is but the passive perception of some individual material forms, but to know or understand, is actively to comprehend a thing by some abstract, free and universal reasonings" (EIM 58).

What, then, can we know? What essential natures can we comprehend? We can know and comprehend only what is "written within" our minds (EIM 60). If we have any knowledge – if there is anything whose essential nature we comprehend – it must be of what is internal to us. As Cudworth puts it, "[T]he primary and immediate objects of intellection and knowledge, are not things existing without the mind, but ideas of the mind itself actively exerted, that is the intelligible reasons of things" (EIM 76). All that we can ever know is our own innate ideas.

Because Cudworth believes that we can have knowledge only of innate ideas and not of things that impress on us from without, it is vitally important for him to prove that innate ideas exist, that the empiricist view of the human soul as carte blanche is mistaken. For if the empiricists are right and we do not possess innate ideas, then Cudworth would have to conclude that it is impossible for us to have knowledge of anything at all.

What does Cudworth have in mind when he speaks of an innate idea? He provides numerous examples, and it is not always clear if there are any coherent organizing principles controlling his disparate lists. But the examples that come up time and time again are: "*Nihil potest esse et non esse eodem tempore* [Nothing can be and not be at the same time]," "*Aequalia addita aequalibus efficiunt aequalia* [Equals added to equals make equals]," and "*Nihil nulla est affectio* [No effect results from nothing]."[11] And the example that he uses most frequently by far – the one that plays the leading, if not the sole, role in his arguments for innatism – comes right out of Euclid: "the geometrical theorem concerning a triangle; that it hath three angles equal to two right angles" (EIM 118). Each of these ideas is a "universal axiomatical truth" (EIM 118) or "scientifical theorem or proposition" (EIM 122). Each of them we know to be necessarily true. And each of them, Cudworth argues throughout Books III and IV of EIM, must have originated not in external sensation but in the active vigor of the mind itself.

It is, however, very difficult to see how the spirit of religion Cudworth glorifies in the sermons would fit into EIM's list of innate ideas. For in the sermons, Cudworth tells us that the spirit of religion cannot be "congealed into ink" nor "blotted upon paper." It cannot be expressed in "words and syllables" nor "written or spoken." The spirit is something that "language and expressions cannot reach." But the theorems and propositions on EIM's list of innate ideas congeal into ink and blot onto paper very well. Words and syllables seem custom-made for their expression. Most of them even have their own Latin names.

Cudworth argues, moreover, that the innate ideas have a *universal* or *public* nature, and this suggests another difficulty in trying to assimilate EIM's innate ideas and the sermons' spirit of religion. To see this we must first trace Cudworth's account of this feature of innate ideas.

Cudworth believes that even though innate ideas "exist only in the mind" (EIM 125), they are nonetheless "exactly the same" for everyone (EIM 131). And when he says that these ideas are "exactly the same" for everyone, he does not mean merely that the ideas have the same content, but rather that each person's rational faculty has as its object the same *public* things.

Cudworth's argument for the public nature of innate ideas starts from the claim that the objects of reason are "fixed and immutable" (EIM 122). We all realize, for instance, that the essence of a triangle has always been and will always be exactly the same. This follows from the necessity of the essential characteristics of a triangle. But our particular individual minds are not fixed and immutable in the way that the essence of a triangle is. For there was a time before our particular individual minds ever existed, and yet there never was a time when the essence a triangle did not exist (EIM 127). There are, as well, times when we "do not actually think of" the essential features of a triangle, and yet the essential features still exist at all times nonetheless, possessing "a constant and never-failing entity ... whether our particular minds think of them or not" (EIM 127). But these truths are purely intelligible, and as such can exist only within a mind. They "are things that cannot exist alone," for as they are nothing but "modifications of mind" they must always inhere in some intellect (EIM 128).

So the objects of reason have an eternal and immutable existence, and those objects can exist only within a mind. But all of our particular created minds are temporal and mutable. We must conclude, therefore, that there is some other mind that is eternal and immutable and that is forever and always thinking of all the objects of reason. This mind, of course, is none other than God. As Cudworth explains:

> Now the plain meaning of all this is nothing else, but that there is an eternal wisdom and knowledge in the world, necessarily existing which was never made, and can never cease to be or be destroyed. Or, which is all one, that there is an infinite eternal mind necessarily existing, and that actually comprehends himself, the possibility of all things, and the verities clinging to them. In a word, that there is a God, or an omnipotent and omniscient Being, necessarily existing, who therefore cannot destroy his own being or nature, that is, his infinite power and wisdom. (EIM 128)

All the objects of reason exist always in the mind of God. And when we exercise our rational faculty, we gain access to those objects. Each of us, moreover, gains access to the very same objects, for each of us, through the use of reason, participates with the mind of God itself. God's mind is the public arena in which the rational thought of everyone is conducted. As Cudworth writes:

> Moreover, from hence also it comes to pass that truths, though they be never so many several and distant minds apprehending them, yet they are not broken, multiplied,

or diversified thereby, but that they are one and the same individual truths in them all. So that it is but one truth and knowledge that is in all the understandings in the world. Just as when a thousand eyes look upon the sun at once, they all see the same individual object. Or as when a great crowd or throng of people hear one and the same orator speaking to them all, it is one and the same voice, that is in the several ears of all those several auditors. So in like manner, when innumerable created understandings direct themselves to the contemplation of the same universal and immutable truths, they do all of them but as it were listen to one and the same original voice of the eternal wisdom that is never silent.... (EIM 131–2)

So Cudworth holds that when we truly understand something – when we have real knowledge – we participate with the mind of God. This is a very significant idea for several reasons.

First of all, it points toward a deep explanation of the epistemological implication Cudworth draws from the necessity of morals thesis. The episte-mological implication, recall, is that we have knowledge or a science of some-thing only if we understand why it is necessarily so. The seventeenth-century philosophers who held this epistemological position seemed to believe that the mind of God knows almost no contingency. God's understanding of the most important things, these philosophers believed, is perfect, and to under-stand something perfectly is to understand why it *has* to be the way it is. It follows, then, that if we are participating with the mind of God, our under-standing will be perfect too. So if our knowledge is God-like, and if God-like knowledge consists of necessary understanding, our beliefs can constitute knowledge only if they too impart necessary understanding.[12] This is why math and logic are, for many seventeenth-century philosophers, such apt models for science – because our understanding of the fundamental math-ematical and logical principles is so full and complete that God Himself cannot improve on it. EIM explains as clearly as any seventeenth-century work this idea that to do math and logic – or, indeed, truly to understand anything at all – is to become one with the mind of God. This is a posi-tion – rooted in a Positive Answer based on the deiformity of the human mind – that unites epistemology and religion, a position according to which the exercise of rationality is nothing less than a sacrament, a way truly to partake of the Divine .

Cudworth's claim that whenever we attain true understanding we partic-ipate with the mind of God is also significant because it allows him to draw the conclusion that when we attain true understanding we participate with the minds of one another. Cudworth is thus able to provide an account of the universal or public nature of reason. He is able to explain how rationality enables us to understand each other's thought, how we are able to "con-fer and discourse together ... presently perceiving one another's meaning" (EIM 131). Everyone is able to comprehend Euclid's theorems and discuss them with others, no matter where or when he or she lives. But this would be impossible unless everyone had in mind the same geometric ideas, unless all of us geometers were truly of one mind. As Cudworth puts it:

> Whereas it is plain that the subject of this theorem [that a triangle has three angles equal to two right angles] is such a thing as every geometrician, though in never such distant places and times, hath the very same always ready at his hand, without the least imaginable difference. And they all pronounce concerning the same thing. (EIM 118)

So reason is universal or public in that its objects are the same for everyone. These objects are publicly accessible intellectual items that everyone can simultaneously apprehend. And "whenever any theoretical proposition is rightly understood by any one particular mind whatsoever, and wheresoever it be, the truth of it is no private thing, nor relative to that particular mind only" (EIM 137).

Now that we have a picture of Cudworth's commitment in EIM to the public nature of the innate ideas that would enable us to attain moral knowledge, let us return to the question of how EIM's account relates to the 1647 sermons. Recall that in the sermons Cudworth repeatedly insists that the spirit of religion is a mystery, that there is something irreducibly mysterious about Christ's kindling of our hearts. But the most natural interpretation of the claim that something is mysterious is that the thing is *not* publicly accessible. A mystery is typically something about which all people *cannot* "confer and discourse" together. So once again, EIM and the 1647 sermons seem, at least prima facie, to imply different positions on the nature of morality. This problem becomes sharper, moreover, when we look closely at the kind of moral theory for which EIM was intended to pave the way.[13]

It might seem that EIM isn't much concerned with morality, its title notwithstanding, as the bulk of the book consists of epistemological arguments for the existence of innate ideas. But these epistemological arguments are clearly tied to a conception of what a proper moral theory would look like, and it's easy enough to infer the latter from the former.

Cudworth's ultimate goal, he tells us in the first chapter of EIM, is to show that we can and do have moral knowledge. In order to show this, he first has to explain what knowledge is, for moral knowledge is one part of knowledge in general. He then goes on to argue that to know something is to understand the necessity of it. He also argues that we can understand the necessity only of what is internal to our own minds, and that as a result, we can have knowledge only if we possess innate ideas. It then becomes necessary for Cudworth to establish that innate ideas do in fact exist in the human mind. And the example of geometry is supposed to establish that. But this still leaves a crucial job undone. For although the example of geometry shows that we can have knowledge (that our minds are not completely incapable of knowing, as they would be if they were blank slates), it does not show that we have knowledge of morality. The fact that our geometric ideas pass epistemic muster does not on its own imply that our moral ideas do.

Cudworth himself makes it clear that EIM leaves undone this job of establishing that our moral ideas are objects of knowledge. That job, he says in the final chapter of EIM, is something that he "shall show afterwards" (EIM 145). EIM has shown that since persons do have some innate ideas of necessary truths arising from within their own souls (as the example of geometry proves), it is possible for them to have knowledge. But showing this general fact about the human soul is only prefatory work to the more specific task of showing that our moral ideas are actually objects of knowledge. EIM disposes of one preliminary objection to the claim that we have moral knowledge, the objection being that we are incapable of having any kind of knowledge at all. But EIM does not positively establish that we do have moral knowledge itself. As Cudworth puts it (once again in the final chapter of EIM):

> Wherefore since the nature of morality cannot be understood, without some knowledge of the nature of the soul, I thought it seasonable and requisite here to take this occasion offered and *to prepare the way to our following discourse* by showing in general that the soul is not a mere passive and receptive thing, which hath no innate active principle of its own, because upon this hypothesis there could be no such thing as morality. (EIM 145; italics added)

So Cudworth sees EIM as prolegomena to a work that will explain "the nature of morality." EIM demonstrates that "if there be anything at all good or evil, just or unjust, there must of necessity be something naturally and immutably good and just," while the discourse to follow EIM will "show what this natural, immutable, and eternal justice is, with the branches and species of it" (EIM 16).

What will this later work look like? What kind of "discourse" will explain "the nature of morality" and show "the branches and species of it"? It's hard to say for sure. Cudworth's voluminous unpublished manuscripts suggest various pictures, and it seems that many more of his manuscripts – including "a discourse concerning Moral Good and Evil" or "Natural Ethicks" – have been lost (see Birch xiii). But the arguments in EIM give us very strong reason to believe that the sequel would have been a moral geometry that starts from self-evident moral axioms and moves on to demonstrations of specific moral duties. EIM implies that the way to establish that we have moral knowledge is to explain clearly and distinctly what our moral ideas are and to show that they are just as clear and certain as geometry. A work that produces a theory such as this would establish the science of morality in the same way that Euclid's principles established the science of geometry.

This idea that a true moral theory will resemble Euclidean geometric theory is evident in Samuel Clarke, John Balguy, and Book IV of John Locke's *Essay concerning Human Understanding* (see Raphael 1991, 192–209, 399, 159) Most relevant to our discussion of Cudworth, however, is that both

Benjamin Whichcote and Henry More – Cudworth's closest friends and philosophical comrades – were also both proponents of the geometric model of moral philosophy.

Whichcote develops his system of morality in several related sermons. He begins from the claim that all of morality is grounded in the self-evident principle that actions should be "fit and just" or "fair and equal." Whichcote does not spend much time explaining this principle of fitness, probably because he thinks of it as so obvious and fundamental that it neither needs nor admits of explanation. He does provide some glosses, though, maintaining in a couple of places that the principle of fitness "consists in this; the congruity and proportion between the action of an agent and his object. He acts morally that doth observe the proportion of an action to its object; that is, he doth terminate a due action upon its proper object" (Whichcote II 236). In a similar vein, Whichcote says that all moral actions are instances of "*giv[ing] every one their own*" (Whichcote II 52).

Whichcote does not leave matters at this very general level of fitness, however. He goes on to derive from that general principle specific rules of conduct, formulating "demonstration[s] in morals, that [are] as clear and as satisfactory as any demonstration in the mathematicks" (Whichcote IV 307). The first things he derives are four general tenets. They are:

1. To reverence and acknowledge the deity. 2. To live in love, and bear good will towards one another. 3. To deal justly, equally and fairly in all our transactions and dealings each with other. 4. To use moderation and government of ourselves, in respect of the necessaries and conveniences of this state. (Whichcote IV 351)

From these four tenets, Whichcote proceeds to demonstrate three general classes of duties: Godliness, or duties to God (from 1); Righteousness, or duties to others (from 2 and 3); and Sobriety, or duties to self (from 4) (Whichcote I 383–4). Whichcote claims to show how these duties imply particular rules that dictate how one ought to conduct oneself in matters of worship, speech, contracts, diet, and the running of a household, including instructions on how parents are to treat their children, husbands their wives, masters their servants, and men their dogs and horses (Whichcote I 253–5, II 218–19, IV 351–61).

More develops his moral system in the *Enchiridion Ethicum*, which was published in 1668.[14] He begins by presenting twenty-three "Moral Noemata" or "Noema's" (More 21). These Noemas, More tells us, fill the same role in the study of morality that "first undeniable Axioms" fill in "Mathematical Demonstrations" (More 20). They are "[a]xioms...into which almost all the Reasons of Morality may be reduced" (More 20) or self-evident general moral propositions from which specific moral duties may be derived. The Noemas consist of definitions of good and evil (Noemas I and II), descriptions of the degrees of which good and evil admit (Noemas III, IV, VII, VIII, IX), methods for maximizing the ratio of good to evil (Noemas V, VI, X,

XI, XII, XIII, XVIII, XIX), various statements of the Golden Rule (Noemas XIV, XV, XVI), and basic ethical claims ("'Tis good to obey the Magistrate in things indifferent" [Noema XX], "'Tis better to obey God than Men" [Noema XXI]).

After presenting his Moral Noemas, More goes on to derive from them extensive lists of duties and virtues, such as those of justice (More 112–25), prudence, sincerity, patience (More 98–108), temperance, and fortitude (More 133). More attempts to bring these derivations down to very specific levels (just as Whichcote had done), claiming, for instance, to have established the particular duties that are owed to magistrates, different family members, and private men who are equals (More 123–5). More makes it clear, moreover, that in deriving these duties he takes himself to be conducting a moral science that is analogous to geometry (More 81), one that consists of demonstrations of eternal and immutable ethical truths (More 115).

The moral system of More's *Enchiridion* fits perfectly with the epistemology of EIM. The Moral Noemas at the foundation of that system are purported to have the same status as the innate ideas Cudworth presents as the foundation of other branches of knowledge. And the demonstrations that proceed from More's Noemas purport to have the same structure as the proofs of geometry, which is Cudworth's paradigm for a science.

In addition to the philosophical confluence of Cudworth's EIM and More's *Enchiridion Ethicum*, there is extratextual evidence that More's ethical system is just the kind of thing Cudworth himself planned to produce. The extratextual evidence consists of several letters from Cudworth and More to John Worthington (all the relevant parts of which are quoted in Birch xiii–xv). They describe a quarrel that took place between Cudworth and More in 1664–5. Cudworth says in the first letter that a year previously he had begun a discourse on "Good and Evil, or Natural Ethicks," and that More had strongly urged him to complete and publish the work. But eight months later, to his dismay, Cudworth learned that More himself "had begun a discourse on the same argument," a discourse that More called his *Enchiridion Ethicum*. Cudworth talked with More about the matter, showing, as More put it, "disgust, &c." and contending "that if I [More] persisted in the resolution of publishing my book he [Cudworth] would desist in his." Out of deference to Cudworth, More agreed to "desist, and throw his into a corner," although he was not happy about it, as he had by this time finished "all but a chapter." Unfortunately, Cudworth did not publish his discourse promptly, although he had told More that "he had most of it then ready to send up to be licensed that week." And so, a few months later, More went ahead and proceeded to publish his book, even though he realized that doing so could very well "disgust Dr. Cudworth, whom I am very loath any way to grieve." Of course, we can't be sure of the reason for Cudworth's disgust (nor can we know whether his discourse on natural ethics, which has since been lost, really was ready to be "set to the press," as he told More). But it seems to me that the best explanation of Cudworth's reaction is that he thought that the *Enchiridion* would steal his thunder – that by publishing the *Enchiridion*, More would gain credit for ideas that actually belonged to Cudworth. The fact that Whichcote *also* presented a view of morality modeled on geometry makes the idea that EIM coheres with a geometric model of morality more likely still.[15]

So I think there are very strong philosophical, textual, and historical reasons for taking Whichcote's ethical demonstrations and More's *Enchiridion* to be the logical extensions of EIM.[16] But if I am right in thinking that in EIM Cudworth is arguing for a conception of moral knowledge modeled on Euclidean geometry, then we are faced with yet another difficulty in bringing into a single harmonious whole EIM and the 1647 sermons. For while the moral geometry for which EIM paves the way is essentially discursive, propositional, and public, the spirit of religion the sermons insist on is essentially intuitive, inexpressible, and mysterious. EIM's raison d'être is to show that morality is a branch of knowledge or "theoretical truth" (EIM 141). But the sermons come very close to dismissing the religious importance of theoretical knowledge altogether.[17]

C. The Civil War and Cudworth's Philosophical Development

It seems to me unlikely that Cudworth failed to notice the difference between EIM and the 1647 sermons. The sermons return again and again to mystery, love, and the heart without ever bringing comparisons to geometric theorems into the picture. EIM returns again and again to geometric theorems and barely mentions mystery, love, or the heart. The rhetoric of the sermons pushes rational thought to the wings, while the terminology of EIM gives it the starring role. A full account of Cudworth's thought must explain these differences.

Such an explanation should, I believe, take account of the historical events that occurred between 1647, when Cudworth delivered the sermons, and the 1660s, when he wrote EIM. My description of these historical events is very brief, but I think that even a sketchy historical picture will help to shed light on the differences between the 1647 sermons and EIM.

The English Civil War began in the summer of 1642. The Royalist and Parliamentary forces battled on and off until 1645, when the Parliamentary forces won several decisive victories, leading to the surrender of King Charles's forces in the spring of 1646. Charles would in the end never reach a peace settlement with Parliament, but Cudworth could not have known that when he was giving his sermons in early 1647. The second half of 1646 and the first few months of 1647 were hardly tranquil times, but Cudworth would have had reason to believe that the worst of the civil strife was over. He would have had reason to believe that the moderate factions within Parliament would, before too long, win the day and establish a peaceful, stable society.

But in late May and early June 1647 – just two months after Cudworth gave his sermon to the House of Commons – events took a drastic turn. Extremist elements within the New Model Army (which had been fighting on the Parliamentary side) severed their relationship with the moderate factions in Parliament and began to make increasingly bellicose demands. In August 1647, the radicalized army occupied Westminster and the City of London. In the spring and summer of 1648, there was a resumption of violent military conflict. In December, the army purged Parliament of all those who might have sought a peace settlement with the king. And in January 1649, Charles was tried, convicted, and beheaded. In retrospect, the months in which Cudworth delivered his sermons might have seemed to him not entirely dissimilar to how September 10, 2001, currently seems to many New Yorkers.

Cudworth's sermons made it clear that he was in favor of a peaceful settlement and greatly opposed to continued fighting. The violent turn of events from 1647 to 1649 must have horrified him. He must also have been horrified by many of the radical religious and political movements that threatened the social order in the 1650s – movements that were in some cases associated with the extremist elements that had spurred the New Model Army toward the violent second phase of the Civil War. I cannot present a detailed picture of these radical movements, but a very brief account of three of them will, I hope, give some indication of the times during which Cudworth's philosophy was evolving.

One of the most politically subversive movements was that of the True Levellers, or Diggers, the most influential of whom was Gerrard Winstanley. Winstanley and his followers (who were probably connected to the radical elements of the New Model Army who instigated the violence of 1647–9) were radical egalitarians who sought to abolish the institution of property and eliminate all class distinctions and hierarchy. Their egalitarian goals included demolishing the traditional structure of the universities by opening them up to all citizens and stripping them of their "emphasis on the classics and divinity" in favor of a concentration "on vocational and scientific subjects" (Coward 1994, 243). Winstanley identified his radical Digger program, which came to him in a vision he had while in a trance, with the spirit of Christ and saw the overthrowing of conventional society as his religious duty, the way to lead all humans to regain the righteousness that had been lost by the Fall. Winstanley said that his Digger program was in accord with reason, but he equated reason not with the discursive geometric rationality of EIM but with an intuitive feeling of love for all humanity, echoing the non-discursive "law of love" Cudworth endorsed in the sermons.

Winstanley's radical egalitarianism certainly disturbed men of property. But even more alarming were the Ranters, who took belief in the deiformity of human nature to a bizarre extreme (see Hill 1972, 163–8). The Ranters (or perhaps merely the hostile characterization of them, which might have been all that people like Cudworth would ever have known) insisted that they possessed an internal natural light that was the spirit of Christ infusing their hearts. The Ranters then drew the conclusion that since they themselves were in a sense God, it was impossible for them to commit sin, regardless of the outward actions they performed. They thus saw no need to respect civil laws or societal restrictions of any kind. To prove their belief in their own divinity and their disdain for mere outward conformity, the Ranters performed (or so it was said) all manner of egregious acts, engaging in public blasphemy, cursing, nudity, and fornication.

The Quakers were less violent than the True Levellers and generally better behaved than the Ranters (although Nayler's re-enactment of Christ's entry into Jerusalem, which consisted of his riding into Bristol on an ass with women strewing palm leaves before him, was considered just as blasphemous as anything the Ranters did). But the Quakers were lumped together with the other dangerous radicals of the 1650s nonetheless, and not without reason (Coward 1994, 241–2). For they too had powerful egalitarian tendencies, as evidenced by their refusal to remove their hats in the presence of superiors and their aggressive use of the familiar "thou." And they too elevated personal conscience above civil law. Quakers listened to the "spirit within" first and foremost, and they made it clear that if that internal spirit pointed toward a course of action forbidden by the magistrate, they would disobey the magistrate and follow the spirit.

Now what's important for our purposes is that there were crucial aspects of the thought of the True Levellers, Ranters, and Quakers that would have been perfectly at home within Cudworth's sermons of 1647. Indeed, their language was at times virtually indistinguishable from Cudworth's. They all exalted the "inner spirit," the "inner light" and "Christ within" while condemning those who overvalued the "dead letter." They all trumpeted the importance of the "law of love" and contrasted it with a fixation on "external observances." And these statements were not platitudinous boilerplate dicta but the bold expression of provocative ideas that signaled the speakers' rejection of central beliefs of mainstream society. It is, consequently, very unlikely that Cudworth failed to notice the similarity between his language in the sermons and the rhetoric of these radical groups.

But while Cudworth's sermons give us very good reason for thinking that in 1647 he would have sympathized with some aspects of enthusiasm, there is no reason to think he would have embraced the radicalism of the 1650s that the True Levellers, Ranters, and Quakers exemplified. An early advocate of religious liberty though he was, Cudworth gives no indication that he would have condoned extremist threats to law and order. Christopher Hill has said that "the early months of 1649 had been a terrifying time for the men of property" (Hill 1972, 88), and it seems very likely that Cudworth had been just as scared as the other members of his class. The wish of the radicals to turn the world "upside down" was not something Cudworth shared. Indeed, he goes out of his way in EIM to explain how his anti-voluntarist view of morality is consistent with a real moral obligation to obey the civil authorities, who must be granted "lawful authority of commanding" so that they may preserve "political order amongst men" (EIM 20).[18]

What is crucial to realize, however, is that it would have been understandable if someone drew a connection between the threat to "political order" posed by the radicals and the heart-based, enthusiastically inclined view of religion Cudworth espoused in his 1647 sermons. For the radicals revealed how a passionate emphasis on the "inner light" can quite easily lead to a disregard for civil authority and a breakdown of societal coherence. This is because the inner light is self-justifying in a very robust sense of the term. It's self-justifying, first of all, in that it is the spirit of God, and thus inherently of a higher authority than the word of any merely civil power. And it's also self-justifying in that it justifies only to a self – only to the person to whom the light appears. As it is beyond the reach of written and spoken language, the inner light is inescapably mystical and private. Its message cannot be the subject of discourse and discussion, but must remain locked within the heart of the individual recipient. The inner light transcends – and subverts – all public justification.

In his sermons of 1647, Cudworth endorsed the mystical inner light and seemed willing to accept some of the enthusiastic features that it implied. But there's every reason to think that he rejected the subversive activities that could reasonably have been associated with these ideas in the 1650s. So what was Cudworth to do?

One possible response was the Hobbesian one. Hobbes took the violence and disorder of the Civil War to be clear evidence of the dangerous selfishness of human nature. Left to their own devices, Hobbesians believed, human beings will inevitably come into conflict, as their basic natural motives are incompatible with a safe, harmonious coexistence. Rampant individual judgment is a recipe for disaster, as the rebellion and enthusiastic lawlessness of the late 1640s and early 1650s plainly revealed. The Hobbesian solution is thus to take judgment away from each individual and give it to an absolute sovereign, who will force everyone to live lawfully by meting out the severest punishment for those who don't. The only way to prevent people from coming into violent conflict, according to Hobbesians, is to place them all under an external power.

It's highly significant that Cudworth did not take this route. He witnessed firsthand the kind of lawlessness Hobbesians took to be their best evidence. But he refused nonetheless to take judgment away from the individual. He continued to insist that righteous conduct can and must be grounded in principles internal to every person. He continued to insist that all people have within themselves all the resources necessary to live as they ought. In short, he continued to insist on the goodness of human nature even in the face of the kind of violent conflict that drives many toward the idea that human nature is fundamentally corrupt.

How did he do it? How did Cudworth distinguish himself from the radicals, whose absolute faith in the inner light bore a striking resemblance to his 1647 insistence on the inward heart of religion, without falling into the authoritarianism of Hobbes? How could he continue to insist that ultimate justification must come from within without condoning heart-felt rebellion? How could he maintain his Positive Answer while distancing himself from the disorderly enthusiasts?

Cudworth managed all this by shifting the seat of righteousness without moving it outside the individual. The shift he effected was from the mystical passions of the sermons to the geometric rationality of EIM: from the heart to the head. This shift solved the problem because rationality, as Cudworth conceived of it, is a faculty that is perfectly suited to lead people to agree and live harmoniously with each other. This is because for individuals to think rationally is for them literally to think with other people. It is for them to comprehend the very same ideas that other people are comprehending – to "confer and discourse together . . . presently perceiving one another's meaning" (EIM 131). By moving from the spirit of love to universal rationality, Cudworth found a way to maintain an inward criterion of righteousness while also holding that all true justification must be publicly accessible. He found a way to abandon a dangerous faith in self-justifying inner light while continuing to affirm his commitment to individual judgment and the Positive Answer.

Cudworth's shift from the heart to the head also set the template for much of the rationalist moral theory that was to come in the eighteenth century and beyond.[19] Future rationalists followed Cudworth in seeking to ground morality in something that was both internal and public – in something that would enable all people to make moral judgments for themselves and yet to make them in a way that would necessarily lead them to make the same moral judgment as every other rational being. Rationalists would also follow Cudworth in endorsing a restricted view of the goodness of human nature, one that placed great confidence in humans' rational capacities while also harboring deep suspicions about the lawlessness of the passions.

5

The Emergence of Non-Christian Ethics

In the past two chapters, we've charted the role played by Whichcote and Cudworth's Positive Answer in the development of religious liberty and moral rationalism. We will now see that their version of the Positive Answer was instrumental to another intellectual development as well – a development at least as momentous as the other two. But unlike religious liberty and moral rationalism, this third development was something to which Whichcote and Cudworth may have contributed unintentionally. Indeed, this third development was something that Whichcote almost certainly would have preferred to squelch. Cudworth's attitude may have been more ambivalent.

The third development was the disengagement of moral philosophy from Christian Protestantism. Theological commitments remained always at the center of Whichcote and Cudworth's view of morality and human nature. But their Positive Answer proved to be incompatible with the conception of Christianity that had defined the mainstream of seventeenth-century English thought. So as Whichcote and Cudworth's Positive Answer gained philosophical ground, the mainstream Christian view began to recede.

In this chapter, I explain the conflict between the mainstream Christianity of seventeenth-century England and Whichcote and Cudworth's Positive Answer. In Section A, I give a general overview of the conflict. In B, I explain how the conflict manifested itself in Whichcote's sermons and his (determined but ultimately failed) attempts to resolve it. In C, I explain how the conflict manifested itself in the work of Cudworth and his (less determined but equally failed) attempts to resolve it.

A. Cambridge Platonism and Seventeenth-Century English Protestantism

Essential to mainstream seventeenth-century English Protestantism was the idea that a person could achieve salvation only if he or she accepted that

Christ died for his or her sins. To be a Christian, on this view, was to believe that salvation would have been impossible without the sacrifice of Christ, and that heaven is open only to those who acknowledge the indispensability of Christ's sacrifice.

It's easy to see how the mainstream view fits with a Negative Answer. For the mainstream view is built on the idea that all human beings are sinful in a way that they themselves cannot overcome. That is why the help of an external agent (Christ) is necessary: he does for us what we could never have done for ourselves. This also goes a long way toward explaining why the Calvinists thought it so important to stress the great sinfulness of humanity. To their minds, the more extreme the denigration of human nature, the greater the glory of Christ's sacrifice.

The Positive Answer, in contrast, maintains that human nature is basically good. That does not mean that adherents of the Positive Answer have to deny that people ever sin. But it does mean that they will deny that sin is a necessary, defining feature of humanity. Adherents of the Positive Answer will hold that people have within themselves the capacity to overcome sin – that righteousness is internally accessible to all human beings. But the more one emphasizes this internal capacity for righteousness, the harder it becomes to explain the indispensability of Christ's sacrifice. As human nature rises up the scale of goodness, the need for Christ to come to earth diminishes.

The issue can be put in terms of *mediation* (which is, as we see in the next section, how Whichcote often put it). Adherents of the kind of Negative Answer central to seventeenth-century English Protestantism believed that there is a vast moral distance between God and humans. So vast is this distance – so far removed from the perfection of God are sinful human beings – that no human can ever hope to traverse it by himself. No human can ever hope to bring about his own unity with God because every human's ineluctable sinfulness always places him apart from God. So if we are to be reconciled to God, the reconciliation must be effected by a *mediator*. A mediator (i.e., Christ) must bridge the distance between God's perfection and humans' sinfulness. Adherents of the Positive Answer central to Cambridge Platonism, in contrast, believed that humans have within themselves the capacity to become righteous. But if humans have within themselves the ability to become righteous – if they can traverse the moral distance between themselves and God – then the mediator's role becomes less important. If through our own efforts we can become one with God, then the bridging function of Christ's mediation loses its indispensability.

Specific aspects of Whichcote and Cudworth's thought made it particularly difficult for them to accommodate the idea that Christ's sacrifice was indispensable for human salvation. Consider, for instance, their view that heaven and hell are essentially not places at all but mental states, or the consciousness of one's own virtue and vice. This conception of heaven and hell was not peripheral to Whichcote and Cudworth's thought but followed directly from the anti-voluntarism at the core of their philosophy. Their anti-voluntarism implied that the natures of righteousness and unrighteousness are necessary features of reality that God himself cannot alter. It is, according to Whichcote and Cudworth's anti-voluntarism, just as impossible to separate heavenly happiness from righteousness and hellish misery from unrighteousness as it is to separate oddness from the number 7. But it's very difficult to see how this deeply rooted conception of heaven and hell leaves any role for Christ's mediation to play. For if a person is righteous, then Christ's mediation is not needed, as it is logically impossible for someone to be righteous and not experience heaven. And if a person is unrighteous, then Christ's mediation will not do any good, as it is logically impossible for someone to be unrighteous and not experience hell.

Consider, as well, Whichcote and Cudworth's profound opposition to the Calvinist doctrines of predestination and supralapsarianism, according to which everyone except the elect is doomed before the time of his or her birth to eternal damnation. As we saw in Chapter 2, opposition to this idea was the fundamental starting point for the development of Cambridge Platonism as a whole. The Cambridge Platonists rejected predestination and supralapsarianism because they thought those doctrines had the absurd implication that God was guilty of the injustice of condemning people for something they could not avoid. But now consider people who lived before the sacrifice of Christ. It was, of course, impossible for them to accept that Christ died for their sins. So if God would never condemn people for failing to do something it was impossible for them to do, God would not have condemned the people who lived before Christ for failing to accept that Christ died for their sins. Whichcote and Cudworth's most basic idea of God's moral nature implies that it must have been possible for those who lived before Christ to achieve salvation. But if that is so, then Christ's sacrifice cannot be indispensable.

Whichcote and Cudworth's reverence for the pre-Christian Greek philosophers only ratchets up the problem. Whichcote and Cudworth gave every indication that they thought that Socrates and Plato achieved the pinnacle of righteousness. They showed no inclination to sign on to the mainstream Protestant idea that the pagan philosophers must have ended up in hell. But if pagans can avoid hell, then, once again, it's hard to see why Christ had to suffer.

The root cause of the difficulty is Whichcote and Cudworth's belief in the deiformity of human nature. Every human, they believed, has within himself or herself the capacity to become God-like. The resources for salvation are internally accessible to all, as Whichcote and Cudworth's conception of heaven as an internal mental state makes perfectly clear. And Whichcote and Cudworth believed this to be a necessary truth about all human beings. They took deiformity to be an essential feature of human nature. As Whichcote put it, God's law is "inherent to human nature" (Whichcote IV 434). The principles of righteousness are so much a part of humans' "intellectual nature" that it is as impossible for a person to lack them "as it is impossible for the water to be without its natural quality that belongs to it, or the sun without light, or fire without heat" (Whichcote II 59). But since these are claims about the essence of human nature, about its necessary features, they imply that the resources for salvation must be internal to all human beings, before Christ as well as after.

Whichcote says that the "business of religion" is to "imitate and resemble" God (Whichcote I 32; cf. I 311), and that through such imitation and resemblance we will become "partakers of the divine nature" (Whichcote I 54). But if we can succeed through our imitation and resemblance in partaking of the divine nature – and Whichcote's rendering of the deiformity claim implies that we can succeed at this – why are the mediating efforts of Christ necessary for a reconciliation with God?

B. Whichcote's Positive Answer and the Need for Christ

Whichcote struggled mightily with this problem.[1] We have already seen that he was committed at the deepest level to the Positive Answer. But he also explicitly endorsed the mainstream Protestant view that humans could achieve salvation only by accepting that Christ died for their sins. "For," as he says, "there is no other way of acceptance with God for fallen man, but through Christ; by Christ only we are recommended" (Whichcote II 293). Whichcote goes on to say that those who do not accept Christ will "be punished, in the lake of fire and brimstone, which burns for ever," availing himself of the traditional hellish imagery that he almost always otherwise eschewed (Whichcote II 293). At times, moreover, Whichcote maintained that "Christ is not only of convenience, but down-right necessity. If a man could have come to God in another way, the son of God needed not to have died" (Whichcote II 301). And he also maintained that it was impossible to know of Christ's sacrifice before it happened – that the revelation of the Gospel was necessary for us to learn of and accept Christ. The "*use* we are to make of *Christ*," as he puts it, is a "matter, which otherwise than by revelation, could never have been known. . . . A man might have thought thousands of years, and never have thought of this way" (Whichcote II 285–6).[2]

Whichcote certainly tried to reconcile the mainstream view of Christ's sacrifice with his more heterodox Positive Answer. At various points in his sermons, he stretches, pulls, squashes, and shoves his ideas in the attempt to bring them all together into a coherent whole. In the end, however, the Positive Answer simply refuses to cohere with the "down-right necessity" of Christ's sacrifice, and Whichcote is left holding disparate and contradictory pieces.

One manifestation of Whichcote's inability to bring his ideas into coherence is his contradictory views of the principle of ought-implies-can. The principle of ought-implies-can, as we saw in Chapter 2, holds that people can be legitimately blamed for failing to do something only if it was possible for them to do it – or, put another way, that it is wrong to punish people for doing things if it was impossible for them not to. Here is Whichcote's perfectly clear application of this principle to the will of God:

[T]he word of God . . . tells us, That *if the wicked man turns from his wickedness, and doth that which is lawful and right, he shall save his soul alive.* Neither let any man say, that these words signify no more, than if one should say to an impotent man, remove this mountain, and thou shalt have such or such a reward: or to bid a man to comprehend the ocean in the hollow of his hand, and it shall so or so be done unto him. These are ludicrous ways of speaking: and such as must not be put upon God, nor in any case attributed unto him. God doth not mock and derive his poor creatures, when he doth invite them to him. This were to reproach one that were impotent, to bid him come to him, when as he knew he could not stir a step. (Whichcote I 205–6)

Whichcote's ought-implies-can principle implies that people cannot be punished for not accepting Christ if acceptance of Christ was impossible for them. And this is an implication that Whichcote himself explicitly draws, maintaining that we can expect to see "*Socrates* and *Plato* received into heaven" and "that ignorance doth greatly excuse, and therefore . . . where men have never heard and are without the pale of the church, we leave them to God's mercy, and exclude them not" (Whichcote I 40). Whichcote is telling us that people who lived before the time of Christ or in regions in which the news of Christ has not yet arrived cannot be blamed for not going to God through Christ, for they could not have known of Christ. For them, the requirements of morality constitute all of religion. And so if they lived moral lives (as Whichcote thought Socrates and Plato had done), they will have been saved, even though they were not Christians.

Elsewhere, however, Whichcote asserts that the path to salvation must go through Christ. "For there is no other way of acceptance with God for fallen man, but through Christ; by Christ only we are recommended" (Whichcote II 294; cf. II 297). At the very same time that he asserts the "down-right necessity" of Christ, moreover, Whichcote also maintains that knowledge of Christ is impossible without the "gospel-revelation" (Whichcote II 301; cf. II 285–6, 176). Whichcote emphasizes the necessity of the gospel-revelation when he tells us that even the "wisest of the men among the philosophers" did not understand that Christ was the only way to God and that these wise philosophers thus made the "mistake" of trying to go to God through some other mediator (Whichcote II 302).

But since it was impossible for the wise philosophers to avoid this mistake, it's hard to see how an advocate of the ought-implies-can principle can conceive of it as involving any culpability. More specifically, it's hard to see how an endorsement of the ought-implies-can principle can be compatible with the idea that an unavoidable mistake had to be corrected before anyone could achieve salvation. And yet, Whichcote does contend that the sacrifice of Christ was absolutely essential, asserting that if "man could have come to God in another way, the son of God needed not to have died" (Whichcote II 301; cf. II 314). In short, Whichcote claims both that it was impossible for people before the time of Christ to go to God through Christ and that people can be saved only by going through Christ: a conjunction in flat contradiction to his application of the ought-implies-can principle to the will of God.

Another manifestation of Whichcote's inability to bring his ideas into coherence is his changing position on the Fall of Man. When he is expounding the Positive Answer, Whichcote soft-pedals the Fall nearly to the point of inaudibility, telling us that we are all "God-like" and thus capable of participating directly with the divine mind here and now, in this world. Heaven, Whichcote tells us, consists of "an *internal reconciliation to the nature of God, and to the rule of righteousness*" (Whichcote III 140), and this heavenly state is something we can be "acquainted with in this world," something we can "lay title to now" (Whichcote II 156–7). But when he is explaining the need to accept Christ, Whichcote strikes a very different chord, hammering away at human sinfulness in language that would be at home in one of Perkins's sermons. "[W]e are all under an universal forfeiture," he says; "we have prejudiced the interest we have in God as our creator; we cannot have confidence in the relation to God as the original of our being, because we have given him offense; we have forfeited our happiness, by consenting to iniquity; we have worsted our faculties, and marred our spirits" (Whichcote II 305). It's rather hard to see, however, how Whichcote can bring into harmony such expressions of ineluctable sinfulness and his optimistic statements about our capacity to attain an internal reconciliation with God. For Whichcote says in numerous places that all of our duties fall into one of two categories: the moral part of religion (which constitutes nineteen-twentieths of religion) and the acceptance of Christ (the last twentieth, which Whichcote calls "the instituted part of religion"). Now the reason we need to accept Christ is that we are sinful, and so our sinfulness cannot consist simply of our failure to accept Christ. The duty of accepting Christ presupposes prior sinfulness. Whichcote must hold, then, that this prior sinfulness consists of a failure to live up to the moral part of religion, as he has told us that morality constitutes all the duties of religion besides the duty of accepting Christ. Whichcote often says, however, that many people (Socrates and Plato among them) have succeeded in realizing their moral duty. But if the need to accept Christ presupposes immorality, and if Whichcote thinks people can and do conduct themselves morally, how can he make the Perkinsian statements of ineluctable sin and the need for Christ?

The underlying problem here is Whichcote's religious rationalism. Whichcote argues throughout his sermons that something can be essential to religion – and thus necessary for salvation – only if it is rational. And when Whichcote says that the essence of religion is rational, he means that it consists only of things that are as demonstrably certain as the most fundamental of mathematical truths; this is a religious version of the epistemological implication of the necessity of morals thesis that we discussed in Chapter 4. As Whichcote puts it, religion concerns only matters that are "clear," "intelligible," and "self-evident" to us. If something does not have "pure reason to commend itself . . . to our judgments and to our faculties," then, according to Whichcote, acceptance of it cannot be necessary for our salvation (Whichcote I 71).

Whichcote repeatedly uses the idea that only demonstrably certain things are essential to religion to argue against the importance of various things that other people took to be necessary for salvation. He argues, for instance, that the rituals and trappings of organized religion must be inessential because they are "doubtful and uncertain" (Whichcote IV 117), while the essentials of religion are "clear, and plain" to all "good men" (Whichcote II 2). He also maintains that it is not essential to believe what the Bible says about "matters of *ancient records*, the history of former times," "matters of deep *philosophy*, as also matters of *philology*" and "matters of *prophecy*" (Whichcote I 179). Whichcote is not saying that what the Bible tells us about these matters is false. His point, rather, is that the Bible's claims about these things "do not belong to the business of religion" because they are not "perspicuous" to us; we cannot "fully understand" them; they are not demonstrably certain (Whichcote I 179–80).

The idea that religion consists only of what is demonstrably certain is, as well, demanded by the deiformity claim that is the cornerstone of Whichcote's Positive Answer. The deiformity claim holds that when we fully exercise our rational faculties we become God-like – that through our religious understanding we become one with the mind of God. But of the truths of religion God possesses absolute certainty. If, therefore, our religious understanding is literally divine, it must involve certainty of the very highest order. And such certainty, for Whichcote, is the certainty of mathematical demonstration. Now the deiformity claim should not be pushed too far. Human rationality has limitations that the reason of God does not have. But Whichcote believes that these limitations restrict only the *quantity* of things humans can understand, not the *quality* of understanding humans can achieve. There are some things that God fully understands that we do not. But there are also some things that we do fully understand, and our understanding of such things is just the same – just as clear, just as full – as God's. It is those things, for Whichcote, and those things alone, that constitute the essence of religion. Anything we cannot completely comprehend we are not required to believe.[3]

But how can Whichcote combine this unalloyed rationalism with his claim that acceptance of Christ's sacrifice requires the gospel-revelation? How can he consistently maintain both that all the essentials of religion are self-evident to us and that the essential belief in Christ is a "matter, which otherwise than by revelation, could never have been known"? How can the same person who said that "we are as capable of religion, as we are of reason" (Whichcote I 37) also say that Christianity "is a matter of supernatural revelation: here you cannot convince men by reason, which is the only way to deal with men in other matters. And so the apostle hath told us: because these are the results of God's will, therefore it follows that they are only knowable by God's revelation to them"? (Whichcote I 176).

Here's another way of putting the problem. When stressing the rationality of religion, Whichcote maintains that all the essentials of religion can be discerned through the use of a priori reason alone. When affirming the truth of Christianity, Whichcote maintains that it is essential that we believe that Christ died for our sins. But the sacrifice of Christ was an event, something that occurred at a specific place and time. And belief in the occurrence of an event cannot be arrived at through the use of a priori reason alone. We need the assistance of the gospel-revelation for that.

The problem begins to look even worse when Whichcote tries to explain why it was impossible for pre-Christians to know that God would send Christ as a mediator. It was impossible, he says, because the decision to send Christ was God's "secret." Unlike the "materials of *natural knowledge*," Whichcote tells us, the distinctly Christian aspects of religion are "the resolutions of the divine will, and only knowable by God's voluntary revelation and discovery; and to this purpose the bible is God's instrument in the world; and concerning these no man can know, but by revelation from God. Secrets of *men* none knows, but he to whom he will reveal them; so of *God*" (Whichcote III 167). Or as he puts it when describing the distinctly Christian aspects of religion and distinguishing them from the "natural" aspects that even the heathens know, "[T]he mysteries of religion were the secrets of [God's] will before they were revealed, but after they are told us, they cease to be mysteries" (Whichcote II 290).

This talk of God's "secret" makes matters worse for Whichcote because a secret is typically the sort of thing on which reason cannot find purchase. A typical secret (and if God's secret is "mysterious" and "unknowable," then it is typical in this way) is something we can learn only if we are told. We cannot discover it through the use of demonstrable reason alone. It seems, then, that if God's decision to send Christ was a secret (or one of the "mysteries of religion"), then it would have been something for which God had no reason we can discern. But to attribute to God an incomprehensible decision – and to make our acceptance of that decision an essential aspect of religion – would seem to violate the most fundamental commitment of Whichcote's rationalism. For it would seem to place at the essential core of religion a matter that we cannot figure out on our own, while the starting point for Whichcote's rationalism is that religion comprises only those things that we can fully understand through the use of our rational faculty alone. There seems to be, in other words, a sharp incompatibility between Whichcote's

claim that our salvation depends on our belief in a revealed secret and his
claim that God does not require belief in anything that is not discernible by
reason alone.

Whichcote was aware of this problem. He realized that there was a serious
difficulty in making religion completely rational and also including in it a
secret knowable only through revelation. His solution was to claim that while
this secret of God's was unknowable before revelation, it became completely
understandable after revelation – that while we could not have discerned the
nature of Christ's sacrifice before God revealed it, it became utterly rational
and completely obvious to us once He had. As he explains:

> And though some men do pretend that religion is not intelligible, they dishonour
> God very much; for that which God hath now revealed, is as plain and as intelligible
> as any other matter: the mysteries of religion were the secrets of his will before they
> were revealed, but after they are told us, they cease to be mysteries. And it is no more
> a mystery that God (in and through Christ) will pardon sin to all that repent if they
> have done amiss, than it is a mystery that a man that is rational and intelligent ought
> to live soberly, righteously and godly: and I do understand it as well that I ought to
> repent and believe the gospel, as I understand that I ought to love and fear God. All
> religion is now intelligible: the moral part of it was intelligible from the creation: that
> which was pure revelation by the gospel, is intelligible ever since, and not a mystery.
> Therefore we be-fool ourselves to talk that religion is not knowable, and we cannot
> understand it: for understand it we may, if we will; for if it be revealed, it is made
> intelligible; if not intelligible, it is not revealed. (Whichcote IV 290–1)

Whichcote wants to maintain that the Christian part of religion is now just
as intelligible to us as the natural part of religion, and that we only needed
to be told about the former in order to realize it. This idea is far from clear,
but perhaps what Whichcote has in mind is that the relationship between
the Christian part of religion and our understanding is the same as the
relationship between a successful mathematical proof and a mathematician
who understands the proof but was unable to formulate it by himself. The
mathematician accepts the proof not simply because someone else tells him
to or because it was printed in a book but because he himself realizes that it
must be correct – because he himself fully understands it. Still, the proof had
to be told or printed for the mathematician to come to that understanding.
In the same way, the defining feature of Christianity is now as certain to us
as the most fundamental principles of natural religion, and that is why we
should accept it. Still, we could not have figured out that principle entirely
by ourselves, even if it's the case that we know it to be necessarily true as
soon as we are told of it.

Does this conception of God's secret succeed in reconciling Whichcote's
rationalism and the "down-right necessity" of Christ? I don't think so. For
the secret has to have two characteristics that seem awfully hard to combine.
First, the secret has to be such that humans, no matter how brilliant, could
never have discovered it on their own. And second, the secret has to be

such that every human, no matter how dim, can immediately understand its rational necessity upon hearing it for the first time. But if the secret is so self-evident now (if it is as obvious to everyone as $2 + 2 = 4$), it seems implausible to say that it was impossible for anyone to discover it on his own before. And if it was really impossible for anyone to discover the secret on his own before, it seems implausible to say that its intelligibility is immediately self-evident to everybody now.

Moreover, even if the analogy with the mathematical proof does open up conceptual space for the idea that a thing can be unknown to us one moment and then completely self-evident to us the next, Whichcote would still have a big problem trying to explain why the specifics of Christ's sacrifice are self-evident. For it's not enough for Whichcote simply to say that it's possible that something we didn't know before could be self-evident to us now. What Whichcote has to show is that we now have purely rational reasons to believe in Christ's sacrifice – that while the testimony of the Bible helped us to learn about it, our current belief in Christ's sacrifice can be completely supported by purely rational considerations. But Whichcote himself doesn't even seem to believe that, at least not when he says that Christianity "is a matter of supernatural revelation: here you cannot convince men by reason, which is the only way to deal with men in other matters" (Whichcote I 176).

And even if that problem can be solved, there is yet another. If it really was impossible for anyone to learn of Christ's sacrifice without the benefit of revelation, then people before Christ cannot be blamed for not accepting Christ. But if Christ's sacrifice is self-evident to us now that we have revelation, we *can* be blamed for not accepting Christ. The obligation of religion thus seems to have undergone a change: something that is necessary for salvation now was not necessary for salvation in the past. That such a change occurred is something that Whichcote himself allows in a few passages (Whichcote III 166–7, IV 289–90). He says, for instance, that "as the secrets of a man are known only to the man himself, till he doth reveal them; so the secrets of God are known only to God, till God reveal them, and till then we are not charged with them; for negative infidelity damns no man" (Whichcote I 169). His allowing religious obligation to change, however, is tantamount to Whichcote's taking a hatchet to both his rationalism *and* his Christianity. For the existence of changing obligations topples the basic rationalist idea of religion's being eternal and immutable, turning religious obligations into things that are relative to a person's position in space and time (see Aphorisms 1107). And the fact that pre-Christians could achieve salvation ("negative infidelity damns no man") topples the basic Christian idea that Christ had to die before anyone could be saved (see Whichcote II 301).

In the end, Whichcote simply cannot reconcile his rationalism with his Christianity, and frankly, it's somewhat painful to watch him try. It's worth noting, however, that there are a few passages in which he seems to quietly withdraw from a commitment to the distinctively Christian aspects of religion, suggesting that natural morality alone, without the added aspects of the gospel-revelation, is sufficient for true religion. "For these [moral principles]," as he says at one point, "do import the *fullest imitation of God*, and the exactest *participation* of the divine nature: for by these we are made partakers of the divine nature. And to resemble God in these [moral] perfections . . . is to partake of it. *This* is the gospel obtaining in effect; and in the ultimate issue, this is to have *Christ formed in us*; and the gospel in its final accomplishment" (Whichcote II 61). Because this statement makes mention of "Christ formed in us," it may initially appear to be consistent with a strict belief in the absolute need to accept Christ's sacrifice. But close attention to the passage reveals that Whichcote is talking about moral principles that he believes to be entirely accessible to all humans, pagan as well as Christian. And if these principles are both accessible to pagans and sufficient for the "fullest imitation of God," then it seems as though a person without any knowledge of Christ's sacrifice can achieve the "exactest participation of the divine nature." It seems as though the ultimate goal of Christianity can be achieved even without the benefit of the gospel-revelation.

In a couple of sermons, moreover, Whichcote suggests a view according to which Christ's sacrifice was very helpful but not absolutely indispensable. On this view, Christ did not make possible a unity with God that was impossible before. What Christ did, rather, is provide *assurance* that this unity is possible. He assuaged our doubts. As Whichcote puts it, "As for those that lived before Christ, and out of the pale of the church visible, they did imagine that infinite goodness was placable, and would be reconciled in some way or other; but to be *assured* of it, as we are, that they could not be" (Whichcote II 136–7). And again: "We indeed have extraordinary assurance [of the choice points of religion]; because we have gospel-revelation, they are certain to us christians: but they were but of hope, and fair persuasions, and belief, to the philosophers, who had no scripture. Yet many of them wrote excellently upon these subjects; they *hoped* all these were true: but we are *satisfied* and *assured*" (Whichcote II 239). Whichcote suggests here that all humans have had within themselves at all times a nature that made it possible for them to become one with God. But until the gospel-revelation, they found it difficult to be absolutely sure that this was so. The gospel didn't change our situation vis-à-vis God and salvation so much as provide assurance that that situation wasn't as bad as we'd feared and could be as good as we'd hoped.

On this view, Christ's taking human form did not open a way to God that had not existed before, but rather revealed that human nature is itself compatible with the nature of God. The story of Christ is useful because it makes clear to all of us what we are (and always have been) capable of (see Aphorisms 1104). And what is importantly true about Christianity is its affirmation of the intrinsic goodness of human nature. This view of Christianity would have been antithetical to Whichcote's Calvinists forebears, and it must be said that Whichcote himself often shies away from it, opting instead to endorse the absolute need for mediation between perfect God and fallen man. But ultimately it is only this view of Christ as helpful but not indispensable that fits with Whichcote's Positive Answer.

How aware was Whichcote of the irresolvable conflict between his Positive Answer and his endorsement of the mainstream Protestant view of Christ's sacrifice? I honestly don't know. He may very well have thought that the conflict was completely resolvable – that, for instance, there was no particular difficulty in saying that the requirements of religion changed after Christ's sacrifice, and that God's secret was indiscernible to everyone before the gospel-revelation and self-evident to everyone afterward. Then again, he may have known that things were not so easily resolved but refrained from saying so because of his circumstances.

Between 1626 and 1660, Whichcote held a number of increasingly important posts at Cambridge: tutor and fellow of Emmanuel College, provost of King's College, and eventually vice-chancellor of the university. He was ousted from Cambridge at the time of the Restoration but landed on his feet, being appointed minister of St. Anne's Blackfriars Church in London in 1662 and holding several prestigious positions thereafter. And throughout his life – right up to his death in 1683, in Cambridge while visiting his one-time student and long-time friend Cudworth – one constant feature of Whichcote's career was sermonizing. It's sermons – many of them given in the nonacademic setting of the London churches – that made Whichcote an immensely popular figure outside the confines of the university, and it's sermons that are the source for most of what we know of Whichcote's thought. But Whichcote's goal in giving sermons was to reach his audience, and to reach them from the pulpit. It would have been inappropriate for Whichcote, in his position as minister, to explore in detail the possible non-Christian implications of a rationalist belief in the goodness of human nature. His duty as minister was to edify and uplift, and to do so in a Christian context. It should come as no surprise, consequently, that he didn't ever say clearly that his Positive Answer undermined mainstream English Protestantism.

C. Cudworth's Positive Answer and the Need for Christ

When Cudworth gave sermons, he too worked hard to reconcile his Positive Answer with the mainstream view of the indispensability of Christ's sacrifice.[4] This effort is most apparent in Cudworth's 1647 sermon at Lincolnes-Inn, in which he tries to explain how Christ made it possible for humans to gain "victory over sin " (Lincolnes 14–15).

Now it turns out that in the Lincolnes-Inn sermon Cudworth finds it much easier to say what Christ *didn't* do for humans than to say what He did. What Christ *didn't* do, Cudworth tells us, was effect human salvation simply through the act of His sacrifice. For the act of Christ's sacrifice is "external" to each human's spirit (Lincolnes 15, 19); it's something that someone else did. And we cannot be made worthy of salvation by someone else's actions any more than "a Sick man should be made Whole by another's imputed Health" (Lincolnes 21). "Imputed righteousness" – or the idea that the righteous act of someone else will gain for us a "victory over sin" – is a "phantastical and imaginary" notion (Lincolnes 22). So long as our spirit remains sinful, the righteousness of someone else (even Christ) can never save us. Salvation will come only to those who are themselves "inwardly quickened and Sanctified" by a righteous spirit (Lincolnes 27) – only to those with "Real Inward Righteousness" (Lincolnes 25). We will be saved if and only if the spirit of righteousness is "In us" – if and only if righteousness is "inherent" in our character (Lincolnes 26). But the "*Good Thoughts* and *Vertuous Dispositions*" that constitute a righteous spirit cannot be "POURED and BLOWN *into men* by God" (Lincolnes 32). They must originate not in "a mere *External Force* acting upon the Soul" but in an "*Innate Principle*" (Lincolnes 37). True righteousness can come only from "the Soul's acting from an inward Spring and Principle of its own Intellectual nature, not be a mere outward Impulse, like a Boat that is tugged on by Oars or driven by a strong blast of Wind" (Lincolnes 37).

So Cudworth argues in the Lincolnes-Inn sermon that salvation must come from within; that righteousness can originate only in an internal active principle of one's own nature; that no external force, not even Christ, can make a person righteous and thus worthy of salvation. But his insistence on "Inward Righteousness" – and his corresponding disdain for "Imputed righteousness" – makes it very difficult for him to explain how Christ's sacrifice made it possible for us to gain a "victory over sin" that we could not have gained before. His insistence on inward righteousness seems to imply that every human being has within himself the necessary and sufficient means for salvation, and that the actions of another (even Christ) are neither necessary nor sufficient.

At one point, Cudworth trots out a version of the "assurance" account we saw in Whichcote, according to which Christ's sacrifice did not create a path to God that did not exist before but merely assured us that the path we are already traveling can get us where we want to go. "The reasons of Philosophy," Cudworth says at that point, demonstratively "prove the *Soul's Immortality*" (Lincolnes 5). But "vulgar apprehensions" lead some people to doubt their immortality nonetheless (Lincolnes 5). Christ's resurrection thus serves the purpose of giving assurance to "Vulgar minds" (who cannot properly attend to "Philosophical Reasons and Demonstrations") that indeed they can survive their own deaths (Lincolnes 6). It's clear, however, that Cudworth does not think that this assurance account captures the full importance of Christ's sacrifice (Lincolnes 51–2). Cudworth wants to explain "the Necessity of Christ's Meritorious and Propitiatory Sacrifice for the Remission of Sins" (Lincolnes 21). And he doesn't think that that "Necessity" is captured simply by the idea that Christ's sacrifice gave assurance to the weak-minded of what had always been plainly discernible to the philosophically astute.

Cudworth's official position in the Lincolnes-Inn sermon is that while our "*Active*" participation is necessary for salvation, it is not sufficient (Lincolnes 40). Also necessary (according to his official position) is "a Divine Operation" working upon us, "so that in a certain sense we may be said to be *Passive*" as well (Lincolnes 40). Cudworth uses an agricultural metaphor to illustrate this idea, pointing out that vegetables cannot grow without the "Spirit of God in Nature," but that it is also necessary that "the Husbandman plow the Ground and sow the Seed" to prepare the way for "the Spirit of God in Nature" to do its work (Lincolnes 40–1). "In like manner," he continues, "unless we *plow up the Fallow-ground of our hearts and sow to our selves in Righteousness* (as the Prophet speaks) by our earnest endeavours; we cannot expect that the Divine Spirit of Grace will showr down that Heavenly increase upon us" (Lincolnes 41). The problem with this official position is that the necessity of God's grace just doesn't fit with anything else Cudworth says about "Real Inward Righteousness." The externality and passivity of this need clash with the insistence on internality and activity that underlies everything else he says in the Lincolnes-Inn sermon. The image of having to wait for a "Heavenly showr" appears to be pasted in from someone else's sermon.

The fundamental problem is this. In the Lincolnes-Inn sermon, Cudworth deploys the full force of his formidable rhetorical and philosophical skills to establish that one's eternal state depends entirely on one's internal constitution. It is, he argues, equally impossible for God to refuse salvation to a righteous person and for Him to grant salvation to an unrighteous one, for salvation follows necessarily from righteousness and damnation follows necessarily from unrighteousness (Lincolnes 21). Cudworth's conception of heaven and hell implies, in fact, that salvation simply *is* the consciousness of one's own righteousness and damnation simply *is* the consciousness of one's own unrighteousness. God, then, has no choice as to whether to grant us salvation or mete out damnation, as salvation and damnation are essentially just our own states of mind. To claim that God does have a choice – to claim that salvation and damnation depend on God's will – is to side with the voluntarists in a manner that would turn "*Righteousness* and *Holiness*" into "mere Phantastical and Imaginary things" (Lincolnes 21). So if righteousness is a real thing at all, it must be sufficient for salvation. Righteousness cannot, moreover, be "poured or blown into men by God"; it must come entirely from within. How, then, can the shower of God's grace (in the form of Christ's sacrifice) find any necessary role to play? Why isn't righteousness both entirely within one's control and all one needs to achieve reconciliation with God?

Cudworth's sermon before the House of Commons doesn't do any better at answering that question. Cudworth maintains there that salvation depends on both an internal principle and the spirit of Christ. But he never explains how salvation can follow necessarily from something internal to each person *and* require that another party (namely, Christ) perform an action. What Cudworth says is that the essence of Christianity must remain ineluctably "mystical" – that Christ's spirit working within us is ultimately a "mystery" (Commons 375, 380, 387, 390). In saying that Christ's role in our salvation is a mystery, however, Cudworth is in effect saying simply that he can't explain it.

So in his sermons Cudworth doesn't do any better than Whichcote at dealing with the conflict between his Positive Answer and the mainstream view of Christ's sacrifice. But unlike Whichcote, Cudworth produced a copious amount of philosophical writing never intended for sermons. Perhaps Cudworth's greater philosophical production is due in part to the fact that he managed to keep his academic position at Cambridge after the Restoration. But what was probably a bigger factor was that Cudworth was simply more philosophically inclined than Whichcote. Cudworth was a grand systematizer, someone driven to discover the origins and implications of every idea and to bring all of them together into a single coherent whole. He stated that his philosophical goal was to describe the "true intellectual system of the universe," and this project was every bit as ambitious as it sounds. He could never have fit all his thinking into audience-friendly, stand-alone Sunday sermons, and his philosophical writing cannot be broken down (as were Whichcote's sermons) into hundreds of bite-sized aphorisms.

Cudworth published volume 1 of his *True Intellectual System* in 1678. It was a mammoth work purporting to contain conclusive proof of God's existence and an exhaustive refutation of all forms of atheism. It is very likely that Cudworth conceived of his *Eternal and Immutable Morality* and his *Treatise of Freewill* as additional parts of his "intellectual system," but only the first volume was published during his lifetime. *Eternal and Immutable Morality* came out in 1731 and *Freewill* in 1838.

Why didn't Cudworth publish these other works? One reason may have been the reception of the *True Intellectual System*, which some people bizarrely mistook to be a piece of surreptitious atheism. The ludicrous charge was that Cudworth did not actually intend to refute all the arguments against God's existence but rather gathered them all together to compile a covert atheistic sourcebook. Another reason may have been Cudworth's obsessive concern to chart every historical influence, track down every logical consequence, and address every counterargument. Cudworth may have been one of those perfectionists whose compulsion for comprehensiveness makes it almost impossible for them to decide that a work is finally complete and ready for publication.

Sarah Hutton also points out, however, that it "is not beyond the bounds of possibility that a combination of native caution along with political and ecclesiastical factors served to exacerbate his painstaking and prolix manner of argument, and thereby delay publication" (EIM xiii). I believe that Hutton's suggestion is very plausible, and that one of the aspects of Cudworth's thought that he may have deemed it prudent to keep under wraps was the difficulty of finding within his system a necessary role for the sacrifice of Christ. The *True Intellectual System*, for instance, contains a brief discussion of the Christian Trinity, but the vast majority of the work consists of theistic arguments that would fit perfectly well into a pre-Christian worldview. The God for which Cudworth argues has no overt connection to the story of the gospel. The proofs of His existence are supposed to be purely rational, completely independent of revelation.

The *Treatise of Freewill* would have been even less palatable to mainstream Protestants. In that work, Cudworth argues that humans are able to determine themselves, that they have "self-power" or "liberty of will" (EIM 175). He explicitly compares this feature of human nature to God's ability to be a self-mover and self-actor (EIM 198). Each of us, he says, has a "self-forming and self-framing power, by which every man is self-made, into what he is" (EIM 178). Now this position on free will is in direct conflict with the predestinarianism central to much of seventeenth-century English Protestantism (EIM 204–7). But rather than hide from this implication, Cudworth openly embraces it. Indeed, he says that if predestination were true, it would "destroy the reality of moral good and evil, virtue and vice, and make them nothing but mere names or mockeries" (EIM 205).

Cudworth is also aware that many of his contemporaries would object that his position on "liberty of will is inconsistent with Divine grace and will necessarily infer Pelagianism" (EIM 208). Pelagianism is the view that an emphasis on the doctrine of original sin is a mistake, that human nature is inherently good, and that all people have the ability to "initiate the process of salvation by their own efforts, without the aid of Divine Grace" (EIM 160). Pelagianism thus constitutes a Positive Answer, and it also explicitly includes the idea that humans' free will and goodness make it possible for them to achieve salvation on their own, without the benefit of Christ's sacrifice and the gospel-revelation. It's easy to see why seventeenth-century English Protestantism branded Pelagianism heretical and why it would have been very dangerous for a seventeenth-century thinker to be associated with it. It's also easy to see why Cudworth's contemporaries might have thought that his view of free will would lead to the Pelagian heresy.

So what does Cudworth do in *Freewill* to distinguish his view from Pelagianism?[5] The truth is: not very much. He addresses the issue, but he does so only in two paragraphs of the penultimate chapter. And both paragraphs are woefully lacking in philosophical reasoning, in stark contrast to the closely argued character of the rest of Cudworth's work in his treatises.

In one paragraph, he repeats the Lincolnes-Inn claim that our active participation is a necessary condition of our salvation but is not sufficient. "The use of their own freewill is required," he says, but the "endeavours and activity of freewill are insufficient without the addition and assistance of Divine grace" (EIM 208). But he doesn't even bother to give any philosophical reason for this claim. He backs it up simply by quoting unexplicated bits of scripture, a justificatory method completely at odds with his entire philosophical project and temperament.

The other paragraph of Cudworth's attempt to distance himself from Pelagianism is no better. He says there that his view doesn't collapse into Pelagianism because

> those angels which by their right use of liberty of will stood when others by the abuse of it fell, though by that same liberty of will they might still possibly continue without falling, yet for all that it would not be impossible for them to fall, unless they had aid and assistance of Divine grace to secure them from it. Wherefore it is commonly conceived that as, notwithstanding that liberty of will by which it is possible for them never to fall, they had need of Divine grace to secure them against a possibility of falling, and that they are now by Divine grace fixed and confirmed in such a state as that they can never fall. (EIM 208)

This passage has no philosophical merit whatsoever, and it's hard to imagine that Cudworth didn't realize it. Cudworth is simply repeating a tale about beings with free will who required divine grace, without even attempting to provide a rational basis for believing it. To see the anomalous nature of this passage, we have only to compare it to Cudworth's refutations in the same treatise of the Hobbesian and scholastic conceptions of will (EIM 197–200 and 168–75, respectively), for whether or not one agrees with those refutations, it is plainly apparent that their intellectual power is miles beyond the question-begging appeal to unfallen angels that constitutes Cudworth's attempt to distance himself from Pelagianism.

So in *Freewill*, Cudworth makes only a token gesture toward reconciling his position with the indispensability of Christ. But in EIM, he doesn't even bother to do that. EIM sets the high water mark for rationalist, theistic versions of the Positive Answer, and this is because EIM develops the most complete and uncompromising picture of how, through the use of reason, human minds can participate with the mind of God. But in that picture, Christ does not appear. Christianity is not mentioned even once. EIM tells us how we can become one with the mind of God through the use of reason alone. There is no need, on this account, for Christ to mediate between humans and God, because the rational faculty inside each human turns out to be a means of direct access to the mind of God itself. Indeed, the connection between human rationality and the divine mind is so close, on the account developed in EIM, that it's hard to see how there could be any room at all between them for the mediator Christ to occupy.

PART TWO

SHAFTESBURY

6

Shaftesbury and the Cambridge Platonists

A. Damaris Cudworth, John Locke, and Anthony Ashley Cooper

Cudworth married a woman named Damaris, and they had several children. One of these was a daughter, also named Damaris, born 18 January 1659. There is no indication that any of the other Cudworth children was interested in philosophy, but Damaris certainly was. By the time she was in her early twenties, she had absorbed the views of her father and Henry More, was well versed in the sermons of John Smith, and knew at least the basics (and probably more than that) of the philosophy of the Stoics and Descartes. That Damaris came to this knowledge despite the formidable obstacles to education placed before women of the seventeenth century attests to her native intelligence, to her love of ideas, and to her close relationship with a philosophically gregarious and relatively enlightened father.

Later in life Damaris became an active player in the philosophical debates of her day. She wrote two books – *A Discourse concerning the Love of God*, published in 1696, and *Occasional Thoughts in Reference to a Vertuous or Christian Life*, published in 1705 – in which she outlined positions on morality, religion, and education and developed sharp critiques of the views of a number of her contemporaries. In 1704–5 she engaged in an extended philosophical correspondence with Leibniz. And Damaris's dearest friend was John Locke, with whom she discussed philosophy on a regular, long-term basis.

Damaris's philosophical career deserves more attention than it has received, and her relationship with John Locke is fascinating on both a philosophical and a personal level.[1] But we cannot canvass the sweep of Damaris's life and works here. Instead, let us zoom in on one weekend in 1691, when Locke brought for introduction to Damaris a young man named Anthony Ashley Cooper. Cooper's father was the second Earl of Shaftesbury, and in time Cooper, who was the eldest child, would become the third Earl.

Locke had been attached to Cooper's family since 1667, during which time Cooper's grandfather had entrusted Locke with numerous responsibilities, one of the most important of which was to ensure the continuance of the Cooper line itself. The first Earl's son was weak, ineffectual, and sickly, and there was concern about his ability to marry and produce an heir. The first Earl thus told Locke to arrange an early marriage for his son. And when in 1671 that marriage produced a child – the future third Earl of Shaftesbury – Locke was put in charge of his upbringing. Locke oversaw the hiring of young Cooper's tutors and was involved in all aspects of the boy's early education. Until he had to flee to Holland in 1683, Locke was also a personal presence in young Cooper's life, a kind of favorite uncle. In 1687, as he was beginning his grand tour of Europe, Cooper stayed with Locke in Holland for several months. And when Locke returned to England in 1689, he and Cooper engaged in frequent philosophical discussion, sometimes bantering, sometimes intense, but always affectionate.

So young Cooper and Locke were virtually family. And Damaris and Locke were intimate friends. All of them, moreover, were philosophically gifted, and Damaris and Cooper were wonderful conversationalists. It's no surprise, consequently, that the three of them had a terrific time together and that Damaris and Cooper found in each other a fellow spirit.

The future third Earl of Shaftesbury would have encountered the thought of the Cambridge Platonists even if he hadn't met Damaris Cudworth. And it's likely that he would have been favorably impressed regardless of the circumstances in which he encountered it. But his friendship with Damaris must have made Cambridge Platonism come alive for him with especial verve. And there can be no doubt that Cambridge Platonism played a formative role in the third Earl of Shaftesbury's intellectual development, nor that his philosophical affinity with the Cambridge Platonists remained strong and deep throughout his life.

I do not mean to suggest that Cambridge Platonism was the only important intellectual influence on Shaftesbury (which is how I will refer to Anthony Ashley Cooper from now on). Shaftesbury soaked up the thought of many philosophers, modern and ancient, and his attachment to Stoicism, in particular, was at least as strong as his attachment to Cambridge Platonism. Nor do I mean to suggest that all of Shaftesbury's ideas are perfectly consistent with every aspect of Cambridge Platonism. He extended and modified their ideas in ways that eventually led him to views they would not have shared. But Whichcote, Cudworth, and More – and in particular their Positive Answer to the Human Nature Question – so molded the general shape of Shaftesbury's thought that it is fitting to think of his philosophy as a continuous outgrowth of Cambridge Platonism itself.[2]

B. Shaftesbury's Preface to Whichcote's Sermons

We do not need to look far to find evidence of Shaftesbury's indebtedness to Cambridge Platonism. The first thing he published – in 1698, when he was twenty-seven years old – was a collection of sermons by Benjamin Whichcote.

Of chief importance for our purposes is the preface Shaftesbury wrote to the collection. For there Shaftesbury makes clear the importance he places on Whichcote's unwavering commitment to the Positive Answer.

At the beginning of his preface, Shaftesbury poses a question: why is there so much immorality in Christian nations when Christianity is itself a perfectly moral religion (Preface ii)? And the culprit Shaftesbury identifies – the cause of immorality in Christian nations – is the Negative Answer. Inundated by statements of the inherent wickedness of human nature, people in Christian nations begin to treat each other as wicked beings, and in so doing become wicked themselves. The belief that people are wicked turns out to be a self-fulfilling prophecy.

Shaftesbury holds two parties responsible for the recent propagation of the destructive idea that humanity is inherently evil. The first party is Thomas Hobbes, whose egoistic conception of human nature "has done but very ill service in the moral world" (Preface iv). The second party is the Calvinists and other Puritans, who maintain that Christianity can be stable only if it is built on the "ruin" of human nature (Preface v; cf. vii–viii). Shaftesbury contends that it is vitally important to "oppose this current" of the Negative Answer, which has decried human nature and destroyed belief in the existence of real virtue (Preface viii). And Whichcote is just the man to do it. For in his sermons, Whichcote clearly exhibits the Positive Answer and shows that humans have within themselves inherently virtuous principles that lead them directly toward virtuous action (Preface vii–xi).

The feature of Whichcote's Positive Answer that Shaftesbury chooses to highlight is the internality of heaven and hell (which I discussed in Chapter 2). According to Whichcote, as we have seen, the essential aspect of heaven is not the externally bestowed reward of residing after death in a pleasant place, but rather the joyous internal mental state of knowing that one has done the right thing. And the essential aspect of hell is not the externally inflicted punishment of residing after death in an unpleasant place, but the tormented internal mental state of knowing that one has done the wrong thing. As Shaftesbury puts it when summing up Whichcote's view, "*There is* inherent punishment *belonging to all* vice; *and no power can divide or separate them. For, tho' God should not, in a* positive way, *inflict punishment; or any instrument of God punish a sinner; yet he would* punish himself; *his misery and unhappiness would arise* from himself" (Preface viii). Shaftesbury highlights this feature of Whichcote's thought because he wants to claim that humans can possess thoroughly nonselfish motives that make it possible for them to achieve real virtue. Whichcote's position on the internality of heaven and hell serves this purpose because it tells us that we should care about virtue and the welfare of others for their own sake, and not simply because of the external benefits acting virtuously and sociably may bring. Whichcote's position tell us that the (non-derivative) value we may place on virtue and sociability can be the (antecedent) cause of the "peace and happiness" we feel when we act virtuously and sociably, which amounts to a denial of the egoist claim that the benefits we receive from acting virtuously and sociably are always the (antecedent) cause of the (derivative) value we place on virtue and sociability (Preface viii). Whichcote's "defence of *natural goodness*" thus implies that the human heart can contain the love, charity, and kindness that alone make actions "*lovely*" in the sight of God and man and "deserving" of notice and kind reward (Preface vii–viii).

According to Whichcote, then, humans are capable of real virtue and sociability. And Shaftesbury claims that Whichcote established this claim about human nature not merely through the propositional content of his sermons but also by the example of his own character. For Whichcote's "excellent spirit" – his sparkling "goodness and humanity" – shone brightly through everything he said and did (Preface xii). Shaftesbury cites Tillotson's laudatory funeral sermon as evidence of Whichcote's "God-like disposition" (Preface ix), but it is reasonable to suppose that he had also learned of Whichcote's character from Damaris Cudworth, who would have heard her father talk about Whichcote and who almost certainly knew the man herself.

Shaftesbury's thought changed over the course of his lifetime, and he adopted different personae in different works. Those factors, combined with his disdain for philosophical "systems," make it difficult to attribute to Shaftesbury a single set of coherent ideas. But from the two central points of his preface to Whichcote's sermons he never deviated.[3] From his earliest writing to his last, he continued to oppose voluntarism and egoism, consistently maintaining (1) that virtue does not originate in positive, arbitrary commands and (2) that humans are not wholly selfish but are capable of caring about virtue for its own sake. These rock solid commitments of Shaftesbury's are the core of his Positive Answer.

Shaftesbury also continued to think that because belief in the Negative Answer was self-fulfilling, convincing people of the truth of the Positive Answer was vitally important to the cause of virtue. A person who believes that all people are entirely selfish will be more likely to act selfishly himself or herself, while a person who believes in true sociability will be more likely to act sociably. Belief in the impossibility of virtue is an almost insurmountable barrier to acting virtuously, while confidence in the possibility of virtue is a spur. In this, too, Shaftesbury was similar to Whichcote and the other Cambridge Platonists, who thought that the Negative Answer of the Calvinists promoted a conception of God and humanity that was incompatible with morality and religion.

C. The Negative Answer Shaftesbury Opposed

Hobbes is the only representative of the Negative Answer to whom Shaftesbury explicitly referred in his Preface. But it's easy to spot in the line of thought he opposes the voluntarist views of the Calvinists and other Puritans.

There was, however, another representative of the Negative Answer Shaftesbury also had in mind, but his opposition to this person Shaftesbury took more care to conceal. That person was John Locke.[4]

In two letters from 1709, Shaftesbury launched blistering attacks on Locke's philosophy, linking him in both letters to "Tom Hobbes." As he put in at one point:

In general truly it has happened, that all those they call *free writers* now-a-days have espoused those principles which Mr. Hobbes set a-foot in this last age. Mr. Locke, as much as I honour him on account of other writings (viz., on government, policy, trade, coin, education, toleration, &c.), and as well as I knew him, and can answer for his sincerity as a most zealous *Christian* and believer, did, however, go in the self-same tract. . . . It was Mr. Locke that struck the home blow: for Mr. Hobbes's character and base slavish principles in government took off the poison of his philosophy. It was Mr. Locke that struck at all Fundamentals, threw all *Order* and *Virtue* out of the World, and made the Very Ideas of these . . . *unnatural* and without foundation in our Minds. (Regimen 403)[5]

Shaftesbury made it clear, moreover, that he had long disapproved of Locke's philosophy, although he had taken pains never to make his negative opinion explicit in his published works. He writes, for instance, "Thus have I ventured to make you the greatest confidence in the world, which is that of my philosophy, even against my old tutor and governor, whose name is so established in the world, but with whom I ever concealed my differences as much as possible" (Regimen 416).

The root of Locke's philosophical failure, as Shaftesbury saw it, was his denial of innate ideas (a point on which Damaris Cudworth also took issue with Locke). Locke might have been right to deny that "the very philosophical propositions about right and wrong" are innate, but he went wrong by suggesting that "the passion or affection towards society" is non-innate as well (Regimen 415). For, according to Shaftesbury, sociable human affections, such as the desire to form friendships and a concern for the public good, are obviously innate, or, since that word was skunked by Locke, "connatural" or "instinctive" (Regimen 404). Sociable affections are just as much a part of human nature, and not simply the result of "art" or "the catechism," as it is part of a bird's nature to fly, or a bull's nature to attack with its horns, or a male's nature to be sexually attracted to a female (Regimen 404, 415).

But Locke nonetheless denied that sociability was natural, probably because he mistakenly believed that allowing instinctive sociability would undermine his denial of innate "philosophical propositions" and because he was too "credulous" of "barbarian stories of wild nations" (Regimen 403–4). And Shaftesbury thought that this led Locke inexorably into the voluntarism of the Puritans and the egoism of Hobbes. For in denying innate sociability, Locke committed himself to holding that morality (which, as we will see, Shaftesbury equated with sociability) comprises rules that have no basis in human nature but are arbitrarily created by God or the sovereign. And the only reasons we could possibly have for obeying an entirely arbitrary rule are the desire for reward and the fear of punishment. But the desire for reward and fear of punishment are utterly selfish motives. So by committing himself to holding that reward and punishment are the only reasons to act morally, Locke became just as guilty as Hobbes and the voluntarists of decrying human nature and destroying belief in the existence of real virtue.

I am not sure that Shaftesbury was entirely fair in attributing to Locke these Hobbesian and voluntarist positions. In *The Reasonableness of Christianity*, which was published in 1695, Locke did emphasize "unspeakable rewards and punishments in another world," and apparently as he grew older he spoke more and more of rewards and punishments in the afterlife as the reasons to be moral. In earlier writings, however, Locke advanced a rationalist conception of morality that implies non-arbitrary and non-selfish reasons to be moral. But however that may be, it's clear that Shaftesbury believed that Locke was guilty of Hobbesian and voluntarist offenses. And the first embodiment of Shaftesbury's anti-Lockean views was his collection of Whichcote's sermons. We find, then, that Whichcote – and his Positive Answer – spurred Shaftesbury's break from his intellectual forebear, just as he had led the young Ralph Cudworth, sixty years earlier, to reject the religion of his father.

7

Shaftesbury's *Inquiry*

A Misanthropic Faith in Human Nature

In 1699, a year after Shaftesbury completed his edition of Whichcote's sermons, an anonymous version of Shaftesbury's *Inquiry concerning Virtue, or
Merit* was published. Shaftesbury would later claim that he did not think
that the 1699 manuscript was fit for public consumption and that the person who had the book published (probably John Toland) acted against his
wishes. Shaftesbury even went so far as to buy up and destroy all the copies of
the book he could find. Or so he said. At the same time, Shaftesbury seems to
have allowed a fair number of people to read the unpublished manuscript in
the years prior to 1699. And there is good evidence that in 1701 Shaftesbury
himself initiated a French translation of the book, a copy of which he had
sent to his friend Pierre Bayle, "to whom I fancy it will be agreeable" (Klein
1999, x). So there is some reason to question his later protestations that
the 1699 edition was "an unshapen *Foetus*, or false birth" whose publication
was entirely "contrary to the Author's design" (Klein 1999, x). In any event,
Shaftesbury revised the *Inquiry* and published authorized versions in 1711
and 1714.

In this chapter, I examine claims that are central to both the early and
late versions of the *Inquiry*, using passages that (unless otherwise noted)
appear virtually unchanged in all editions. So the ideas I'll discuss in this
chapter are ones that Shaftesbury developed quite early in his intellectual
career and never disowned.

A. Virtue and Religion

The beginning of the *Inquiry* is continuous with Shaftesbury's preface to
Whichcote's sermons. The preface addressed the question of how there can
be so much immorality in Christian nations when Christianity is itself such a
moral religion. And the *Inquiry* begins by casting doubt on the widely held
idea that religion and virtue are "so nearly related, that they are generally

presum'd inseparable Companions" (Virtue or Merit 3). "We have known People," Shaftesbury says,

who having the Appearance of great Zeal in *Religion*, have yet wanted even the common Affections of *Humanity*, and shewn themselves extremely degenerate and corrupt. Others, again, who have paid little regard to Religion, and been consider'd as mere ATHEISTS, have yet been observ'd to practise the Rules of *Morality*, and act in many Cases with such good Meaning and Affection towards Mankind, as might seem to force an Acknowledgment of their being *virtuous*. (Virtue or Merit 3–4)

Shaftesbury says that he will solve the puzzle of how religious people can be vicious and atheistic people virtuous by determining the nature of virtue "by it-self" and how it is "influenc'd by Religion" (Virtue or Merit 4). That Shaftesbury placed this point front and center in both the *Inquiry* and the Whichcote preface is telling: It reveals that the issue was of paramount concern to him in the 1690s, it foreshadows his later arguments for a conception of morality that can be disengaged from religion, and it hints at a fierce antipathy toward pious hypocrites who claimed the moral high ground while treating other people like dirt.

In the next section, I discuss in more detail Shaftesbury's account of virtue. But let us first look at what he says about how virtue is "influenc'd by" the differing attitudes people take toward religion or God. He describes four such attitudes: perfect theism, which is the belief that the world is "govern'd, order'd, or regulated *for the best*, by a designing Principle, or Mind, necessarily good and permanent"; perfect atheism, or the belief that there is no designing principle or mind; polytheism, or the belief in multiple designing minds; and daemonism, or belief in a designing mind or minds "not absolutely and necessarily good, nor confin'd to what is best, but capable of acting according to mere Will or Fancy" (Virtue or Merit 6).

Shaftesbury maintains that perfect theism contributes greatly to virtue. This is because belief in a "*Worthy*" and "*Good*" God serves as an excellent "Example" that can "raise and increase the Affection towards Virtue, and help to submit and subdue all other Affections to that alone" (Virtue or Merit 32–3). Perfect theism also contributes to virtue by imparting "FEAR *of future Punishment*, and HOPE *of future Reward*" (Virtue or Merit 33). Shaftesbury takes great pains to state that a theist's motives to virtue should not be self-interested. If fear or hope of an afterlife constitute "essential" or "considerable" motives of one's actions, then one's actions will lack moral worth (Virtue or Merit 33). In order to be truly virtuous, one must be motivated to virtue for its own sake, distinct from the benefits to oneself. Still, belief in a God who ultimately gives everyone his just deserts can help "support" one's commitment to virtue, especially when one is faced with "ill Fortune" or "unjust Censure" in this world (Virtue or Merit 35, 33).

Shaftesbury believes that atheism neither contributes to nor detracts from virtue. Atheism lacks the advantages of perfect theism in that an atheist cannot gain inspiration from the salutary example of a worthy and good God, nor lean in times of trouble on the thought that there is a supreme being who will ensure that everything eventually works out for the best (Virtue or Merit 32–3). But an atheist can realize virtue nonetheless. It's more difficult for an atheist to be virtuous than it is for a theist, but it's possible (Virtue or Merit 40–3). Atheism is thus preferable to "corrupt religion" and "superstition." For while corrupt religion and superstition can cause someone to think that hideous activities such as cannibalism and bestiality are "good and excellent," atheism will never "be the cause of any estimation or valuing of any thing as fair, noble, and deserving, which was the contrary" (Virtue or Merit 27). Atheism does not set up "a false Species of Right or Wrong," and so atheists can be just as proficient as theists at judging virtue and vice (Virtue or Merit 27; cf. 31). Religion "is capable of doing great Good, or Harm; and ATHEISM nothing positive in either way" (Virtue or Merit 30).

Shaftesbury's belief that atheists could have a proper "sense of right and wrong" and be "capable of Virtue" was highly provocative (Virtue or Merit 31). The Cambridge Platonists had argued that non-Christians could be fully moral, and that was enough to place them in opposition to the mainstream of English Protestantism. But even Whichcote and Cudworth didn't go so far as to affirm the possibility of a fully moral atheist. Indeed, Whichcote maintained that one of our three fundamental moral duties is to be "Godly," which is to believe in and show gratitude toward God. In the *Inquiry*, however, Shaftesbury is willing to disengage virtuous conduct from belief in God. This is one of the chief reasons many of Shaftesbury's contemporaries called him a "free thinker" – a label often used in a pejorative fashion to identify atheistic threats to the Christianity and morality. This is also one of the chief reasons Shaftesbury is crucial to the birth of modern secular ethics. Shaftesbury himself, as we will see, had profound theological commitments, and one of the dominant strands of his thought was based on a conception of morality and human nature that implies God's existence. But Shaftesbury did not think every person had to believe in God in order to be virtuous. He did not think virtue essentially involved any of the sorts of duties we would typically classify as religious. Shaftesbury's position is thus a halfway house between a religio-theological ethics and an ethics that is thoroughly secular.

But as provocative as Shaftesbury was to religious thinkers in general, he reserved his sharpest barbs for the Calvinists in particular, as the *Inquiry*'s discussion of polytheism and daemonism makes clear. Polytheism and daemonism, Shaftesbury says, can corrupt the natural moral sense by instructing people to worship gods who commit immoral acts, which inevitably leads the people to approve and respect the immoral acts that the "ador'd and reverenc'd" gods commit. As an example of such corruption, Shaftesbury cites worship of the "amorously inclin'd" Jupiter, whom history represents as liable to permit his sexual desires "to wander in the loosest manner" (Virtue or Merit 27). "[T]is certain," Shaftesbury says, "that his Worshippers, believing this History to be literally and strictly true, must of course be taught a greater Love of amorous and wanton Acts" (Virtue or Merit 27–8). Shaftesbury also alludes to other religions that teach their adherents to love gods who engage in deceit, treachery, and resentful vengeance. And he contends that "'tis evident that such a Religion as this being strongly enforc'd, must of necessity raise even an Approbation and Respect towards the Vices of this kind, and breed a sutable Disposition, a capricious, partial, revengeful, and deceitful Temper. For even *Irregularitys* and *Enormitys* of a heinous kind must in many cases appear illustrious to one, who considers them in a Being admir'd and contemplated with the highest Honour and Veneration" (Virtue or Merit 28).

With this characterization of pagan religions the Calvinists would have agreed. Shaftesbury goes on, however, to place Calvinism itself in the category of daemonism, arguing that the Calvinist representation of God can be just as destructive to the natural moral sense as the most superstitious paganism. Shaftesbury doesn't mention the Calvinists by name, but he clearly has them in mind when he speaks of the voluntarist–supralapsarian view of a "supreme Being" who decided "arbitrarily, and without reason, [that] some Beings were destin'd to endure perpetual Ill, and others as constantly to enjoy Good" (Virtue or Merit 29). For recall that the Calvinists held that God decided before the moment of creation who would go to heaven and who would go to hell and that God's decisions were unrestrained by independent moral principles. Recall, as well, that Cudworth said that it was just this voluntarist–supralapsarian view of God that turned him and the other Cambridge Platonists against Calvinism because it implied that God, by punishing people for things they could not avoid, was immoral. Well, Shaftesbury says the same thing – that the Calvinist view of God implies that He performs immoral acts. Honor and veneration of the Calvinist God are, thus, just as likely to corrupt the natural moral sense as is worship of the most "captious" pagan deity. As Shaftesbury puts it directly after his allusion to voluntarism and supralapsarianism, "And thus it appears, that where a real Devotion and hearty Worship is paid to a Supreme Being, who in his History or Character is represented otherwise than as really and truly just and good; there must ensue a Loss of Rectitude, a Disturbance of Thought, and a Corruption of Temper and Manners in the Believer. His honesty will, of necessity, be supplanted by his Zeal, whilst he is thus unnaturally influenc'd, and render'd thus immorally devout" (Virtue or Merit 29).

Shaftesbury's attack on Calvinism and other "daemonisms" dovetails with his preface to Whichcote's sermons. For in the preface, as in the *Inquiry*, Shaftesbury argues that religious misconception breeds moral corruption. In the preface, Shaftesbury also highlights the morally destructive effects of egoistic views of human nature. And he makes the same point in the *Inquiry*, explaining how a person with an excessive self-interested concern to reach heaven will have little room left in his soul for "other Affections towards Friends, Relations or Mankind" (Virtue or Merit 39). The "more there is of this violent Affection towards *private Good*," Shaftesbury writes, "the less room is there for the other sort towards *Goodness it-self*, or any good and deserving Object, worthy of Love and Admiration for its own sake" (Virtue or Merit 34).

But while the *Inquiry*'s attack on religious error is much the same as the Whichcote preface, in other parts of the *Inquiry* Shaftesbury develops a more expansive criticism of human folly. Indeed, the *Inquiry* describes a veritable plethora of immoral activities and vicious habits – cowardice, revengefulness, treachery, ingratitude, luxury, avarice, vanity, ambition, sloth, gluttony, and covetousness, to name only a few. He examines the ways in which "a settled Idleness, Supineness, and Inactivity... must produce a total Disorder of the Passions, and break out into the strangest Irregularities imaginable" (Virtue or Merit 77); how "a constant ill Humour, Sourness, and Disquiet [must produce] perverse Inclinations and bitter Aversions" (Virtue or Merit 48); and the "UNNATURAL *and* INHUMAN DELIGHT *in beholding torments*, and in viewing Distress, Calamity, Blood, Massacre and Destruction, with a peculiar Joy and Pleasure" (Virtue or Merit 93). And as much as there is on moral deformity in the 1711 and 1714 versions of the *Inquiry*, the 1699 edition had even more. In 1699, in passages that he would later excise, Shaftesbury expounded further on anger, rage, revengefulness, resentment, pique, vexation, frowardness, sloth, and laziness (Virtue or Merit [1st ed.] 115–17). Particularly conspicuous in the 1699 edition is a virulent screed on sexual perversion, a typical sentence of which runs thus: "All other Creatures in the world are for their orderliness in this, a reproach to Man: since they, of what kind soever they are, have regular and proportion'd Appetites, and have the use of Venery according to fit and proper Seasons and Subjects; whilst Man alone knows neither season, nor bound, nor fitness of Subject, but breaks into all horridness of unnatural and monstrous Lusts, regarding neither Sex nor Species" (Virtue or Merit [1st ed.] 118).

The *Inquiry*, then, is rife with examples of wickedness, vice, and the evil men do to each other and themselves. And Shaftesbury's presentation of these examples manifests an attention to detail and an excitability that wouldn't have been out of place in one of Perkins's own proclamations of human depravity. All of this might make us wonder whether Shaftesbury really ought to be counted a proponent of the Positive Answer. Shaftesbury supposedly agrees with the Cambridge Platonists' optimistic view of humanity and disagrees with the pessimism of Hobbes and the Calvinists. But at various points in the *Inquiry*, disgust for human beings is the dominant note.

Nonetheless, Shaftesbury still has to be counted a proponent of the Positive Answer, his capacious disgust notwithstanding. That's because definitive of the Positive Answer is the belief that each human being has within himself all the resources necessary to achieve the height of morality. Or, to put the same point another way, proponents of the Positive Answer deny that each of us, if left to our own devices, will necessarily come to moral ruin. And Shaftesbury certainly fits this description. Even in the 1699 version of the *Inquiry*, with all of its expressions of disgust, Shaftesbury makes it clear that he believes that human beings can be fully virtuous even without the assistance of an absolute sovereign or a revealed religion. Indeed, for Shaftesbury, real virtue can and must come entirely from within each person's own soul. And in making this point, Shaftesbury explicitly rejects both the Hobbesian idea that self-interest is our only motive and the Calvinist idea that pervasive sin is ineluctable to the soul of every human. According to Shaftesbury, human nature is fundamentally aligned to virtue, and that's why a virtuous person is internally balanced, harmonious, and happy, his "MIND *or Reason well compos'd and easy within it-self*" (Virtue or Merit 68; cf. 66). That humans are naturally aligned to virtue also explains why vicious people invariably suffer intense internal torment – it's because their vicious action is a violence to their own nature (see Virtue or Merit 45–50, 66–70, 96–8; [1st ed.] 116).

So Shaftesbury did not think internal corruption was inevitable. But he did think it was distressingly common. And he thought this was a peculiarly human calamity. No other creature, he contends, was designed to achieve real virtue; humans alone have the capacity to reach so high. At the same time, no other creature violates its nature so grievously; humans alone can sink so low. "For as the highest Improvements of Temper are made in Human Kind; so the greatest Corruptions and Degeneracys are discoverable in this Race" (Virtue or Merit 55). Shaftesbury was equally impressed by the moral beauty of human nature and the moral ugliness of particular human beings. "Virtue or Merit," he proclaims, "is allow'd to *Man* only" (Virtue or Merit 16). But it's often almost impossible, he says with bitter disappointment, "to find a Man who lives NATURALLY, and as a Man" (Virtue or Merit 56).

The Positive Answer of Shaftesbury's *Inquiry* thus has a distinctively misanthropic flavor. All humans have the ability to be virtuous and happy, the *Inquiry* tells us. But many of them succeed only in making themselves vicious and miserable.[1]

B. The *Inquiry* Account of Virtue

The account of virtue in the *Inquiry* had a greater impact on twentieth-century Anglo-American philosophy than anything else Shaftesbury wrote. That's due in large part to twentieth-century Anglo-American philosophers' bestowing on the *Inquiry* the honor of being the first moral sense theory. Anglo-American philosophers identified the *Inquiry*, that is, as the initial blow in the battle waged by moral sentimentalists, such as Hutcheson and Hume, against moral rationalists, such as Whichcote and Cudworth.

This view of the *Inquiry* is simplistic in two respects. First, the *Inquiry* was not the first work to place sentiment at the heart of morality. As we've seen in Chapter 4, Cudworth himself emphasized the role of sentiment in his sermons from the 1640s, and John Smith made equally emphatic sentimentalist points in his discourses from the same period. Henry More's "boniform faculty" is, if anything, an even clearer antecedent of Shaftesbury's moral sense. And those are just the Cambridge Platonists. I don't doubt that convincing cases can be made for other pre-Shaftesburean sentimentalists as well. The typical view of the *Inquiry* as moral sense prototype is also inaccurate because the *Inquiry*, as we will see in this chapter, contains unmistakably rationalist elements that confound any attempt to place Shaftesbury squarely in the sentimentalist camp.

That said, there is still a crucial kernel of truth to the typical twentieth-century view of the *Inquiry*. For Shaftesbury's account of morality in the *Inquiry* does contain elements that are undeniably sentimentalist, even if it also contains elements that are undeniably rationalist. And Shaftesbury's statements of these sentimentalist elements are clearer than many that came before. The sentimentalist aspects of the *Inquiry* were also instrumental to the philosophical development of Francis Hutcheson, and Hutcheson, as we will see in Chapter 12, would eventually produce one of the eighteenth century's most well-defined versions of the moral sense theory. Shaftesbury, moreover, makes it clear that when he is talking about morality he is talking about something that can be cleanly distinguished from religion, while most of his predecessors assiduously refused to countenance such a distinction. And this feature of Shaftesbury's thought made him particularly suitable for use by secular twentieth-century Anglo-American moral philosophers.

In this section, I examine the *Inquiry*'s account of virtue and attempt to elucidate both its sentimentalist and rationalist elements. We will see that Shaftesbury wanted morality to touch the private heart of every individual and yet also be objective and public. We'll also come to see that the tension between these two goals – which echoes the tension that existed between Cudworth's 1647 sermons and EIM (as I discussed in Chapter 4) – is something the *Inquiry* fails to resolve.

Shaftesbury begins his *Inquiry* account of virtue by telling us that he is going to "determine what that Quality is to which we give the Name of *Goodness*, or Virtue" (Virtue or Merit 9). Something is good, according to Shaftesbury, if it contributes to the "Existence or Well-being" of the system of which it is a part. Every animal, for instance, is a part of its species. So a particular animal, say a tiger, is a good member of its species – it's a good tiger – if it contributes to the well-being of the tiger species as a whole. There is also "a System of all Animals," which consists of the "order" or "economy" of all the different animal species (Virtue or Merit 11). So a good animal is one that contributes to the well-being of "Animal Affairs" in general (Virtue or Merit 11). The system of all animals, moreover, works with the system "of Vegetables, and all other things in this inferiour World" to constitute "*one system* of a Globe or Earth" (Virtue or Merit 11). So something is a good earthly thing if it contributes to the existence of earthly things in general. And the system of this earth is itself part of a "Universal System" or "a System *of all things*" (Virtue or Merit 11). So to be "*wholly* and *really*" good, a thing must contribute to the existence of the universe as a whole (Virtue or Merit 11).

This progression of ever-larger systems is a bit dazzling, and we might wonder how we can ever know (or even make sense of) whether something is contributing to the well-being of the universe as a whole. But Shaftesbury avoids this problem by discussing in detail only that which makes "a sensible Creature" a good member of its species – by focusing almost exclusively on whether an individual creature is promoting the well-being of its species as a whole (Virtue or Merit 12).[2] Perhaps Shaftesbury believed that a creature that contributes to the well-being of its species will also always contribute to the well-being of the universe as a whole, in which case being a good member of one's species would be equivalent to being "*wholly* and *really*" good.

Shaftesbury begins his discussion of goodness in sensible creatures by making a crucial point. The goodness or evilness of a sensible creature, he says, is based on the creature's motives, and not simply on the results of the creature's actions.

We do not however say of any-one, that he is an *ill Man*, because he has the Plague-Spots upon him, or because he has convulsive Fits which make him strike and wound such as approach him. Nor do we say on the other side, that he is *a good Man*, when having his Hands ty'd up, he is hinder'd from doing the Mischief he designs; or (which is in a manner the same) when he abstains from executing his ill purpose, thro a fear of some impending Punishment, or thro the allurement of some exteriour Reward. So that in a sensible Creature, That which is not done thro any Affection at all, makes neither good nor Ill in the nature of that Creature; who then only is suppos'd *Good*, when the Good or Ill of the System to which he has relation, is the immediate Object of some Passion or Affection moving him. (Virtue or Merit 12)

The anti-egoism of this passage is completely in accord with Shaftesbury's preface to Whichcote's sermons. A person who does the right thing only through fear of punishment or hope of reward is morally no better than a person who refrains from doing ill only because he's tied up. Indeed, a person who does the right thing only through fear of punishment or hope of reward is just as morally despicable as a person who does the wrong thing in order to further his "Self-Good" (Virtue or Merit 14). Shaftesbury hammers away at this anti-egoist point throughout the *Inquiry*, maintaining over and over again that a person who does good from selfish motives is morally equivalent to a person who does ill from selfish motives.

There is, however, another aspect of the passage quoted in the previous paragraph that would not have fit so well in a preface to the sermons of the rationalist Whichcote. Shaftesbury is arguing in this passage that a sensible creature's moral status is determined entirely by its motives. But he also says that sensible creatures have as motives only passions or affections. And this is not an anomaly or slip of the pen. Throughout the *Inquiry*, Shaftesbury is perfectly consistent in calling every motive to action an affection or passion. Reason alone cannot motivate. As Shaftesbury writes:

> It has been shewn before, that no Animal can be said properly *to act*, otherwise than thro Affections or Passions, such as are proper to an Animal. . . . Whatsoever therefore is done or acted by any Animal *as such*, is done only thro some Affection or Passion, as of Fear, Love, or Hatred moving him. . . . So that according as these Affections stand, a Creature must be virtuous or vitious, good or ill. (Virtue or Merit 50; cf. 23–6)

So in the *Inquiry*, the moral status of sensible creatures is a function of their motives, and their motives depend on their passions – a position that echoes some of Cudworth's rhetoric in the 1647 sermons and anticipates some of the most influential anti-rationalist arguments of Hutcheson (see Chapter 12) and Hume (see Chapter 16). Let us now examine in somewhat more detail Shaftesbury's view of the morally relevant passionate motives and how they fill out his picture of morality as a whole.

In the *Inquiry* Shaftesbury draws a distinction between goodness and virtue. Goodness is something that is within the reach of all sensible creatures, not only humans but also nonhuman animals such as tigers. This is because a creature is good if its affections promote the well-being of the system of which it is a part, and nonhuman animals are just as capable of possessing this type of affection as humans. "Virtue or Merit," on the other hand, is within the reach of "Man" alone (Virtue or Merit 16). And that is because virtue or merit is tied to a special kind of affection that only humans possess.

This special kind of affection is a second-order affection, an affection that has as its object another affection. We humans experience these second-order affections because we, unlike nonhuman animals, are conscious of our own passions. Not only do we possess passions, but we also reflect on or become aware of the passions we have. And when we reflect on our own passions, we develop feelings about them. Imagine, for instance, that you feel the desire to help a person in distress. In addition to simply feeling that desire, you may also become aware that you are feeling that desire. And when you become aware of that, you may experience a positive feeling (or "Liking") toward your desire to help. Or imagine that you feel the desire to harm a person who has blamelessly bested you in a fair competition. In addition to simply feeling the desire to harm, you may also become aware that you are feeling that desire. And when you become aware of that, you may experience a negative feeling (or "Dislike") toward your desire to harm. These are the kinds of phenomena Shaftesbury has in mind when he says that "the *Affections* of Pity, Kindness, Gratitude, and their Contrarys, being brought into the Mind by Reflection, become Objects. So that, by means of this reflected Sense, there arises another kind of Affection towards those very

Affections themselves, which have been already felt, and are now become the Subject of a new Liking or Dislike" (Virtue or Merit 16).

Shaftesbury calls this capacity to feel second-order affections the "*Sense of Right or Wrong*" (Virtue or Merit 18) or the "*moral Sense*" (Virtue or Merit 27). The moral sense is that which produces in us feelings of "like" or "dislike" for our own (first-order) affections. When the moral sense is operating properly, it produces positive feelings toward affections that promote the well-being of humanity and negative feelings toward affections that detract from the well-being of humanity. The second-order feelings that the moral sense produces can themselves motivate one to action. And people are virtuous if they act from those second-order feelings. In contrast, nonhuman animals, because they lack the powers of reflection necessary for consciousness of their own affections, do not possess a moral sense. So nonhuman animals are incapable of achieving virtue. As Shaftesbury explains:

> Upon the whole. As to those Creatures who are only capable of being mov'd by *sensible Objects*; they are accordingly *Good* or *Vitious*, as the sensible Affections stand with them. 'Tis otherwise in Creatures capable of framing *rational Objects* of moral Good. For in one of this kind, shou'd the *sensible Affections* stand ever so much amiss; yet if they prevail not, because of those other *rational Affections* spoken of [i.e., the affections of the moral sense]; 'tis evident, the Temper still holds good in the main; and the Person is with justice esteem'd virtuous by all Men. (Virtue or Merit 21)

For Shaftesbury, creatures are virtuous only when their actions involve a conscious concern to benefit their species. Virtue belongs only to those creatures who can reflect on the public good and who act from the affection that reflection produces. Simply possessing an affection that is beneficial to its species may make a creature good, but if the creature lacks a conscious "Notion of a publick Interest" it cannot be virtuous (Virtue or Merit 18).

That said, we should take care not to overstate Shaftesbury's distinction between virtue and goodness. Virtue, as Shaftesbury understands it, is a subset of goodness, not a distinct quality. A sensible creature is good if it is motivated by an affection that benefits its species as a whole. And the moral sense, as Shaftesbury conceives of it, produces affections that benefit the human species. So since a virtuous person is one who is motivated by the affections of the moral sense, a virtuous person is also (necessarily) good (see Virtue or Merit 45). The affections of the moral sense are unlike other good affections in that they have a unique reflective or second-order quality, but they are like all other good affections in that they are beneficial to the species and affective. Shaftesbury is quite clear about this: what the moral sense produces is a "Sentiment" or "Exercise of the Heart" (Virtue or Merit 17–18). It's true that only rational beings can possess a moral sense. This is because only rational beings are capable of reflecting on their own affections. But the moral sense is a passionate faculty nonetheless. It is more akin to the enthusiastic, heart-felt love of Cudworth's 1647 sermons than to the propositionally, geometrically certain rationality of Cudworth's EIM.

In his sermons, recall, Cudworth was moved to base righteousness on heart-felt love because he believed that the essence of righteousness lay in the motivating principles behind one's actions. Also recall, however, that by the time he wrote EIM Cudworth had become sharply concerned to accommodate a principled, peaceful way of adjudicating between people who came into conflict about what to do. And this led him to develop an account of morality based in reason alone, as such an account implied that people who acted rationally would always be able to resolve their conflicts.

Shaftesbury's *Inquiry* contains a distinctly sentimentalist version of the motivational point of Cudworth's sermons: passions motivate us to action, not reason alone, and our motives are what are morally significant about us. But Shaftesbury was also concerned about the possibility of one person's passions conflicting with another person's, about the possibility that the moral sense of one person might "like" what the moral sense of another person "dislikes." And, like Cudworth of EIM, Shaftesbury was unwilling to allow that these conflicts were rationally irresolvable. He wanted to hold that if one person's moral sense comes into conflict with another person's, then at least one of the persons must be wrong and that there must be a rational way of establishing it. The problem with the overzealous enthusiasts of the seventeenth century had been that each of them had claimed to have privileged, private access to the word of God, and Shaftesbury did not want his moral sense theory to collapse into the chaotic and violent subjectivism such enthusiasm induced. He wanted to base virtue in a moral sense, but he also wanted to maintain that there was a principled and public way of showing that the deliverances of a person's moral sense were correct or incorrect. He wanted his account of virtue to be affective, but he also wanted to anchor it in something objective.

The objective anchor Shaftesbury relies on is his account of goodness. As we've seen, Shaftesbury claims that a thing is good only if it promotes the well-being of the system of which it is a part. And Shaftesbury conceives of virtue as a subset of goodness, which means that humans (as parts of humanity) can be virtuous only if they promote the well-being of humanity as a whole. So if two people ever come into moral conflict, there is in principle a rational way of settling the dispute. If the moral sense of one of them "likes" something that detracts from the good of humanity as a whole, then that person is wrong. His moral affections cannot be good, and so he cannot be virtuous. As Shaftesbury puts it:

We have found, that to deserve the name of *Good* or *Virtuous*, a Creature must have all his Inclinations and Affections, his Dispositions of Mind and Temper, sutable, and agreeing with the Good of his *Kind*, or of that *System* in which he is included, and of which he constitutes a PART. To stand thus well affected, and to have one's Affections *right* and *intire*, not only in respect of one's self, but of Society and the Publick: This is *Rectitude, Integrity,* or VIRTUE. And to be wanting in any of these, or to have their Contrarys, is *Depravity, Corruption,* and VICE. (Virtue or Merit 45)

Shaftesbury's account of goodness thus constitutes an independent standard against which we can measure everyone's moral sense. If a person's moral sense tracks the account of goodness, it is functioning correctly; if a person's moral sense veers from the account of goodness, it is functioning incorrectly.

But where does the account of goodness come from? It cannot originate in the moral sense, as it is used as an independent standard against which the moral sense itself is measured. Nor does Shaftesbury ever give the impression that his account of goodness is based on the "likings" or "dislikes" of his own moral sense. Shaftesbury presents his account of goodness, rather, as something he has discovered through the use of reason alone (see Virtue or Merit 8–16). Goodness, as Shaftesbury conceives of it, is an objective property, one that is independent of all human minds, and reason tells us of what that property consists.

So even if every member of society were to approve of something harmful to humanity, it would still be vicious. For that which is destructive of the species can never be "*Virtue*, of any kind, or in any sense; but must remain still horrid Depravity, notwithstanding any Fashion, Law, Custom or Religion; which may be ill and vitious *it-self*; but can never alter the *eternal Measures*, and immutable independent Nature of *Worth* and VIRTUE" (Virtue or Merit 21). Fashion, law, custom, and religion can cause people to develop positive affections toward things harmful to humanity. But the development of such affections will never make such things right. The "eternal *Measures*" of right and wrong are not constituted by human affections. Right and wrong have an "immutable independent Nature." And we are virtuous just to the extent that our affections lead us to act in accord with these eternal and immutable moral truths.

In the *Inquiry* account of virtue, then, reason and sentiment both play essential roles. People are virtuous if and only if their actions flow from properly functioning moral sentiments. And reason tells us that moral sentiments are functioning properly if and only if they promote the well-being of the species as a whole. Shaftesbury thus captures the spirit of the sermon before the House of Commons, in which Cudworth insisted that one's moral state depended on the movements of one's heart, and the objectivity of *Eternal and Immutable Morality*, in which Cudworth argued that morality had to be grounded in rationally discernible truth.

C. Problems with the *Inquiry* Account of Virtue

Combining reason and sentiment is, in any event, what Shaftesbury tried to do in his *Inquiry* account of virtue. But the elements he attempts to combine do not rest easily together. The fundamental problem is that Shaftesbury's sentimentalist moral psychology conflicts with his rationalist moral ontology. We can illustrate this point by examining what Shaftesbury says about vicious people.

According to Shaftesbury, there are three types of vicious people. One type is the person who knows what is virtuous, whose moral sense "likes" what is virtuous, but whose corrupt non-moral affections have opposed and overwhelmed his motivation to virtue (Virtue or Merit 30). Because his moral sense and rational faculty are in accord with those of a virtuous person, this first type does not directly concern our present discussion. The second type of vicious person has an operative moral sense, but his moral sense "likes" the wrong kinds of things (Virtue or Merit 26–30). The third type has lost the operation of his moral sense altogether. He has become so corrupted that he no longer possesses his natural sense of right and wrong at all (Virtue or Merit 24–6). Let us look first at the second type and then at the third.

The second type is the person whose moral sense "likes" or approves of things that fail to promote the well-being of humanity. Within this type, Shaftesbury draws yet another distinction (Virtue or Merit 16–21). Some of these people approve of harmful things only because they are mistaken about some non-moral fact, and some approve of harmful things because their moral sense has been corrupted. People who approve of harmful things only because they are mistaken about a non-moral fact are victims of a morally blameless "Mistake . . . *in Fact*" (Virtue or Merit 20). But people who approve of harmful things because their moral sense has been corrupted are guilty of a morally blameworthy "Mistake *of Right*" (Virtue or Merit 20).

It's easy enough to think of an example of a person who is misled by a morally blameless mistake of fact, someone who approves of or follows a course of action that he has every reason to think will benefit humanity but that ends up harming humanity as a result of factors he could not have known about. A person who does the wrong thing only because of "Weakness or Imperfection in the Senses," for instance, is not vicious because "his Failure is not in his principal or leading Part" (Virtue or Merit 19). And a "Man who loves and esteems another, as believing him to have that Virtue which he has not, but only counterfeits, is not on this account vitious or corrupt" (Virtue or Merit 20).

But a person guilty of a morally blameworthy mistake of right is mistaken in a way other than simply getting the non-moral facts wrong. Shaftesbury gives as one example of such a mistake a person who eats "the Flesh of his Enemys" because he thinks it "both right and honourable; as supposing it to be of considerable service to his Community and capable of advancing the Name, and spreading the Terrour of his Nation" (Virtue or Merit 27). He also discusses people who, as a result of worshipping a "furious" and "revengeful" God, come to feel "Approbation" for the vices of "resentment," "Wrath and Anger" (Virtue or Merit 27–9). These people, according to Shaftesbury, do not simply miscalculate. What is wrong with these people is that their moral affections are corrupt. And this corruption has resulted from affective or non-rational influences. Belief or opinion, Shaftesbury maintains, cannot on its own cause someone to approve of cannibalism, vengefulness, and the like. Rather, "the wrong sense or false imagination of right and wrong...can proceed only from the Force of Custom and Education" (Virtue or Merit 26). Shaftesbury elaborates on this point when he explains that mere belief or nonbelief in God will not on its own alter one's moral sense. One's moral sense will become corrupted only "where a real Devotion and hearty Worship is paid to a Supreme Being, who in his History or Character is represented otherwise than as really and truly just and good" (Virtue or Merit 29). Mistakes of right result from ill-placed "Love" and "Esteem" (Virtue or Merit 27).

Shaftesbury's discussion of people who have lost their sense of right and wrong (the third type of vicious person) is further evidence of his view that one's moral character essentially depends on the shape of one's passions. There he says explicitly that it is impossible for "Belief or Opinion" to efface "the Sense of Right and Wrong" (Virtue or Merit 25–6). As he puts it:

Sense of Right and Wrong therefore being as natural to us as *natural Affection* itself, and being a first Principle in our Constitution and Make; there is no speculative Opinion, Persuasion or Belief, which is capable *immediately* or *directly* to exclude or destroy it. That which is of original and pure Nature, nothing beside contrary Habit or Custom (a second Nature) is able to displace. And this Affection being *an original one* of earliest Rise in the Soul or affectionate Part; nothing beside a contrary Affection, by frequent check and controul, can operate upon it, so as either to diminish it in part, or destroy it in whole. (Virtue or Merit 25–6)

Belief alone will not diminish or destroy a person's moral sense. If a person is vicious as a result of a diminished or destroyed moral sense, it is because of non-rational influences, or changes to his passionate nature.

So Shaftesbury's view implies that there is no purely rational way of correcting the mistakes of some vicious people. If people do not disapprove of cannibalism and vengeance, it is because they have corrupted passions, and rational discussion will not on its own bring these passions back into line. But the non-rational nature of these vicious mistakes raises two worries for Shaftesbury.

One worry is that there may be no common rational ground between people who come into moral conflict. According to Shaftesbury's account, two people who disagree about what is right may have different moral affections, and there may be no reason to think that they will be able to resolve their disagreement through rational means. This is a serious problem given Shaftesbury's desire for a principled, peaceful method for resolving moral disputes – given his desire for an anchor in objectivity. Cudworth's EIM manifested a rationalist optimism about the resolution of moral conflict in that it held that morality comprises public principles that are always accessible to every human mind. But Shaftesbury's *Inquiry* is comparatively pessimistic in that it tells us that moral disagreement may be based on affective corruption that rational thought cannot undo. Shaftesbury has to face the fact that his anchor in objectivity will not keep zealous enthusiasts from drifting out to sea.

But perhaps even more serious is the worry that Shaftesbury's theory of goodness will itself become lost. Shaftesbury presents his account of goodness as objectively true, a discovery of reason, not a feeling of the heart. Indeed, Shaftesbury's account of goodness must be independent of all the affections, as he takes that account to be the standard against which all affections (including the affections of the moral sense) must be measured. Shaftesbury's moral psychology implies, however, that persons' moral judgments necessarily conform to the affections of their moral sense. If a person's moral sense "likes" something, she'll think it's morally good; if her moral sense "dislikes" something, she'll think it's morally bad; and if her moral sense has been destroyed, she won't make moral judgments at all. That's the inevitable conclusion of Shaftesbury's discussion of vicious people and mistakes of right (Virtue or Merit 24–31). But if every person's moral judgments depend on his or her moral sense, why think that it is possible for anyone – Shaftesbury included – to discover the nature of morality through the use of reason alone? To repeat, Shaftesbury presents his account of goodness as objectively true, as a description of eternal and immutable principles that are independent of all human affections. But he also argues that humans' moral ideas depend on the affections of their moral sense. So how can he claim that his own ideas of goodness are independent of the affections of the moral sense? Shaftesbury's account of goodness constitutes his attempt to stake out an affection-free moral high ground, a vantage point from which he can pass judgment on all affections. But his moral psychology implies that such a vantage point is impossible for human beings to attain.

One might object that I am misconstruing Shaftesbury by conflating his concept of goodness with his concept of virtue.[3] Shaftesbury's teleological concept of goodness, one might think, is simply a description of the natural function of living beings. So when Shaftesbury says that an individual is good if it promotes the good of the species of which it is a part, he is making a claim that is more biological than moral. He is telling us about the natural state of living beings, about the design and healthy functioning of organisms. It is, then, on this way of thinking, incorrect for me to hold that Shaftesbury's account of goodness constitutes an ad hoc moral judgment. His account of goodness is, rather, a teleological claim about the biological design of living beings.

This way of viewing Shaftesbury's concept of goodness is not completely off-base. Shaftesbury probably did believe that his account of goodness constituted a biological-like description of the natural functioning of living beings. But he *also* believed that his account of goodness constituted a standard against which an individual's moral status could be measured. For Shaftesbury uses his account of goodness to distinguish between correct and incorrect moral judgments. He uses his account of goodness to distinguish between, on the one hand, a person whose moral sense is operating properly and is thus virtuous and, on the other hand, a person whose moral sense is operating improperly and is thus vicious. And in drawing such distinctions, Shaftesbury is himself making moral judgments.

Someone objecting to my interpretation might go on to argue, however, that Shaftesbury intended his account of human goodness to be just as much about natural function – just as teleologically biological – as his account of the goodness of other species. Shaftesbury, according to this view, believed that the difference between a properly functioning moral sense and a dysfunctional moral sense is just the same as the difference between a properly functioning eye and a dysfunctional eye. But distinguishing between a functional eye and a dysfunctional one is not a moral judgment, so Shaftesbury's application of this theory of goodness to the human moral sense should not be taken to be a moral judgment either.

This way of thinking of Shaftesbury's concept of goodness is, once again, not completely off-base. Shaftesbury probably did want his distinction between a functional moral sense and a dysfunctional one to have the same status as the distinction between a functional and a dysfunctional eye.[4] But he does not have the resources to give the former distinction the same status as the latter. The problem lies in his definition of goodness, which is what he uses to draw the distinction. Shaftesbury says that a creature is good if and only if its affections promote the "the publick Good" or the "good of the Species in general" (Virtue or Merit 13). But the obvious deficiency of this definition is that "good" appears in both the definiendum and the definiens. This is a problem because virtually everyone will claim that the things he or she approves of promote the public good. That is not to say that Shaftesbury's definition of "good" is tautologous: it does imply that certain kinds of egoism are false. But many of the views Shaftesbury wanted to condemn (e.g., Calvinism, enthusiasm) did not take themselves to be egoistic. These views claimed to support that which promoted the public good; it's just that Shaftesbury disagreed with their view of what that good was. Even Hobbes's view can be construed as an attempt to produce that which best promotes the public good. If Shaftesbury is to explain why these moral views are wrong, he is going to have to rely on his own judgment of what is and is not good for people. And his moral psychology implies that this judgment of his will be based on his affections, not on reason alone.

This creates a nasty dilemma for Shaftesbury. The moral differences between people are almost always due to their differing views of what the public good is. And so Shaftesbury either has to let the "public good" remain vacuous, and thus present us with an account of goodness that provides virtually no basis for distinguishing between a functional moral sense and a dysfunctional one, or he has to use a substantive notion of the public good to distinguish between functional and dysfunctional moral senses, but rely on his own moral sense for the substance that allows him to draw those distinctions.[5]

I believe this problem stems from Shaftesbury's trying to combine the rationalist anti-voluntarism he inherited from Whichcote with the sentimentalist moral psychology he developed in the *Inquiry*. The anti-voluntarism led him to affirm the existence of an eternal and immutable system of value (Virtue or Merit 20–1, 8–12). The sentimentalist moral psychology led him to claim that every moral judgment depends on the affections of the judger (Virtue or Merit 23–30). But human affections, far from being eternal and immutable, are subject to all manner of alteration and corruption (as Shaftesbury himself argued). So if the moral judgments of each of us are necessarily tied to our affections, we can never have principled grounds for claiming that our judgments align with an affection-independent standard of value, while the judgments of those who disagree with us do not. Or, to put the point in terms we used in Chapter 4, Shaftesbury seems to want both to embrace the necessity of morals thesis and to advance a sentimentalist moral psychology. But if our judgments depend on our affections, as the sentimentalist moral psychology implies, then we cannot be certain that they are tracking principles that are eternal and immutable, which certainty the necessity of morals thesis implies we must have if we are to have any confidence in our moral judgments.

There's no clear evidence that Shaftesbury himself identified this conflict between the *Inquiry*'s "eternal and immutable" standards and its sentimentalist moral psychology. In the years after completing the first version of the *Inquiry*, he downplayed the book's significance, but he usually suggested that its shortfalls were stylistic rather than substantive. In Chapter 9, however, we'll see that an addition Shaftesbury made to later versions of the *Inquiry* tipped the balance away from the eternal and immutable standards and toward the sentimentalist moral psychology. But before taking up that issue, let us turn to an account of virtue that Shaftesbury never downplayed or apologized for, the account presented in *The Moralists, a Philosophical Rhapsody*.

8

The Moralists; a Philosophical Rhapsody

If you had said to Shaftesbury that you could read only one of his books, *The Moralists* is what he would have given you. He thought of it as his magnum opus, the work that best captured both the essence and scope of his thought. So we can fully understand Shaftesbury only by exploring *The Moralists*, even if that work has had considerably less influence on contemporary philosophy than the *Inquiry*.[1]

A. Form and Purpose in *The Moralists*

One of the most obvious reasons *The Moralists* has fared less well with contemporary philosophers than the *Inquiry* is the difference between the forms of the two works. The *Inquiry* has the form of a typical philosophical treatise. Systematic and discursive, it states its theses at the start and then presents arguments to establish their truth. Distinctions are drawn, objections are answered. The connection between each idea and the next is explicitly articulated.

To read *The Moralists*, in contrast, is to enter a narrative world. It is a story told in the first person by Philocles to his friend Palemon. The story is of Philocles' two-day visit to the country estate of a man named Theocles, a visit that converted Philocles from skepticism to a rare type of reasonable enthusiasm. In telling his story, Philocles recounts several long conversations he had with Theocles and other men visiting the estate. But these long conversations notwithstanding, *The Moralists* is not one of those barebones philosophical dialogues in which the dramatically unrealized speakers are transparent mouthpieces for disembodied philosophical positions.[2] Shaftesbury had much higher literary ambitions than that. The characterizations of Philocles, Palemon, and Theocles are expansive, and several minor characters are also sharply drawn. There is a plotted arc to the relationships between the various visitors to the estate, with friendships budding and hostilities brewing. And then there are the settings. Shaftesbury devotes a tremendous amount of energy to the settings. We are always aware of the rooms in which Shaftesbury's characters dine, the gardens in which they stroll, the woods through which they traipse. We are also always aware of the time of day – of when the last rays of light are fading from the sky, of when the sun is readying itself to draw off the curtain of night, and so on (see, for instance, Moralists 193–4).

Whatever our opinion of the stylistic success of *The Moralists*, there can be no doubt that its dramatic form was a conscious choice. And this choice tells us a lot about what Shaftesbury was trying to accomplish.

Shaftesbury intended *The Moralists* to be a work of *practical* philosophy.[3] He wanted the book to improve its readers' character and conduct. His goal was not simply to explain virtue but to instill it. Shaftesbury did not want *The Moralists* to be a work of merely *speculative* or *theoretical* philosophy. Someone who engages in merely speculative or theoretical philosophy may discover new facts, but he will do little if anything to improve the character of his readers. Theoretical philosophy seeks only to describe the world; practical philosophy tries to make it a better place.

Shaftesbury thought that in the past philosophy had been primarily a practical enterprise. The betterment of society, Shaftesbury believed, used to be virtually every philosopher's goal. But in recent times, philosophy had been hijacked by speculative thinkers, who were more concerned to construct elaborate intellectual edifices and satisfy their picayune curiosities than to improve the lot of humankind. As the narrator of *The Moralists* puts it:

You must allow me, PALEMON, thus to bemoan *Philosophy*; since you have forc'd me to ingage with her at a time when her Credit runs so low. She is no longer *active* in the World; nor can hardly, with any advantage, be brought upon the public *Stage*. We have immur'd her (poor Lady!) in Colleges and Cells; and have set her servilely to such Works as those in the Mines. Empiricks, and pedantic Sophists are her chief Pupils. The *School-syllogism*, and the *Elixir*, are the choicest of her Products. So far is she from producing Statesmen, as of old, that hardly any Man of Note in the publick cares to own the least Obligation to her. (Moralists 105)

The Moralists is supposed to change all that. It's supposed to set philosophy back on its rightful path. And because he aims to edify with *The Moralists*, Shaftesbury has to be just as concerned with form as the sculptor and the poet. To be truly practical – to reach people in a way that can really improve them – a book of philosophy has to have "Strength and Boldness," "Body and Proportions," "good *Muscling*" (Moralists 106). It must be conceived as a moral painting. All of which, Shaftesbury maintains, is manifestly absent from the pedantic, enervated treatises in which "we Moderns" so abound.

Shaftesbury's ardor for *practical* philosophy also helps explain his affinity with Benjamin Whichcote. Whichcote did not write "*Treatises* and *Essays*." He did not construct philosophical systems nor speculate about recondite empirical matters. Whichcote gave sermons and taught students. And in his sermonizing and his teaching, he always had as his overriding goal the moral improvement of his listeners. Indeed, it is the practical nature of Whichcote's thinking that Shaftesbury stresses in his preface to Whichcote's sermons: he justifies the publication of Whichcote's sermons on the basis of the salutary effect they can be expected to have on the character of the audience.

By Shaftesbury's own reckoning, his *Inquiry* had failed to be truly practical. It was too dry and systematic, too akin to the barren theoretical philosophizing of the scholastics and of Locke. So in *The Moralists*, Shaftesbury gave the ideas of the *Inquiry* a dramatic makeover.

There is, in fact, one section of *The Moralists* that is entirely devoted to a discussion of the *Inquiry*. The setting is a dinner party at Theocles' country estate. Dinner has just ended. Wine is being served. The guests discuss several philosophical topics, but they eventually focus on the question of atheism. Philocles, the narrator, says that it is difficult to write about atheism without being branded an atheist oneself, no matter what one actually believes. Perhaps it is true, he jokes, "That none *writ well* against the Atheists beside the *Clerk*, who drew the Warrant for their Execution" (Moralists 146). As an example of someone who was unfairly branded in this way, Philocles points to Ralph Cudworth, who was "acus'd of giving the upper hand to the Atheists, for having only stated their Reasons, and those of their Adversarys, fairly together" (Moralists 148) Philocles goes on to say, "And among other Writings of this kind, you may remember how a certain *Fair* INQUIRY (as you call'd it) was receiv'd, and what offence was taken at it." Theocles says that he is sorry that the *Inquiry* was misconstrued as an atheist tract, and that he feels compelled to enter "the Lists in defense of a Friend unjustly censur'd for this philosophical Liberty" (Moralists 148). Theocles then delivers a seven-page speech in which he explains what "our Friend" really intended in writing the *Inquiry*. Theocles tries to explain, in particular, that while "our Friend" does make virtue independent of religion, he does not for that reason commit himself to either atheism or deism. Indeed, a careful reading of the *Inquiry* will reveal that its author is just as much "*a Realist* in DIVINITY" as he is "*a Realist* in MORALITY" (Moralists 151).[4]

Philocles chides Theocles, saying that his speech almost turned into a "Discourse," so that "had this been at a University, Theocles might very well have pass'd for some grave Divinity-Professor, or Teacher of *Ethics*, reading an Afternoon Lecture to his Pupils" (Moralists 146). Theocles himself deems it necessary to beg his companions' patience and ends by apologizing for coming "well nigh to *Preaching*" (Moralists 158). But these depreciating framing comments notwithstanding, Theocles' account of "his Friend's" purpose in writing the *Inquiry* is still much more conversational than the presentation in the *Inquiry* itself. Theocles is, moreover, the most charismatic person in *The Moralists*, and one whose theism and character are above reproach. In this way, Shaftesbury deploys literary technique in an attempt to make the ideas of the *Inquiry* more palatable.

But it would be a mistake to think of *The Moralists* as simply a spruced-up version of the *Inquiry*. For while Shaftesbury holds to the same basic view of morality and religion in both works, there are, in addition to the stylistic choices, some philosophically substantive differences. The most significant new development is *The Moralists'* aesthetic construal of morality, which we will discuss in the next two sections. But *The Moralists* also paints a more optimistic picture of human nature. The *Inquiry* constitutes a Positive Answer in that it maintains that all humans are naturally disposed toward goodness and that all humans have within themselves all the resources needed to achieve virtue. But as we've seen, the *Inquiry* is in many ways a misanthropic book nonetheless. For in the *Inquiry* Shaftesbury spends a great of time expounding the ways in which humans mar their own nature and plunge themselves into the depths of degeneracy.

The bitter view of humanity expressed in certain *Inquiry* passages is represented in *The Moralists* by Palemon. Palemon is a "well-bred" young man whose courtly upbringing has fitted him "for the greatest Affairs" but who has taken an "unaccountable" and "violent" turn toward philosophy (Moralists 103–4). Palemon is the sort of person who, on a ride through the park on a fine spring day, will break out in a rant that begins, "O wretched State of Mankind! – Hapless Nature, thus to have err'd in thy chief Workmanship! – Whence sprang this fatal Weakness?" (Moralists 109). Palemon says that he feels the bond of humanity within him and that he wants to love his fellows. "But O," he laments, "what Treacherys! what Disorders! And how corrupt is all!" (Moralists 112). Palemon's attitude toward humanity is what *The Moralists* seeks to refute. Palemon delivers his angry harangue in the first few pages of the book. The rest of the book consists of Philocles' telling Palemon the story of his visit to Theocles' estate. And the final moral of Philocles' story is that Palemon's pessimism is unwarranted.

So while the *Inquiry* says that humans can achieve virtue, much of the weight of the book falls on their failure to do so. And while *The Moralists* doesn't deny that people can fail to live up to their full potential, its overarching theme is the glorious moral heights human beings can attain. While the *Inquiry* points out that some forms of human corruption are irreversible, *The Moralists* beckons its readers to what is true and good. In the preface to Whichcote's sermons, Shaftesbury warned that giving a Negative Answer can be self-fulfilling: if you convince people that human nature is evil, you may very well make them more vicious than they were before. But when he was writing *The Moralists*, Shaftesbury seemed to be more impressed by the possibility of a self-fulfilling Positive Answer: convince people that human nature is good, and you may spur them to greater virtue.

Crucial to *The Moralists'* attempt to instill virtue is the person of Theocles, the hero of the story and Shaftesbury's exemplar of the Positive Answer. Philocles (the narrator) often remarks on Theocles' character, on how the force of Theocles' arguments was more than matched by the appeal of his personality. And Shaftesbury's readers are supposed to feel the same thing. Theocles is supposed to affect us in the way vividly charismatic characters from successful works of literature do. He's supposed to be someone we would want to emulate, someone we would want for a friend. Let us now examine Theocles in more detail.

B. Theocles' Reasonable Enthusiasm

Shaftesbury's aim in *The Moralists* is to steer between two positions he found equally intolerable. One is the barrenly rationalistic position of the pedantic schoolman, and the other is the rabidly immoderate position of the fanatical enthusiast. The pedantic schoolman places greatest value on syllogisms and demonstrations. But since such dry intellectual exercises bear no relation to conduct and character, the schoolman who fixates on them will inevitably neglect matters of real moral importance. The fanatical enthusiast places greatest value on his own private revelatory passions.[5] But since he has no way of distinguishing between passions that are divinely inspired and passions that are delusively superstitious, he inevitably flies off in the wrong direction. Both the schoolman and the enthusiast, moreover, have an ineluctably divisive effect on human society, the former because he focuses his energies on captious philosophical argument and the latter because his irrational faith in private passion leaves room for nothing but conflict with those who disagree.

The character of Theocles is Shaftesbury's attempt to show us how both pitfalls can be avoided – how one can be passionate *and* reasonable. Theocles' leading passion is his profound love for the natural world, which transports him to ecstatic states of high-flown rapture (Moralists 193–4). But he is also a deft philosophical interlocutor, fully capable of mounting a convincing rational defense of his beliefs. Perhaps most importantly, Theocles exudes a personal warmth and serene friendliness that brings all the members of his company into harmony (Moralists 123–4). He works like a balm on social interaction, soothing nascent hostilities between his guests rather than inflaming them. His effect on people is exactly opposite to the divisiveness of the pedant and fanatic.

Shaftesbury's original title for the book was *The Sociable Enthusiast*. Theocles says that his is "a fair and plausible *Enthusiasm*, a reasonable *Extasy* and *Transport*" (Moralists 224). Philocles says that Theocles has converted him to a type of "*Philosophical Enthusiasm*" (Moralists 119). And these phrases, which are supposed to sound oxymoronic, capture succinctly the position Shaftesbury intends the character of Theocles to embody.[6] At the time Shaftesbury was writing, enthusiasts were typically thought of as superstitious, unhinged, and divisive, the farthest thing from "reasonable," "philosophical," and "sociable." But Theocles is not only consumed by passion but also completely reasonable. Indeed, what Shaftesbury ultimately wants to show is that Theocles' consuming passion is itself fully reasonable. Theocles is supposed to exemplify the marriage of the affective and the rational.

So Shaftesbury had high hopes for what the character of Theocles could accomplish. And he used all of his literary talents to help Theocles succeed. But what exactly are Theocles' views? Of what does his reasonable passion consist?

Theocles explains his views throughout *The Moralists*, but his fullest exposition comes in Part III, the final part, during the course of a meandering conversation he and Philocles have as they walk out of Theocles' estate and through the woods, fields, and hills of the surrounding countryside. Their conversation starts in the very early hours of the morning, when it is still dark, and finishes at noon.

Theocles' first goal is to convince Philocles that the universe is "*One Intire Thing*" (Moralists 195). The world, he says, "is simply *One*"; everything in it "hangs together, *as of a Piece.*" There is a "*Coherence*" or "*Sympathizing*" of all parts (Moralists 203), a "plain Concurrence *in one common end*" (Moralists 196). All things participate in "*a uniting Principle*" (Moralists 200), a "*universal UNION*" (Moralists 203).

This idea of the world as one is not new to *The Moralists*. Shaftesbury made the same point in the *Inquiry* when he spoke of a "SYSTEM *of all things*" and the "*general one* of the *Universe*" (Virtue or Merit 11). What is new is Theocles' understanding of how the oneness of the universe can be apprehended. In the *Inquiry*, the claim that there is a universal system was treated as a deliverance of reason. But Theocles maintains that we cannot apprehend the universal oneness through the use of dry, systematic reason alone. According to Theocles, we can grasp the universal oneness only by means of a perception that is inherently affective.

According to Theocles, one's perception of the oneness of the universe must be an aesthetic experience. This is because the unity of all things in the universe is of the same type as the unity of all the elements of a great work of art. The unity of a great work of art is not something we can grasp simply through the use of non-affective, a posteriori reasoning. We can grasp a work's unity only through the perception of its beauty. True understanding of how the elements of a great work of art fit together is inseparable from the feeling of joy one experiences when truly appreciating its greatness. Someone who felt nothing when he or she looked at a great work of art – no pleasure, no passion – could not really be perceiving the profound coherence that constitutes its beauty. Similarly, someone who felt no joy when contemplating the universe could not really be perceiving the universal oneness. To understand the oneness of the world, according to Theocles, is to have the passionate experience of perceiving the world's beauty. Understanding is inseparable from appreciation.

Shaftesbury's belief in the inherently affective aesthetic nature of a true apprehension of the oneness of the universe goes a long way toward explaining the form and style of Theocles' speeches. Theocles is someone who truly grasps the universal oneness. His appreciation of the deep coherence of things is full and robust. He is, moreover, trying to spark the same appreciation in Philocles. He wants to persuade Philocles to abandon his detached skepticism and embrace the world's beauty. So it makes sense that Theocles emits a rhapsody instead of constructing a treatise. The flow of poetry is much better suited to his purposes than is the discursiveness of a philosophical system. Indeed, great swaths of Theocles' speeches have very little propositional content at all but are unabashed expressions of aesthetic passion. As he gushes in one typical rapture, "How beautiful is the WATER among the inferior Earthly Works! . . . Stubborn and un-yielding, when compress'd, but placidly avoiding Force, and bending every way with ready Fluency! . . . How vast are the Abysses of the *Sea*, where this soft Element is stor'd; and when the Sun and Winds extracting, raise it into Clouds!" (Moralists 211–12). Hurrah for this! Theocles exclaims, hurrah for that! I love nature! Do so as well!

But Shaftesbury is far from being an emotivist or anti-realist about beauty and the oneness of the universe, Theocles' rapturous transports notwithstanding. The position Theocles represents, inherently affective though it is, is supposed to be thoroughly objective as well. It is supposed to be objective precisely because it is enthusiastic. Now as I mentioned earlier, the idea of an objective enthusiasm should seem oxymoronic or paradoxical. For "enthusiasm," in Shaftesbury's time, was typically used as a label for wildly subjective flights of fancy. But Shaftesbury intends Theocles' enthusiasm to be a *reasonable* enthusiasm. He intends Theocles' enthusiasm to be enthusiastic in the original, literal sense.

In the original, literal sense, an enthusiast is someone who is inspired by, or full of, the spirit of God. But the spirit of God is that which has created and structured everything in the universe. It would follow, then, that if Theocles' rapturous delight in the natural world is literally enthusiastic, it is not simply a subjective feeling reflecting his own private affections but an apprehension of the objective basis of reality itself.[7]

Of course, all enthusiasts claim that their enthusiasm is of the literal kind. All enthusiasts claim that their passions do not reflect merely their own idiosyncratic psyches but are unmediated messages from God. Shaftesbury was as aware of this as anyone, as his *Letter on Enthusiasm* makes clear (Characteristics I 1–36). So on what basis can he claim that Theocles' passions are godly, while the passions of other would-be enthusiasts' are delusive? Why should we think that Theocles' enthusiasm is real while others' are false?

Theocles frequently allows himself to be transported by passion. But he also regularly pulls himself out of his enthusiastic ecstasies and calmly examines their content, consistently assuring Philocles and himself that his enthusiasm accords with a rational view of things. After one of Theocles' rhapsodic speeches, for instance, Philocles reports: "Here he stop'd short and, starting, as out of a Dream; 'Now, PHILOCLES, said he, inform me, How have I appear'd to you in my Fit? Seem'd it a sensible kind of Madness, like those Transports which are permitted to our *Poets*? or was it downright Raving?'" (Moralists 194; cf. 212–3, 218–9). Theocles then proceeds to engage Philocles in rational philosophical discussion. In the next two sections, we will examine the arguments Theocles presents. For now, it suffices to say that the conclusions Theocles claims to reach through rational philosophical discussion fully support his enthusiastic ecstasies. There is a God, Theocles claims to show. The universe is God's creation. And the universe that God created is perfect, and perfectly beautiful. It is, therefore, entirely reasonable to feel for the universe the highest kind of aesthetic love, to see the universe as the greatest work of art imaginable. Theocles thus convinces Philocles that his enthusiasm is reasonable. And we, as a result, are supposed to realize that there is every reason to think that Theocles' enthusiasm is objective, every reason to think that Theocles' enthusiasm really is a partaking of the mind of God. As Philocles puts it at the end of one philosophical interlude, and just before Theocles starts in on another enthusiastic rave, "Enough, said I, THEOCLES. My Doubts are vanish'd. . . . You are Conqueror in the cool way of *Reason*, and may with Honour now grow warm again, in your *poetick* Vein" (Moralists 205).

Theocles' reasonable enthusiasm plays a role in Shaftesbury's philosophy that is similar to the role played by innate ideas in Cudworth's EIM. Cudworth believed that it was through our innate ideas of eternal and immutable truths that we could participate with the mind of God. Similarly, Shaftesbury believes that Theocles becomes one with God through his enthusiasm (Moralists 200–2). *The Moralists* thus embraces the Cambridge Platonist idea that a human being here on earth can unite with God – that we can ourselves be godly, deiform. This is the noonday sun of the theological Positive Answer, and it is just as fulgent in *The Moralists* as it was anywhere in Cambridge Platonism.[8]

But while EIM and *The Moralists* share a profound – and profoundly theistic – optimism about human nature, they diverge from each other in one crucial respect. In EIM, God is a geometer. In *The Moralists*, God is an artist.

The feature of God that dominates EIM is His perfect understanding of eternal and immutable truths. EIM holds, as a result, that to be God-like involves possessing perfect understanding. Of course, being finite, we cannot understand everything that exists. But we can attain God-like understanding of geometry. We can fully comprehend the truth of a geometric theorem, realizing that it is not only true but necessarily so. And when we fully comprehend the necessary truth of a theorem, we have in our mind an idea of the theorem that is exactly the same as the idea of it that exists in the mind of God. Our moments of absolute certainty unite us with God. Geometry is a sacrament.

The feature of God that dominates Shaftesbury's *Moralists*, in contrast, is the consummate artistry with which He created the world. An artist makes things that he finds beautiful, and the more successful the artist, the closer to his idea of beauty his creation will be. But God is a perfect artist, and the world is His creation. So from God's perspective, the world (in its entirety) must be absolutely beautiful. We become God-like, then, just to the extent that we see the world as beautiful. Our appreciation of the beauty of the universal oneness is what unites us with the mind of God. Aesthetic appreciation of the natural world is Theocles' sacrament.

Bound up with this idea of how we can unite with God is a particular view of aesthetic appreciation. To appreciate a work of art, according to this view, is to get into the head of the artist who created it. When I fully appreciate a great painting, I see it the same way the painter did. When I fully appreciate a great novel, I understand it as the novelist did. I comprehend the artists' intentions, realizing why they made the decisions they did and why those decisions were the right ones. But when I am in the throes of this realization – when I am struck by the utter rightness of the decisions the artists made – I am in the same state of mind the artists themselves were in when they were engaged in artistic creation. Thus, to the extent that I appreciate the universe's beauty, I enter into the mind of God, the universe's artist-creator.

Cudworth wanted to assimilate morality to geometry. That's why his book entitled *A Treatise on Eternal and Immutable Morality* ends up reading like an epistemological tract on the innate idea of a triangle. Shaftesbury wanted to assimilate morality to beauty. That's why his book entitled *The Moralists* ends up reading like a poetic novel about aesthetic experience. Indeed, Shaftesbury makes explicit his desire to assimilate morality and beauty, having Theocles state on three different occasions that beauty and goodness are one and the same (Moralists 223, 232, 235–6).

C. Moral Judgment and the Content of Virtue

At this point, it's fair to wonder how Theocles' holistic enthusiasm for the beauty of the universe relates to the judgments that constitute the fabric of morality as we encounter it in daily life. The moral phenomena that most of us encounter most often involve judgments of actual situations, people, and actions. Does *The Moralists* have anything to say about this type of everyday moral assessment? This was a question we also asked about Cudworth's EIM. I argued that Cudworth planned to say more about specific moral rules that were supposed to guide our everyday lives, but that he never completed that part of his project. *The Moralists*, on the other hand, is a finished work, and while it would never pass for a book on applied ethics, it does include a general account of the making of particular moral judgments.

Theocles contends that every person has an internal sense that distinguishes the orderly and beautiful from the disorderly and ugly (Moralists 162, 230–1). This internal sense causes us to feel pleasure when we perceive harmonious sounds and regular shapes, and to feel displeasure when we perceive disharmonious sounds and irregular shapes. We thus judge that harmonious sounds and regular shapes are beautiful and that disharmonious sounds and irregular shapes are not (Moralists 160–2, 230–1). In addition to sounds and shapes, the internal sense causes us to feel pleasure when perceiving things that are more typically thought of as morally significant, such as sentiments, resolutions, principles, determinations, and actions (Moralists 228). So just as we naturally think that certain kinds of sounds and shapes are beautiful, so too we naturally think that certain kinds of actions and characters are beautiful. As Theocles rhetorically asks, "Is there then ... a natural Beauty of *Figures*? and is there not as natural a one of ACTIONS? No sooner the Eye opens upon *Figures*, the Ear to *Sounds*, than straight *the Beautiful* results, and *Grace* and *Harmony* are known and acknowledg'd. No sooner are ACTIONS view'd, no sooner the *human Affections* and *Passions* discern'd (and they are most of 'em as soon discern'd as felt) than straight *an inward* EYE distinguishes and sees *the Fair* and *Shapely*, *the Amiable* and *Admirable*, apart from *the Deform'd*, *the Foul*, *the Odious* or *the Despicable*" (Moralists 231).

The Moralists' internal sense of beauty (which is, clearly enough, the counterpart to the *Inquiry's* moral sense) serves two closely related moral functions. First, it causes us to feel the pleasures and pains that are the basis of our judgments of other persons' virtue and vice. But, crucially, the internal sense causes us to feel these pleasures and pains not merely about other persons' actions and characters but also about our own. Just as we feel pleasure when we view others' "*Amiable* and *Admirable*" qualities, so too we feel pleasure when we view what is amiable and admirable about ourselves. And just as we feel displeasure when we view others' "*Deform'd*" and "*Foul*" qualities, so too we feel displeasure when we view deformed and foul qualities in ourselves. Of course, we prefer the pleasure of viewing what is amiable and admirable to the displeasure of viewing the deformed and foul (just as we prefer to view beautiful things rather than ugly ones). So our internal sense of beauty gives us a reason to try to make our actions and character as amiable and admirable as possible. And this is the second moral function of our natural internal sense of beauty: to motivate us to virtue and rectitude. Just as an artist's aesthetic sense leads her to try to create beautiful figures, so too our internal sense of beauty leads us to try to produce qualities in ourselves that are morally beautiful. As Philocles puts it, "My Study therefore shou'd be to grow *beautiful*, in [Theocles'] way of *Beauty*; and, from this time forward I wou'd do all I cou'd to propagate that lovely Race of mental Children [i.e., sentiments, resolutions, principles, determinations, and actions], happily sprung from such a high enjoyment and from a union with what was fairest and best" (Moralists 229).

Once again, then, we find that in *The Moralists* Shaftesbury draws a very tight connection between morality and beauty, going so far as to make the former a subset of the latter. Our moral judgments, *The Moralists* maintains, are just like our aesthetic judgments of shapes and sounds in that we find certain mental qualities and certain shapes and sounds pleasurable to perceive and other mental qualities and other shapes and sounds displeasurable – and the pleasures and displeasures in both the moral and aesthetic cases are the same, based as they are on the same internal sense. Our drive to be moral, moreover, is the same as an artist's drive to create beautiful works of art; our reason to make of ourselves a beautiful character is the same as a painter's reason to make a beautiful painting and a musician's reason to make beautiful music. Indeed, in addition to explicitly equating the quest for goodness with the quest for beauty, Shaftesbury contends that becoming moral involves becoming a kind of "self-improving Artist" (Moralists 238). And the term "self-improving Artist" is particularly apt, as it captures Shaftesbury's idea that living well involves taking oneself to be a work of art that one should strive to make as beautiful as possible. Or, as Shaftesbury has Theocles put it, the "*wise* and *able* Man" is he who "having righter Models in his Eye, becomes in truth *the Architect* of *his own Life* and *Fortune*" (Moralists 238).

Drawing this tight connection between morality and beauty was one of Shaftesbury's major contributions to the history of ideas.[9] And it seems that he first came to this line of thought when he was writing *The Moralists*. In the 1699 edition of the *Inquiry*, Shaftesbury said that we feel pleasure when we perceive good characteristics and displeasure when we perceive bad characteristics. But he didn't equate this pleasure and displeasure to aesthetic experience. Moreover, the *Inquiry* calls the pleasure of perceiving virtue "approbation" and attributes the pleasure to a "moral sense" or "sense of right and wrong," terms that can suggest a distinction between morality and aesthetics and that are notably absent in *The Moralists*. But after completing *The Moralists* Shaftesbury added to the *Inquiry* five paragraphs that did explicitly connect morality and beauty (Virtue or Merit 16–17, 43). These added paragraphs (especially the one on page 43) read almost like a synopsis of Theocles' views.[10]

The Moralists and the first edition of the *Inquiry* do, however, present the same view of the content of virtue. In both works, virtue consists of the impartial disposition to benefit humanity. We have already seen that in the *Inquiry* Shaftesbury said that the virtuous person is one who is disposed to promote the public interest or the good of the human species in general. Similarly, in *The Moralists* Shaftesbury says that the highest good is an impartial love of humanity as a whole, or "an equal, just, and universal Friendship" for all people (Moralists 137). In keeping with his conflation of morality and beauty, Shaftesbury has Theocles maintain that this love for humanity is beautiful to behold: "Answer me, PHILOCLES," he says, "you who are such a Judg of *Beauty*, and have so good *a Taste* of Pleasure; is there any thing you admire, so fair as *Friendship*? or any thing so charming as *a generous Action*?" (Moralists 135).

The Moralists also shares with the *Inquiry* the claim that virtue is natural to human beings. Our natural disposition, Shaftesbury maintains in both works, is to act sociably, or for the benefit of humanity, and when we perceive affections that are sociable or beneficial to humanity, we naturally feel pleasure (Moralists 135–7, 176–81). Shaftesbury is careful to avoid saying that morality is "*innate*," as he wants to steer clear of the epistemological debate over innate ideas.[11] But he does say that the internal sense of beauty that is the origin of our moral notions is an "*Instinct*," and that instinct is "that which *Nature* teaches, exclusive of *Art, Culture* or *Discipline*" (Moralists 229–30). Our moral capacity is implanted in us by our maker, "imprinted on our Minds" (Moralists 160). This belief of Shaftesbury's that humans are naturally virtuous is yet another clear manifestation of his Positive Answer.

So according to *The Moralists*, our moral judgments and our moral actions both have their basis in an internal sense. And that internal sense is natural to us, instinctive, imprinted on our minds by God. When we judge and act from our natural internal sense, therefore, we conduct ourselves in the way that God designed us. But God's design is objectively good and beautiful, in perfect accord with goodness and beauty as they really exist (Moralists 151–2, 164–5, 203–4). So when we judge and act from our natural internal sense, we are conducting ourselves in accord with the reality of goodness and beauty. Our moral judgments and actions can, therefore, achieve perfect objectivity. They can accord with reality as God created it (Moralists 232–6; cf. 144–5, 151).

We can now see how *The Moralists* attempts to establish both the affectivity and objectivity of morals. It does so by subsuming morality into beauty. By making virtue into a type of artistic creation, Shaftesbury thinks he can explain how morality can have an essential grip on our emotions and exist independently of our particular human minds.

Now I imagine that to some twenty-first-century readers this attempt of Shaftesbury's will sound only half-plausible. I imagine, that is, that some twenty-first-century readers will think that equating morality to artistic creation is a good strategy for establishing morality's affective grip but a bad strategy for establishing its objectivity. Consider, for instance, Shaftesbury's idea that we should treat our lives as in-progress works of art, that a truly virtuous person is a self-improving artist. Some contemporary readers will agree that artistic creation is essentially affective. They may also allow Shaftesbury to describe artistic creation in terms of the transporting enthusiastic passions that Theocles gives voice to. But I suspect they will be less likely to accept that artistic creation is an endeavor that aims for objectivity, that an artist is someone who strives to make something that accords with a pre-established universal standard. For a common contemporary conception of an artist is of a person who is trying to produce a new creation, someone who is trying to make something that is different, distinctively his or her own. The notion that we should view our lives as a work of art is likely to conjure up in some contemporary minds an essentially subjective picture of how we ought to live; it is likely to suggest that we live with a particularly idiosyncratic flair.

But Shaftesbury is a thoroughgoing objectivist about beauty. This objectivism may not be amenable to some contemporary readers, but it is integral to his position. He believes that there is an eternal and immutable standard of beauty and that God created the world in accord with it. And he believes that when we produce something beautiful, we too create in accord with the eternal and immutable standard of beauty and thus become God-like. For Shaftesbury, artistic creation is not primarily about making a new thing down here on earth. It is first and foremost about raising oneself up to heaven. As Theocles explains:

> [There is a] *third* Order of Beauty, which forms not only such as we call mere Forms, but even *the Forms which form.* For we our-selves are notable Architects in Matter, and can shew lifeless Bodys brought into Form, and fashion'd by our own hands: but that which fashions even Minds themselves, contains in it-self all the Beautys fashion'd by those Minds; and is consequently the Principle, Source, and Fountain of all *Beauty.* . . . Therefore whatever Beauty appears in our *second* Order of Forms, or whatever is deriv'd or produc'd from thence, all this is eminently, principally, and originally in this *last* Order of *Supreme* and *Sovereign* Beauty. . . . Thus Architecture, Musick, and all which is of human Invention resolves it-self into this *last* Order. (Moralists 227–8)

Shaftesbury advances a theistic aesthetic objectivism: that's what Theocles' reasonable enthusiasm is supposed to exemplify.

D. Problems with *The Moralists*

There is much to praise in *The Moralists.* It is an enormously ambitious attempt to produce a new and comprehensive view of goodness, virtue, and beauty, and it also contains trenchant discussion of numerous other topics I have not even scratched the surface of (e.g., a critique of belief in miracles, a refutation of egoism, a critique of social contract theories, an exploration of the concept of happiness). Moreover, Shaftesbury does a valiant job of pulling all the elements of the book together into a coherent whole, uniting them in both substance and style. But does Shaftesbury's characterization of Theocles ultimately succeed? Does Shaftesbury create a position that successfully captures affection and rationality, love and objectivity?

Perhaps there is a sense in which *The Moralists* does succeed on a literary level, in that it may paint a picture of virtue that is vivid and attractive enough to arouse in the reader an aspiration, both fervent and sober, to become a better person.[12] But it leaves a number of critical philosophical issues unsettled.

Shaftesbury's position in *The Moralists* relies on the existence of a perfect artist-God who created the world in the best and most beautiful way possible. It's Theocles' communion with such a perfect artist-God that makes his enthusiasm reasonable, and it's the reasonableness of Theocles' enthusiasm that is the ground of *The Moralists'* most important claims.

Shaftesbury puts into the mouth of Theocles two arguments for the existence of a perfect artist-God. The first argument is a version of the argument from design, according to which the "wise and perfect Order" of the world constitutes irrefutable evidence of a "*supreme Mind* or DEITY" (Moralists 155). Here's how Theocles puts it:

For can it be suppos'd of any-one in the World, that being in some Desert far from Men, and hearing there a perfect Symphony of Musick, or seeing an exact Pile of regular Architecture arising gradually from the Earth in all its Orders and Proportions, he shou'd be persuaded that at the bottom there was no *Design* accompanying this, no secret Spring of *Thought*, no active *Mind?* Wou'd he, because he saw no Hand, deny the Handy-Work, and suppose that each of these compleat and perfect Systems were fram'd, and thus united in just Symmetry, and conspiring Order, either by the accidental blowing of the Winds or rolling of the Sands? What is it then shou'd so disturb our Views of *Nature*, as to destroy that Unity of Design and Order of *a Mind*, which otherwise wou'd be so apparent? All we can see either of the Heavens or Earth, demonstrates Order and Perfection.... (Moralists 164)

Theocles' second argument for the existence of a perfect God is less clear than his argument from design. He says that unlike his previous argument, which had been a posteriori and thus could establish only the overwhelming "presumption" of a perfect God, his second argument constitutes an irrefutable "*Demonstration*." He then presents the following:

[Theocles:] "The *Appearances* of ILL, you say, are not necessarily that ILL they represent to you." [Philocles:] "I own it." [Theocles:] "Therefore what they represent may possibly be GOOD." [Philocles:] "It may." [Theocles:] "And therefore there may possibly be no *real* ILL in things: but all may be perfectly concurrent to one Interest; the Interest of that Universal ONE." [Philocles:] "It may be so." [Theocles:] "Why, then, if it may be so, (be not surpriz'd), 'It follows that it must be so', on the account of that great *Unit*, and simply *Self-principle*, which you have granted in *the* WHOLE. For whatever is possible *in the Whole*, the Nature or Mind of the *Whole* will put in execution for *the Whole's Good*: And if it be possible to exclude ILL, it will exclude it. Therefore since notwithstanding the *Appearances*, 'tis possible that ILL may actually be excluded; count upon it, 'That actually it is excluded.' " (Moralists 204)

This appears to be a version of the ontological argument, although it is so condensed that it's hard to say for sure.

This is not the right place to examine in detail the argument from design or the ontological argument. But my cursory assessment is that Theocles'

version of the argument from design runs smack dab into Philo's devastating
criticisms in Hume's *Dialogues on Natural Religion* and that Theocles' version
of the ontological argument (if that's what it is) is too scant to support its
weighty conclusion. Of course, there have been many other attempts to
prove the existence of a perfect God, and perhaps we could offer Theocles
the most successful of those. The main point to remember, however, is that
his position does require a *rational proof* of God's existence. Theocles' enthusiasm is supposed to be *reasonable*. His passionate love of nature is supposed
to be anchored in a rational view of things. If he cannot show that his passionate love has a rational basis, then he has no grounds for claiming that it
connects with the world as it really is and that others' differing passions are
delusive.[13] He would thus have no principled way of distinguishing his supposedly literal enthusiasm from the spurious enthusiasm of superstitious,
melancholy fanatics.

Furthermore, even if he can prove the existence of a perfect God, Shaftesbury still has another burden to shoulder. Theocles' reasonable enthusiasm
does not consist merely of the belief that a perfect God exists. It also consists
of a feeling of joy that comes from appreciating the beauty of the entire universe. But it's unclear that an argument for the existence of God can produce
such a feeling. Even if we come to believe that everything in the universe is
ultimately for the best, we still may not feel aesthetic joy when we consider
it. And Theocles wants us to feel aesthetic joy not merely toward individual things but toward the universe as a whole, toward the "Universal ONE"
(*Moralists* 204). This is a very tall order, and a rational proof of the existence
of God may not fill it. Now I suppose Shaftesbury might say that this feeling
of joy toward the universal ONE is something we have to strive for, that it's not
something we can expect simply to appear in us but will develop only if we
consciously train ourselves and our passions. Perhaps he'd say that we have
to learn to love the universe. But I wonder whether love for the universe as a
whole (as distinct merely from the belief that everything is ultimately for the
best) is even humanly possible. Is our affective makeup expansive enough
to feel an emotion toward this universal ONE? Early on in *The Moralists*,
Philocles expresses similar doubts, wondering whether it's possible for him
to feel love toward a huge conglomeration. In response, Theocles suggests
that Philocles is underestimating his own emotional capacity, and that over
the course of their succeeding conversations Philocles will come to realize
that such an expansive love is possible (*Moralists* 134–9). It doesn't seem to
me, however, that Philocles ever makes good on this promise. Theocles is
transported by emotional ecstasies, and he claims that all of these ecstasies
are fully grounded in rationally established beliefs. But I question whether
it's plausible to think that the ecstasies can arise from the beliefs.

Moreover, success at instilling heart-felt appreciation for the beauty of the
universal ONE would create another, perhaps even more serious problem

for Shaftesbury's position. It would raise the worry that Theocles' enthusiasm may conflict with his view of the virtuous life. If a person loves the universe as a whole – if he thinks that everything in it, like all the components of a great work of art, is exactly as it should be – why would he ever try to change things? It seems that a person who has really succeeding in appreciating the design of the world as a whole would accept things just as they are. He would not try to make the world a better place, because he would believe (and feel) that the world is already the best it can be. But a wholly resigned and accepting person does not fit Shaftesbury's conception of the virtu-ous life. In both the *Inquiry* and *The Moralists*, Shaftesbury says that virtue consists of promoting the good of humanity. Virtuous people, according to Shaftesbury's official position, are active players in the world. They do not stand on the sidelines, sanguinely taking it all in. They play a leading role in human affairs. They work to improve things. As Shaftesbury put it in a letter from 1706, the true philosophy is "civil" and "social" because it recommends "action, concernment in civil affairs, religion, etc" (Regimen 355–66).

But would Theocles live up to Shaftesbury's active conception of virtue? Or would his appreciation of the world just as it is siphon off his "concern-ment in civil affairs, religion, etc"? Theocles' arguments for a perfect God make this question particularly sharp. For when making these arguments, Theocles acknowledges that some things that exist in the world might seem to us to be "vitious or imperfect" (Moralists 203). But he claims to show that things look that way to us only because we are finite (Moralists 204–9). From God's infinite perspective, everything really is perfect. And the true enthusiast is the person who trains himself to feel God-like appreciation for all of it (Moralists 163–5). At least on the face of it, this appears to be an injunction to Panglossian acceptance, not a call to active participation in civil affairs.[14]

I believe, moreover, that this tension between trying to appreciate the world as it is and trying to change the world for the better runs deep in Shaftesbury's thought and is not simply a minor quirk of *The Moralists*.[15] Consider, for instance, Shaftesbury's great admiration for the Stoics. He says in his 1706 letter that the Stoics were part of the true philosophy that "recommended action [and] concernment in civil affairs." And one of his two Stoic heroes is Marcus Aurelius, who, as Roman emperor, was obviously engaged in the civil life of his country. But his other Stoic hero was Epictetus, who advises us to withdraw our concern from worldly matters. And in his notebooks, Shaftesbury often endorses Epictetus' idea that the highest goal of philosophy is to teach us to accept the world as it is, not to try to change it, to become tranquil, resigned, reconciled to things just as they are. This ambivalence about the proper role to play in worldly affairs is also evident in Shaftesbury's life, as he alternated between periods of intense public ser-vice and periods of reclusive resignation. For several years, he would be as

actively engaged in human affairs as one could imagine, throwing himself
into national politics and taking a hands-on approach to the day-to-day running of his family estate. Then, for several years, he would retreat to the
Netherlands, shutting down his household, avoiding politics and refusing
visitors.[16]

It's possible that this ambivalence was rooted in the fate of Shaftesbury's
grandfather, the first Earl of Shaftesbury. The first Earl helped create the
Whig Party and led it in Parliament from 1679 to 1681, spearheading the
resistance to James II that would eventually culminate in the Glorious Revolution of 1688. But the Earl himself did not live to see the Revolution.
Arrested for treason in 1681, he was imprisoned in the Tower of London
and just barely escaped execution. He managed to secure release from the
Tower, but his opposition to the king put him in constant danger of reimpris-
onment. He went into hiding, and then, in November 1682, fled to Holland,
where he died two months later, broken and disgraced. After his death, the
first Earl's reputation plummeted. Many Britons came to think of him not
only as a failure but also as an object of scorn, an example of the worst kind
of conniving, manipulative, opportunistic politician.

Shaftesbury (our Shaftesbury, the third Earl) grew up in the first Earl's
house, and the first Earl was more like a father to him than a grandfather.
There is, as well, every reason to believe that Shaftesbury was very fond of his
grandfather. So Shaftesbury must have been sharply affected by his grandfather's sullied reputation. While at school in his early teens, he probably had
to endure personal ridicule from his classmates, and throughout his life he
must have continued to encounter the scorn his grandfather's name provoked. Close as he had been to his grandfather, these expressions of hostility
must have seared Shaftesbury's heart. (This is, perhaps, a partial explanation for the conspicuous misanthropy of the 1699 version of Shaftesbury's
Inquiry concerning Virtue, or Merit.)

It seems to me likely that Shaftesbury had conflicting responses to this
dubious legacy. On the one hand, he wanted to vindicate his grandfather.
He wanted to achieve the political goals his grandfather stood for, and live a
life of such scrupulous honesty and civil service that people would be compelled to honor the Shaftesbury name. But on the other hand, he resented
the shoddy way his grandfather (and, by association, he himself) had been
treated, and this produced in him a disdain for service and politics. Thus,
he also wanted to rise above society's prejudice and corruption, to attain
an elevated philosophical perspective from which his tranquility would be
wholly unaffected by the vicissitudes of public opinion and affair. Shaftesbury wanted to be a leader in making the lives of his countrymen the best
they could be – and he also wanted to wash his hands of them entirely. He
wanted the public to respect the Earl of Shaftesbury, and he also wanted not
to give a damn what the public thought.[17]

E. Theistic, but Not Christian

About another matter, however, *The Moralists* is clear and unambiguous. It is a profoundly theistic work, but the theism that pervades it is has no distinctly Christian elements. The God that Theocles embraces is within immediate reach of Christian and non-Christian alike. Humans can unite with God, according to *The Moralists*, without the help of Christ.

The Moralists does contain a few perfunctory remarks about Christianity and "the sacred Mysterys of Religion" (Moralists 118). But its substantive views of God, humanity, and the relationship between them leave no room for the mediation of Christ. Theocles' aesthetic ecstasies are a way of directly uniting with the designing mind of the universe. Nor does Theocles' belief in a perfect God depend on faith or scripture. It is based entirely on philosophical argument.

This dispensing with Christ is an inevitable consequence of the Positive Answer to which Shaftesbury subscribes. Theocles represents the Positive Answer in that he has within himself all the resources necessary to achieve the height of virtue and to experience the spirit of God. But from that characterization it follows that Theocles has no need for external assistance, no need to look to scripture or to call on Christ's sacrifice. And Theocles is the sort of person we are all supposed to aspire to be.

We saw that in his sermons Whichcote struggled mightily with the idea that we could achieve salvation without the mediation of Christ. He realized that his Positive Answer might seem to imply that Christ's mediation was unnecessary, but he was profoundly reluctant to accept that implication. So he pushed, pulled, twisted, and bent his ideas in various attempts to reconcile his belief in the deiformity of man with the indispensability of Christ's sacrifice. Shaftesbury, in contrast, seems largely unconcerned. Theocles, his paragon of religion and virtue, never calls on Christ. And Shaftesbury never apologizes for Theocles' lack of Christian commitment, nor does he try to explain it away. It is plain to see, for anyone who cares to look.

This difference between Shaftesbury and Whichcote marks a tectonic shift. In 1600, few British thinkers would have admitted that being virtuous can be distinguished from being Christian. But by the beginning of 1700, Shaftesbury was describing virtue without invoking anything distinctly Christian, and such descriptions became steadily more common as Shaftesbury's thought grew in influence. For Shaftesbury, God is still the cornerstone of morality. But Christ has left the building.

9

Shaftesbury's Two Reasons to Be Virtuous

A Philosophical Fault Line

As I've already noted, Shaftesbury's *Inquiry concerning Virtue, or Merit* first
came out, in an unauthorized edition, in 1699. An official edition didn't
appear until 1711, when Shaftesbury included the *Inquiry* in his *Characteristics of Men, Manners, Opinions, Times,* a three-volume set containing most of
his previous writings and a new miscellaneous commentary. The philosophical skeleton of the *Inquiry* remained unchanged from 1699 to 1711. But
Shaftesbury cut some of the most acerbic passages and added a number of
points that he had thought through in the intervening years.

In this chapter, I examine one of the ideas that first appeared in the 1711
version of the *Inquiry.* Shaftesbury presents the idea in two different places
in the revised *Inquiry* and in the section of his miscellaneous commentary
that explicitly addresses that work. Shaftesbury's attitude toward this new
idea is casual, almost offhand. He doesn't mark it as terribly important.
But this casualness is either disingenuous or a miscalculation. For the new
idea, carried to its logical conclusion, amounts to an abandonment of the
prevailing concept of moral objectivity and ushers into British philosophy a
radically new conception of morality and human nature.

The new idea appears when Shaftesbury is explaining the reason we have
to be virtuous.[1] Shaftesbury actually gives two different accounts of our reason to be virtuous, and the new idea emerges in his discussion of how these
two accounts relate to each other. So let me first describe one account of the
reason to be virtuous, next describe the other account, and then examine
Shaftesbury's provocative description of the relationship between them.

A. The Teleological Account

According to the first account of the reason to be virtuous, humans will be
happiest if they live virtuously because virtue is the end or telos for which they
were designed. Now virtue, according to Shaftesbury, consists of impartial
benevolence toward the human species as a whole. It follows, therefore,

that humans will be happiest if they consistently act to benefit humanity. Call this the "teleological account" of our reason to be virtuous. Here is one representative passage of it:

It has been already shewn, that in the Passions and Affections of particular Creatures, there is a constant relation to the Interest of *a Species*, or *common Nature*. This has been demonstrated in the case of *natural Affection*, parental Kindness, Zeal for Posterity, Concern for the Propagation and Nurture of the Young, Love of Fellowship and Company, Compassion, mutual Succour, and the rest of this kind. Nor will any-one deny that this Affection of a Creature towards the Good of the Species or common Nature, is as *proper* and *natural* to him, as it is to any Organ, Part or Member of an Animal-Body, or mere Vegetable, to work in its known Course, and regular way of Growth. 'Tis not more *natural* for the Stomach to digest, the Lungs to breathe, the Glands to separate juices, or other Intrails to perform their several Offices; however they may by particular Impediments be sometimes disorder'd or obstructed in their Operations. (Virtue or Merit 45)

A human's "*natural Affections*," Shaftesbury says here, are those that benefit other humans, and it is as "*proper* and *natural*" for a human to live by these affections as it is for "the Stomach to digest." Just as digestion is the purpose of the stomach or the end for which it was designed, so too is the promotion of the good of humans the purpose of humans or the end for which they were designed.[2]

Shaftesbury offers this claim about the "*proper* and *natural*" end of humans as a specific instance of the general claim that the proper and natural end of every creature is to promote the good of the members of the system (or species) of which it is a part. As he explains it in his "Miscellaneous Reflections" on this part of the *Inquiry*, the "Design or End of Nature in each Animal System, is exhibited chiefly in the Support and Propagation of the particular Species," and so the affections of a creature are "natural" just to the extent that they "contribute to the Welfare and Prosperity of that *Whole* or *Species*, to which he is by Nature join'd" (Reflections 135).

The claim that it is the proper and natural end of each human to be benevolent is not the same as the claim that each human will be happiest if he is benevolent. But according to Shaftesbury's teleological account, the step between these two claims follows ineluctably from obvious facts. All our observations of other species show that a creature is happiest when it fulfills its proper and natural end. And so, since nature and happiness are connected in the life of every other creature, there is every reason to think that they are connected in the lives of humans as well. To think otherwise is to hold the

extraordinary Hypothesis [according to which] "That in the System of a Kind or Species, the Interest or *the private Nature* is directly opposite to that of *the common one*; the Interest of *Particulars* directly opposite to that of *the Publick in general*." — A strange Constitution! in which it must be confess'd there is much Disorder and

Untowardness; unlike to what we observe elsewhere in Nature. As if in any vegetable or animal-Body, the *Part* or Member cou'd be suppos'd in a good and prosperous State *as to it-self*, when under a contrary Disposition, and in an unnatural Growth or Habit *as to its* WHOLE. (Virtue or Merit 47)

Shaftesbury believes that only sophistical skeptics and egregious blockheads would ever doubt that creatures are happiest when they fulfill their natural ends. He thus ridicules the "sportly" and "airy gentlemen" who deny the connection between nature and happiness in humans while plainly affirming it in all other species.

Ask one of these Gentlemen, unawares, when sollicitously careful and busy'd in the great Concerns of his *Stable*, or *Kennel*, "Whether his *Hound* or *Greyhound*-Bitch who eats her puppys, is as *natural* as the other who nurses 'em?" and he will think you frantick. Ask him again, "Whether he thinks the *unnatural* Creature who acts thus, or the *natural-one* who does otherwise, is best in its kind, and enjoys itself the most?" And he will be inclin'd to think still as strangely of you. (Reflections 133)

That these "gentlemen" deny the connection between happiness and nature in humans just goes to show that for all their knowledge of horses, dogs, game cocks, and hawks, they "never had it in their thoughts *to study* NATURE in their *own* Species" (Reflections 132).

So Shaftesbury's teleological account establishes the connection between benevolence and happiness for humans on the basis of two claims. The first claim is that benevolence is the natural and proper end for humans. The second claim is that humans will be happiest if they pursue their natural end and miserable if they do not. Both of these claims are offered as particular instances of general claims that Shaftesbury believes follow obviously from our observations of other species: the first, of the general claim that the natural end of every creature is to promote the good of the system of which it is a part; and the second, of the general claim that a creature will be happiest if it pursues its natural end.

The teleological account is supposed to have a clear anchor in moral objectivity, as it is based on a commitment to an order of value that is independent of human affections. As we noted in Chapter 7, Shaftesbury holds that a creature is good if it fulfills its natural or proper end, and he also holds that a creature fulfills its natural or proper end when it promotes the interests of the members of the system of which it is a part (Virtue or Merit 8–16). But the fact of whether a creature is promoting the interests of the members of the system of which it is a part is independent of human affections.[3] Shaftesbury goes on to say that a creature cannot be *virtuous* unless it possesses a moral sense (Virtue or Merit 16–21). But that sentimentalist position on virtue is built on a non-sentimentalist account of goodness. For the goodness of the conduct one's moral sense approves of is inherent in "the System of the Universe" and thus ontologically prior to the approval itself.[4] The ontological origin of value lies in the universal system, not in our approval. Shaftesbury's teleological account presupposes that the origin of value lies not in human affections but in the human mind-independent structure of the universe.

But the teleological account is not Shaftesbury's only attempt to show that we have reason to be virtuous. He develops another one as well, which we can call the "mental enjoyment account."[5] Let us look at this second account now.

B. The Mental Enjoyment Account

Shaftesbury begins this second account by stating that all "*Pleasures* or *Satisfactions*" are either "*of the Body*, or *of the Mind*" (Virtue or Merit 57). The pleasures of the body are typically those of eating, drinking, and sex. The pleasures of the mind – which Shaftesbury calls "mental Enjoyments" – are of two main types, the first consisting of the "*immediate Operation*" of certain affections and the second consisting of the "*Effects*" of the operation of those affections (Virtue or Merit 58). Shaftesbury next shows that the particular affections that produce the mental enjoyments (either immediately or by their effects) are just those that are characteristic of virtue. He also argues that the mental enjoyments are far superior to the pleasures of the body, that living by the former is in fact "the only means" of procuring "a certain and solid *Happiness*" (Virtue or Merit 58). He can then conclude that one can be happy if and only if one lives by the affections that are characteristic of virtue.[6]

The particular affections that produce the mental enjoyments are "*Benignity and Goodness*" (Virtue or Merit 61). We can be sure that the operation of these affections is immediately pleasurable to an extent far superior to eating, drinking, and sex, Shaftesbury argues, since being benign and good is the essence of love and friendship, and one has only to experience love and friendship to realize that they are much more pleasurable than mere bodily sensation (Virtue or Merit 58–60).

What common sense tells us about "the *compleat* immoral State" confirms the importance of this first kind of mental enjoyment (Virtue or Merit 48). Everyone realizes that a person "wholly destitute of a communicative or social Principle" will be perfectly miserable, constantly suffering "dark Suspicion and Jealousy," "Fears and Horrour," and "continual Disturbance, even in the most seeming fair and secure State of Fortune, and in the highest degree of outward Prosperity" (Virtue or Merit 47–8). But since we acknowledge that "this *absolute* Degeneracy, this *total* Apostacy from all Candour, Equity, Trust, Sociableness or Friendship" leads to complete misery, it is unreasonable to deny that some degree of degeneracy will lead to at least some misery (Virtue or Merit 48). Thus he dismisses as absurd the notion that

to be *absolutely* immoral and inhuman, were indeed the greatest misfortune and misery; but that to be so, in *a little degree*, shou'd be no misery nor harm at all! Which to allow, is just as reasonable as to own, that 'tis the greatest Ill of a Body to be in the utmost manner distorted and maim'd; but that to lose the use only of *one* Limb, or to be impair'd in some *one single* Organ or Member, is no Inconvenience or Ill worthy the least notice. (Virtue or Merit 48)

Just as anyone with even the slightest knowledge of biology should realize that a person is harmed by losing a limb, so too anyone with even the slightest knowledge of "our *inward Constitution*" should realize that a person sacrifices happiness to the extent that he forgoes benevolence. (Virtue or Merit 49).

The second type of mental enjoyment Shaftesbury describes is an "effect" one experiences as a result of having been benevolent, which is the pleasure of having a "*Mind or Reason* [that is] *well compos'd, quiet, easy within it-self, and such as can freely bear its own Inspection and Review*" (Virtue or Merit 66). If, conversely, one is not benevolent, one will be unable to bear freely his own inspection and review – one will inevitably experience the mental pain of self-condemnation (Virtue or Merit 68–73).[7]

Why will the benevolent person be able to bear freely his own inspection and the non-benevolent person not be able to do so? It is because, first of all, every person "is, by his Nature, forc'd to endure the *Review* of his own Mind, and Actions; and to have Representations of himself, and his inward Affairs, constantly passing before him, obvious to him, and revolving in his Mind" (Virtue or Merit 69).[8] And it is because, secondly, every person has a "*moral* or *natural Conscience*" or moral sense, which causes him to like or approve of that which benefits others and dislike or disapprove of that which harms others (Virtue or Merit 69). So a benevolent person is bound to like or approve of himself, and a non-benevolent person is bound to dislike or disapprove of himself.

Throughout both his published works and his unpublished journals, Shaftesbury takes great pains to emphasize the superior pleasure of being able to bear freely one's own inspection and the "grievous" pain of not being able to do so. At times he gives the impression that these self-reflective mental pleasures and pains are more important to one's happiness than even the immediate social pleasures of love and friendship, as for instance when he says that this aspect of the mental enjoyment account is "the chief Principle of Philosophy" (Characteristics I 115). I think part of the explanation for Shaftesbury's emphasizing this point is that he happened to be an intensely self-critical person, one whose obsessive scrutiny of his own conduct regularly occasioned terrible pangs of shame, guilt, and disgust. Another part of the explanation is that Shaftesbury was deeply impressed by the idea that one's ability to bear one's own inspection is entirely under one's own control, perfectly insulated from the vicissitudes of "Fortune, Age, Circumstances, and Humour" (Moralists 242).[9] As Theocles rhetorically asks, "How can we better praise the Goodness of *Providence*, than in this, 'That it has plac'd our Happiness and Good in things *We* can bestow upon *ourselves*?'"

(Moralists 242–3). This stress on our control over the outcome of our self-reviews grows out of Shaftesbury's commitment to Epictetus's injunction to concern oneself only with what is within one's own power and constitutes a very conspicuous strand of stoicism in his thought.[10]

A third part of the explanation of Shaftesbury's emphasis on this self-reflective pleasure is that he seemed to think that being able to bear freely one's own inspection is a condition for having a unified self at all.[11] Identity of self, Shaftesbury suggests, is not something that we all have as a matter of course. It requires resolution of will from one moment to the next, and resolution of will is forged only through one's own internal "*Inquisition*" or self-review (Characteristics I 116). It is this internal Inquisition that will

> keep us the *self-same* Persons, and so regulate our governing Fancys, Passions, and Humours, as to make us comprehensible to our selves, and knowable by other Features than those of a bare Countenance. For 'tis not certainly by virtue of our Face merely that we are *our-selves*. 'Tis not WE who change, when our Complexion or Shape changes. But there is *that*, which being wholly metamorphos'd and converted, WE are thereby in reality transform'd and lost. (Characteristics I 176)

So when Shaftesbury says that virtue is necessary for "Self-enjoyment" (Virtue or Merit 80), we can take him to mean not merely that the virtuous will find life more enjoyable than the vicious, but also that virtue – because it is necessary for successful self-reflection – is something one needs in order to be one self at all.[12]

C. The Fault Line between the Two Accounts

Shaftesbury, then, presents a well-developed and emphatic version of the mental enjoyment account. But what is the relationship between it and his equally well-developed and emphatic version of the teleological account? Do they fit together?

From one point of view, the two accounts appear to fit together very well indeed. Both accounts conclude that a human will be happiest if he is benevolent. The teleological account reaches this conclusion on the basis of the teleological claims that creatures are happiest when they live in accord with their design and that humans were designed to be benevolent. The mental enjoyment account reaches this conclusion through an examination of specific human affections. But the examination of human affections, so it might seem, just constitutes further confirmation of the teleological principles. The relationship between Shaftesbury's two accounts appears, in other words, to be analogous to the relationship between two ways of arriving at the conclusion that, say, wallabies will be better off if they climb into their mothers' pouch immediately after birth. Suppose that before discovering wallabies we had studied all the other Australian marsupial species and found that in every one of those other cases the marsupial infant was better off if it climbed into its mother's pouch immediately after birth. We then discovered the wallabies, realized that they too were Australian marsupials, and so formed the belief that they too would be better off it they climbed into their mothers' pouch immediately after birth. To confirm this belief we then examined the particulars of wallaby development, which revealed that in fact the wallabies did do better when they climbed into their mothers' pouch immediately after birth. Our study of the wallaby would then establish independently the particular claim about what is best for wallabies while at the same time constituting further confirmation of the general claim about what is best for Australian marsupials.

Shaftesbury himself suggests at times that the relationship between his two accounts is complementary in just this way – that they reach the same conclusion through consistent and mutually reinforcing channels. But then he goes on to present an idea that rends this tidy package. This idea is the new one that I alluded to at the beginning of this chapter, the idea that was absent in the 1699 version of the *Inquiry* but present in the 1711 version.

The new idea is that the mental enjoyment account will be equally compelling whether our perceptions of the external world are truthful or illusory. As Shaftesbury puts it in a passage that he added to the 1711 version of the *Inquiry*, just after he has claimed that vice leads to misery and virtue leads to happiness:

> For let us carry *Scepticism* ever so far; let us doubt, if we can, of every thing about us; we cannot doubt of what passes *within our-selves*. Our Passions and Affections are known to us. *They* are certain, whatever the *Objects* may be, on which they are employ'd. Nor is it of any concern to our Argument, how these exteriour Objects stand; whether they are Realitys, or mere Illusions; whether we wake or dream. For *ill Dreams* will be equally disturbing: And a good *Dream*, if Life be nothing else, will be easily and happily pass'd. In this Dream of Life, therefore, our Demonstrations have the same force; our *Ballance* and *OEconomy* hold good, and our Obligation to VIRTUE is in every respect the same. (Virtue or Merit 99; cf. 25)

We will experience the mental enjoyments if we are benevolent, Shaftesbury tells us here, even if everything we believe about the external world is false. So since the mental enjoyments are the only means of procuring a certain and solid happiness, our reason to be virtuous is entirely independent of the truth of any of our beliefs about the external world.

According to this added passage, then, the mental enjoyment account constitutes a reason to embrace virtue that is impervious to even the most extreme forms of skepticism. In his commentary on the *Inquiry*, he calls this account "the *inward* way" because it relies entirely on "our very *Perceptions, Fancys, Appearances, Affections*, and *Opinions* themselves, without regard to anything of *an exterior* WORLD, and even on the supposition that there is *no such World in being*" (Reflections 129). Shaftesbury makes it very clear, moreover, that this inward way differs from his teleological account, as the latter is grounded in claims about the way the world really is. As he puts it in the section entitled "Passage from *terra incognita* to the visible world," just after recounting "the inward way":

> [O]ur late dry Task [has been] to prove MORALS without *a World*, and *establish a Conduct of Life* without the Supposition of *any thing living or extant* besides our immediate *Fancy* and WORLD of *Imagination*. But having finished this *mysterious* Work we come now to open *Day*, and *Sunshine*. . . . We are, henceforward, to trust our Eyes, and take for real *the whole Creation*, and *the fair Forms* which lie before us. We are to believe the Anatomy of our *own Body*, and in proportionable Order, the *Shapes, Forms, Habits*, and *Constitutions* of other Animal-Races. . . . To deny there is anything properly *natural*, (after the Concessions already made) wou'd be undoubtedly very preposterous and absurd. NATURE and the *outward* World being own'd existent, the rest must of necessity follow. The *Anatomy* of Bodys, the *Order* of the Spheres, the *proper Mechanisms* of a thousand kinds, and the infinite *Ends* and sutable *Means* establish'd in the general Constitution and Order of Things; all this being once admitted, and allow'd to pass as certain and unquestionable, 'tis as vain afterwards to except against the Phrase of *natural* and *unnatural*, and question the Propriety of this Speech appl'd to the particular Forms and Beings in the World, as it wou'd be to except against the common Appellations of *Vigour* and *Decay* in Plants, *Health* or *Sickness* in Bodys, *Sobriety* or *Distraction* in Minds, *Prosperity* or *Degeneracy* in any variable part of the known Creation. (Reflections 129–30)

Once we allow that our perceptions inform us accurately of an external world, we will be able to show that virtue is an end as proper and natural to humans as vigor is for plants and health is for bodies. But we cannot show this if we are in doubt about our beliefs about the external world. So while the mental enjoyment account is compatible with extreme skepticism, the teleological account is not.[13]

Shaftesbury's new idea, then, is that even if all our beliefs are false, we will still have a conclusive reason to be virtuous. This reason to be virtuous, because it is based on the mental enjoyment account, is entirely independent of the epistemic value of our beliefs.

As I said at the beginning of this chapter, Shaftesbury's overt attitude toward this new idea is nonchalant. He presents it as though it is simply a nifty way of circumventing Descartes' skeptical arguments without being pulled into the messy epistemological fray. But whether he realizes it or not, Shaftesbury's method of defanging extreme skepticism has momentous implications for our way of thinking about normativity and moral ontology.

In the previous two chapters, we've seen that Shaftesbury wanted to develop an account of virtue that was both necessarily connected to human affections and firmly anchored in objective reality. His goal was to show that virtue essentially involved both being moved by certain kinds of passions *and* acting in accord with the universal system designed by God. But this new idea amounts to an abandonment of the second part of that goal, in that it reneges on the commitment to a correspondence between our moral affections and the systematic design of the universe. It is as though Shaftesbury is pulling up the anchor in objectivity and allowing affection to blow morality wherever it will. For Shaftesbury is saying that our reason to be virtuous will have the same normative status even if all our beliefs are false, even if there is no universal system, even if there is no external world, even if there is no God. This implies that our reason to be virtuous is constituted entirely by our own subjective, affective states. But this kind of subjective basis for the normativity of morals is something that British philosophers prior to Shaftesbury had always sought to distance themselves from. Indeed, this kind of subjective basis for the normativity of morals was typically thought of as a reductio ad absurdum of either a theory or morality: show that a theory implies that our reason to be virtuous is based on subjective affections, and you succeed in showing either that the theory is false or that we have no real reason to be virtuous. But in the 1711 revision of the *Inquiry*, Shaftesbury claims that subjective affections on their own really do provide a reason to be virtuous.

Cudworth certainly wouldn't have accepted this idea. If morality exists at all, Cudworth argued in EIM, it must consist of eternal and immutable truths (EIM 16). This means that if our ideas of morality are to have any legitimacy, they must represent accurately the way the world really is. According to EIM, if our moral ideas are illusory – if moral terms are simply names that fail to correspond to any real entities – then our reason to be moral will evaporate. As a result, Cudworth deemed it necessary to soundly defeat the hypothesis of extreme skepticism (EIM 138–42). Skepticism about all our beliefs, according to Cudworth, is just as incompatible with our commitment to morality as it is with our confidence in geometry or any other science.

Theocles shouldn't have accepted the implication, either. For Theocles believed it imperative to establish the reasonability of his enthusiasm. He thought it imperative to show that there is a principled, rational way of distinguishing his ruling passions from the superstitious, fanatical emotions of the false enthusiasts. Theocles drew this distinction by proving that God exists and that his own ruling passions corresponded to the creative principles in the mind of God. If we accept the extreme skeptical hypothesis, however, we cannot accept Theocles' proofs. We would have to proceed on the assumption that God does not exist, or at least acknowledge that we have no reason to think that our ideas of God are veridical. But in the same instant that Theocles' proofs lose their soundness, his enthusiasm must relinquish its claim to reasonability. Indeed, Theocles explicitly commits himself to the same kind of moral realism that Cudworth argues for in EIM (Moralists 144–51). Theocles also goes on to say that "whoever sincerely defends VIRTUE, and is a *Realist* in MORALITY, must of necessity, in a manner, by the same Scheme of Reasoning, prove as very a *Realist* in DIVINITY" (Moralists 151). But the extreme skeptical hypothesis is incompatible with Theocles' rational belief in the divinity. Theocles' claims imply that the extreme skeptical hypothesis would undermine his defense of virtue.[14]

And yet, in the passages he added to the 1711 version of the *Inquiry*, Shaftesbury maintains that the extreme skeptical hypothesis leaves the cause of virtue unaffected. Our "obligation to virtue," he says, will be "in every respect the same" even if we carry skepticism so far as to doubt "every thing about us" (Virtue or Merit 99). Or as he puts it in another passage added to the *Inquiry*, "If there be no *real* Amiableness or Deformity in moral Acts, there is at least *an imaginary one* of full force" (Virtue or Merit 25).

The difference between Shaftesbury's earlier position on the reality of virtue and his later concession to the extreme skeptic can be helpfully put in terms of Hume's distinction between representations and original existences.[15] When the teleological account is on line, we should attribute to Shaftesbury's moral sense a representational character, since on that account the affections of the moral sense accurately reflect the world. Shaftesbury himself seems to endorse the idea that the moral sense has such a representational character when he speaks of a "Misconception or Misapprehension of the Worth or Value of any Object" (Virtue or Merit 19), implying that the worth or value is grounded in the affection-independent universal system and that the job of the moral sense is to represent that worth or value accurately. But Shaftesbury also claims that according to the mental enjoyment account, our moral affections will still ground our obligation to virtue even on the assumption that we fail in all our attempts to produce truthful representations of the external world (Virtue or Merit 99). Or as he puts it in his other expression of this new idea, "If there be no *real* Amiableness or Deformity in moral Acts, there is at least *an imaginary one* of full force" (Virtue or Merit 25). Our moral affections will still have full force even if they come from "Imagination or Fancy" and do not tell us how things are "in Nature" (Virtue or Merit 25). In these passages, Shaftesbury attributes to the moral sense a kind of normativity or obligatoriness that is independent of representational quality.

Of course, it is anachronistic to read the Humean distinction between representations and original existences back into Shaftesbury. Shaftesbury did not draw the distinction himself and, as we've just seen, his claims about the moral sense turn out in fact to straddle it. I think, though, that the distinction reveals a crucial divide that exists in nascent form in Shaftesbury's thought. And Shaftesbury's failure to place the moral sense clearly on one side of this divide or the other may have been part of the motivation behind Hume's deployment of the distinction (Second Enquiry 74). So it might not be at all anachronistic to read Shaftesbury's claims about the moral sense forward onto Hume's distinction between representations and original existences. Focusing on how this distinction cleaves Shaftesbury's conception of the moral sense also helps to make clear that what is at issue here is not principally the threat of extreme skepticism. What is at issue, rather, is the ground of our reason to be virtuous, or the source of the normativity of morals. And while the hypothesis of extreme skepticism can bring this issue into a helpfully stark light, the issue will nonetheless remain pressing even after the skeptical hypothesis has been dismissed.

By putting these ideas in terms of the self, we can bring into even sharper focus the contrast between the Cambridge Platonists and Shaftesbury of the teleological account, on the one hand, and Hume and Shaftesbury of the mental enjoyment account, on the other. The Cambridge Platonists, Shaftesbury, and Hume all believed that one had to be virtuous in order to have a fully realized self.[16] Shaftesbury, as we've seen, even suggests that without virtue one cannot be one self at all. Now according to the Cambridge Platonists, the fully realized self that virtue enables us to acquire corresponds to the mind of God. This view is grounded in the belief that God's conduct is determined by His ideas of virtue and that our ideas of virtue derive directly from God's mind. Thus, we become God-like just to the extent that our conduct is determined by ideas of virtue. Or as the Cambridge Platonists sometimes put it, by being virtuous we come to "participate" in a limited but nonetheless real way with the divine nature itself. I have tried to show that Theocles' view and the teleological account are fundamentally consistent with this Cambridge Platonist view. For when he is characterizing Theocles and proposing his teleological account, Shaftesbury maintains both that our ideas of goodness originate in God and that we become God-like when our conduct accords with those ideas (see Characteristics I 21–3). And these two claims are in perfect accord with the Cambridge Platonist view that through virtuous conduct we can participate with the divine mind. As Theocles puts it, "[C]onvinc'd . . . of my own Being, and of this *Self* of mine, 'That 'tis a *real Self*, drawn out, and copy'd from another principal and *original* SELF (the *Great-one* of the World)' I endeavour to be really *one* with it, and conformable to it, as far as I am able" (Moralists 201).

Shaftesbury's mental enjoyment account, however, must involve a conception of self that is significantly different. For the self that virtue enables us to realize, on the mental enjoyment account, will not necessarily correspond to or participate with the divine mind, since that account can allow that there may be nothing external to the self to correspond to or participate with. It must be possible for the conception of self that the mental enjoyment account involves to be untethered from all theological belief, left to float free in a world without design.[17]

This divide in Shaftesbury's thought can also be charted by his use of the notion of integrity. Shaftesbury (like Whichcote) says on numerous occasions that a virtuous person will have integrity, while a vicious person will not. He points out, as well, that the word "integrity" is derived from "intire" or "entire." There are, however, two different ways of understanding this idea of being entire. On one understanding, one's affections are entire when they constitute a concern for the well-being of the entire system of which one is a part. This is what Shaftesbury has in mind when he says that "*Rectitude, Integrity*, or VIRTUE" consists of agreement with "that *System* in which [one] is included, and of which [one] constitutes a PART" or having "one's Affections *right* and *intire*, not only in respect of one's self, but of Society and the Publick" (Virtue or Merit 45). It is also what he has in mind when he contrasts "narrow or *partial* Affection" – that is, concern for only some of those within the system of which one is a part – with "*intire Affection*" – that is, concern for all those within the system of which one is a part (Virtue or Merit 65). And this understanding of integrity fits perfectly well with the teleological account, as it equates the possession of integrity to the state of being in harmony with the system of the universe, or to living "*according to Nature*, and the Dictates and Rules of *supreme Wisdom*" (Virtue or Merit 65–6).

But on the other understanding of integrity, one's affections are entire simply when they harmonize with one another or form one self-consistent whole. One's integrity, on this understanding, concerns how one's parts relate to each other, not how one relates to things outside of oneself. And this second understanding coincides with Shaftesbury's mental enjoyment account of virtue, as that account relies simply on internal consistency and not on any correspondence between one's internal principles and the external world.

This ambiguous notion of integrity, I believe, marks Shaftesbury as a harbinger of contemporary moral thinking, for a similar ambiguity continues to surround our use of the term today. Sometimes we use "integrity" to describe that which is possessed by a person who lives according to independently determined moral principles, and sometimes we use "integrity" to describe that which is possessed by a person who lives in a manner consistent with her own principles, whatever they may be. And like Shaftesbury, we usually don't bother to disambiguate these two senses of integrity, letting the word slide back and forth between them. Perhaps we don't draw the distinction clearly because of a hopeful belief that the two senses are coextensive. But while Theocles and the Cambridge Platonists invoked theological commitments that ensured such a coextension, positions that allow that human nature may not be built to a perfect, benevolent design – such as Shaftesbury's mental enjoyment account – must face the possibility that the two senses of integrity will diverge.

Shaftesbury's mental enjoyment account thus marks the beginning of yet another momentous shift in the history of ethical thought. We've seen that at the start of the seventeenth century, English Protestants believed that for humans to escape the wages of sin, the sacrifice of Christ was indispensable. The Cambridge Platonists had great difficulty accommodating the need for Christ, but Whichcote and Cudworth continued to maintain that human morality depended on the divine mind. Indeed, Whichcote and Cudworth

argued that it was literally inconceivable that morality could exist without
God. By the beginning of the eighteenth century, Shaftesbury had decided
that Christ was dispensable, but in *The Moralists* he held, as had the Cambridge Platonists, that the existence of morality implied the existence of
God. But then, in 1711, Shaftesbury made claims that implied that our obligation to virtue would remain just as compelling even if we assumed that
God does not exist. These claims suggest (whether Shaftesbury realized it or
not) that morality may be independent not only of religion but also of God.
And thus, intentionally or not, Shaftesbury opened the door to a thoroughly
secular ethics.

As this shift occurs, moreover, the Human Nature Question begins to
lose its footing. The Question is whether human nature is essentially good
or sinful, whether human beings naturally incline toward virtue or vice.
For seventeenth-century thinkers, this Question had an obvious point. It
was obvious to them that there was a standard of goodness against which
human nature could be measured. That's because it was obvious to them
that there existed a God who was the origin and paragon of goodness. But
now imagine that we are proceeding on the assumption that our obligation
to virtue depends entirely on our own mental states; that our ideas of morality are "original existences" whose normativity does not depend on their
representing or corresponding to anything else; that our moral ideas are
facts only about ourselves; that they do not tell us anything about parts of
reality that exist outside ourselves. When you imagine this (as Shaftesbury
does when he says that the mental enjoyment account is insulated even from
extreme skepticism), the seventeenth-century understanding of the Question collapses. For now there is no longer an independent moral standard
against which human nature can be measured. Morality becomes a fact of
human nature, and only a fact of human nature. In a kind of Copernican
Revolution in moral philosophy, the study of morality becomes a subset of
the study of human nature.

This Copernican Revolution does not make it senseless to ask whether
people are good or evil. But answering the question will now involve comparing one part of human nature to another part (e.g., comparing one's own
moral sentiments to one's own actions or comparing one person's character
to the character of others). The moral status of humans will be a function of
how they measure up to something that is itself an aspect of human nature.

One way of elucidating the importance of these developments is by noting the different responses Shaftesbury's two accounts of virtue allow us to
offer to someone who asks why she shouldn't try to rid herself of her moral
sense. Someone might ask such a question because she is tempted by vice
but knows that if she is vicious her moral sense will disapprove. She wants to
avoid self-condemnation but wonders why this goal is better served by avoiding vice instead of by quashing her moral sense. Now Shaftesbury believes

that the moral sense is so deeply ingrained in each of us that eradicating it entirely is almost impossible (although he does think it can become corrupted by superstition and false religion [Virtue or Merit 24–30]). When the teleological account is on line, however, Shaftesbury can say more than simply that one's attempts to quash one's moral sense will almost certainly fail. Shaftesbury can go on to tell a person tempted by vice that her moral sense is in fact aligned to the system of the universe, and that living in accord with it will bring her into harmony with God's design. But when he is relying only on the mental enjoyment account, Shaftesbury will not be able to call on such considerations. He will be able to say only that it is a brute fact that we are instinct-driven to approve of one kind of conduct and disapprove of another, and that consequently we will be happy if we live a certain kind of life and unhappy if we do not. He will not be able to situate this fact in an affection-independent, theologically grounded universal system of value.[18] With the claim that humans happen to be constituted in a certain way, Shaftesbury's account of the reason to be virtuous will simply bottom out. That's just the nature of being human, he'll have to say. That's just the way we are.

It might seem that I've overemphasized the brief passages on extreme skepticism that Shaftesbury added to the 1711 version of the *Inquiry*. Perhaps, if Shaftesbury had come to agree with me about the implications of these passages, he would simply have deleted them. In his earlier writings, he didn't try to insulate the obligation to virtue from extreme skepticism, and if pushed he might have been willing to concede that extreme skepticism threatened our reason to be moral just as much as it threatened our reason to trust the senses. But he can't get off the hook that easily. For the truth is, even if he hadn't added these passages, his philosophy would still rest on a fault line between a seventeenth-century way of thinking that insists that there exists a realm of value independent of human minds and an eighteenth-century way of thinking that makes all moral reasons depend on humans' own mental states. In Chapter 7, we saw that one manifestation of these different ways of thinking was the tension between the *Inquiry*'s moral ontology, which affirmed "*eternal Measures*, and [an] immutable independent Nature of *Worth* and Virtue," and its moral psychology, which held that our moral judgments are based in a sense that produces a "Sentiment" and that no one acts "otherwise than thro Affections or Passions." In Chapter 8, we saw that the *Moralists*' figure of Theocles was supposed to resolve this tension by simultaneously embodying both ways of thinking. But there are reasons to doubt whether Shaftesbury succeeded at this task. And this doubt – doubt about coherently and plausibly combining a human mind-independent realm of value and a human mind-dependent account of moral reasons – would exist even if Shaftesbury had never added the new passages to the 1711 version of the *Inquiry*.

Besides, whether he meant to or not, Shaftesbury ended up inspiring Hutcheson and Hume to develop their own sentimentalist accounts of morality. And the moral ontology of their accounts is clearly incompatible with a realm of human mind-independent value. Examining these later sentimentalist accounts and their relationship to the Human Nature Question will be the topic of the second half of this study.

PART THREE

HUTCHESON

10

Early Influences on Francis Hutcheson

The Scottish philosopher Francis Hutcheson lived almost a century after Whichcote and Cudworth. But his early intellectual trajectory paralleled the Cambridge Platonists' in fascinating ways. Hutcheson, like Whichcote and Cudworth, was born into a household dominated by a Calvinist Negative Answer to the Human Nature Question. And Hutcheson, again like Whichcote and Cudworth, found his way, in his early college years, to a clear and shining version of the Positive Answer, which then served as the spark to his greatest philosophical achievements.

In Section A of this chapter, I outline Hutcheson's religious upbringing. In B, I describe the role one of his college professors had in leading Hutcheson to a new view of religion, morality, and human nature. And in C, I sketch the intellectual milieu of Dublin in the 1720s, which is where Hutcheson wrote the philosophical works we will examine in more detail in the following four chapters.[1]

A. The Negative Answer of the Scottish Presbyterians

Hutcheson was born in 1694 in Armagh, in the north of Ireland. His family was Scottish, and he grew up in the Scotch-Irish community. Hutcheson's grandfather was a Presbyterian minister who "came from Scotland to attend to the spiritual wants of the Scottish colony in Ireland" (Scott 1900, 4). Hutcheson's father was also a minister, and he too served the Scots in Ireland.

The Scottish Presbyterianism Hutcheson's father and grandfather preached bears a striking resemblance to the English Calvinism of the early 1600s. For Scottish Presbyterianism insisted, as had the earlier Calvinism, that human nature was wholly corrupt and degenerate. We can gain a glimpse of the kind of Negative Answer that would have pervaded the upbringing of the young Francis by looking briefly at the two official statements of the Scottish religion, the Scottish Confession of Faith[2] and the Westminster Standards,[3] to which Hutcheson's father and grandfather would have sworn allegiance.

The Confession introduces the subject of human nature by describing the Fall of Man, "by which transgression, commonly called Original Sin, was the image of God utterly defaced in man; and he and his posterity of nature became enemies to God, slaves to Satan, and servants to sin." The Confession goes on to maintain that our sin is so complete and pervasive that it is impossible for any of us, on our own, to do what is necessary to achieve righteousness and salvation. "[O]ur nature is so corrupt, so weak, and so imperfect," the Confession tells us, "that we are never able to fulfill the works of the law in perfection. Yea, if we say we have no sin (even after we are regenerate), we deceive ourselves, and the verity of God is not into us." As a result of our ineluctable sin, we all deserve to be "cast in the dungeon of utter darkness," where the worm shall not die nor the fire be extinguished. The Confession also describes the way in which a few people will manage to avoid hell, and that is by going to God through Christ. But Christ's assistance, the Confession makes clear, is something a human being can never be worthy of. We are all thoroughly sinful, and sinful we will all always remain. The grace that Christ might bestow on us is completely "undeserved." "For of nature we are so dead, so blind and so perverse, that neither can we feel when we are pricked, see the light when it shines, nor assent to the will of God when it is revealed, unless the Spirit of the Lord Jesus quicken that which is dead, remove the darkness from our minds, and bow our stubborn hearts to the obedience of his blessed will."

The Westminster Standards begin with an equally vehement assertion of man's fallen nature, vividly describing the "original corruption" that has made us all "utterly indisposed, disabled, and . . . opposite to all good." Because we are so corrupt, the Standards tell us, we all deserve the "wrath of God, and curse of the law, and . . . death with all miseries spiritual, temporal, and eternal." None of us, moreover, has any capability whatsoever of transforming himself into a more worthy being. "Man, by his fall into a state of sin, hath wholly lost all ability of will to any spiritual good accompanying salvation: so as, a natural man, being altogether averse from that good, and dead in sin, is not able, by his own strength, to convert himself, or to prepare himself thereunto." There is an "infinite distance" between "us and God," a distance that we, on our own, could never even begin to traverse. The external assistance of Christ, in the form of His undeserved grace, is thus absolutely essential for salvation. Indeed, the assertion that a non-Christian could ever be saved is "very pernicious, and to be detested." The Standards also insist on the necessity of our attending to the revealed word of the scriptures, as the "light of nature" we find within ourselves is "not sufficient to give that knowledge of God and of His will, which is necessary unto salvation." As well, the Standards affirm predestinarianism and supralapsarianism, two

Calvinist doctrines that help round out as robust a version of the Negative Answer as one could hope to find.

B. The Positive Answer of John Simson

It's impossible to know whether Hutcheson resisted the Negative Answer when he was a child or young teenager. The biographical information suggests that he was, from an early age, unusually gentle, loving, and benevolent, and we might conjecture that such a personality would find less than amenable the fierce sin-and-corruption view of human nature contained in the Confession and the Westminster Standards. However that may be, we do know that in 1711, at age seventeen, Hutcheson entered the University of Glasgow, and that once there he fell under the influence of a person clearly opposed to central aspects of Scottish Presbyterianism's Negative Answer.

That person was John Simson, professor of divinity.[4] In 1713, Simson was brought before the "ecclesiastical courts upon charges of holding doctrines inconsistent with the 'Confession of Faith.' It was purported that he was doubtful about punishment for original sin and to have believed in 'Free-Will and the possibility of salvation of the heathen'" (Scott 1900, 15). These supposed heresies of Simson, which led his enemies to label him "Arminian," "Pelagian," and "Deist," are all indicative of a commitment to the Positive Answer. Simson was charged, that is, with holding that human nature was not as wholly corrupt as the Confession of Faith maintained and that individuals had within themselves the resources necessary for achieving salvation.

Hutcheson studied with Simson before and during the latter's trials for heresy. And soon after leaving the University of Glasgow, Hutcheson was quoted as making claims about the goodness of God and human nature that were "an almost verbal reproduction of the heresies of Simson" (Scott 1900, 21). There is, therefore, good reason to believe that Simson played a seminal role in Hutcheson's early intellectual development. Cudworth had the good fortune to be assigned Whichcote as a tutor when he first got to Emmanuel. So too, it seems, Hutcheson found at university a teacher who led him from the gloomy Calvinist religion of his father to the bright ideas of the Positive Answer.

After receiving his degree from the University of Glasgow and teaching there for several years in the Department of Theology, Hutcheson returned to Ireland in 1717. He was probably expected to become a minister in the Presbyterian Church, to follow in the footsteps of his grandfather and father. But things did not go according to plan. It took him longer to gain a probationary minister license than might have been expected, and he never did become a full-time minister. Scott suggests, plausibly, that a large part of the problem was Hutcheson's affinity with Simson's ideas, which placed him sharply at odds with his father and the rest of the old guard of Scottish Presbyterianism. Hutcheson seemed to believe that human beings had within themselves the resources to achieve righteousness. But the belief that human nature was ineluctably sinful, corrupt, and deserving of God's punishment was the religious cornerstone for many of the Scots in Ireland. The following anecdote is a colorful illustration of this clash between Hutcheson's belief in the Positive Answer and the Negative Answer of his father and his father's congregation.

At Armagh, his father, who laboured under a slight rheumatic affection, deputed him to preach in his place upon a cold and rainy Sunday. About two hours after Francis has left Ballyrea (his father's residence) the rain abated – the sun shone forth – the day became serene and warm – and Mr Hutcheson, who found his spirits exhilarated by the change, felt anxious to collect the opinions of the congregation on the merits of his favourite son and proceeded directly to the city. But how was he astonished and chagrined, when he met almost the whole of his flock coming from the Meeting-house with strong marks of disappointment and disgust visible in their countenances. One of the elders, a native of Scotland, addressed the surprised and deeply mortified father thus – 'We a' fell muckle wae for your mishap, Reverend Sir, but it canna be concealed. Your silly loon, Frank, has fashed a' the congregation wi' his idle cackle; for he has been babbling this oor aboot a gude and benevolent God, and that the sauls o' the heathens themsels will gang to Heeven, if they follow the licht o' their ain consciences. Not a word does the daft boy ken, speer, nor say aboot the gude auld comfortable doctrines o' election, reprobation, original sin and faith. Hoot mon, awa' wi' sic fellow.' (Scott 1900, 20–1)

But despite Hutcheson's lack of enthusiasm for the central tenets of the Confession and the Westminster Standards, he was neither condemned nor ostracized by the Presbyterian Scottish community.[5] This is probably partly because there was in the first part of the eighteenth century growing dissent within the Scottish Church about doctrinal matters. Simson and Hutcheson were not the only ones questioning the traditional understanding of Presbyterianism and trying to update the Church's sixteenth- and seventeenth-century theology. Indeed, Simson himself initially escaped his trials with the relatively lenient punishment of the temporary suspension of his university post, an indication of at least some degree of toleration for his views. It seems, moreover, that Hutcheson had the kind of character that enabled him to remain on good terms even with those with whom he disagreed. He was widely acknowledged to be exceedingly intelligent and learned. And he was also thought to be truly well intentioned and upright, someone whose ideas grew out of sincere reflection on important matters rather than a desire for selfish gain. He did not attack other people or put disagreements in personal terms, and his morals were above reproach. Like Whichcote, who openly rejected Puritan doctrine and yet was still greatly esteemed within Puritan circles, Hutcheson remained within the fold of the Scottish Presbyterian community even while he was developing a philosophical position sharply at odds with Presbyterianism's official Negative Answer.

Accordingly, in 1719, a group of Scotch-Irish Presbyterian clergymen asked Hutcheson to set up a private academy in Dublin to serve the sons of prominent Protestant families. Hutcheson accepted the offer, and in 1720, when he was twenty-six, he moved to Dublin, where he would stay for the next ten years.

C. Hutcheson in Dublin and Shaftesbury's Positive Answer

Hutcheson was lucky to be where he was in the 1720s. Dublin was at that time an intellectually very fertile place with a thriving community of philosophically engaged young men.[6] Few of these men left a lasting mark on the history of ideas, but they were in the vanguard of many of the movements of their day. Thus, Hutcheson quickly became immersed in discussion of such topics as Deism, Cartesianism, the empiricism of Locke and Berkeley, and the egoism of Hobbes and Mandeville. But the subject that probably had the most buzz within Dublin's intellectual community of the 1720s was the philosophy of Anthony Ashley Cooper, the third Earl of Shaftesbury.

The influence of Shaftesbury's writings on the Dublin scene was due to a large extent to the efforts of Robert Molesworth, the second Lord Viscount. Wealthy, powerful, and keenly interested in philosophy, Molesworth brought together young Dublin intellectuals, provided fora for their discussions, and used his influence to see that their essays were published in the *Dublin Weekly Journal*. Molesworth did not leave many writings of his own, but his opinions were much respected by the thinkers of his time, and all accounts portray him as an astute and persuasive philosophical conversationalist.

Molesworth had been a contemporary of Shaftesbury's, and the two of them had been political allies in Parliament, confidants in matters of the heart, and sounding boards for each other's ideas. Indeed, to hear Molesworth tell it, Shaftesbury's moral philosophy was deeply indebted to Molesworth's instruction. Voitle, Shaftesbury's biographer, thinks this is a bit of an exaggeration, but he acknowledges that Molesworth and Shaftesbury were close personal friends and that at least in some respects Shaftesbury was "Molesworth's disciple" (Voitle 1984, 71). It is clear, in any event, that Molesworth had a powerful, almost proprietary, commitment to Shaftesbury's ideas, and it's easy to imagine his efforts to impress those ideas on his circle of bright young men.

It was probably through Molesworth and his friends that Hutcheson first became acquainted with Shaftesbury's works.[7] Hutcheson's sympathy with the heresies of Simson gives us reason to believe that he would have reacted positively to Shaftesbury's ideas regardless of the setting in which he first encountered them. But his membership in Molesworth's circle almost certainly made him even more receptive.

Shaftesbury's influence on Hutcheson's early work is impossible to miss.[8] The title page of Hutcheson's first book, published in 1725, reads: *An Inquiry into the original of our ideas of beauty and virtue; in two treatises. In which the principles of the late Earl of Shaftesbury are Explain'd and Defended, against the Author of the Fable of the Bees: and the Ideas of Moral Good and Evil are establish'd, according to the Sentiments of the Antient Moralists* (Beauty and Virtue [1st ed.] ii). In the preface to the second edition of his *Inquiry*, moreover, Hutcheson emphasized his admiration for Shaftesbury's work. "To recommend the Lord Shaftesbury's Writings to the World," he wrote, "is a very needless Attempt. They will be esteemed while any Reflection remains among men" (Beauty and Virtue xxi). Hutcheson also praised Molesworth's "Conversation" and "Civilitys" at great length, contending that the publication of the Inquiry "was owing to [Molesworth's] Approbation of" it (Beauty and Virtue xix). He acknowledged "his Obligations" to Molesworth "for admitting him into his Acquaintance, and giving him some Remarks in Conversation, which have very much improv'd these Papers beyond what they were at first" (Beauty and Virtue [1st ed.] ix–x). And it seems very likely that the "Remarks" of Molesworth to which Hutcheson refers here were of a distinctively Shaftesburean nature.

What was it in Shaftesbury that so inspired Hutcheson? The standard answer is that reading Shaftesbury convinced Hutcheson of the anti-rationalist moral sense account of moral judgment. But there are two reasons to question this answer. First, Shaftesbury's account of morality is as at least as much rationalist as it is a moral sense theory. And second, the first edition of Hutcheson's *Inquiry* contains almost no arguments against what we would now take to be moral rationalism. What seems more likely is that the "principles" of Shaftesbury that Hutcheson was concerned to "explain" and "defend" were those that constituted Shaftesbury's Positive Answer. We examine this explanation and defense in the next chapter.

11

Hutcheson's Attack on Egoism

In this chapter, I explain Hutcheson's attack on egoism, or the view that humans are always ultimately motivated by self-interest. In Section A, I discuss why Hutcheson thought it so important to defeat egoism. In B, I describe the central aspects of Hutcheson's anti-egoist position. And in C, I examine one particular anti-egoist argument and its relationship to the anti-rationalist arguments for which Hutcheson would eventually become most well known.

A. The Negative Answer of Bernard Mandeville

Almost all of us at least sometimes distinguish between those who are virtuous and those who are not. Almost all of us think that certain things people do are moral and that other things people do are not moral. This is a plainly observable feature of human life.

According to Hutcheson, when we distinguish between virtuous and non-virtuous people, we do so on the basis of motive (Beauty and Virtue 162–8, 191, 197, 229, 266–7). Specifically, we judge people to be virtuous when we believe they are motivated by benevolence (or the desire to benefit others), and we judge people to be non-virtuous when we believe they are motivated by desires that are not benevolent. As Hutcheson puts it, "If we examine all the Actions which are counted *amiable* any where, and enquire into the Grounds upon which they are *approv'd*, we shall find, that in the Opinion of the Person who approves them, they always appear as Benevolent, or flowing from *Love of others*, and a Study of their Happiness, whether the *Approver* be one of the Persons belov'd, or profited, or not" (Beauty and Virtue 162; cf. Passions and Affections 37).

This picture of virtue-as-benevolence could have come directly from Shaftesbury. It was apparent as early as 1699, when Shaftesbury's *Inquiry concerning Virtue* first came out, and was perfectly clear by 1711, when Shaftesbury's *Characteristics* was published. But in the years between the publication of the *Characteristics* and Hutcheson's *Inquiry*, the virtue-as-benevolence picture had come under powerful attack.

The attack was spearheaded by Bernard Mandeville, a "brilliant free-thinking doctor" who was born in Rotterdam in 1670 and lived in London from 1692 until his death in 1732 (Mandeville I xxi). Mandeville's chief work was *The Fable of the Bees: or, Private Vices, Publick Benefits*. This book was first published in 1714, but Hutcheson probably read the second edition, which came out in 1723.

Mandeville is a fascinating thinker, and his account of human nature is more nuanced and penetrating than most of his contemporaries gave him credit for. (As we will see in Chapter 18, Hume's account of human nature owes a great deal to Mandeville.) But for now, let us focus on Hutcheson's reading of Mandeville. As Hutcheson saw it, Mandeville advanced an unqualified form of egoism, according to which all humans are always motivated exclusively by self-interest. Everyone, according to this reading of Mandeville, cares about his or her own happiness and only about his or her own happiness. We are all selfish, through and through.

Hutcheson took this egoist position to imply that no one is ever virtuous. For to be virtuous, on Hutcheson's view, is to act on a benevolent motive – that is, a nonulterior motive to benefit others, a motive that has others' happiness as its ultimate end. But Mandevillean egoism implies that no one ever has such a motive. Hutcheson also took Mandevillean egoism to imply that the moral distinctions we draw are all based on error. For when we distinguish the virtuous from the non-virtuous, on Hutcheson's view, we do so because we think that the former act on a motive that the latter do not act on. But Mandevillean egoism implies that everyone always acts on the same (ultimate) motive. We judge some people to be saints and other people to be knaves because we think the former act on motives that are different from the motives of the latter. But if Mandevillean egoism is true, the (ultimate) motives of saints and knaves are exactly the same: they are all thoroughly selfish. So the saints aren't virtuous, and the distinction we draw between saints and knaves is mistaken.[1]

Mandevillean egoism does allow for a distinction that might be coextensive with Hutcheson's conception of the difference between virtue and vice. This is the distinction between agents whose view of their own self-interest leads them to perform actions that benefit other people and agents whose view of their own self-interest leads them to perform actions that harm other people. But Hutcheson held that this distinction was not enough to fund a real moral difference between saints and knaves. For when we distinguish between the virtuous and the vicious, according to Hutcheson, we are trying to mark the difference between ultimate motives. That's why we think that the good an agent does for other people has no moral worth so long as the agent has an ulterior, self-interested motive.[2] So since Mandevillean egoism implies that all actions are based in the ultimate motive of self-interest,

Hutcheson believed that he could vindicate the moral distinctions we draw – and establish that humans can be virtuous – only if he could defeat Mandevillean egoism. Hutcheson had to show that we can act on an ultimately benevolent motive, on a motive that "is not an Intention to obtain . . . *sensible Pleasure*, much less the *future Rewards* from Sanctions of Laws, or any other *natural Good*, which may be the Consequence of the *virtuous* Action; but an entirely different Principle of Action from *Interest* or *Self-Love*" (Beauty and Virtue 116).

Hutcheson's relationship to Mandeville was thus very similar to Shaftesbury's relationship to Hobbes. Hobbes was Shaftesbury's bete noire, the exemplar of the egoistic Negative Answer that Shaftesbury found anathema. And similarly, Mandeville, who was explicitly indebted to Hobbes, was bete noire to Hutcheson, who was explicitly indebted to Shaftesbury. Hutcheson's reason for thinking it so urgent to defeat Mandeville, moreover, was the same as Shaftesbury's reason for thinking it so urgent to defeat Hobbes: Hutcheson and Shaftesbury both thought the egoistic Negative Answer was self-fulfilling.

Shaftesbury contended that those who were persuaded by Hobbes that self-interest and fear are the only real human motives would be more likely to treat others in selfish and violent ways. Thus Shaftesbury wrote that Hobbes "*made war* (if I may say so) even on *virtue* itself" (Preface vii). And Hutcheson expressed the same concern, contending that those persuaded by the egoistic Negative Answer would harbor dark thoughts about humanity that would inevitably lead to dark deeds. As Hutcheson put it, "If any Opinions deserve Opposition, they are such as raise Scruples in our Minds about the *Goodness* of Providence, or represent our Fellow-Creatures as *base* and *selfish*, by instilling into us some ill-natur'd, cunning, shreud Insinuations, 'that our most generous Actions proceed wholly from *selfish Views*.' This wise *Philosophy* of some *Moderns*, after Epicurus, must be fruitful of nothing but *Discontent*, *Suspicion*, and *Jealousy*" (Beauty and Virtue 208–9; cf. Beauty and Virtue 170–3, Passions and Affections v, 89, 140–1, and Moral Sense 320–2).[3]

Shaftesbury and Hutcheson's foremost purpose in attacking the egoistic Negative Answer was, then, *practical*.[4] Egoism, as they saw it, was not merely a mistaken theory but a destructive moral influence. Convincing people of the Positive Answer – convincing them that benevolence and (thus) virtue can and do exist – was a way to improve people. It was a way to instill virtue. Shaftesbury and Hutcheson both believed, as well, that this practical goal was philosophy's province. Philosophy, they held, ought ultimately to serve the purpose of making us lead better lives. Truths that have no bearing on how to live are trifling, unimportant, scarcely the worth the effort of discovering. Shaftesbury asserted his belief in the practical purpose of philosophy when, in *The Moralists*, he had Philocles "bemoan philosophy" because it was "no longer active in the world" (Moralists 232). And Hutcheson made the same point in the first paragraph of the preface of the first edition of his first book, when he criticized the philosophy of his day for seeking "speculative Knowledge" instead of pursuing "Wisdom" (Beauty and Virtue ix; cf. Passions and Affections v).

But while Shaftesbury and Hutcheson both said they were trying to reach their readers in a way that would instill virtue, the works they produced were noticeably different in form. Shaftesbury made use of literary genre and personae, deploying the techniques of novels, poems, and plays. Hutcheson was much more methodical. He did not use narrative, character, or irony to seduce us to his position. That's not to say that Hutcheson was a clumsy or infelicitous writer. His sentences are always adept and sometimes quite graceful. But when reading Hutcheson, we are never in danger of forgetting that we are making our way through a philosophical treatise in which arguments are being presented in support of one thesis and against another. Shaftesbury consistently sought to distance himself from the dry, systematic form in which he first put his ideas in the *Inquiry*. But that dry, systematic form suited Hutcheson to a tee.

This is a difference in style between Shaftesbury and Hutcheson, but it's a difference that had some substantive repercussions. Shaftesbury's concern with the flow and proportion of his books prevented him at times from following the consequences of a position through to the bitter logical end, and the engaging surface of his prose allowed him to finesse his way of out of having to make some difficult conceptual choices. Hutcheson, in contrast, would follow a position all the way through, to bite the bullet and accept the consequences, even if it meant a less entertaining – and less intuitive – result. Where the argument led is where Hutcheson would usually go. So while Hutcheson started out with Shaftesburean ideas, he ended up pushing them into new philosophical territory. Hutcheson is more pedestrian than Shaftesbury, less inspiring. But the logic of his position is clearer and more consistent. I am tempted to say that what makes Shaftesbury a better writer is also what makes Hutcheson a better philosopher. But that would be to beg some important questions about what philosophy should be. So let me say instead only that the form of Hutcheson's philosophizing is much closer than Shaftesbury's to that of contemporary Anglo-American analytic philosophy.

Hutcheson's philosophical method is on full display in his attack on egoism in his *Inquiry into the Original of Our Ideas of Beauty and Virtue*. There he advances argument after argument after argument, assaulting egoism from every side, cutting off every avenue of escape. It's an exhaustive, suffocating strategy, and describing it in its entirety would be a ponderous task. Hutcheson's *Inquiry* certainly lacks the flair of Shaftesbury's literary exploits. If they were woodworkers, Shaftesbury would hide all the joints connecting his finely carved pieces, while Hutcheson would hammer in plenty of large, conspicuous nails. But while Hutcheson's method lacks Shaftesbury's elegance, it does get the job done. He may make his case in a battery of arguments instead of in an amusing epistle or a dramatic narrative. But in the end, Hutcheson succeeds in constructing one of the most decisive refutations of egoism that exists in the English language.

B. Hutcheson's Attack on Mandeville's Egoistic Negative Answer

Hutcheson attacked two different aspects of Mandevillean egoism. First, he attacked the claim that all of our *moral distinctions* are based in self-interest, and second, he attacked the claim that all of our *actions* are motivated by self-interest. Let us look at these in order.[5]

The claim concerning our moral distinctions that Hutcheson tried to refute is that we judge others' conduct to be virtuous when and only when we think it benefits us. According to this egoistic claim, there is no difference between the conduct of others that we morally approve of and the conduct of others that we think will promote our own interests. Everything we do is ultimately based on our desire for our own happiness, and the activity of passing moral judgment on others is no exception. I react positively towards others' benevolence only because I believe that their benevolence is likely to benefit *me*. The good others' conduct may do for humanity as a whole, distinct from the good it does for me, is none of my concern.

Hutcheson begins his attack on this egoistic account of our moral distinctions by first developing a non-egoistic account of *aesthetic* judgment.[6] The pleasure we experience when we view a beautiful object, he argues, can be completely independent of any advantage we might hope to gain from it.[7] Our aesthetic judgment is based on our sense of beauty, and our sense of beauty is entirely distinct from our perception of our own interests. But given that we possess one faculty of judgment that is entirely distinct from self-interest (a disinterested sense of beauty), it is eminently plausible to suppose that we also possess another faculty of judgment that is entirely distinct from self-interest (a disinterested moral sense).[8] The existence of disinterested aesthetic judgment forces us to abandon the psychologically global claim that self-interest underlies everything we think, say, and do. But once we abandon that global claim and observe what people are actually like, we will see that a non-egoistic account explains our moral judgments much better than an egoistic one (Beauty and Virtue xvii).[9]

A non-egoist account better explains, first of all, the fact that there are many things that promote our self-interest that we do not judge to be virtuous. Inanimate objects, for instance, can be just as advantageous to us as sensible beings, but we never judge inanimate objects to be virtuous (Beauty and Virtue 117–18). Similarly, we do not judge people to be virtuous if we believe their motives are entirely selfish, no matter how much we may benefit from their actions (Beauty and Virtue 119, 124). A foreign traitor, for instance, may benefit our country as much as the most valorous hero, but we still do not think the traitor virtuous (Beauty and Virtue 130). At times, moreover, we ourselves may have the option of performing actions that harm others, but coming to believe that those actions will be to our own advantage will not necessarily lead us to judge that they are virtuous (Beauty and Virtue 126–7). And when we do give in to temptation and perform actions harmful to others, we may continue to condemn those actions even after we have reaped the benefits (Beauty and Virtue 127).

A non-egoist account also better explains the fact that there are many things that do *not* promote our self-interest that we *do* judge to be virtuous. We judge as virtuous, for instance, people who performed good deeds long ago in distant lands, even though there is no chance that their actions will have any bearing on our own welfare (Beauty and Virtue 117, 121). And we also judge as virtuous people who have attempted to benefit others, even if, as a result of circumstances outside their control, no good whatsoever came of their actions (Beauty and Virtue 123). Indeed, it is not uncommon for us to judge as virtuous people who have performed actions that actually conflict with our self-interest, such as when we approve of someone with good intentions who harms us by mistake, or when we approve of a magistrate who pronounces a just sentence against us, or when we approve of a "gallant Enemy" who serves his country well even though it does great damage to our own cause (Beauty and Virtue 120, 130, 133).

Hutcheson is aware that egoists will try to show that the seemingly unselfish character of such moral judgments can be explained by ultimately selfish principles. But the egoists' circuitous psychological stories, Hutcheson argues, fail to provide a plausible account of the observable phenomena. Egoists claim, for instance, that our approval of virtuous actions performed long ago and far away is best explained by our imaginatively placing ourselves in the position of those who were directly affected by the action, and that we then approve of the action only because we imagine that we ourselves are reaping the benefits. But, Hutcheson points out, the "parsimony of a miser" produces just as much benefit for his heirs as the "generosity of a worthy man" produces for his friends (Beauty and Virtue [5th ed.] 116). And we could just as easily imagine ourselves "heirs to misers" as we could "favourites of heroes." But we don't approve of the former and we do approve of the latter. Similarly, we approve of "brave unsuccessful Attempts, which we see prove detrimental both to the Agent, and to those for whose Service they were intended" and disapprove of successful traitorous endeavors, even if large groups of people benefited from the treachery (Beauty and Virtue [5th ed.] 117). As Hutcheson puts it, "[H]ad we no Sense of *moral Good*, in *Humanity, Mercy, Faithfulness*, why should not *Self-Love*, and our Sense of *natural Good* engage us always to the victorious Side, and make us admire and love the successful *Tyrant*, or *Traitor*? . . . It is plain we have some *secret Sense* which determines our Approbation without regard to *Self-Interest*; otherwise we should always favour the *fortunate* Side without regard to *Virtue*, and suppose ourselves engaged with that Party" (Beauty and Virtue 122).

The only plausible account of the pattern of our moral judgments is that we approve of actions as virtuous when we apprehend that they proceed from benevolence, or an "Instinct, antecedent to all Reason from Interest, which influences us to the Love of others" (Beauty and Virtue 155). The egoistic explanation is simply not credible.

Hutcheson next attacks the egoist claim that all of our actions are motivated entirely by self-interest. By way of transition, he notes that it would be very strange for us to base our moral judgments on whether people are motivated by benevolence if we ourselves had never experienced such a motive. For how could "a Person who is wholly selfish" ever come "to imagine others to be publick-spirited" (Beauty and Virtue 132)? How could we ever come to think that there is such a thing as moral goodness, and that people sometimes instantiate it, if none of us had ever perceived firsthand that of which it consists?

Hutcheson then goes on to argue that we commonly try to benefit others without giving any thought at all to the possible connection between their happiness and ours (Beauty and Virtue 145, 155). And the egoists' attempts to reduce or assimilate such conduct to the pursuit of self-interest are miserable failures.

One of Hutcheson's principal examples is the benevolence parents exhibit toward their children, which can lead them to do all sorts of things that don't seem to be in their self-interest at all (Beauty and Virtue 155–8). Egoists try to undermine this example by attributing all sorts of selfish motives to parents who benefit their children. But Hutcheson does an excellent job of establishing the inadequacy of the selfish interpretations of parental conduct. Such interpretations, he shows, either tacitly presuppose that parents have a disinterested ultimate desire for the happiness of their children, mistake metaphors for literal truths, or define "selfishness" in a way that makes the claim that parents act selfishly a mere tautology. Hutcheson clinches the point by deploying the following thought experiment: imagine that God has declared that a person is about to be "suddenly *annihilated*, but at the Instant of his Exit it should be left to his Choice whether his Friend, his Children, or his Country should be made happy or miserable for the future, when he himself could have no Sense of either Pleasure or Pain from their State" (Beauty and Virtue [5th ed.] 147). Would such a person lack the motive to promote his children's happiness? Of course not. If anything, a person's motivation to promote the future well-being of his children will grow stronger as his death draws near.

Nor is it only one's child whose happiness one may care about for its own sake. At "the Instant of his Exit," one may be motivated to make one's friends happy as well. Indeed, this benevolent motive is readily apparent in many actual human interactions. We often act benevolently towards "Neighbours" even when we have "receiv'd no good Offices" from them, and we desire the happiness of our countrymen even when we are not in any position to share in it (Beauty and Virtue 158). We even care about the happiness of people in the "*most distant* parts of the Earth," as is evident from the distress we feel on hearing of the misery of people in faraway lands and the joy we feel on hearing of their good fortune (Beauty and Virtue 159).

Hutcheson acknowledges that benevolence comes in weaker and stronger forms, and that our desire to benefit those who are close to us is stronger than our desire to benefit those who are distant (Beauty and Virtue 216–21). He also acknowledges that when people believe that benevolence is in conflict with their self-interest, it is not uncommon for them to act self-interestedly (Beauty and Virtue 161). Hutcheson is not claiming that we always act benevolently. He is not claiming that everyone is always virtuous. To defeat the egoists, he needs to show only that human nature does include the motive of benevolence and that people sometimes act on it. That is enough to establish that it makes sense to speak of a distinction between virtue and vice and that virtue is sometimes instantiated.

As further proof of our benevolent nature Hutcheson points to "compassion" or "pity," which leads us "to study the *Interest* of others without any Views of *private Advantage*" (Beauty and Virtue 237). Every human is "made uneasy" by the pain of others. And unless other factors intrude, we will try to relieve others' pain when we see it, without any thought of whether it will benefit us. This is an automatic response, something our constitution compels us to immediately. When we witness another's pain our distress "immediately appears in our *Countenance*" and we "*mechanically* send forth *Shrieks* and *Groans*" (Beauty and Virtue 238). Human nature must, then, include a "*natural, kind Instinct*" (Beauty and Virtue 239).

Hutcheson also responds to Hobbes' egoistic account of compassion and pity. According to this account, we are motivated to relieve the pain of others only because we imagine that we ourselves are feeling the pain they are feeling. We care about relieving other persons' pain, according to the Hobbesian egoist, only because it is a means to the ultimate end of relieving our own (imaginatively induced) pain. But, Hutcheson argues, if the only reason for our compassion were the desire to relieve our own pain, we would be at least as likely to take measures to stop thinking about people who are suffering as we would be to try to help them. In fact, however, we often take active measures to find out *more* about the circumstances of persons in pain so that our efforts to help them will be more effectual. As Hutcheson puts it, "If our sole Intention, in *Compassion* or *Pity*, was the Removal of our Pain, we should run away, shut our Eyes, divert our Thoughts from the miserable Object, to avoid the Pain of Compassion, which we seldom do" (Beauty and Virtue 153).[10] Hutcheson once again clinches this point by means of a thought experiment: imagine that God gave you the option of either relieving the pain of a person in distress or wholly blotting out your memory of such a person. If our "sole End" were to free ourselves of distress, we would be indifferent between these two options (Beauty and

Virtue [5th ed.] 147). But we're not indifferent. We all prefer to relieve the person's pain.

Another influential egoist argument Hutcheson addresses is that we try to help others only because of the satisfaction we feel when we succeed in helping them (Beauty and Virtue 115–16, 154). The idea here is that we experience joy when we get what we desire, and that the ultimate goal of our benevolent actions is the selfish one of experiencing the joy of fulfilling the desire to help others. But, as Hutcheson points out, the fact that we derive satisfaction from helping others shows that we have an antecedent non-selfish desire for their happiness. If we did not have an antecedent non-selfish desire for their happiness, we would experience no joy when we succeeded in helping them. That is to say, we experience joy when we help others because we want to help them; it's not the case that we help them only because we want to experience joy. So this supposedly selfish explanation of our benevolence actually presupposes that we have a prior disinterested concern for others' well-being.

A related egoist objection that Hutcheson addresses is that we try to help others only because we crave self-approval, or the "secret Sense of Pleasure accompanying such of our own Actions as we call Virtuous" (Beauty and Virtue 115). The egoist claim here is that we experience a certain kind of self-satisfied pleasure, a warm glow of self-congratulation, when we do something we think is virtuous, and that the selfish desire to experience that pleasure is the ultimate reason for all virtuous action. Hutcheson responds by arguing that virtue is not always pleasant. Virtue involves concern for others' well-being, and such concern is as likely to give rise to unease as to pleasure. He also argues that the fact that we feel satisfied when we perform virtuous actions itself reveals that we have a prior concern for virtue (this argument has the same form as the one described in the preceding paragraph). The claim that we act virtuously because of the pleasure we receive from reflecting on our virtue "plainly supposes a *Sense* of *Virtue* antecedent to Ideas of *Advantage*, upon which this Advantage is founded" (Beauty and Virtue 152).

In a similar vein, Hutcheson attacks the view that we pursue virtue only because of a selfish desire for honor. This was the position most closely associated with Mandeville, and Hutcheson's opposition to it was probably the impetus for his anti-egoist project as a whole. Against Mandeville, Hutcheson argues that we think people are honorable only when we think they are virtuous (Beauty and Virtue 221–30). So since our sense of honor itself presupposes a prior sense of virtue, our sense of virtue cannot be derived entirely from our sense of honor. Furthermore, our desire for others to think us honorable presupposes that we care about virtue itself and not simply about the advantages we might gain from others' opinions of us. That is why we would not necessarily give up an honorable reputation in order to gain a shameful but more profitable one. Hutcheson also points out that people are motivated to pursue virtue and avoid vice even when they have no reason to believe that anyone else will ever learn of their actions (Beauty and Virtue [5th ed.] 235). Our concern for virtue can exist entirely independently of our beliefs about others' opinions of us. So Mandeville must be wrong when he claims that our concern for virtue is based entirely on the desire for others to think us honorable.

Another one of Mandeville's claims that Hutcheson attacks is that those in power have manipulated us into caring about virtue (Beauty and Virtue 130–3). According to this view, it is in the self-interest of political leaders to convince the rest of us that there is great value in promoting the public good, and it is only as a result of politicians' propaganda that we have come to admire and imitate public benefactors. In response, Hutcheson contends that if we had never had any prior admiration for or motive toward benevolence, political leaders could never have convinced us that anyone else had ever acted benevolently or that we should act benevolently ourselves. It would be as impossible for Mandevillean political leaders to create our benevolent motives and our idea of virtue as it would be for one blind person to give another blind person the perception of redness.[11]

C. Hutcheson's Attack on the Reflective Egoism of Cumberland and Pufendorf

Let us turn now to one more of Hutcheson's anti-egoist arguments. This final argument is historically important because it marks the transition between Hutcheson's anti-egoism and the anti-rationalist arguments for which he would eventually become best known.

Hutcheson's final anti-egoist argument is aimed at the view, which he attributed to Cumberland and Pufendorf, that our positive concern for virtue is based entirely on self-interest and a careful, detailed examination of human affairs. What a careful, detailed examination of human affairs reveals, according to this view, is that both my own virtue and the virtue of others always ends up promoting my own self-interest. As Hutcheson puts the view, "There is no Need of supposing such a *Sense* of *Morality* given to Men, since *Reflection,* and *Instruction* would recommend the same Actions from Arguments of *Self-Interest,* and engage us, from the acknowledg'd Principle of *Self-Love,* to the Practice of them" (Beauty and Virtue 270–1).

As we've seen, Hutcheson wants to deny that any form of egoism provides a credible general explanation of our approval of others' virtue or of our own virtuous conduct. Interestingly, however, he is willing to concede that a careful, detailed examination of human affairs establishes the connection between virtue and happiness. As we will see in Chapter 14, Hutcheson really did believe that a person who acts virtuously will be happier than one who doesn't. He was more dubious about attempts to show that every instance of the virtuous actions of other people somehow redounds to the benefit of each of us. He thus pokes fun at Cumberland and Pufendorf for trying "to shew by their nice Train of Consequences, and Influences of Actions by way of Precedent in particular Instances, that we in this Age reap any *Advantage* from Orestes's killing the *treacherous* Aegysthus, or from the Actions of Codrius or Decius" (Beauty and Virtue 124–5; cf. 133). But for the sake of the argument, Hutcheson is willing even to grant that Cumberland and Pufendorf's Rube Goldberg–like stories succeed in showing that every virtuous action that has ever been performed has somehow ended up promoting my personal happiness.

So how can Hutcheson respond to the egoists if he's willing to grant them this connection between virtue and happiness? If he concedes that acting virtuously always promotes the agent's own happiness, isn't he opening the door to the egoist view that people are motivated to virtue only because it serves an ultimately selfish end? And if he allows that others' virtue promotes a moral judge's own happiness, isn't he opening the door to a similarly selfish account of why moral judges approve of virtue?

Hutcheson doesn't think so. He argues that even if we do suppose that there is a consistent connection between virtue and happiness, the egoistic account will still fail to capture our positive regard for virtue. For to understand the connection between virtue and happiness, one needs to follow the many complicated steps of sophisticated philosophical arguments about the long-term, wide-ranging effects of certain kinds of actions. But we all love virtue immediately, the moment we see it. Our love of virtue does not arise only after we have gone through lengthy ratiocinations, such as those produced by Cumberland and Pufendorf. Indeed, most people have never read these authors, and many would not be able to follow their arguments if they did. But most people have virtuous motives and approve of virtue anyway. So even if Cumberland and Pufendorf succeed in showing that virtue in distant ages has benefited everyone living today, they will have only proved "that after long Reflection, and Reasoning, we may find out some Ground, even from Views of Interest, to approve the same Actions which every Man admires as soon as he hears of them; and that too under a quite different Conception" (Beauty and Virtue 125). They will have only shown "that *Reason* and *calm Reflection* may recommend to us, from *Self-Interest*, those Actions, which at first View our *moral Sense* determines us to admire, without considering this *Interest*" (Beauty and Virtue 133).[12]

Hutcheson, then, is willing to allow that the set of all virtuous actions and the set of all actions that promote our self-interest are coextensive. But he thinks that we clearly have a different sense of what is virtuous and what is in our self-interest. And we love virtue in the sense that it is virtuous, not simply in the sense that it is in our self-interest. Indeed, many people who love virtue do not even realize that virtue and self-interest are coextensive. The connection between virtue and self-interest was a momentous intellectual discovery, something that Cumberland and Pufendorf exerted great effort to establish. But since Cumberland and Pufendorf had to use their prodigious mental talents to discover the connection, we cannot explain the universal regard for virtue by attributing to all humans the belief in the connection. The more philosophically impressive Cumberland and Pufendorf's discovery, the less tenable it is as an account of the motivation behind everyday human behavior. As Hutcheson puts it:

> But must a Man have the Reflection of Cumberland, or Puffendorf, to admire *Generosity, Faith, Humanity, Gratitude?* Or reason so nicely to apprehend the *Evil* in *Cruelty, Treachery, Ingratitude?* Do not the *former* excite our *Admiration,* and *Love,* and *Study* of Imitation, wherever we see them, almost at first View, without any such Reflection; and the *latter,* our *Hatred, Contempt* and *Abhorrence?* Unhappy would it be for *Mankind,* if a *Sense of Virtue* was of as narrow an Extent, as a Capacity for such *Metaphysics.* (Beauty and Virtue 125–6)

The fact that virtue is in our self-interest is analogous to the fact that certain foods we find tasty also turn out to be good for our health. Nutritional science may show that a certain food is good for us, but that does not mean that all the people who find the food delicious eat it because of their belief in its nutritional value. Indeed, many of the people who eat healthy, tasty food may know nothing about nutritional science at all. Nutritional science does not explain away the immediate gustatory pleasure people take in certain foods. Similarly, the Byzantine arguments of Cumberland and Pufendorf do not explain away the immediate moral pleasure people take in benevolence.

> It is perhaps true, that *Reflection* and *Reason* might lead us to approve the same Actions as *advantageous.* But would not the *same* Reflection and Reason likewise, generally recommend the same *Meats* to us which our *Taste* represents as pleasant? And shall we thence conclude, that we have no *Sense* of *Tasting?* Or that such a *Sense* is *useless?* No: The use is plain in both Cases. Notwithstanding the mighty *Reason* we boast of above other Animals, its Processes are too slow, too full of doubt and hesitation, to serve us in every Exigency, either for our own Preservation, without the *external Senses,* or to direct our Actions for the *Good* of the *Whole,* without this *moral Sense.* (Beauty and Virtue 271)

Hutcheson's point here could also be put in terms of color recognition. Scientists may be able to show that all red things produce certain kinds of light waves. But that obviously does not prove that people lack a sense of sight. And just as it would be ridiculous to attribute to everyone who recognizes redness the scientific knowledge of light waves, so too is it ridiculous to attribute to everyone who loves virtue the metaphysical knowledge of the connection between virtue and self-interest.

Hutcheson placed great emphasis on this argument against the reflective egoism of Cumberland and Pufendorf. He tells us in the preface to the *Inquiry,* for instance, that his "principal design" is to establish that our positive regard for virtue is instinctive, independent of rational considerations of interests. "The weakness of our Reason," he writes, is "so great, that very few Men could ever have form'd those long Deductions of Reason, which shew some Actions to be in the whole advantageous to the Agent, and their Contrarys pernicious" (Beauty and Virtue xiv–xv). The only explanation of our positive regard for virtue, Hutcheson says he will show, is that we all possess virtuous "affections." The love of virtue does not originate in the "calm dull Reflections of *Self-Interest*" but in "delightful Sensations" by which we are "strongly determin'd" (Beauty and Virtue 271).

So when Hutcheson contends in the *Inquiry* that the view that "virtue arises from reason" is incorrect, what he means is that virtue does not originate in "long Deductions of Reason, which shew some Actions to be in the whole advantageous to the Agent, and their Contrarys pernicious." What he means is that our approval of benevolence and our own benevolent motives are not based on the belief, arrived at through conscious ratiocination, that benevolence promotes our interests. When he is arguing against those who would derive morality from reason, he is arguing against rational *egoists*, or those who maintain that our only reason for caring about virtue is that it increases our own happiness (Beauty and Virtue 190–4). Thus, he tells us that by showing that morality originates in a moral sense, he has shown that we have an instinct toward virtue that is "antecedent to all Reason from Interest" (Beauty and Virtue 159). And the view that "*Virtue* arises from *Reason*" he summarizes by saying: "What is *Reason* but *that Sagacity we have in prosecuting any End?* The *ultimate End* propos'd by the common *Moralists* is the *Happiness* of the *Agent* himself, and this certainly he is determin'd to pursue from *Instinct*" (Beauty and Virtue 192).

Why am I making such a big deal out of the fact that when Hutcheson is attacking the view that "*Virtue* arises from *Reason*" in the *Inquiry* he is attacking an *egoist* view? I am doing so because the anti-rationalist arguments for which Hutcheson would eventually become most well known are directed at another kind of rationalism. This other kind of rationalism, represented by Cudworth, Samuel Clarke, and John Balguy, holds that morality originates in reason alone, which is very different from the egoist view that morality originates in reflective, considered judgments about what will best promote one's long-term self-interest. According to the egoist view Hutcheson attacks in the *Inquiry*, whenever I am reasoning I am trying to determine what will most benefit me. Reason, on this egoist view, is slave to self-interest. But the reason alone rationalists such as Cudworth, Clarke, and Balguy took reason to be a disinterested, God-like faculty through which we gain access to eternal and immutable truths. On the reason alone view, when I am reasoning about morality I am engaged in a process that can be cleanly separated from all affection, self-interested or otherwise.

Because Hutcheson's place in the history of philosophy has largely been defined by his arguments against positions such as Cudworth's, Clarke's, and Balguy's, it is easy to form the impression that his opposition to reason alone rationalism was the impetus and centerpiece of his philosophical thinking as a whole. Selby-Bigge certainly promoted this way of viewing Hutcheson when he placed Hutcheson in the "moral sense" volume of his *British Moralists*. And Stafford, writing almost 100 years after Selby-Bigge, adheres to the same historiographical approach when he says that Hutcheson's staunch opposition to rationalism militates against placing him in the "same philosophical tradition" as Cudworth and Clarke (Stafford 1985, 136). But once we see that the overwhelming weight of Hutcheson's *Inquiry* was directed against egoism – and that none of it was directed against reason alone rationalism – we realize that from the start Hutcheson was much more concerned to defeat the Negative Answer of Hobbes and Mandeville than he was to refute the rationalism of Cudworth, Clarke, and Balguy.[13]

Why was the anti-egoist goal foremost for Hutcheson? It was foremost because, as I've already noted, Hutcheson thought that moral philosophy was properly a *practical* endeavor. And reason alone rationalism did not constitute the threat to virtue that egoism did. Rationalists such as Cudworth, Clarke, and Balguy believed that there was a real difference between moral good and moral evil, and they believed that human beings could aspire to real moral goodness. They argued *for* the Positive Answer. But Hutcheson's main goal in the *Inquiry* was to defeat the Negative Answer. So for Hutcheson's purposes, distinguishing his view from that of the moral rationalists was relatively unimportant. Insofar as he wanted to combat the self-fulfilling Negative Answer of the egoists, Hutcheson would have taken the rationalists to be on the same side. There is, then, a single deep philosophical commitment to which Hutcheson, Cudworth, Clarke, and Balguy (and Shaftesbury) all adhered: the Positive Answer to the Human Nature Question.[14] And it seems to me that an historiographical approach that attends to this common ground – an approach rooted in thinkers' attitude toward the Human Nature Question – better captures what the philosophers of the period themselves took to be most important, as well as making their writings more continuous with the moral questions people in general have perennially asked.

That said, there can be no doubt that Hutcheson did produce a book, *Illustrations upon the Moral Sense*, that is almost entirely devoted to arguments against reason alone rationalism. And this book (which we will examine in the next chapter) did exert a significant influence on subsequent moral philosophy. Most saliently for our purposes, the anti-rationalist arguments of the *Moral Sense* led Hutcheson to further what we have called a Copernican version of the Positive Answer (this will be the topic of Chapter 13), and the same arguments played a crucial role in the eventual development of Hume's rejection of the Human Nature Question altogether (this will be the topic of Part Four).

But Hutcheson himself did not place as much importance on the *Moral Sense* as subsequent philosophers have done. *The Moral Sense* came out attached to the *Essay on the Nature and Conduct of the Passions and Affections*. And there are no arguments against reason alone rationalism in the *Essay*.

The *Essay*, like the *Inquiry*, is focused on disproving egoism and on providing instruction on how to lead a happy, virtuous life, goals Hutcheson would have expected the reason alone rationalists to agree with. Of course, the *Essay* is attached to *Illustrations upon the Moral Sense*, which does contain arguments explicitly addressed to reason alone rationalism. But in his introduction, Hutcheson suggests that the *Moral Sense* is something of an appendix, if not an afterthought, to the *Essay* (Passions and Affections xiii–xiv). It is the *Essay*, with its practical aim of instilling virtue, that contributes to what Hutcheson took to be the most important goal of moral philosophy. The *Moral Sense* is more of a rear-guard action, Hutcheson's attempt to rebut objections to his view (one of the most important of which is that a moral sense theory damages our commitment to virtue and thus detracts from moral philosophy's practical goal). And that is because Hutcheson did not think the question of whether or not morality originated in reason alone had nearly as much practical importance as the question of whether egoism was true. He didn't seem to think that our commitment to virtue would be greatly affected by the outcome of the reason alone versus moral sense debate.[15] Moreover, in the years between the composition of the *Moral Sense* and his death in 1746, Hutcheson seemed to be more concerned – in his teaching and in the writings that grew out of his teaching – with instilling virtue by advancing the Positive Answer. His conception of the origin of our moral ideas, moreover, seemed to lose some of its strict moral sense character, becoming more similar to the faculty of conscience that Joseph Butler presented as a middle ground between rationalism and the moral sense theory. In examining the *Moral Sense*, consequently, we should probably take ourselves to be looking at only a snapshot – and maybe one of Hutcheson in a pose he did not frequently hold – of Hutcheson's dynamic career.

12

Hutcheson's Attack on Moral Rationalism

In April 1725, shortly after the publication of Hutcheson's *Inquiry*, the rationalist philosopher Gilbert Burnet published a letter in the *London Journal* in which he raised a number of objections to Hutcheson's position. Hutcheson responded to Burnet's letter, Burnet responded to Hutcheson's response, and Hutcheson responded once again. Hutcheson then incorporated much of what he said in the letters in his *Illustrations upon the Moral Sense*, which was published in 1728.

In Section A of this chapter, I outline Burnet's initial rationalist criticisms of Hutcheson's moral sense theory. In B, I explain Hutcheson's first response to Burnet, which is based on a claim about morality that is a clear descendant of Cudworth's 1647 sermons and Shaftesbury's sentimentalist moral psychology and an even clearer ancestor of Hume's "motivational argument" in 3.1.1 of the *Treatise of Human Nature*. In C, I show how Burnet countered Hutcheson's response, with an eye toward elucidating the similarity between Burnet's rationalism and the moral rationalism of Cudworth's EIM. And in D, I explain Hutcheson's response, which consists of an argument that is not only a clear precursor to Hume's "content" arguments of 3.1.1 of the *Treatise* but itself a devastating blow to that rationalist position.

A. Burnet's Initial Rationalist Criticism of Hutcheson's Moral Sense Theory

In the *Inquiry*, Hutcheson had contended that the moral distinctions we make are based on our moral sense: when something elicits from our moral sense the pleasurable feeling of approval we think it virtuous, and when something elicits from our moral sense the painful feeling of disapproval we think it vicious. But in his first letter to Hutcheson, Burnet argued that sense is too uncertain to provide a foundation of moral judgment. Senses can "mislead," Burnet pointed out. They can be "deceitful and wrong," tingeing objects "with false and glaring colors" (Burnet vs. Hutcheson 204).

We can, therefore, put stock in our sensations only after we have determined that they are accurate. We must measure the deliverances of sense against an antecedent rule or standard. But that antecedent rule or standard is something we discern through the use of reason alone. So in the case of morality, we determine whether something is right or wrong through the use of reason alone. We then deem a feeling of approval to be correct if it is elicited by something we have antecedently determined to be virtuous, and deem it to be incorrect if it is elicited by something we have antecedently determined not to be virtuous. Reason gives us the "standard" to judge whether our moral sense is itself "right or wrong" (Burnet vs. Hutcheson 236). As Burnet put it, "The perception of pleasure, therefore, which is the description [Hutcheson] has given of his moral senses, seems to me not to be a certain enough rule to follow. There must be, I should think, something antecedent to justify it, and to render it a real good. It must be a reasonable pleasure before it be a right one or fit to be encouraged or listened to" (Burnet vs. Hutcheson 204).

Burnet also claimed that the feeling of approval presupposes a prior non-feeling-based judgment of moral goodness. We feel approval of something, he argued, only because we have antecedently judged it to be morally worthy. In Burnet's words, "But things do not seem to us to be true or right because they are beautiful or please us, but seem beautiful or please us because they seem to us to be true or right. . . . Thus, in a theorem or problem in geometry we perceive beauty. But we first discern truth or we should never find out any beauty in it. And so in moral science we first conclude that certain action is right and then it appears to us likewise beautiful" (Burnet vs. Hutcheson 205).

For Burnet, then, moral judgment is based in reason. It is reason that tells us whether things are morally good and evil, as well as whether our feelings of approval and disapproval are correct or incorrect. And reason is the faculty that tells us what is true or false. It is through reason that we determine how things really are. So morality must be "founded on truth" (Burnet vs. Hutcheson 200). It cannot be founded on sense, as Hutcheson maintained.

B. Hutcheson's First Response: Reason Alone Cannot Provide Ultimate Ends

Hutcheson responded by first defining reason as "our power of finding out true propositions" (Moral Sense 213; cf. Burnet vs. Hutcheson 209). He next distinguished between two types of true propositions reason can discover: speculative and practical. He dismissed the possibility that speculative reason could be the origin of morality, because morality is practical, or a "rule of conduct" (Burnet vs. Hutcheson 209). And he then explained why practical truths cannot be the origin either.

According to Hutcheson, practical reason is always merely instrumental. Practical reasoning can only inform us of the means to attain ends given to us by our desires. About our ends themselves reason is completely silent (Burnet vs. Hutcheson 209).[1]

Or, rather, about *ultimate* ends, reason is completely silent. About *subordinate* ends, reason can have quite a lot to say. A subordinate end is something we pursue because it is itself the means to another goal. But it's impossible for all of our ends to be subordinate. There has to be an ultimate end at the end of every chain of subordinate ends. There has to be something we want for its own sake, and not only for the sake of something else. And Hutcheson's anti-rationalist claim is that all of our ultimate ends – all the things we pursue for their own sake – are ends for us only because we are affectively disposed to pursue them. No ultimate end is any more reasonable or unreasonable than any other. As Hutcheson put it:

> But are there not also exciting Reasons, even previous to any end, moving us to propose one end rather than another? To this *Aristotle* long ago answered, "that there are *ultimate Ends* desired without a view to any thing else, and *subordinate Ends* or Objects desired with a view to something else." To *subordinate Ends* those *Reasons* or *Truths* excite, which shew them to be conducive to the *ultimate End,* and shew *one Object* to be more effectual than another: thus *subordinate Ends* may be called *reasonable.* But as to the *ultimate Ends,* to suppose *exciting Reasons* for them, would infer, that there is no *ultimate End,* but that we desire one thing for another in an infinite Series. (Moral Sense 217; cf. Burnet vs. Hutcheson 227)

This non-rationalist conception of ultimate ends leads directly to Hutcheson's non-rationalist view of virtue. For Hutcheson believed that virtue consists of acting on one particular ultimate end: the happiness of humanity. Now it's possible that one person might be more effective in pursuing his ultimate end than another person, and so one person might in that sense be more reasonable than the other. But this attribute of reasonability is not what distinguishes the virtuous person from the non-virtuous. A vicious person could be more adept at satisfying his selfish desires than a virtuous person may be at benefiting others. What distinguishes the virtuous person is his ultimate end – that is, that he pursues the happiness of humanity. So since no ultimate end is more reasonable than any other, a virtuous person is not necessarily any more reasonable than a non-virtuous person. Because reason is completely silent about which ultimate ends to pursue, reason cannot tell us that we ought to be virtuous rather than vicious.

Hutcheson made perfectly clear his belief that the virtuous person is not necessarily any more reasonable than the non-virtuous. He said, for instance, that it is just as reasonable for a wholly selfish person to pursue his own satisfaction as it is for a benevolent person to pursue the happiness of others (Moral Sense 224; cf. Burnet vs. Hutcheson 209–10). He also said that if there were fully rational beings who lacked a moral sense, they would have no moral reason whatsoever to prefer a benevolent person to a selfish one (Burnet vs. Hutcheson 211). He even went so far as to say that a malicious being (such as "the Devil") would have just as much reason to harm others as a benevolent being has to benefit them (Moral Sense 242).

I think it's remarkable that Hutcheson produced such an unabashed statement of moral anti-rationalism. For Hutcheson, as we've seen, intended not merely to describe virtue but to instill it. He intended to engage in *practical* philosophy, which means that he intended for his readers to be more committed to morality as a result of reading his books. This goal is just as clear in the preface to the book of which the *Moral Sense* is a part as it is in the preface to the *Inquiry* (Passions and Affections iii–vi, xviii–xix, 320–1; cf. Beauty and Virtue ix–x, 170–3). Hutcheson knew, moreover, that a very common way of recommending morality was to hold that acting virtuously is more reasonable than acting viciously. He knew that belief in the reasonability of virtue was one of the tools most frequently used by those trying to convince people to act virtuously. And we might expect that his desire to instill virtue would lead him to balk a bit at claiming so baldly that selfishness (and malice!) could be just as reasonable as benevolence. Certainly the other practical philosophers we've discussed up to this point would not have countenanced such a claim. But an outright rejection of moral rationalism is where the argument led, and that's where, unabashedly, Hutcheson went.

As we've seen, Burnet objected that sense was too unreliable to be the basis of morality. In responding to this objection, Hutcheson acknowledged that senses can deceive, that we sometimes have to correct our first impressions. But he then went on to present an extensive account of how our moral ideas can originate in sense and yet also be susceptible of correction. This account makes up the better part of the *Essay on the Nature and Conduct of the Passions and Affections*, to which *Illustrations upon the Moral Sense* is attached.

In Chapter 14, we will examine in more detail Hutcheson's account of how to correct moral affections. But for now, when our topic is Hutcheson's initial rejection of moral rationalism, the details can be put aside. The crucial point for our current discussion is Hutcheson's claim that when we correct our moral judgments we are doing something that is fundamentally the same as when we correct our color judgments. And just as the fact that we correct our color judgments doesn't prove that we perceive color through reason alone, so too the fact that we correct our moral judgments doesn't prove that we perceive morality through reason alone. Our color and moral judgments are, corrections notwithstanding, still based in sense.

[L]et us consider the Arguments brought to prove that there must be some Standard of moral Good antecedent to any Sense. Say they, "*Perceptions of Sense* are deceitful, we must have some Perception or Idea of *Virtue* more stable and certain; this must be *Conformity to Reason: Truth* discovered by our *Reason* is certain and invariable: *That* then alone is the Original Idea of Virtue, *Agreement with Reason*." But in like manner our *Sight* and *Sense of Beauty* is deceitful, and does not always represent the true *Forms* of Objects. We must not call that *beautiful* or *regular*, which pleases the *Sight*, or an *internal Sense*; but Beauty in external Forms too, consists in *Conformity* to *Reason*. So our *Taste* may be vitiated: we must not say that *Savour* is perceived by *Taste*, but must place the original Idea of grateful *Savours* in *Conformity to Reason*, and of *ungrateful* in *Contrariety to Reason*. (Moral Sense 230–1)

And again:

But must we not own, that we judge of all our Senses by our Reason, and often correct their *Reports* of the *Magnitude, Figure, Colour, Taste* of Objects, and pronounce them *right* or *wrong*, as they agree or disagree with *Reason*? This is true. But does it then follow, that *Extension, Figure, Colour, Taste*, are not *sensible Ideas*, but only denote *Reasonableness*, or *Agreement with Reason*? Or that these Qualities are perceivable antecedently to any *Sense*, by our *Power of finding out Truth*? . . . All these Sensations [of figure, color, and taste] are often corrected by *Reasoning*, as well as our *Approbations* of Actions as Good or Evil: and yet no body ever placed the *Original Idea of Extension, Figure, Colour, or Taste*, in *Conformity to Reason*. (Moral Sense 236–7)

To be fully convincing, this response needs to be supplemented by a full account of how corrections of the moral sense can occur. But even the simple point of these passages – that an analogy can be drawn between the corrections of the moral sense and the corrections of other senses – succeeds in parrying the initial thrust of Burnet's objection.

C. Burnet's Second Rationalist Criticism

Burnet did not drop the issue, however. He added another aspect to his objection and raised it again, this time focusing his attack directly on the analogy at the core of Hutcheson's response. The analogy Hutcheson relied on was between moral judgment and judgments of color and taste. But, Burnet argued, between these two types of judgments there is a crucial *disanalogy* that Hutcheson failed to appreciate. According to Burnet, if morality exists at all it must exist *necessarily*. "[M]oral good and evil must be immutably fixed" (Burnet vs. Hutcheson 201). And if we have knowledge of morality, it must be knowledge that is absolutely certain. Our moral ideas must be grounded in truths that are "self-evident," "certainly demonstrable," or impossible to doubt, truths that "we cannot but acquiesce in," truths about which we have "as much certainty as we are capable of" (Burnet vs. Hutcheson 223). Morality must be based in propositions that are necessarily true, and to have knowledge of morality we must fully understand that necessity. But the deliverances of sense are not necessarily true propositions, and thus we cannot understand why they *must* be so. The deliverances of sense are, rather, simply contingent results of the interaction between things and our affective mechanisms, and we can experience them as nothing other than brute facts. And correcting our first impressions will not make the deliverances of sense any more necessary nor any more understandable.[2]

Burnet's claim that morality had to be based on necessary truths and that moral understanding has to comprehend that necessity is something we've encountered before. It was the central point of Cudworth's *Eternal and Immutable Morality*, as we saw in Chapter 4. And Burnet's reasons for holding to the necessity of morals thesis and its corresponding epistemological implication were much the same as Cudworth's.[3] They both believed that we can have knowledge of a thing only if we know how it is in and of itself. Knowledge consists of the understanding of a thing's absolute nature, of its necessary characteristics. But what we learn through our senses of color and taste is only how a thing affects us, which may be quite different from how it affects another creature. So our senses of color and taste cannot tell us what is necessarily true of a thing. They cannot give us knowledge of the thing's eternal and immutable nature. Hutcheson's moral sense is, however, just as much a sense as are our senses of color and taste. Our moral sense thus tells us only how we are affected by a thing. It does not tell us how the thing is in and of itself. Our moral sense cannot, therefore, give us moral knowledge. As Burnet put it, "[Hutcheson's] description will only hold as to relative good and evil. It is very true that what affords us pleasure is good relatively to us, and what brings us pain is evil to us. But still what is good to us may be, notwithstanding its being relatively good to us, very evil in itself" (Burnet vs. Hutcheson 201).

So Burnet, like the Cudworth of EIM, believed that if morality exists, it must be necessarily true. And to have moral knowledge, according to Burnet and the Cudworth of EIM, is to be absolutely certain of a moral proposition. Burnet and Cudworth thus both held morality to the epistemic standards of mathematics and logic. Burnet thought, moreover, that our moral judgments could live up to the epistemic standards of math and logic. He thought we could be absolutely certain of certain moral propositions. And this shows, according to Burnet, that Hutcheson was wrong when he claimed that our moral judgments are based in sense.

Burnet backed up his criticism of Hutcheson by presenting moral propositions that, he claimed, are necessarily true and about which we can be absolutely certain. One such proposition was "that it is better that the species should be happy than that it should not" (Burnet vs. Hutcheson 238). Another was "that the public good should be preferred to private good" (Burnet vs. Hutcheson 219). A third was "that every rational agent should study the public good" (Burnet vs. Hutcheson 219). These propositions, Burnet maintained, are self-evident and undeniable, on a perfect epistemic par with the most basic principles of mathematics and logic. As Burnet put it, "If anyone asks why [the public good is preferable to the private good], I would answer him as I would do if he asked me why four is more than two. It is self-evident" (Burnet vs. Hutcheson 233). Or as he said elsewhere, "But if it be farther asked why it is best that the species should be happy, I own no reason can be assigned for it, no more than a reason can be assigned why the whole is equal to all its parts, or a part is less than the whole, or things equal to the same third are equal to one another" (Burnet vs. Hutcheson 238; cf. 219). Every rational being understands these things "immediately with one glance" (Burnet vs. Hutcheson 206). And such understanding has nothing to do with affections. A rational being with entirely malicious affections, or with no affections at all, would still immediately assent to all these moral propositions (Burnet vs. Hutcheson 217–18, 237). We all realize, through the use of reason alone, that these moral propositions are necessarily true. And it is these necessary truths, according to Burnet, that are the origin of our moral ideas and the foundation of virtue.

D. Hutcheson's Second Response: Reason Alone Cannot Provide the Content of Morality

Burnet and Hutcheson agreed about much of the general content of morality. They both believed that to be virtuous is to be committed to benefiting humanity, and not simply to trying to fulfill one's own self-interested desires. But while Burnet believed that that benevolent commitment had to be based on eternal and immutable truth that we ascertain through the use of reason alone, Hutcheson believed that it had to depend on non-rational affection.

How did Hutcheson argue against Burnet's rationalist view? He did so on the basis of a two-pronged strategy. The first prong was a direct toe-to-toe attack on the idea that the content of morality is rationally necessary. The second prong was an attempt to cut off an avenue of rationalist retreat.

The direct toe-to-toe attack consisted of a flat denial that reason alone tells us that it is better to promote the happiness of the many rather than the few. One makes no purely rational mistake, Hutcheson argued, if one prefers the happiness of the few to the happiness of the many. This will appear to be a mistake only to those who have a prior preference for the happiness of the many. As Hutcheson puts it:

If one should still farther inquire, 'Is there not something absolutely reasonable to any possible mind in benevolence or a study of public good? Is it not absolutely reasonable that a being who does no evil to others should not be put to pain by others?' It is very probable every man would say that these things are reasonable. But then all mankind have this moral sense and public affections. But if there were any natures disjoined from us who knew all the truths which can be known but had no moral sense nor anything of a superior kind equivalent to it, such natures might know the constitution of our affairs and what public and private good did mean, they would grant that equal intenseness of pleasure enjoyed by twenty was a greater sum of happiness than if it were enjoyed only by one, but to them it would be indifferent whether one or more enjoyed happiness if they had no benevolent affections. (Burnet vs. Hutcheson 211; cf. 213)

And again:

> In like manner, where [Burnet] says that to a being void of public affections, the pursuing the happiness of twenty rather than his own is reasonable, I want to know the truth exciting such a nature to pursue it. Sure it is not this, that the sum of twenty felicities is a greater quantity than any one of them. For unless by a public affection the happiness of others be made desirable to him, the prospect of a great sum in the possession of others will never excite him more than the knowledge of this truth, that one hundred equal stones are a greater bulk than one, will excite a man who had no desire of heaps to cast them together. (Burnet vs. Hutcheson 228–9; cf. Moral Sense 222–3)[4]

The happiness of twenty people is a greater quantity of happiness than the happiness of one person. But that fact alone does not explain why we should prefer the happiness of twenty to the happiness of one. That fact explains why we should prefer the happiness of twenty only if it is assumed that we have a prior preference for more happiness rather than less. For it makes sense to say that a greater quantity of something is preferable only when there exists a prior preference for that thing. If there is no prior preference for it, then there is no reason to think that a greater quantity of it is preferable. Thus, a being who has no prior preference for happiness does not make a rational mistake when he prefers a lesser quantity of happiness, just as a person who dislikes stones makes no rational mistake when he prefers a lesser quantity of them. Preferring a lesser quantity of happiness doesn't contradict a necessary truth any more than preferring a lesser quantity of stones does. Opting for less of something appears to be unreasonable only if we presuppose that the person doing the opting has a prior preference for more.

But what if a rationalist such as Burnet continued to assert that there *is* something rationally necessary about preferring the happiness of twenty to the happiness of one? What if Burnet continued to assert that preferring the happiness of one to the happiness of twenty *is* self-contradictory? Does Hutcheson's denial amount to simply a counterassertion?[5] Have we reached a stalemate in which the rationalist side insists that a claim is rationally necessary, the moral sense side insists that it isn't rationally necessary, and there is no principled way of choosing between them? I don't believe so. I believe, rather, that the second prong of Hutcheson's anti-rationalist argument gives him the upper hand .

Hutcheson's second prong begins with the question of what we mean by "happiness." Do we mean something that can be cashed out in terms that are entirely non-moral or do we mean something that must remain in morally loaded terms?

Hutcheson conceived of happiness in the first way. He took the happiness of an individual to be the satisfaction of the individual's desires, and he thought the desires of an individual can be cashed out in entirely non-moral terms (Moral Sense 205–6, 228–9; cf. Beauty and Virtue 113).[6] Now if we conceive of happiness in this morally neutral way, then Hutcheson's attack on the rationalism of Burnet looks to be very strong, at least insofar as that rationalism implies that morals must possess the same necessity as mathematics and logic. For Hutcheson's "heap of stones" passage does an excellent job of making the case that the kind of rational necessity possessed by mathematical and logical truths is not possessed by moral principles such as the one that tells us to pursue the happiness of the many rather than the happiness of the few. It is not self-contradictory (or at least not in the way that it is self-contradictory to deny a logical theorem) to prefer the happiness of the few. Reason alone – when it is conceived of entirely on the model of that which underlies mathematics and logic – does not seem to tell us to prefer the happiness of the many.

Others, however, may conceive of happiness in the second way. They may take the happiness of an individual to be roughly equivalent to the good for a person, and they may understand "good" in a sense that is necessarily morally positive. (Taking happiness in a necessarily morally positive sense may be encouraged by the word "benefit," which can do double duty as a morally neutral and morally positive term.) Someone whose notion of happiness already includes a morally positive element, however, has smuggled moral preferability into "happiness."[7] But the important, substantive question is whether the morally neutral happiness of others is morally preferable. The important, substantive question is whether our positive moral regard for the promotion of the morally neutral happiness of humanity depends on our affective nature or is based in reason alone. And Hutcheson's claim is that when you scrub the morally loaded elements out of the concept of happiness, it becomes clear that our moral judgments depend upon our affective nature. As he puts it:

> If any allege, that this is the *justifying Reason* of the *Pursuit of public Good*, "*that it is best all be happy*," then we approve Actions for their *Tendency to that State which is best*, and not for *Conformity to Reason*. But here again, what means *best*? *morally best*? or *naturally best*? If the *former*, they explain the same Word by itself in a Circle: If they mean the *latter*, that "it is the most happy State where all are happy;" then *most happy*, for whom? the *System*, or the *Individual*? If for the *former*, what Reason makes us *approve the Happiness of a System*? Here we must recur to a *Sense* or *kind Affections*. Is it most happy for the *Individual*? Then the Quality moving *Approbation* is again *Tendency to private Happiness*, not *Reasonableness*. (Moral Sense 228–9)

The only way we can give the claim "that it is best all be happy" any substance is by bringing affections into the picture. If we try to understand it by reason alone, we get nowhere.

Here's another way of putting the point. If we conceive of happiness in morally neutral terms, then the claim that the happiness of twenty is, all things being equal, morally preferable to the happiness of one is a synthetic claim. But this synthetic claim is not self-contradictory to deny. It's a claim that lacks the rational necessity of mathematics and logic. If, on the other hand, we conceive of happiness as something that is necessarily morally positive, then the claim that the happiness of twenty is, all things being equal, morally preferable to the happiness of one is an analytic claim. Now analytic claims are self-contradictory to deny, but that is because they are circular, tautological, without substance. So if we take the claim that the happiness of twenty is, all things being equal, morally preferable to the happiness of one in a substantive way, then it will not be rationally necessary; it will have to involve a non-rational affective preference. We can turn the claim into something that is rationally necessary only by emptying it of substantive content (see Moral Sense 229).

Hutcheson did not always make this argument explicit in his discussion of quantities of happiness. But it was clearly what he had in mind when he discussed other moral principles that his rationalist opponents held up as rationally necessary. Clarke, for instance, contended that the following is a self-evident, rationally necessary truth: "whoever first attempts, without the consent of his fellows, and except it be for some public benefit, to take to himself more than his proportion, is the beginner of iniquity" (Raphael 1991, 218). Similarly, William Wollaston contended that it is a self-evident, rationally necessary truth that it is wrong for a man to live "as if he had the estate which he has not" (Raphael 1991, 242). What Clarke and Wollaston were saying is that reason alone tells us that we ought to respect others' property. They were saying that the principles of morality that condemn theft are rationally necessary. Now Hutcheson did not deny the self-evidence of Clarke and Wollaston's statements of the morality of respect for property and the immorality of theft. He pointed out, however, that if these statements are self-evident, it is only because the positive moral status of respect for property and the negative moral status of theft have been smuggled into the descriptions of the relevant actions.

It were to be wished that writers would guard against, as far as they can, involving very complex ideas under some short words and particles which almost escape observation in sentences, such as 'ought,' 'should,' 'as,' 'according' – nay, sometimes in our English gerunds, 'is to be done,' 'is to be preferred,' and such like. Some writers treat the pronoun 'his' as if it were the sign of a simple idea and yet involve under it the complex ideas of property and of a right to natural liberty, as the Schoolmen made space and time to vanish into nothings by hiding them in the adverbs when and where or by including them in the compound words coexistent, corresponding, etc. (Burnet vs. Hutcheson 213–14)

Clarke said that it was wrong, all things being equal, for someone to take more than is *"his."* Wollaston said that it is wrong for someone to make use of something "which he *has* not." But Clarke's "his" and Wollaston's "has" presuppose the morality of respect for property and the immorality of theft. So their principles are rationally necessary only because they are circular or tautologous, without substance (see Moral Sense 228–30, 272–3 and Burnet vs. Hutcheson 213). Substance will come only if we bring a non-rational affective preference into the picture. As Hutcheson put it when summing up his attempt to cut off the rationalist retreat into analytic moral propositions, "Whoever explains *Virtue* or *Vice* by *Justice* or *Injustice*, *Right* or *Wrong*, uses only more ambiguous Words, which will equally lead to acknowledge a *moral Sense*" (Moral Sense 252).

So according to Hutcheson, approval of the promotion of the happiness of humanity is not necessary in the same way that the basic elements of mathematics and geometry are. We can imagine someone with different affections from ours lacking entirely a positive regard for the promotion of humanity's happiness. Imagining such a person is not like trying to imagine the truth of a contradiction, nor like trying to conceive of what it would be like to believe the truth of a contradiction. The lack of positive regard for the promotion of the happiness of humanity is a state of affairs we can make sense of in a way we can't make any sense of the denial of $2 + 2 = 4$ or p or not p. Our moral distinctions, therefore, because they are based on our positive regard for the promotion of the happiness of humanity, must be based in something other than the faculty that informs us of the rationally necessary truths of mathematics and logic. Hutcheson acknowledges that there are some moral principles that might appear to be as impossible to deny as $2 + 2 = 4$ and p or not p. A prime example is the principle that it is wrong to take what does not belong to you, which rationalists often presented as a rationally necessary truth. But such a principle can be necessary only if it is construed in a way that makes it tautological or circular. So while everyone who understands the meaning of the word "belong" might agree that it is wrong to take what does not belong to you, there could still be rational agents who have no positive regard whatsoever for the human institution of property. Perhaps such alien rational agents, once they came to learn English, would agree that when persons say "x does not belong to A" they imply that "A should not take x." But the rational aliens could learn this fact about English and still lack a positive regard for the institution of property. Thus, our positive regard for respect of property cannot be based in reason alone, as beings who shared our rational faculties and who assented to tautological propositions about property could nonetheless lack that regard. Our regard for property must be based in something other than our analytic understanding of the meaning of words such as "belong."

The arguments I've described do not constitute the entirety of Hutcheson's criticisms of moral rationalism. He used different versions of these arguments, mutatis mutandis, to assail many of the specific formulations of moral rationalism that various contemporaries of his presented; Hutcheson was nothing if not thorough. He also spent an inordinate amount of time pummeling the peculiar view of William Wollaston in what was really a pretty unfair fight between a philosophical middleweight and a philosophical featherweight. I believe, however, that we've already seen enough to understand why Hutcheson's attack was so damaging to the kind of early modern moral rationalism that was based on the necessity of morals thesis and its epistemological implication. After Hutcheson, it was very difficult to maintain that our moral judgments are based in propositions that possess the same kind of rational necessity as the most basic mathematical and logical truths. Of course, other versions of moral rationalism would develop, versions that Hutcheson did not anticipate. I do not mean to suggest that we can find in Hutcheson preemptive refutations of the moral rationalism of, say, Reid, Kant, Thomas Nagel, or Michael Smith. But the view that morality must possess the same kind of necessity as mathematics and logic, and that to understand morality is to comprehend that necessity, Hutcheson all but demolished. (This form of moral rationalism thus proved to be less hearty than egoism, which kept returning year after year despite Hutcheson's trenchant criticisms.)

13

A Copernican Positive Answer and an Attenuated Moral Realism

In this chapter, I discuss several important features of Hutcheson's moral sense theory and the worries they gave rise to. In Section A, I explain why Hutcheson thought his theory was a moral realist one and one that secured the Positive Answer – as well as explaining why his rationalist predecessors would have denied that Hutcheson was right about either of these points. In B, I discuss the worry that Hutcheson's theory was incompatible with Christianity and compatible with atheism. In C, I discuss the worry that Hutcheson's theory could not ground a principled resolution to interpersonal moral conflict and thus implied a kind of moral relativism. In D, I discuss the worry that Hutcheson's theory could not ground a principled resolution to conflict within a person and thus left us with no reason to privilege our moral affections over our non-moral ones. And in E, I contrast Hutcheson's strategy for dealing with the last of these worries with the strategy used by Joseph Butler.

A. Attenuated and Robust Moral Realism; Ptolemaic and Copernican Positive Answers

Hutcheson's *Moral Sense* was cause for alarm among rationalists, and not just because it opposed a metaphysical position they had defended. For as the rationalists saw it, morality could not exist unless it was based in eternal and immutable truth. So according to the rationalists, if Hutcheson's anti-rationalist theory were true, we would have to conclude that morality does not exist. And if it turned out that morality did not exist, there would then be no reason to refrain from all manner of selfish, licentious, and violent behavior. We've seen that Hutcheson thought that if people came to believe in Mandevillean egoism, it would have a destructive effect on their conduct. Well, the rationalists thought that belief in Hutcheson's moral sense theory would be similarly deleterious.[1] As the rationalists saw it, every view that implied that moral distinctions were based in affection was equally a threat to morality. It didn't matter to the rationalists whether the affection was selfish or benevolent. The threat was the same.

Hutcheson, of course, did not take himself to be precipitating a moral calamity. He thought that our commitment to morality would be unshaken by the news that there are no eternal and immutable moral truths. Our moral judgments and actions had always been based on our affections, and those affections, Hutcheson believed, would not change just because the rationalist explanation of the origin of moral distinctions had been refuted.

Hutcheson's unconcern about the putatively dire practical consequences of his moral sense theory is particularly evident in his responses to Burnet and in *The Moral Sense*. Moral distinctions, he argues there, originate in the approval or disapproval we feel when we observe others' actions. These approvals and disapprovals do not inform us of "invariable eternal or necessary Truths" (Moral Sense [2nd ed.] 163). They do not necessarily resemble or correspond to anything in the "external" world (Moral Sense 281, 283). They are simply affections we experience. But the discovery that moral distinctions originate in affections does not lessen morality's importance. Virtue and vice will still have all the "reality" we could wish them to have. Their affective origin does not "diminish" them at all.

The *Perception of Approbation or Disapprobation* aris[es] in the Observer, according as the *Affections of the Agent* are apprehended *kind* in their *just Degree*, or *deficient*, or *malicious*. This *Approbation* cannot be supposed an *Image of any thing external*, more than the *Pleasure of Harmony, of Taste, of Smell*. But let none imagine, that calling the *Ideas of Virtue* and *Vice* Perceptions of a *Sense*, upon apprehending the *Actions* and *Affections* of another does diminish their *Reality*, more than the like *Assertions* concerning all *Pleasure* and *Pain, Happiness* or *Misery*. (Moral Sense 283)

Hutcheson's unconcern about his theory's effect on our conduct is also evident in his *Inquiry*. In the first part of the *Inquiry*, Hutcheson explains that all aesthetic judgments originate in the affections of the aesthetic judge. There is, Hutcheson maintains, no absolute beauty, if what we mean by "absolute beauty" is a quality that would be beautiful regardless of the affections of observers. Moreover, our aesthetic affections do not necessarily resemble or correspond to anything in the external world. As Hutcheson put it:

[By] beauty is not understood any Quality suppos'd to be in the Object, which should of itself be beautiful, without relation to any Mind which perceives it: For Beauty, like other Names of sensible Ideas, properly denotes the *Perception* of some Mind; so *Cold, Hot, Sweet, Bitter*, denote the Sensations in our Minds, to which perhaps there is no resemblance in the Objects, which excite these Ideas in us, however we generally imagine that there is something in the Object just like our Perception.... [W]ere there no Mind with a Sense of Beauty to contemplate Objects, I see not how they could be call'd beautiful. (Beauty and Virtue 14–15)

And again:

> There seems to be no necessary Connection of our pleasing Ideas of Beauty with the
> Uniformity or Regularity of the Objects, from the Nature of things, antecedent to
> some Constitution of the Author of our Nature, which has made such Forms pleasant
> to us. Other Minds may be so fram'd as to receive no Pleasure from Uniformity; and
> we actually find that the same regular Forms seem not equally to please all the
> Animals known to us. . . . (Beauty and Virtue 47)

Beauty is mind-dependent. Nothing is beautiful in itself. But this discovery
will not make beauty any less important to us. We will continue to care just
as much about beautiful music and art after coming to believe Hutcheson's
sense-based explanation of beauty, just as we will continue to find certain
foods just as delicious even after we have learned that their deliciousness is
due to the particular structure of our taste buds. And the case of morality,
according to Hutcheson, is the same. Beauty and morality both originate
in our affections. But just as this discovery will not lead us to care any less
about beauty, neither will it enervate our commitment to morality.

So Hutcheson did not take himself to be advancing an error theory. He
did not think that his view threatened the "reality" of morals at all. And
this reveals very clearly that he held to an attenuated conception of the
reality of morals and not to another, more robust conception.[2] According
to the attenuated conception Hutcheson held, there is a real difference
between virtue and vice just so long as there is a difference between the
motives of a virtuous person and the motives of a vicious person. Egoists
denied this sense of the reality of morals in that they held that everyone
is always motivated by self-interest. Hutcheson, of course, argued strenuously against this egoist position, contending that virtuous people are motivated by benevolence, which distinguishes them from vicious people, who
are motivated by selfishness. And so when Hutcheson says that morals are
"real," we can (usually) take him to be asserting that there is a meaningful distinction to be drawn between the motives of the people we correctly
judge to be virtuous and the motives of the people we correctly judge to be
vicious.

At times, Shaftesbury held to the same attenuated conception of the
reality of morals. The attenuated conception was most prominent when
Shaftesbury was attacking Hobbesian egoism (Virtue or Merit 14) and when
he was arguing that morality would maintain all its importance for us even if
we doubted all our beliefs about the external world (see Virtue or Merit 25,
99, which we examined in Chapter 9). At other times, however, Shaftesbury
held to the other, more robust conception. According to the robust conception, morality is real if and only if it originates solely in necessary, eternal, and
immutable truth. Morality, if it is real in this robust way, must be absolute,
independent of every human mind. It is this robust kind of moral reality

that Shaftesbury tried to establish when, in his *Inquiry concerning Virtue, or Merit*, he embedded human conduct in a "system of all things" (Virtue or Merit 11), and it is this robust kind of moral reality that Theocles argued for throughout *The Moralists* (see, for instance, Moralists 266–7).

I have suggested that Shaftesbury was a Janus-faced thinker in that he looked back to a robust, seventeenth-century conception of moral reality and forward to an attenuated eighteenth- and twentieth-century view. When we get to Hutcheson, however, there's no looking back.[3] The kind of moral reality most seventeenth-century rationalists sought – a morality originating entirely in rationally necessary, eternal and immutable, mind-independent truth – Hutcheson completely abjures.

Closely related to the difference between robust and attenuated conceptions of the reality of morals is the difference between the Ptolemaic and Copernican versions of the Positive Answer. Once again, Shaftesbury was Janus-faced toward these two different Positive Answers. And here too we find that Hutcheson clearly looks in only one direction.

According to the Ptolemaic Positive Answer, human nature is good in that it accords with a moral standard that is independent of human nature itself. The Ptolemaic Positive Answer holds that there is a moral measure that exists outside of human minds and that human beings can succeed in living up to that measure. The moral status of human beings is based on how they stand in relation to principles that would exist whether or not any human beings existed.

According to the Copernican Positive Answer, in contrast, there are no moral standards that are independent of human nature. The Copernican Positive Answer holds that human beings can and often do succeed in living up to the standards of morality. But the moral standards human beings can and do succeed in living up to are determined by human nature itself.

The Copernican nature of Hutcheson's Positive Answer is perfectly clear in his answer to one of Burnet's most vociferous objections. Burnet agreed with Hutcheson that we approve of benevolence. But Burnet contended that this affection of approval could be misleading or in need of correction. So the challenge to Hutcheson was to provide a reason for thinking that we're *right* to approve of benevolence – to provide a reason for thinking that approval of benevolence is morally *correct*.

Hutcheson didn't take up this challenge so much as refuse to accept it, contending that it just did not make sense to ask whether our approval of benevolence is right or morally correct. The moral distinctions one draws are based on one's moral sense, and no one can "either *approve* or *disapprove* as *morally good or evil* his own *moral Sense*" (Moral Sense 237). As Hutcheson put it, "But none can apply *moral Attributes* to the very *Faculty* of perceiving *moral Qualities*, or call his *moral Sense morally Good* or *Evil*, any more than he calls the *Power of Tasting, sweet* or *bitter*, or of *Seeing, straight* or *crooked, white* or *black*" (Moral Sense 234). For Hutcheson, the affections of our moral sense determine the standard by which we measure good and evil, and so we cannot morally measure these affections themselves.

Hutcheson accepted that his theory implied that morality depends on an affection we have no reason to believe in. He accepted that he gave us no grounds for thinking that we're right to approve of benevolence. But approval of benevolence, for Hutcheson, is the foundation of morality nonetheless. The foundation of morality is simply a brute fact about human nature. We happen to be constituted in a certain way, and morality issues from our constitution. Beyond this brute fact about human nature there is nowhere for our moral philosophizing to go.[4] Hutcheson thus advances further the Copernican Revolution in moral philosophy that began with Shaftesbury's mental enjoyment account of the reason to be virtuous. According to Hutcheson, we cannot measure human nature against a moral standard that is independent of human nature because all of our moral judgments are rooted in our nature itself. The question of whether humans are good or evil can only be asked *within* human nature. It cannot be asked *about* human nature as a whole.

B. The Moral Sense Theory and God

There were, however, some worries about the moral sense theory that Hutcheson did take very seriously. One of these worries was that the theory was irreligious. Even in this case, however, Hutcheson was concerned to respond only to one version of the worry, and not to two other versions that vexed many of his contemporaries.

A version of the worry that Hutcheson did not seemed concerned about was that the moral sense theory was incompatible with the Scottish Presbyterianism of his father and grandfather. As we've seen, that religion revolved around a Calvinist Negative Answer. According to this view, human nature is so thoroughly corrupt that no one can hope to realize righteousness by relying on his own internal resources. One can learn the requirements of religion only through the revealed word of the Bible, and one can gain salvation only through the external assistance of Christ.

Hutcheson did not say much about specifically religious duty and salvation in his early works. But it's clear that he thought that morality, at least, is internally accessible to every person. He did not think human beings needed Christ or the Bible in order to understand and realize virtue. This is because Hutcheson thought that morality for a person is based on the deliverances of his or her own moral sense. And one will possess the same moral sense whether or not one has had the benefit of Christ or the Bible. Hutcheson did believe that a person's moral sense could become altered for the worse (a topic we'll discuss in detail in Chapter 14). But he did not think everyone's moral sense was ineluctably corrupt. According to Hutcheson, most people in most times and places – Christian and pagan – have possessed moral senses that are basically okay.

Indeed, there is very little in Hutcheson's early works that has any distinctly Christian content at all. Hutcheson said in the preface to his first book that he intended to correct Shaftesbury's one great fault: his "prejudices . . . against Christianity" (Beauty and Virtue xxi; cf. Moral Sense [2nd ed.] 109). And it's true that Hutcheson did not manifest the hostility to Christianity that sometimes percolated up through Shaftesbury's writings. But the only aspect of his own view that Hutcheson explicitly connected to Christianity was the emphasis on benevolence. He claimed, that is, that the benevolence at the center of his moral theory was the same as the love for others that was the essence of Christian virtue (Beauty and Virtue [5th ed.] 151–2). But Hutcheson's route to his assertion of the moral importance of benevolence was incompatible with the religion of his father and grandfather. For while Hutcheson reached that conclusion by attending to humans' actual affective responses, his father and grandfather's Scottish Presbyterianism insisted that human affections were too corrupt to offer any useful guidance to righteousness.

Another version of the worry that Hutcheson seemed unconcerned about was that the moral sense theory allowed that an atheist could be virtuous. It seems that Hutcheson had pretty much the same attitude toward morality and atheism as had Shaftesbury. Both of them thought that belief in a "kind" God was morally useful, that belief in a "wrathful" God was morally destructive, and that atheism was morally neutral (Beauty and Virtue 208; cf. Passions and Affections 175–8, 187–9; Moral Sense 319–29). So Hutcheson did allow that an atheist can be virtuous. And while he did not highlight this feature of his moral sense theory, he did not apologize for it either.

The version of the irreligious worry that Hutcheson did take very seriously was that his moral sense theory was itself atheistic. Hutcheson was willing to allow that atheists could be virtuous, but he also wanted his theory to imply the existence of God.

Hutcheson thus occupied the same halfway house between a religio-theological ethics and a thoroughly secular ethics that Shaftesbury constructed in the first part of his *Inquiry*.[5] He wanted God to play the central role in his account of morality and human nature, even if he was willing to allow that a person did not need to realize that God played this role in order to be virtuous. And Hutcheson wanted his affirmation of God to imply that God's goodness was substantial. He was as disgusted as Whichcote and Cudworth had been with voluntarism's tautological rendering of God's goodness (Beauty and Virtue 274).[6]

Hutcheson tried to show that his theory implied the existence of a morally admirable God by establishing through observation certain a posteriori truths about morality and human nature. But this feature of Hutcheson's thought will stand out most clearly when placed against the backdrop of his responses to two additional worries raised by his moral theory. Let us look at those other worries now.

C. The Moral Sense Theory and Moral Relativism

People come into conflict with each other about moral matters.[7] Moral philosophers have long recognized this fact. But most moral philosophers have also argued that when two people come into conflict about a moral matter, at least one of them must be incorrect.

Rationalists such as Cudworth, Clarke, and Burnet had a very direct and simple way of making this point. Morality, they held, is a purely rational matter. But rationality is universal, objective. If reason alone dictates something to one person, then necessarily it dictates the same thing to every person. So if two people are in conflict about morality, at least one of them must be making some kind of mistake.

There's another position one could take on moral conflict, however: the position of moral relativism. Relativists hold that two people who are in conflict about a moral matter may both be correct in their own way – that there may be no principled, objective grounds for claiming that either person is incorrect. The faultless moral judgment of one person, according to relativists, could bring her into conflict with the faultless moral judgment of another.

There have been philosophical defenses of moral relativism. But traditionally, relativism has been viewed as morally destructive, something that any decent moralist will strive to defeat. If morality exists, according to the traditional view, then it will provide the same objective guidance to every moral agent. If it turns out that some moral conflicts are objectively irresolvable, then we will have to conclude that morality as we conceive of it does not exist or is, at least, something less than we had thought. Relativism has traditionally been taken to imply an error theory of morals.

Hutcheson could not accommodate an a priori rejection of moral relativism. He could not claim that moral relativism was self-contradictory. This is because, for Hutcheson, what is a correct moral judgment for a particular person depends on what that person's moral sense will cause her to feel approval and disapproval for, and because it is logically possible that one person's moral sense will cause her to feel approval for something that another person's moral sense will cause her to disapprove.[8]

Hutcheson also wanted to maintain, however, that it was a contingent but nonetheless true fact that the moral sense of every person takes him or her to the same place as every other. Hutcheson wanted to show that mistake-free moral conflict is logically possible but psychologically impossible. So while he did not start from an objective conception of moral judgment, he tried to reach a position that was its practical equivalent. Or to put the matter another way, the relativist idea that two people in moral conflict may both be correct is something that Hutcheson could not reject on a priori grounds. So he set out instead to show that there were conclusive a posteriori grounds for its rejection. Hutcheson's moral sense was not "universal" if what we mean by that word is that it holds on all possible worlds. But he tried to show that it was "universal" in the sense that it holds for every human on this world (Beauty and Virtue 75, 168, 196, 202, 216).

How did Hutcheson go about trying to show this? He could not do it by armchair introspection based on purely rational principles. He needed, rather, to go out in to the world and observe what people were actually like. He needed to engage in an activity that was closer to psychology (perhaps combined with some sociology and anthropology) than to the rationalists' a priori philosophy.[9]

Of course, it was not a foregone conclusion that Hutcheson's psychological observations would establish conclusive a posteriori grounds for his belief that all humans' moral senses were uniform enough to serve as a practical equivalent of objectivity. We will have to examine the arguments before passing judgment on his response to the worry of moral relativism. Before we do that, however, let us look at another worry to which Hutcheson's moral sense theory gave rise to.

D. The Moral Sense Theory and Internal Conflict

This other worry concerns the possibility of conflict within a single individual. To appreciate the sharpness of this worry for Hutcheson, recall that at the beginning of both the *Inquiry* and the *Essay*, he strenuously insisted on the existence of different sources of affections within each person (Beauty and Virtue x–xiv; Passions and Affections 1–26). He called each of these sources a "sense." Everyone is familiar, of course, with the five external senses. But, according to Hutcheson, there are numerous others senses as well. There is an aesthetic sense, which gives rise to love of uniformity amid diversity; a public sense, which gives rise to the desire to benefit humanity; a moral sense, which gives rise to approvals and disapprovals; a sense of honor, which gives rise to the desire for others' esteem; and perhaps several other kinds of sense besides (Passions and Affections 4–6).[10]

The worry is that the ultimate end of one sense will come into conflict with the ultimate end of another sense. Hutcheson contends that there is no necessary connection between the affections of a sense and the objects that evoke those affections. But by the same token, he also has to allow that there is no necessary connection between the affections of one sense (as provoked by an object) and the affections of another sense (as provoked by the same object). Each Hutchesonian sense is a separate source of affections. And there is nothing in Hutcheson's theory that gives us a priori grounds for thinking that all the natural sources of affection within a person will always be in harmony (Passions and Affections 127–8).[11]

This worry about the possibility of conflict between the senses of a single individual is far from a mere academic quibble. Worrying about such internal conflict is tantamount to worrying about why we should be moral when morality conflicts with our other desires, and that question is central to reflective thinking about how to live.

Hutcheson himself highlighted this issue when he said that if there were an insuperable conflict between our moral and non-moral affections, we would have to deny "the Reality of Virtue" (Beauty and Virtue xi; cf. viii–ix, 269–70, and Moral Sense 277–8). The particular kind of conflict Hutcheson had in mind when he made that comment was between morality and self-interest.[12] But in other places, Hutcheson takes just as seriously the possibility of conflict between the moral sense and the public sense, between the moral sense and the sense of honor, between the public sense and the moral sense, and between those three "social" senses and various other (non-social) internal and external senses as well (Passions and Affections 126–60).

What if one of the other senses does turn out to be in irresolvable conflict with the moral sense? Why should morality have a more authoritative claim on our conduct than, say, self-interest or honor or aesthetic pleasure? Hutcheson's insistence that morality originates in a *sense* threatens to preclude him from giving a principled answer to this question. He cannot, of course, claim that the moral affections are more truthful or reasonable than the other affections, as he had, when arguing against the rationalists, asserted time and time again that vicious affections can be just as "in conformity with truth" and "reasonable" as virtuous ones. Nor can he offer any sense-transcendent justification for granting one source of affections decisive authority over all the others. He cannot allow the existence of a normative ground that is distinct from the senses and thus able to provide principled adjudication between them. So what reason can he give for the moral affections' trumping the non-moral?

Here's another way of putting Hutcheson's problem. Imagine that you have to choose between spending time in one room or another. Everything will be the same regardless of which room you choose, except that one room has wonderful music playing but hideous wallpaper, while the other room has delightful wallpaper but terrible music. In such a case, there is no sense-transcendent reason for you to choose one room over the other. It seems reasonable to hold that your auditory and visual senses have the same normative status. So you might as well choose the room that satisfies your stronger (as opposed to a more authoritative or normatively superior) desire. Well, Hutcheson's insistence that morality is based in a sense puts morality on a normative par with other senses in the same way that your auditory and visual senses are on a normative par with each other. This insistence implies that moral affections cannot normatively trump non-moral ones. And so it seems that in the case of internal conflict,

Hutcheson can give us no reason not to choose to conduct ourselves simply in accord with whichever of our desires – moral or nonmoral – happens to be strongest.[13]

To dispel the worries about internal conflict, Hutcheson had to develop a response that was parallel to his response to the worry of moral relativism. He had to show that while it was conceivable that one's natural sources of affection would conflict with each other, such conflict would never actually occur in practice. He had to argue that while conflict between one's ultimate ends was logically possible, it was psychologically impossible – that it turned out to be a contingent fact but nonetheless true that the room with delightful wallpaper also always happened to have the best music playing. And as we will see, the arguments Hutcheson would use to dispel the worries about internal conflict and moral relativism also turned out to be the basis of his attempt to give a morally admirable God a firm place at the center of his account of morality and human nature. Elucidating those arguments will be the goal of the next chapter.

E. Butler and Hutcheson on Internal Conflict

Let me close this chapter by contrasting Hutcheson's strategy of trying to show the contingent connection between all the senses with Butler's view of the authority of the source of moral distinctions. Butler agreed with Hutcheson that within each person are different sources of motive and concern – particular appetites, benevolence, self-love, and conscience are the sources Butler talked about most often. And Butler also agreed with Hutcheson that these sources all ultimately harmonize with each other (Butler 76, 92–3, 108–9). But Butler differed from Hutcheson in claiming that even if these different kinds of reasons *did* conflict, we would still have conclusive reasons to act morally (Butler 14–16). Unlike Hutcheson, Butler argued that moral reasons do trump other sorts of reasons, that the former do possess a normative status that is intrinsically superior to the latter. The key to Butler's view was his belief that our different internal principles form an "economy," "constitution," or "system" in which certain principles are designed to fulfill functions that others are not, and in which certain principles are designed to have authority over others (Butler 8). Most importantly, Butler claimed that our constitution is one in which conscience has "authority" over every other internal principle – that our nature is a system in which conscience has "supremacy" or normative priority (Butler 9; cf. 10–14 and 51–76).

Hutcheson couldn't avail himself of a Butlerian teleology and thus affirm the normative superiority of moral reasons because Hutcheson committed himself to holding that every source of motive and concern is equally a *sense* – because the origin of moral distinctions in Hutcheson's theory was a sense in a strong, strict way and not merely in a weakly metaphorical way. Hutcheson was driven to equate the origin of our moral distinctions to the external senses at least partly by his accedence to Locke's attack on innate ideas (Beauty and Virtue xv–xvi, 82–3, 135, 200–4, 271–2; Moral Sense 142).[14] Hutcheson did not want the internal principles on which morality is based to be mistaken for the innate ideas that Locke had discredited. He took pains, therefore, to make it clear that the internal principles in question were non-rational, or sensory. He took pains to assimilate them to the external senses (Beauty and Virtue xi–xiii, 11; Passions and Affections 1–6). The same sort of consideration is part of what led Shaftesbury to base virtue in a moral sense. But Shaftesbury's attitude toward this result was considerably more casual than Hutcheson's. Shaftesbury was concerned to refute the Negative Answers of Hobbes and the Calvinists, but he did not seem to care very much about whether the Positive Answer he affirmed involved innate ideas or a moral sense. Indeed, it seems to me that Shaftesbury opted for a moral sense not necessarily because he thought Locke's anti-innatist arguments were sound but simply because he wanted to make his point about the Positive Answer without getting bogged down in abstruse, academic details.[15] Hutcheson, in contrast, was much less likely to avoid abstruse details if that was where he thought the argument led. He, too, had the practical goal of instilling virtue in his readers by convincing them of a self-fulfilling Positive Answer, but once he decided that virtue originated in a moral sense and not in innate ideas, he made a clear and unambiguous commitment to that position. As a result, Hutcheson did more than Shaftesbury to work out the full implications of the view that virtue originates in sense rather than in reason alone, and he got saddled with some of the more profound problems as a result. (Hutcheson's willingness to follow the argument where it led, even if it resulted in unexpected or counterintuitive results, is one more way in which he is a transitional figure between Shaftesbury and Hume; no one was more willing to follow an argument through to unexpected or counterintuitive results than Hume.)

Hutcheson was probably more rigorous than Butler in this respect as well. Butler remained above the fray between innatists and empiricists, and between rationalists and moral sense theorists (Butler 4–5; Raphael 1991, 378–9). He did not commit himself one way or the other on the topics of these debates. And for the practical purposes of his sermonizing, this neutrality might have been appropriate (see Butler 5–6). But it left some philosophical loose ends dangerously dangling. Is the idea that conscience is normatively superior a deliverance of reason, and if so, how is it rationally justified? Or is the idea an affectively grounded judgment, and if so, why does the affection on which it is grounded have a normative status that is superior to that of any other affection? Teleological considerations play a large role in Butler's account of the superiority of conscience. We are, that is, supposed to be able to read the superiority of conscience off of our own internal constitution; we are supposed to be able to grasp conscience's authority from an observation of how we are designed. But Butler's evidence for these teleological claims seems to be almost entirely phenomenological: he relies on our agreeing with him that conscience has "marks of authority" we can perceive from the inside of our moral experience, that conscience presents itself to us in a way that "carries its own authority with it" (Butler 13, 71). And while, once again, this way of proceeding might have been appropriate to Butler's sermonizing context, it leaves some important philosophical questions unanswered. For instance, what would Butler say to those – such as Plato's Thrasymachus, Hobbes' fool, and Hume's sensible knave – who would deny the existence of the phenomenological features on which Butler rests morality's authority? And what would Butler say to people who agree with his description of the phenomenology but are skeptical about whether the phenomenology constitutes any good reason for granting authority to morality? Why should we trust the phenomenology? To provide answers to these questions, one may have no choice but to enter the fray between innatists and empiricists, and between rationalists and moral sense theorists. And that is what Hutcheson, but not Butler, did.

Not surprisingly, Shaftesbury straddled some of these differences between Butler and Hutcheson. Butler claimed that teleological considerations reveal that conscience has a normative status that is superior to our other sources of motive and concern. And Shaftesbury, too, when presenting his teleological account of our moral ideas, implied that our moral ideas have normative authority because they inform us of a human mind-independent moral reality. Hutcheson, in contrast, placed moral ideas on the same normative playing field as other natural sources of motive and concern and then tried to show that none of these sources is actually in competition with another. And Shaftesbury, in his mental enjoyment account of the reason to be virtuous, developed a similarly normatively flattened defense of our obligation to virtue. Now if we take Shaftesbury's primary goal to be the practical one of convincing people to live morally, then perhaps the differences between his two accounts might not be to his discredit. Shaftesbury first presented his teleological account of the reason to be moral, and this may have convinced some people that they ought to live a life of virtue. But he also realized that some people would not accept the metaphysical baggage that came along with the teleological account. So he then presented his mental enjoyment account, which provided a reason to live virtuously that would speak even to those who rejected the teleology Shaftesbury had relied on earlier. Shaftesbury tried to show, in other words, that two people who differ on certain abstruse metaphysical issues would nonetheless both have conclusive reasons to be virtuous. But, as with Butler, this does leave some important philosophical questions unanswered.

Let me note, finally, that Hume seemed to realize that Hutcheson's moral sense theory from the 1720s was incompatible with Butler's privileging of conscience, and he also seemed to realize that in his later years Hutcheson was drawn toward a more Bulterian position. As Hume put it in a 1743 letter to Hutcheson, "You seem [now] to embrace Dr Butler's Opinion in his Sermons on human Nature; that our moral Sense has an Authority distinct from its Force and Durableness, & that because we always think it *ought* to prevail. But this is nothing but an Instinct or Principle, which approves of itself upon reflection; and that is common to all of them" (Letters, 47).

14

Explaining Away Vice, or Hutcheson's Defense of a Copernican, Theistic Positive Answer

In the previous chapter, we saw that Hutcheson's moral sense theory gave rise to a number of worries: the worry of moral relativism, the worry about internal conflict, and the worry about finding a place for God. In this chapter, I examine how Hutcheson tried to dispel these worries. In Section A, I outline the general shape of Hutcheson's response, explaining why he thought that establishing an *explanatory asymmetry* between virtue and vice could dispel all the worries in one fell swoop. In B, I describe the details of Hutcheson's argument for this all-important explanatory asymmetry – an argument that relies on his use of the Lockean notion of the association of ideas. And in C, I sum up Hutcheson's Positive Answer and point to some aspects of it that Hume would later target.

A. Hutcheson's Need for Explanatory Asymmetry

Hutcheson acknowledged that people sometimes have moral conflicts with one another and that individuals sometimes have within themselves conflicting passions (Passions and Affections 127–8, 146–54). But he believed that all of these interpersonal and intrapersonal conflicts were due to one of two things: either a false belief or an unnatural affection.

Hutcheson's view of false beliefs leading to interpersonal moral conflict is pretty easy to explain (Beauty and Virtue 196–202). If one person believes that a course of action will create great happiness for humanity and another person believes that the same course of action will create great unhappiness, then the two of them will have different views about the moral status of that course of action. But at least one of them must have a false belief. They cannot both have the facts right. As Hutcheson explains in a section entitled "All Mankind agree in this general Foundation of their Approbation or moral Actions. The Grounds of the different Opinions about Morals":

We may perhaps commit Mistakes, in judging that Actions tend to the publick Good, which do not; or be so stupidly inadvertent, that while our Attention is fix'd on some *partial good Effects*, we may quite over-look many *evil Consequences* which counter-ballance the *Good*. Our *Reason* may be very deficient in its Office, by giving us partial Representations of the tendency of Actions; but it is still some *apparent species* of *Benevolence* which commands our Approbation....It is therefore to no purpose to alledge here, 'That many Actions are really done, and approv'd, which tend to the *universal Detriment*.' For the same way, Actions are often perform'd, and in the mean time approv'd, which tend to the *Hurt* of the *Actor*. But as we do not from the *latter*, infer the *Actor* to be void of *Self-Love*, or a *Sense* of *Interest*; no more should we infer from the *former*, that such Men are void of a *Sense* of *Morals*, or a desire of *publick Good*. The matter is plainly this. Men are often mistaken in the Tendency of Actions either to *publick*, or *private Good*....(Beauty and Virtue 197–9)

Someone may think something is virtuous while I may think it is not. But that does not show that she and I are in any real *moral* conflict. According to Hutcheson, both of our judgments are almost certainly based on approval of that which promotes the happiness of humankind. It's just that she believes that certain things promote happiness, while I believe they do not. Our conflict is due to "Different Opinions of . . . the most effectual Means to advance" human happiness (Beauty and Virtue 200).

Hutcheson's view of how false beliefs can lead to internal conflict is similar but also depends on an empirical belief of his own. According to Hutcheson, the most common cause of internal conflict is a perceived incompatibility between self-interest and morality: people who suffer internal conflict usually do so because they believe that living in accord with their moral senses is incompatible with promoting their own happiness (Beauty and Virtue 171–2; cf. Passions and Affections vii–ix). Hutcheson maintains, however, that self-interest and morality coincide (Beauty and Virtue 242–69; cf. Passions and Affections 136–65). As he puts it after a long discussion of how an individual's happiness is affected by "the pleasures and pains of the several senses": "We see therefore, upon comparing the several kinds of Pleasures and Pains, both as to *Intention* and *Duration*, that 'the whole Sum of Interest lies upon the Side of *Virtue*, *Publick-spirit*, and *Honour*. That to *forfeit* these Pleasures in whole, or in part, for any other *Enjoyment*, is the most foolish Bargain; and on the contrary, to secure them with the *Sacrifice* of all others, is the *truest Gain*'" (Passions and Affections 165). A person who lives in accord with her moral sense will in the long run be happier than a person who does not. The coincidence of morality and self-interest is not an obvious fact. But, Hutcheson believes, if we conduct a detailed empirical examination of human psychology and the long-term effects of benevolence and selfishness, we will eventually discover that this coincidence of self-interest and morality does hold. Those who believe that what morality asks of them conflicts with their self-interest are factually mistaken.[1]

Hutcheson believed that many interpersonal and internal conflicts were due to these kinds of false beliefs. But he did not think false beliefs could account for *all* conflicts. Some conflicts, he contended, are based in causes that cannot be immediately counteracted by an accurate apprehension of facts. The causes of these more recalcitrant conflicts are *unnatural affections*. According to Hutcheson, while all people who have natural affections and are in possession of the same non-moral facts will be in perfect harmony with each other and within themselves, people who possess *unnatural* affections may experience conflict even when they do know all the relevant non-moral facts. To explain this view, we need first to describe Hutcheson's conception of the difference between natural and unnatural affections.[2]

Hutcheson does not provide a crisp, completely unambiguous account of the difference between natural affections and unnatural ones, but it's pretty clear what he has in mind. A natural affection is a "rooted," "original," or "implanted" part of our constitution, something that is hard-wired in our makeup (Beauty and Virtue 216, 270; cf. Passions and Affections 43, 105, 198–9; Moral Sense 290). It's a disposition "to which we are inclined by some part of our Constitution, antecedently to any *Volition of our own*; or which flow[s] from *Principles* in our Nature, not brought upon us by our own *Art*, or that of others" (Passions and Affections 198–9).[3] A natural affection cannot be explained by experience or by our interactions with the world. It does not result from habit, education, or custom. Natural affections can be used to explain aspects of human behavior, but they themselves cannot be explained by other aspects. Natural affections are the fundamental building blocks of empirical explanation. They are the points at which empirical explanations of human behavior begin. Our empirical explanations cannot get behind them.[4]

An unnatural affection, in contrast, is an affection that is at least partly the result of experience's having changed our original constitution. Unnatural affections have the shape they do because our natural tendencies have been altered by custom, education, and habit. There is thus an *explanatory asymmetry* between natural and unnatural affections. Natural affections do not admit of empirical explanation, while unnatural affections can be explained by the effects of experience on our natural affections.[5]

According to Hutcheson, all of us are naturally constituted to agree with others and to be in harmony with ourselves.[6] Our natural, or original, affections are all in perfect accord. Our natural affections, moreover, are all either benevolent or consistent with benevolence. We are all naturally constituted to care about things in a way that makes our interests coincide with each other and with the interests of other people.[7]

Thus, according to Hutcheson, all moral conflict results either from false beliefs or from our having been wrenched away from our natural affections. And once we see that, we can understand why Hutcheson might have thought that the worries about his moral theory that we described in the previous chapter can be laid to rest.

One of the worries, recall, was that Hutcheson was committed to moral relativism – that he had to hold that individuals with wildly varying moral judgments might at times be equally correct. But if Hutcheson's views about false beliefs and unnatural affections are true, he can claim that whenever individuals are in conflict with each other about whether something is virtuous, at least one of them will possess a false belief or will have responded from an unnatural affection. Hutcheson's theory cannot accommodate the idea that the moral judgments of everyone *necessarily* coincide (Passions and Affections 46). But in its place he can put a weaker kind of moral objectivity, or moral objectivity's practical equivalent. As he explains:

> If [one asks], "How are we sure that what *we* approve, *all others* shall also approve?" Of this we can be sure upon *no Scheme*; but 'tis highly probable that the *Senses* of all Men are pretty *uniform*. . . . Now since the *Probability that Men shall judge truly*, abstracting from any presupposed *Prejudice*, is greater than that *they shall judge falsely*; 'tis more probable, when our Actions are really *kind* and *publickly useful*, that *all Observers* shall judge *truly* of our *Intentions*, and of the *Tendency* of our Actions, and consequently approve what *we* approve our selves, than that they shall judge *falsely* and condemn them. (Moral Sense 280)

That people with true beliefs and natural affections make congruent moral judgments is a contingent fact. It's logically possible that one person could have natural moral affections that conflict with the natural moral affections of someone else. But moral harmony among people who have true beliefs and are responding from their natural affections is a fact nonetheless, and this fact, contingent though it is, is sufficient for dispelling the worry of moral relativism.

Another one of the worries was internal conflict – that Hutcheson's theory of morality and human nature left him no way of satisfactorily resolving conflicts between morality and self-interest.[8] Many moralists have tried to handle such conflicts by developing reasons for privileging morality over self-interest. But, as we have seen, Hutcheson's moral sense theory prevented him from taking that route. So what Hutcheson tried to show instead is that worries about why we should be moral when it conflicts with self-interest need not concern us because if we know all the facts and our affections have their natural shape, such conflicts will never arise. Here's how he described this goal:

> Now the principal Business of the *moral Philosopher* is to shew, from solid Reasons, That *universal Benevolence* tends to the Happiness of the *Benevolent*. . . . Let the Obstacles from *Self-love* be only remov'd, and Nature it self will incline us to *Benevolence*. Let the Misery of *excessive Selfishness*, and all its Passions, be but once explain'd, that so *Self-love* may cease to counteract our *natural Propensity* to *Benevolence*, and when this *noble* Disposition gets loose from these Bonds of *Ignorance*, and false Views of *Interest*, it shall be assisted even by *Self-love* and grow strong enough to make a *noble virtuous Character*. (Beauty and Virtue 269–70; cf. Beauty and Virtue xi-xii and Passions and Affections viii–ix)

Rather than claim that the moral sense trumps, or is in some sense superior to or more authoritative than self-interest, Hutcheson tried to show that even though morality and self-interest are on a normative par, morality still will not be threatened. That's not to say that Hutcheson could hold that the coincidence of morality and self-interest was a *necessary* fact.[9] He thought morality and self-interest coincided, but not because he defined one in terms of the other or claimed that there was some logical link between them. Morality, for Hutcheson, is based in the moral sense. Self-interest involves other senses. And Hutcheson had to allow that it was possible that the deliverances of the moral sense could come into conflict with the deliverances of other senses (Moral Sense 276–7). Moral and non-moral senses are distinct aspects of our psychology that logically could come into conflict. It just so happens, Hutcheson argued, that conflict between them never actually occurs.

Hutcheson's response to the worry about internal conflict thus rested on a contingent fact about the coincidence of psychologically distinct sources of affection, just as his response to the challenge of interpersonal moral conflict did. He did not try to establish that our moral affections possess intrinsic intrapersonal privilege but rather offered a kind of practical equivalent of morality's authority. If our ideas of virtue proceed from true beliefs and our natural moral sense, we will have no reason to act contrary to them.

So Hutcheson's responses to the worries about moral relativism and internal conflict rested on the contingent fact that all of our natural affections are in harmony – that is, that all the natural affections within me are in harmony with each other, and that all of my natural affections are in harmony with all of your natural affections. Now it's important to note that Hutcheson did not and could not provide a naturalistic explanation of the fact that all of our natural affections harmonize, as natural affections were themselves the most basic elements of Hutcheson's naturalistic explanations of human behavior. This lack of any naturalistic explanation for such pervasive affective harmony might seem to be a great weakness of Hutcheson's theory. Indeed, from a thoroughly naturalistic perspective, it is just this feature of Hutcheson's theory that makes Hume's account of morality and human nature superior, for Hume does provide a naturalistic explanation for both the coincidence of virtue and self-interest and the coincidence of the interests and moral judgments of different people. (Another difference is that Hume claims that these coincidences hold only generally, not absolutely; this might be another way in which his account looks to be superior to – truer to the observed phenomena than – Hutcheson's.) From Hutcheson's perspective, however, this apparent weakness was actually a strength, for it was just this feature that enabled him to respond to the remaining worry.

This remaining worry was that God could find no role to play in Hutcheson's account of morality and human nature.[10] This was a worry for Hutcheson because although he was willing to allow that an atheist could be virtuous, he still wanted his philosophy to imply the existence of a morally good God. Now according to Hutcheson's view of human nature, as we've seen, every human has certain natural affections. These affections are "rooted," "original," or "implanted" parts of our constitution. They have not been caused by anything else in the natural world. Hutcheson believed that empirical observation revealed that these natural affections are all in perfect harmony with each other – that if all of our affections were in their natural state, we'd all be benevolent and happy, in perfect accord with ourselves and with others. But how can we account for the wonderfully harmonized character of all of our implanted affections? We cannot attribute it to natural causes, as our natural affections are just those that do not admit of further natural explanation. So we must attribute our natural affective harmony either to chance or to the design of a supernatural Creator. It's wildly unlikely, however, that chance would produce such an exquisite harmony. That would be like throwing 10,000 dice and getting all sixes on our first roll. Overwhelmingly more likely is that our natural constitution was the design of a supernatural Creator (see Beauty and Virtue 47–72). And this Creator must care a lot about our welfare, as He designed us to be in perfectly happy harmony with each other and with ourselves. As Hutcheson put it after explaining the relationship between the public and private senses, "This account of our Affections will, however, prepare the way for discerning considerable Evidences for the *Goodness of the Deity*, from the Constitution of our Nature. . . . [I]f the preceding Account be just, we see [that] every Passion or Affection in its *moderate Degree* is innocent, many are directly *amiable*, and *morally good*: we have *Senses* and *Affections* leading us to *publick Good*, as well as to *private*; to *Virtue*, as well as to external Pleasure" (Passions and Affections 86–7). And as he put it after arguing against Mandeville's empirical explanation of our moral ideas:

"[Our] Perception of *moral Good* is not deriv'd from *Custom, Education, Example,* or *Study*." These give us no new Ideas. . . . [T]hey never could have made us apprehend Actions as *amiable* or *odious*, without any Consideration of our own *Advantage*. It remains then, "That as the Author of Nature has determin'd us to receive, by our *external Senses*, pleasant or disagreeable Ideas of Objects, according as they are useful or hurtful to our Bodies; and to receive from *uniform Objects* the Pleasures of *Beauty* and *Harmony*, to excite us to the Pursuit of Knowledge, and to reward us for it; or to be an Argument to us of his *Goodness*, as the *Uniformity* it self proves his *Existence*, whether we had a *Sense* of *Beauty* in *Uniformity* or not: in the same manner he has given us a Moral Sense, to direct our Actions, and to give us still *nobler Pleasures*; so that while we are only intending the *Good* of others, we undesignedly promote our own greatest *private Good*." (Beauty and Virtue 134–5)

The naturalistically inexplicable harmony of our affections is, for Hutcheson, itself an argument (an abductive or best explanation argument) for the existence of a benevolent God.[11]

Hutcheson also thought he could hold that God is morally good, since he equated moral goodness with benevolence (Moral Sense 239–42). In making this additional point, Hutcheson did not provide a completely non-circular account of God's goodness in that he had to hold both that we judge God to be good because we approve of His benevolence and that we approve of God's benevolence because He has designed us to do so.[12] But Hutcheson seemed to think that since it is impossible for us to seriously doubt that benevolence is morally good, a proof of God's benevolence will be completely adequate for the purposes of inspiring love and admiration for God.[13]

Having explained Hutcheson's responses to the three worries, we can now describe his answer to yet another pressing question. Hutcheson noted that most people "have many Suspicions about Tempers or Dispositions formed by *Art*; but are some way prepossessed in favour of what is *natural*" (Passions and Affections 197). And Hutcheson believed that there was an important sense in which this common belief was true (Passions and Affections 199–203). Hutcheson wanted us to keep our affections in their natural shape. He wanted us to act and judge naturally, to withstand or counteract the effects of custom, education, and habit. But why? What reason do we have for thinking that being natural is better than being unnatural? Hutcheson's answer was this: being natural brings all one's affections into harmony, brings one into harmony with one's fellows, and brings one into harmony with God's original design.

Hutcheson's account of natural human affections is, then, a clear Positive Answer. For according to this account, we are all naturally benevolent, moral, and happy. And if this account is accurate, Hutcheson can claim to have successfully dispelled a number of serious worries about his moral sense theory and also to have vindicated the common belief that our "natural" principles are superior to any tendency that has been brought about by "art."

B. Hutcheson's Fantastick Association of Ideas

So Hutcheson has a lot riding on the claim that if our natural affections are in their natural state they will all harmonize with each other. But is this claim accurate? Are our disagreeable and discordant tendencies always the result of false beliefs or alterations to our original constitution?

Hutcheson supports this claim by arguing that there is an explanatory asymmetry between our harmonious affections, on the one hand, and our disagreeable, discordant affections, on the other: he contends that the former do not admit of empirical explanation and are therefore natural, while the latter can be explained by the corrupting effects of custom, education, and habit and are therefore unnatural. It is this explanatory asymmetry that allows him to rebuff the threats to his moral theory and to assert a Positive Answer that is both Copernican and theistic. But how does Hutcheson go about trying to establish this all-important explanatory asymmetry? How does he try to show that if we have the facts right, natural affections will always lead to harmony, and that any discord must be due to affections that are unnatural?

What Hutcheson cannot do is simply apply the label "natural" to affections that are agreeable and harmonious and the label "unnatural" to affections that are disagreeable and discordant. That would beg all the questions to which he must provide principled answers. Hutcheson himself, moreover, acknowledges that few of our responses are based entirely on our purely natural constitution. Experience has "depraved" almost all of our affections to at least some extent (Passions and Affections xvi). Hutcheson must therefore *infer* the shape of our natural affections from the less-than-purely-natural judgments people actually make, "abstracting from particular Habits or Prejudices" that have altered their original tendencies (Passions and Affections xvi; cf. 29, 181, 201–3). But what principled reason can he give us for thinking that, from his observations of the responses people actually have, he has correctly inferred the character of our natural affections? He says that when we "abstract from particular Habits or Prejudices" we find that all of our natural affections are harmonious and agreeable. But what method does he use to perform this "abstracting" task?

He uses a method that is based on a notion he learned from Locke: the association of ideas. Let us now sketch how Locke developed that notion and then examine the use to which Hutcheson puts it.

Locke believed that all humans possess the "native Faculty to perceive the Coherence, or Incoherence of [their] *Ideas*" (Locke 1975, 671). By the use of this "perceptive faculty of the mind" or "reason" we can, according to Locke, come to see whether any two ideas agree or disagree with each other.

Lockean demonstration consists in tracing these agreements or connections between ideas. Sometimes we see immediately that ideas agree. At other times we must interpose one or more intermediate ideas in order to see the natural connection between two "extreme" ideas. But even in the latter case the demonstration still turns on our native faculty to perceive the coherence or incoherence of individual ideas, since that is the faculty that enables us "to discover what connexion there is in each link of the Chain, whereby the Extremes are held together" (Locke 668). We do not need to be familiar with the rules of logic or the forms of syllogism in order to trace these connections, since those rules and forms only codify types of demonstrations that our native faculty has antecedently affirmed. Rather, when ideas are laid out before us, we can see "what connexion they have, and so [are] able to judge of the Inference, without any need of a Syllogism at all" (Locke 676).

Of course, Locke acknowledges that people err in their thinking, his belief in each person's "native Faculty" notwithstanding. He blames the mistakes on "associations of ideas," which, he says, are "the foundation of the greatest, I had almost said, of all the Errors in the World" (Locke 401).

Associations of ideas cause errors by leading people to believe that two ideas are connected when in fact they are "loose and independent one of another" (Locke 397). Ideas that "have in Nature nothing to do one with another" become, as a result of association, confounded in our mind so that we come to think there is a natural connection between them when in fact there is none (Locke 398).

The causes of these unnatural connections or associations are education and custom. If we frequently conjoin two unrelated ideas, either as a result of instruction, repetition, or traumatic experience, we may come to think of them as naturally connected. A child who becomes sick on an overdose of honey, for instance, may come to believe that honey is naturally connected with illness, although in reality it is not (Locke 397). Similarly, someone whose education constantly reinforced the conjunction of the ideas of infallibility and a particular person may come to associate the proclamations of that person with certain truth. And so too philosophers who repeatedly conjoin two independent ideas "of no alliance to one another" may eventually find it impossible "to separate them in their Thoughts" and so come to claim that they have demonstrated what in fact are the greatest absurdities (Locke 400).

Associating ideas is especially dangerous, according to Locke, because "it hinders men from seeing and examining" things in the correct manner. Since the perceiving faculty of the mind, our reason itself, becomes warped as a result of associations, we cannot rely on that faculty to rescue us from associative errors. "When this Combination is settled and whilst it lasts," Locke writes, "it is not in the power of Reason to help us, and relieve us from Effects of it" (Locke 398). Locke makes it clear, moreover, that these associations are not simply the result of violent moods. We falsely associate ideas, he tells us, "in the steady calm course of . . . life," even when we are not "under the power of an unruly Passion" (Locke 395).

In the *Essay*, Hutcheson adopts Locke's notion of the association of ideas and puts it to work for his own purposes.[14] He uses the association of ideas specifically to try to establish the explanatory asymmetry at the heart of his defense of the theistic, Copernican Positive Answer.

Like Locke, Hutcheson takes association to be the cause of error, mistake, and corruption (Passions and Affections 10–11). We can be sure that Hutcheson is concerned in the *Essay* with the negative effects of association, since he uses a pejorative adjective to describe associations and their effects in almost every case.[15] He calls them foolish, confused, vain, strange, and wild (Passions and Affections 9, 23, 95, 98, 111, 121, 127, 131, 164, 168, 202). He also frequently distinguishes results of associations from what is natural and real (Passions and Affections 93, 23–4, 93–6, 99–100, 120–1, 165–6).

"Fantastick," however, may be Hutcheson's favorite adjective for describing associations of ideas (Passions and Affections 102, 111, 135, 154, 162, 166). The *Oxford English Dictionary* gives as its first definition of "fantastic"

"Existing only in imagination; proceeding merely from imagination; fabulous, imaginary, unreal." One of its example of usage is a sentence from Cudworth: "All those other phantastick Gods, were nothing but several Personal Names." Hutcheson might also have had in mind Locke's section "Of Real and Fantastical Ideas," where Locke writes, "By *real Ideas*, I mean such as have a Foundation in Nature; such as have a Conformity with the real Being, and Existence of Things, or with their Archetypes. *Fantastical or Chimerical*, I call such as have no Foundation in Nature, nor have any Conformity with that reality of Being, to which they are tacitly referr'd, as to their Archetypes" (Locke 372). Locke also says, in "Of associations of ideas," that those antipathies that are not natural come from our "Phancies," or "Phancy" (Locke 397).

Hutcheson is also like Locke in thinking that reason alone is incapable of breaking associations. An association may initially get its grip on you because you hold a false belief. But, Hutcheson believes, if it becomes entrenched enough in your way of thinking, you may continue to fall under the sway of an association even after your false belief has been corrected.

The common Effect of these *Associations* of Ideas is this, "that they raise the Passions into an extravagant Degree, beyond the proportion of real Good in the Object: And commonly beget some secret Opinions to justify the Passions. But then the *Confutation* of these false Opinions is not sufficient to break the *Association*, so that the *Desire* or *Passion* shall continue, even when our Understanding has suggested to us, that the Object is not good, or not proportioned to the Strength of the Desire." Thus we often may observe, that Persons, who by reasoning have laid aside all Opinion of *Spirits being in the dark* more than in the light, are still uneasy to be alone in the dark. Thus the *luxurious*, the *extravagant Lover*, the *Miser*, can scarce be supposed to have the *Opinions* of the several Objects of their Pursuit, proportioned to the Vehemence of their Desires: but the constant *Indulgence* of any Desire, the frequent *Repetition* of it, the *diverting* our Minds from all other Pursuits, the strain of *Conversation* among Men of the same Temper, who often haunt together, the *contagion* in the very Air and countenance of the passionate, beget such wild *Associations* of Ideas, that a sudden *Conviction of Reason* will not stop the Desire of Aversion, any more than an Argument will surmount the *Loathings* or *Aversions*, acquired against certain Meats or Drinks, by Surfeits or emetick Preparations. (Passions and Affections 94–5)

Fantastick associations of a similar sort can afflict our public and moral senses. Although the "Desire of Virtue, upon extensive impartial Schemes of publick Happiness, can scarce be too strong," we may come, "thro' an Association of foreign Ideas," to desire the good of only a part of humanity. Often the origins of this sort of fantastick desire are "*mistaken or partial Views* of publick Good," that is, mistakes of fact about what will help humanity as a whole. But once these associations and the corresponding desires become ingrained in our mind, "a sudden Conviction of Reason" will not break or eradicate them. We may, for instance, have been brought up with mistaken views of the "*Impiety, Cruelty*, [and] *Profaneness*" of a foreign people and this may cause us to desire, for the good of humanity as a whole, their destruction. But if these false views are not corrected early on, they will persist even after we have found out the truth about the foreigners. It is in this way that our "just natural Affection" toward humanity can become "overgrown," and we may come to approve of partial "*Phantoms* of Virtue" even when we are in full possession of the facts (Passions and Affections 97–9; cf. 191–2).

For Hutcheson, then, all of our natural affections are in benevolent harmony, while every harmful or disharmonious affection is the result of associations' corrupting influences. And thus Hutcheson can claim that there does exist an explanatory asymmetry between benevolence and harmony, on the one hand, and harmfulness and disharmony, on the other. For while benevolence and harmony do not admit of empirical explanation, distrust and disharmony can be explained by the effects of association on our empirically inexplicable affections. We are built to be as good as can be. By nature, we are all benevolent, harmonious creatures. All the bad things we do and think are the result of alterations to our original nature.

This raises the question of how we can undo the alterations. Hutcheson's ultimate philosophical goal is the practical one of promoting virtue. But a person can be fully virtuous, on Hutcheson's view, only if she frees her mind of pernicious associations and acts from her natural affections. So how can a person achieve this? What guidance does Hutcheson provide for those who have been corrupted by association?

We've already seen that while Hutcheson believes that some moral mistakes can be corrected simply by learning the facts relevant to the situation, he also believes that simple discovery of the facts won't free us from all of the associations that may lead us into error. Hutcheson maintains, however, that while a simple discovery of facts might be of limited value in distinguishing real virtues from phantoms of virtue, a disciplined and habitual attention to the facts might he more helpful. By attending diligently and consciously to the connections we draw between ideas, we may come to see the foolishness of the associations that grip us. And if we continually call this foolishness to mind, we may eventually be able to free ourselves of the pernicious associations.

Hutcheson points out, for instance, that as a result of association we often come to desire objects out of proportion to their actual goodness. When we gain the objects, we see the disproportionality of our desire, but our association and consequently the desire may still persist. "But," he says, "if just *Reflection* comes in, and tho' late, applies the proper Cure, by correcting the *Opinions* and the *Imagination*, every Experience will tend to our Advantage" (Passions and Affections 123). So imagine that you have a strong desire to drink a cup of coffee after dinner. And it's a desire to drink regular coffee, not decaf. You desire not only the immediate gustatory experience of the drink itself but also the sense of animated well-being the caffeine gives you. You know all too well, however, that when you drink coffee after dinner, you can't get to sleep. And the ills of insomnia – being agonizingly awake in the middle of the night, being painfully exhausted the next morning – are not worth the pleasure of even the finest after-dinner beverage. Hutcheson is aware that your bare knowledge of the consequences will not free you from your desire to drink the coffee. He suggests, however, that if you meditate and reflect on the consequences – if you consciously and conscientiously attend to them, if you ruminate – the desire will eventually fade away.

Hutcheson's view of associations and how to break them thus resembles contemporary cognitive psychotherapy. They both hold that many of our emotional problems can be remedied by continual conscious correction of our distorted thinking. We get into bad mental habits. We form destructive associations. But we can break them, so long as we put our minds to it.

But Hutcheson is concerned not only with improving mental health but also with promoting moral behavior and judgment. Or rather, Hutcheson believes that correct moral behavior and judgment is an essential part of mental health. He maintains, consequently, that we should use the method of meditation and reflection to rid ourselves both of self-defeating desires and of desires that distort our moral thought and conduct (Passions and Affections 30–1, 106–7, 123, 166, 201–2). He has a couple of different kinds of cases in mind.

An example of the first kind of case is a person who has a great passion for a particular moral cause (Passions and Affections 99; cf. Beauty and Virtue 206–8). Working for this cause may generally be a good thing in that it tends to benefit humanity. But the person may, over time, become so singularly committed to the cause that she comes to associate its advancement with morality as a whole. She may come to think that everything that promotes the cause is good, regardless of the harmful effects it may produce, and that everything that thwarts the cause is bad, regardless of the benefits. And this association may lead her to make decisions and judgments that are morally incorrect. In her zeal to promote her particular cause, she may end up performing and approving of actions that harm humanity overall. Hutcheson believes, however, that if she engages in "frequent Meditation and Reflection" on the matter, she can come to realize that her cause is morally worthwhile only to the extent that it benefits humanity, and that continued attention to this fact may eventually bring her desires and judgments back in line with the correct view of morality.

An example of the second kind of case is a person who is opposed to a group he deems immoral (see Passions and Affections 99–100 and Beauty and Virtue 206–8). Hutcheson suggests as an instance of this a person who disapproves of the Roman Catholic Church (Beauty and Virtue 91–3). Now Hutcheson, like many Britons of his day, thought that the Catholic Church did merit considerable disapprobation, and that is because he thought that the Catholic Church had done much to harm humanity. But he also seemed to think that some people had wrongly come to associate moral evil with everything Catholic. And this association could lead a person to hate all Catholics and to engage in and approve of anti-Catholic activities that do more harm to humanity than good. The solution to this morally pernicious habit of mind? Once again: "frequent Meditation and Reflection."

So Hutcheson holds that desires that originate in fantastick associations will wither once we have managed to break the associations in question through meditation and reflection. He also holds that meditation and reflection will *strengthen* desires that are natural. Hutcheson mentions in this regard the desire a person typically has for her family to be happy after her death. He initially points to this desire as a counterexample to Mandevillean egoism. He realizes, however, that his egoist opponents might claim that dying people have through the years come to associate the welfare of their families with their own happiness, and that self-interest therefore can explain their dying wishes. Hutcheson counters:

> Should we alledge, that this Desire of the Happiness of others, after our Exit, is some *confused Association of Ideas*; as a Miser, who loves no body, might desire an Increase of Wealth at his Death; or as any one may have an Aversion to have his Body dissected, or made a Prey to Dogs after Death: let any honest Heart try if the deepest Reflection will break this *Association* (if there be any) which is supposed to raise the Desire. The closest Reflection would be found rather to strengthen it.... 'Tis plain then we feel this *ultimate Desire* of the Happiness of Others to be a most *natural Instinct*, which we also expect in others, and not the Effect of any confused *Ideas*. (Passions and Affections 23–4)

We can be sure that the desire for the happiness of others after our death is natural because meditation and reflection do not eradicate it. If, on the other hand, it did disappear upon meditation and reflection, then it would be the result of fantastick association, unnatural, and necessary to root out.

So whenever we have doubts about whether a desire is natural or unnatural, we can use Hutcheson's method of meditation and reflection to determine the truth of the matter. And we can use the same method to ensure the correctness of our moral judgments. For a correct moral judgment of an object is that which accords with the moral affection one would feel if one knew all the relevant facts about the object and if the moral affection the object arouses in one was natural, original, and uncorrupted by association's corrupting influence. So if we know all the relevant facts and want to determine whether our moral judgment of an object is correct, we need only meditate and reflect on the moral affection the object arouses in us. If (and only if) the moral affection survives our conscious and conscientious meditation and reflection – if (and only if) upon meditation and reflection we continue to feel the same way – then the affection is natural, and the moral judgment that originates in it is correct.

For Hutcheson, then, meditation and reflection is the method for bringing the elements of human nature into alignment and correcting moral judgment. By meditation and reflection, we can free ourselves from the corrupting influences of association, leaving us with only our natural affections. And these natural affections – whether they are grounding moral judgments, motivating us to perform actions that affect other people, or leading us to pursue our own interests – will all be in harmony. On meditation and reflection, my affections will all harmonize with each other, and if you and I both engage in meditation and reflection, then my affections will always harmonize with yours. Meditation and reflection dissolves both interpersonal and internal conflict.

Why do all these affections harmonize with each other? Why are we naturally in such perfect alignment? As we've seen, Hutcheson believes there can be no naturalistic explanation of that fact. But there is an excellent *supernatural* answer that can be given. The best explanation of the harmony of all of our natural affections is that we have been designed by a supernatural being who wants us to be happy. The best explanation is that our natural affections – the affections for which we can provide no empirical explanation – were implanted in us by an intelligent and benevolent God. As Hutcheson puts it in the conclusion to the *Essay*:

But while we feel in our selves so much *publick Affection* in the various Relations of Life, and observe the like in others; while we find every one desiring indeed his *own Happiness*, but capable of discerning, by a little Attention, that not only his external *Conveniency*, or *worldly Interest*, but even the most immediate and lively *Sensations of Delight*, of which his Nature is susceptible, immediately flow from a *Publick Spirit*, a *generous, human, compassionate Temper*, and a suitable *Deportment*. . . . How can any one look upon this World as under the Direction of an *evil Nature*, or even question a perfectly *good* PROVIDENCE?" (Passions and Affections 202)

Hutcheson thus has reason to believe he has dispelled all the worries raised by his moral sense theory. He has managed to paint a picture of human nature in which meditation and reflection, benevolence, morality, mental health, and the existence of God all merge into one coherent whole.

C. Hutchesonian Human Nature

Attractive as it is, however, Hutcheson's picture is not one we can accept, at least not if what we're looking for is an accurate representation of human nature. What survives meditation and reflection is not always original to human nature. What's original is not always good. Meditation and reflection are no guarantee of harmony. And interpersonal and internal harmony, when it does exist, results not simply from naturalistically inexplicable affections but from the interaction of a number of other more basic elements of human nature. Hutcheson's picture may help to inspire a morally salutary optimism, but it's not the best explanation of the observable phenomena of human conduct.

No one saw the deficiencies of Hutcheson's account more clearly than Hume. In the next part of the book, we'll examine how Hume undermined Hutcheson's view, how Hume's alternative account overthrew the traditional way of thinking about the Human Nature Question, and how Hume's new ideas created new moral challenges.

Before moving on to Hume, however, let us bask for a moment in the flattering light of Hutcheson's view of human nature. On that view, benevolence is universal in two ways: all humans are naturally benevolent, and every human is naturally benevolent toward all of humanity (Beauty and Virtue 75, 155, 165, 168, 180, 202, 214, 216). Even the lesser concern we feel toward those distant from us Hutcheson construes as evidence of our benevolence toward all human beings, in that he maintains that we have greater power to make happy those close to us, and thus focusing on them is a more efficient use of our energies, producing greater benefit for humanity overall (Beauty and Virtue 218–19). Hutcheson does acknowledge that mistaken ideas of self-interest can lead us to perform actions that conflict with our benevolent tendencies. But he seems to think that even this happens relatively infrequently. More often, when people harm humanity, they act under the mistaken belief that they are producing an overall benefit (Beauty and Virtue 197–206). Hutcheson believes, for instance, that when people deliberately thwart others, they almost always believe that the others are immoral. Immoral people are people who harm humanity. Thus, when people deliberately thwart others, they almost always believe that they are protecting humanity from harm. And the bad things people do that cannot be accounted for simply by false beliefs Hutcheson explains in terms of the corrupting influences of associations of ideas, which all people, when they put their minds to it, have the capacity and motivation to break. In the same vein, Hutcheson denies that any human being is capable of "malice" or "a sedate ultimate Desire of the Misery of others" (Beauty and Virtue 143–5, cf. 168–9; Passions and Affections 74, 104, 108, 189). What appears to be malice, Hutcheson argues, is almost always an overzealous desire to combat vice, which the seemingly malicious person believes to exist in superabundance in those toward whom he or she seems to be acting maliciously. Hutcheson even takes the time to explain away children's ill treatment of animals, contending that "*Children* delight in some Actions which are *cruel* and *tormenting* to Animals . . . not from *Malice*, or want of *Compassion*, but from their *Ignorance* of those signs of Pain which many Creatures make; together with a *Curiosity* to see the various Contortions of their Bodys" (Beauty and Virtue 241). Once children become "more acquainted with these Creatures, or come by any means to know their Sufferings," their compassion usually becomes very strong.

All of this amounts to an exceedingly optimistic account of human nature. It's a Positive Answer that, within the confines of Hutcheson's moral Copernicanism, is just about as positive as it could possibly be.[16]

Hutcheson's view is certainly extremely different from the Negative Answer of his father's Scottish Presbyterianism.[17] Hutcheson doesn't suggest that any of us will ever achieve the "highest perfection of our kind," and he does (albeit very occasionally) refer to the Fall of Man (Passions and Affections 199–201). But the overwhelming bulk of Hutcheson's early books consists of arguments implying that, far from being ineluctably corrupt, all humans have within themselves the ability not only to discern morality but also to bring all of their affections into righteous harmony. The associative effects of custom, education, and habit have pulled us away from our original, God-given constitution. But they haven't pulled us very far. And through meditation and reflection we can undo almost all of association's unfortunate effects. The basic shape of our Authored nature is, to Hutcheson, still plainly discernible in all of us, and through disciplined effort we can get into even better – that is, closer-to-original – shape.

In certain respects, Hutcheson's view is also more positive than that of the rationalists of the period. The rationalists had, of course, great confidence in human reason. But on human affections they looked considerably more askance. They seemed to think that our affective nature was something that could never be brought entirely into line with morality, and thus that living virtuously must involve resisting rogue desires. Conflict between reason and morality, on the one hand, and passion and immorality, on the other, was, for the rationalists, an inevitable feature of human life. Now Hutcheson wasn't blind to the internal strife people may experience when trying to do the right thing. But he didn't think such strife was inevitable. The natural state of every affection is in perfect accord with the natural state of every other affection, and that includes the affections in which our moral distinctions originate. Moreover, while Hutcheson didn't believe human reason could do what the rationalists said it could, that's not because he thought it was distorted or corrupt. Human reason, for Hutcheson, works just fine at doing what it was designed to do. And the things it wasn't designed to do – such as ground moral and aesthetic judgments and motivate to action – human affection can do perfectly well.

Hutcheson's view of human nature is also more rosy than Shaftesbury's. Like Hutcheson, Shaftesbury believed that the design of human nature reflected the goodness of creation, and that we all had within ourselves every resource necessary to achieve the height of virtue. But Shaftesbury also believed that many, perhaps most, human beings had thoroughly corrupted their originally virtuous constitution. He often emphasized the despicable distance between the goodness of our original nature and the evilness of our current conduct. There's no shortage of vitriol in Shaftesbury's writings. It's clear that he thought that a lot of people are really pretty rotten.

Hutcheson, too, tells a story about how humans fall away from the virtue toward which their original constitution tends, a story in which the association of ideas plays a leading role. But most people, in Hutcheson's view, are pretty close to virtue most of the time. He thus gives charitable interpretations of much that seems wanting in human conduct, trying to convince us that once we understand why people are doing what they do, we'll realize that they're not nearly as bad as we might have thought. And once he gets it in mind to show that most human conduct proceeds from benign motives, Hutcheson follows through on the project with a bulldog-like tenacity.

Earlier, I suggested that Hutcheson's writings can be rather drab and uninspiring, at least when compared to Cudworth's rhetorically elevated sermons or Shaftesbury's literary escapades. But there is an accumulative power in Hutcheson's consistently clear arguments for the goodness of human nature. They can wear down your pessimism. And this serves Hutcheson's underlying, practical goal, which is to instill in people the attitudes toward each other that will lead them to live virtuous lives.

Hutcheson himself, moreover, seemed to live up to his own Positive Answer exceedingly well. The biographical information paints a portrait of a kind and decent person who thought that other people were kind and decent as well. He acted virtuously himself and expected other people to act virtuously. And apparently this expectation was self-fulfilling, in that he brought out the best in his friends and acquaintances. In this respect, Hutcheson was probably personally more similar to Whichcote than to any of the other philosophers we've discussed. And like Whichcote, Hutcheson was a spectacular teacher (Scott 1900, 64–5).

In 1730, after teaching at the academy in Dublin for about ten years, Hutcheson was appointed chair of moral philosophy at the University of Glasgow, where he stayed until his death in 1746.[18] While at Glasgow, Hutcheson's intellectual acuity, his belief in the goodness of his fellows, and his overall moral character apparently inspired his students not only to scholarship but also to virtue. Furthermore, Hutcheson created the template for future occupants of the chair of moral philosophy, which continued to be an institution of moral improvement at the university for years to come. As Scott sees it, in fact, Hutcheson did as much to advance the cause of virtue in his role as a professor as he did as a philosophical writer (Scott 1900, 66). If that is the case, then it would seem that some of the most significant consequences of Hutcheson's Positive Answer can be found not simply in his printed works but in the way he lived his life.

PART FOUR

DAVID HUME

15

David Hume's New "Science of Man"

In the previous parts of this study we examined the works of Whichcote, Cudworth, Shaftesbury, and Hutcheson. There were many differences between those thinkers. But in certain highly significant respects all of them stand together on one side of a philosophical divide, while David Hume stands alone on the other. In this chapter I outline three related ways in which Hume's *Treatise* account of morality and human nature differs from the work of his predecessors. In Chapters 16 to 19 I examine the specific arguments that set the *Treatise* apart. And in Chapter 20 I point to some implications Hume's new account has for our thinking about morality and human nature.

A. Theoretical, Not Practical

The *Treatise* differs from the writings of earlier British moralists, first of all, in being an essentially *theoretical* work, not a practical one. The goal of the *Treatise* is to provide an account that best captures the observable phenomena of human behavior. It does not try to convince people that they ought to act in certain ways. The *Treatise* will succeed if it advances our understanding of human conduct. Its success does not depend on improving our conduct.[1]

Virtually all previous moral philosophy, in contrast, had been explicitly practical. The goal of Hume's predecessors was to improve their readers' conduct. This was true of proponents of both the Negative and Positive Answers.

The practical purpose of the Negative Answer is perfectly clear in the writings of Hobbes and the English Calvinists. The Calvinists thought that belief in the Negative Answer was essential to Christianity. A full awareness of one's own ineluctable depravation, according to the Calvinists, was an inviolable prerequisite for the proper attitude toward God that lies at the core of true religion. Hobbes' commitment to the Negative Answer was never as unambiguous as his contemporaries made it out to be. But there's no question that Hobbes too took himself to be providing a moral prescription for his readers to follow. Hobbes' *Leviathan* was supposed to prove that society ought to be structured one way rather than any other. Hobbes' goal was the practical one of convincing people that rationality demands that they obey an absolute sovereign.

All the proponents of the Positive Answer we've examined – Whichcote, Cudworth, Shaftesbury, and Hutcheson – also clearly intended their writings to serve the practical purpose of instilling virtue. The practical purpose of the sermons of Whichcote and Cudworth is obvious. These were, after all, *sermons*, edifying speeches delivered from the pulpit. But even when he was writing *A Treatise concerning Eternal and Immutable Morality*, Cudworth took himself to be promoting the cause of virtue. For in that book, Cudworth set out to defeat the Hobbesian and voluntarist conceptions of morality. And Cudworth believed this task was of the utmost importance because he thought that Hobbesianism and voluntarism implied that morality had no real existence, and that if people came to believe that morality did not exist they would no longer have reason to be moral. Similarly, Shaftesbury justified his first publication, *Select Sermons of Dr. Whichcot*, by telling us that Whichcote's sermons needed to gain a wider audience precisely because they would help us to withstand the assault on virtue launched by Hobbes and the Calvinists. Throughout his career, moreover, Shaftesbury consistently maintained that the proper end of philosophy is to improve character and better society. Indeed, Shaftesbury thought that any writing that didn't serve such practical ends was not worthy of the noble title of "philosophy" at all. This commitment to practical philosophy was fully endorsed by Hutcheson, who repeatedly condemned those who sought to advance only "speculative knowledge" instead of "wisdom."

I do not mean to suggest that theoretical or speculative philosophy was absent from the works of Whichcote, Cudworth, Shaftesbury, and Hutcheson. These thinkers did not engage only in direct exhortations to virtue, religion, and good citizenship. They did address meta-ethical, metaphysical, epistemological – and sometimes rather recherché – issues. But they believed that such philosophizing was worthwhile only because it ultimately led to an impregnable case for rightful conduct.

When he was writing the *Treatise*, Hume realized that he was engaged in an activity that, because it was non-practical, differed from his predecessors'. Hutcheson realized it too. We know this because in 1739, when Hume was twenty-eight years old, he sent a draft of the as-yet-unpublished Book III of the *Treatise* to Hutcheson. Hutcheson's comments on the draft are not extant, but it is easy enough to infer what he said from the letter Hume wrote in response:

What affected me most in your Remarks is your observing that there wants a certain Warmth in the Cause of Virtue, which, you think, all good Men wou'd relish, & cou'd not displease amidst abstract Enquirys. I must own, this has not happen'd by

Chance, but is the Effect of a Reasoning either good or bad. There are different ways of examining the Mind as well as the Body. One may consider it either as an Anatomist or as a Painter; either to discover its most secret Springs & Principles or to describe the Grace & Beauty of its Actions. I imagine it impossible to conjoin these two Views. Where you pull off the Skin, & display all the minute Parts, there appears something trivial, even in the noblest Attitudes & most vigorous Actions: Nor can you ever render the Object graceful or engaging but by cloathing the Parts again with Skin & Flesh, & presenting only their bare Outside. An Anatomist, however, can give very good Advice to a Painter or Statuary: And in like manner, I am perswaded, that a Metaphysician may be very helpful to a Moralists; tho' I cannot easily conceive these two Characters united in the same work. (Letters 32–3)

Hutcheson criticized the *Treatise* for not doing enough to promote morality. And Hume did not deny that his book lacked "a certain Warmth in the Cause of Virtue." But he did not apologize for that lack. He took himself to be "a Metaphysician," not a "Moralist." The *Treatise* was an attempt to anatomize human nature, to discover the "Springs & Principles" that underlie all human conduct, good and bad. Describing the "Grace & Beauty" of certain actions, rendering virtue "graceful or engaging," was a different job, a job for the "Moralist." The *Treatise* did focus on the theoretical instead of the practical. But that was by design.

Hume must have been satisfied with his response to Hutcheson's letter, because he incorporated it into the concluding paragraph of the *Treatise*. There he repeats that he is an "anatomist," not a "painter," and goes on to say explicitly that his is not a book of "*practical morality*" (THN 3.3.6.6). The *Treatise* consists of "abstract speculations concerning human nature," not "perswasive" exhortations to virtue. It is the work of a metaphysician, not a moralist.[2]

B. Rejection of the Human Nature Question

The second way in which the *Treatise* differs from earlier works is in its rejection of the idea that humans are either naturally virtuous or naturally vicious. This idea, as we've seen in the previous three parts of this study, was absolutely central to the thought of Hume's predecessors. The *Treatise*'s rejection of it thus constitutes a pivotal moment. It is the moment at which the Human Nature Question is forced to relinquish its hold on moral philosophy.[3]

In Chapters 16 through 19, we will look at the details of Hume's dismantling of the Negative and Positive Answers. But we can discern the general shape of Hume's position simply from the fact that he says that Part 2 of Book III of the *Treatise* is his account of the "artificial" virtues and that Part 3 is his account of the "natural" virtues.[4] Hume also maintains, throughout Books II and III, that natural tendencies and unnatural ones can both give rise to vice. So according to the *Treatise*, what's natural can be the source of both vice and virtue, and what's not natural can be the source of both vice and virtue as well. The distinction between virtue and vice, on the one hand,

and the distinction between what is natural to human beings and what is not natural, on the other, are orthogonal. The second distinction, on any meaningful interpretation (i.e., on any interpretation that does not simply define "natural" so as to include all and only that which is virtuous), does not track the first. "The question . . . concerning the wickedness or goodness of human nature" is one that a philosophical account of morality should not try to answer (THN 3.2.2.13).

This aspect of the *Treatise* was just as inimical to Hutcheson as was its lack of warmth in the cause of virtue. Hutcheson believed that our natural tendencies lead to virtue and happiness, and that anything artificial (any custom, education, or habit that alters the original direction of our natural tendencies) leads to vice and unhappiness. Hutcheson also believed that convincing people that the virtuous life is natural and the vicious life is unnatural would help instill virtue, and that instilling virtue had to be the ultimate goal of all truly philosophical reflection.

But once again, Hume did not back down or apologize in the face of Hutcheson's criticism. We've already seen that Hume eschewed the practical goal of instilling virtue that Hutcheson took to be essential to philosophy. And in his 1739 letter to Hutcheson, Hume explains that he also rejects the Positive Answer that Hutcheson took to be the anchor of that practical endeavor. "I cannot agree to your Sense of *Natural*," Hume wrote. "Tis founded on final Causes; which is a Consideration, that appears to me pretty uncertain & unphilosophical. For pray, what is the End of Man? Is he created for Happiness or for Virtue? For this Life or for the next? For himself or for his Maker? Your Definition of *Natural* depends upon solving these Questions, which are endless, & quite wide of my Purpose" (Letters 33). But Hume's most explicit rejection of the idea that virtue is natural and vice unnatural comes in 3.1.2 of the *Treatise*.

At the end of that section, Hume asks "whether we ought to search for these principles [that distinguish moral good and evil] in *nature*, or whether we must look for them in some other origins?" And what Hume says in reply is "that our answer to this question depends upon the definition of the word, *nature*, than which there is none more ambiguous and equivocal" (THN 3.1.2.7). Hume then proceeds to canvass various meanings of the word "nature" and to show that none of them is of any use in distinguishing moral good from evil. On each definition, either vice and virtue are both natural, or they are both unnatural. Hume concludes that "nothing can be more unphilosophical than those systems, which assert, that virtue is the same with what is natural, and vice with what is unnatural. . . . 'Tis impossible . . . that the character of natural and unnatural can ever, in any sense, mark the boundaries of vice and virtue" (THN 3.1.2.10).

Indeed, according to Hume, the concern to show that humans are either naturally good or naturally bad was responsible for many of the distortions of past accounts of human nature. Mandeville, for instance, made some exceedingly astute observations about the role socialization can play in the development of moral sentiments. But then, in an attempt to present a uniformly Negative Answer, he argued for a global egoism that obviously didn't fit the facts, trying to shoehorn altruistic behavior into ridiculously complicated motives of self-interest. Similarly, Hutcheson made some exceedingly astute observations about the non-egoistic character of many of our moral sentiments. But then, in an attempt to present a uniformly Positive Answer, he asserted an ad hoc explanatory asymmetry between virtuous traits and vicious ones. Instead of trying to defend the claim that virtue is or is not natural, Hume implies, philosophers seeking to establish "the science of man" should focus on questions that are more "simple" and "free from ambiguity and obscurity" (THN Introduction 7 and 3.1.2.11). They should think of human nature as something to be explained, not as something either to live up to or to overcome.

Hume denied the Positive Answer. But he denied the Negative Answer too. This is something many of his contemporaries missed. They seemed to think that since Hume failed to affirm the essential goodness of human nature, he must have been affirming the essential evilness – that his not signing on to the edifying optimism of Shaftesbury, Hutcheson, or the moral rationalists could mean only that he was crossing over to the dark side of Hobbes and Mandeville. But in fact Hume's point was that the prevailing taxonomy of positions on morality and human nature – rooted as it was in the distinction between the Positive Answer and the Negative Answer – was ill-conceived. A perfectly clear indication of Hume's rejection of this taxonomy is the point in the *Treatise* introduction where he says that his work will build on that of Shaftesbury, Hutcheson, *and* Mandeville (THN Introduction 5). No one who took the Human Nature Question to be central to moral philosophy could ever have claimed all three of these men as intellectual forbears, as the first two were exemplars of the Positive Answer and the third was an exemplar of the Negative.[5]

C. A Thoroughly Secular Moral Philosophy: The Copernican Revolution Completed

The third way in which the *Treatise* differs from its predecessors is in refusing to give God any role in its account of morality and human nature. Indeed, coming to Book III of the *Treatise* after reading Hume's predecessors, I am consistently struck anew by the conspicuousness of God's almost total absence.

We saw in Parts Two and Three of this study that Shaftesbury and Hutcheson constructed a kind of halfway house between theological and secular ethics. They both thought that although belief in God was a great support to virtue, an atheist could in theory be virtuous – that virtue did not absolutely require theistic belief or any duties to God per se. But they also both thought that the best account of morality and human nature implied the existence of God – that theism was the inevitable result of a full and accurate philosophical understanding of morality and human nature, even if a person did not have to grasp that result in order to be virtuous. Hume, on the other hand, goes fully secular. According to Hume, not only is belief in God unnecessary for virtue, the best account of morality and human nature does not imply God's existence.

The only place in Book III of the *Treatise* where Hume explicitly mentions God is 3.1.1, "Moral distinctions not deriv'd from reason." And when he does so there, it is only to argue that the rationalists' claims about God either fail to establish their account of morality or make their account of morality even harder to establish (THN 3.1.1.22). In this section, in other words, Hume does not himself commit to any claims about God. He merely shows that the claims about God that his rationalist opponents have made do not help their case and may actually hurt it.

Hume does not explicitly mention God in 3.1.2, "Moral distinctions deriv'd from a moral sense." But that section contains an implicit attack on Hutcheson's central theistic argument. As we saw in Chapter 14, Hutcheson argued that our natural constitution is overwhelming evidence that we were created by a benevolent God. Hutcheson argued, specifically, that we are all naturally constituted to be happy and to make others happy, that if we all live according to our natural principles, happiness will abound. Hutcheson then drew the conclusion that happiness is what the author of our nature designed us to achieve. But to say that the author of our nature designed us to be happy is just to say that we were created by a benevolent God.

In arguing that there is no sense in which virtue is natural and vice unnatural, Hume demolishes the basis of Hutcheson's a posteriori inference to a benevolent Creator God.[6] Hume agrees with Hutcheson's general idea that virtue leads to happiness and vice leads to unhappiness (although he doesn't think the connection between virtue and happiness is as direct and unwavering as Hutcheson does). But Hume maintains that it is not just virtue that proceeds from our natural tendencies. Some vices proceed from them as well. Moreover, some of the virtues that are vitally important for human happiness are artificial, proceeding from changes wrought on our natural constitution. So, since our nature includes aspects that tend not only toward virtue and unhappiness but also toward vice and unhappiness, if we set out to draw a posteriori conclusions about the intentions of our Creator from our natural constitution, we will have to attribute to Him not only the desire to produce virtue and happiness but also the desire to produce vice and unhappiness. Hutcheson cannot claim, therefore, that our natural constitution is evidence that we were created by an entirely benevolent God. That is not to say that Hume goes on to draw the conclusion that God doesn't exist or that He possesses malicious as well as benevolent motives. Hume doesn't draw any conclusions about God at all. His point is that our natural constitution is not grounds for any inference about God. For Hume, claims about God and philosophical accounts of morality and human nature simply do not engage.[7]

This stance of Hume's has to count as one of the most important in the history of ideas. For it marks the final full emergence, among British philosophers at least, of thoroughly secular ethics. In 1600, English-speaking theorizing about morality and human nature was done almost entirely within a Christian framework. But now, 140 years later, Hume presents an account that is not only non-Christian but devoid of theological commitment altogether. Hume's secular ethics didn't come out of nowhere, however. There was a long gestation process, aspects of which I've tried to elucidate in the previous parts of this study. Hume's predecessors held deep theological commitments, but they unintentionally paved the way for Hume's secular ethics nonetheless.

We first examined Whichcote and Cudworth. We saw that they apotheosized human reason, making righteousness directly accessible to every person. This eliminated the need for Christ and thus removed thinking about morality and human nature from a distinctly Christian framework. But Whichcote, and probably Cudworth, believed that duty to God constituted a fundamental part of the moral life – that an atheist could not be fully moral. And there can be no doubt that Whichcote and Cudworth's philosophy remained fundamentally theological. For they held that human minds and their moral ideas depended on – were ectypes or partakers of – the mind of God. Whichcote and Cudworth's apotheosis of the human mind was literal.

Next came Shaftesbury, who embraced and expanded the non-Christian aspects of Whichcote and Cudworth's theological view of morality and human nature. In particular, Shaftesbury developed a teleology according to which humans were designed by God to promote the good of the system of which they are a part. But unlike the Cambridge Platonists, Shaftesbury thought that virtue did not necessarily involve theistic belief. Although belief in God is, according to Shaftesbury, the greatest support to virtue, it is at least theoretically possible for an atheist to be virtuous. Moreover, Shaftesbury included in his teleological account a new and psychologically astute description of the moral sentiments. And the existence of these sentiments implied – as Shaftesbury himself mentioned, although perhaps without realizing the full importance of the point – that we would still have reason to be virtuous even if God did not exist.

Hutcheson agreed with Shaftesbury that while belief in God is a great support to virtue, it is at least theoretically possible for an atheist to be virtuous. Hutcheson also latched on to Shaftesbury's claims about the moral sentiments, placing them center stage in a way that crowded out a number of other ideas that had been central to Shaftesbury. An especially noteworthy feature of Hutcheson's emphasis on the sentiments was his corresponding diminution of the role reason can play in the moral and religious life. And because Hutcheson greatly reduced the power of reason, certain paths to theism were closed to him, including ones that Shaftesbury had traveled. Shaftesbury, for instance, sometimes relied on an a priori belief in a comprehensive theistic teleology; at these times, Shaftesbury's claims about the moral sentiments presupposed a purely rational understanding of the teleology of human nature. Hutcheson, in contrast, always started from observations of the sentiments themselves. A priori teleology, and the theism it embodies, were things that Hutcheson would not allow rationality to deliver. But although Hutcheson's philosophy did not begin from claims about God, a claim about God was where it ended. For Hutcheson concluded that his observations of human sentiments provided a posteriori grounds for belief in a God whose motives correspond perfectly to the conception of virtue all of us have.

Hume agreed with Hutcheson's emphasis on the sentiments and corresponding diminution of reason. But he rejected Hutcheson's inference from the observable facts of our sentimental nature to claims about God. He sought to account for the observable facts of human behavior without recourse to any theistic or supernatural causes. The connection between theology and moral philosophy, which by the time we got to Hutcheson had already been winnowed down to a pretty thin thread, is now decisively cut. Nor is there any indication in the *Treatise* that Hume thought that theists were more likely to be virtuous than atheists.

In a 1740 letter to Hutcheson, Hume expressed the belief that moral philosophy should be an entirely human affair – that a proper theory would neither originate in nor lead to any claims about God. He wrote, "[S]ince Morality, according to your Opinion as well as mine, is determin'd merely by Sentiment, it regards only human Nature & human Life" (Letters 40). The human moral phenomena that are the subjects of the *Treatise* tell us nothing about "superior Beings."

Hume thus completes the Copernican Revolution in moral philosophy that was initiated by Shaftesbury's mental enjoyment account of the reason to be virtuous and furthered by Hutcheson's moral sense theory. The study of morality, for Hume, is a subset of the study of human nature. We cannot sensibly ask whether human nature as a whole is good or evil, as good and evil themselves turn on human sentiments and conduct.

16

Hume's Arguments against Moral Rationalism

Like Hutcheson, Hume claims that morality originates not in reason alone but at least partly in sentiment. In this chapter, I do not present a detailed, comprehensive account – much less a defense – of Hume's arguments against moral rationalism. Instead, I sketch in very broad brushstrokes the overall structure of Hume's arguments against moral rationalism and how they fit with the parts of his philosophy that, in the next three chapters, I will examine more closely. There are three reasons I am covering this part of Hume's view so quickly. First, the secondary literature already contains a number of excellent discussions on this topic.[1] Second, many of Hume's anti-rationalist arguments cover the same ground as Hutcheson's arguments in *The Moral Sense*, which I discussed in Chapter 12. And third, I think the other parts of Book III of the *Treatise* contain Hume's most important contributions to the philosophical developments I am charting in this study.

Almost all of Hume's arguments against moral rationalism fall into one of three categories: arguments based on the idea that reason alone cannot motivate, which I will, following Korsgaard (1986), call "arguments from motivational skepticism about practical reason"; arguments based on the idea that reason alone cannot provide the content necessary for moral judgments, which I will, once again following Korsgaard, call "arguments from content skepticism about practical reason"; and arguments based on the idea that sentimentalism constitutes a better explanation than rationalism of the observable moral phenomena.[2]

A. Arguments from Motivational Skepticism

The arguments from motivational skepticism about practical reason occur in paragraphs 5 to 16 of "Moral distinctions not from reason" (THN 3.3.1), although they explicitly presuppose prior arguments made in "Of the motivating influences of the will" (THN 2.3.3). The overall argumentative structure is the following:

1. Necessarily, morality motivates.
2. Reason alone cannot motivate.
3. Therefore, morality does not come from reason alone.

More has probably been written about this overall argumentative structure and the particular arguments that fall within it than about any other aspect of Hume's moral philosophy.[3] I will not add to them here. Allow me, rather, simply to assert without argument that I think that the arguments from motivational skepticism can be construed in a way that amounts to a very powerful objection to the type of moral rationalism that seeks to assimilate moral judgment to geometric-like demonstration. Whichcote, Cudworth, More, Clarke, Balguy, and Burnet all imply this type of moral rationalism in some parts of their works.[4] It is not at all clear, however, that Hume's arguments from motivational skepticism pose a threat to other types of rationalist moral theories, such as those proposed by Kant and latter-day Kantians.[5]

B. Arguments from Content Skepticism

The second category of Hume's anti-rationalist arguments consists of arguments from content skepticism about practical reason. These arguments occur in paragraphs 18 to 26 of "Moral distinctions not from reason" (THN 3.3.1). The leading idea of these arguments is that judgments that come from reason alone are too general or formal to fund the distinctions that our moral judgments are in the business of drawing. According to the content skeptic, two people who are in complete agreement on all purely rational matters can nonetheless disagree in moral judgment, and this is because moral judgments have more substance, or more content, than reason alone cannot provide.

Hume argues for content skepticism, first, by describing propositions that come from reason alone and, second, by casting doubt on whether propositions of this type can provide the substance or content characteristic of moral judgment. The category of rational propositions Hume's content skeptical arguments mainly concern are those that are a priori and either self-evident or follow by demonstratively certain steps from propositions that are self-evident.[6] Logic and mathematics comprise propositions of this kind. All the philosophers who held to what we've called the necessity of moral thesis and its epistemological implication – Whichcote, Cudworth, More, Clarke, Balguy, and Burnet – placed moral judgments in this category. They all maintained that, like p or not p and $2 + 2 = 4$, true moral judgments bear the hallmarks of pure rationality ("hallmarks of pure rationality" is a phrase I will use in the rest of this section as a shorthand for the quality of being a priori and either self-evident or demonstratively derivable from propositions that are self-evident).

In response, Hume maintains that every proposition that bears the hallmarks of pure rationality concerns one of four relations: resemblance, contrariety, degrees in quality, and propositions in quantity and number. But these relations, Hume says, are not substantial or content-ful enough to fund the distinctions moral judgments are in the business of drawing. Hume argues for this claim by first contending that "no one has ever been able to advance a single step" toward showing how these relations might produce moral judgments (THN 3.1.1.18) and by then providing two examples of moral judgments that we make but that we could not make if we restricted ourselves to propositions concerning the four purely rational relations.

Hume's first example is the moral judgment that it is vicious for a child to kill one of his or her parents. Hume argues that all of the purely rational relations that exist in the situation in which a child kills a parent also exist in the situation in which an "oak or elm...by the dropping of its seed...produces a sapling below it, which springing up by degrees, at last overtops and destroys the parent tree" (THN 3.1.1.24). But we do not judge that the sapling has done anything wrong. So, since the relations that reason alone can judge of do not allow for any distinction between the sapling and the child, when we judge that there is a significant difference between the moral status of the sapling and the moral status of the child, our judgment must involve something other than a priori reason alone.

Hume's second example is the moral judgment that "incest in the human species is criminal" (THN 3.1.1.25). Hume argues that all of the purely rational relations that exist in the situation in which close human relatives copulate also exist in the situation in which close animal relatives copulate. But we do not judge that the animals are guilty of even "the smallest turpitude [or] deformity" (THN 3.1.1.25). So, since the relations that a priori reason alone can judge of do not allow for any distinction between human and animal incest, when we judge that there is a significant moral difference between the two, our judgment must, once again, involve something other than a priori reason alone.

There are, of course, differences between the case of the patricidal child and the overtopping sapling, and between the case of human incest and animal incest. But Hume contends that none of these differences concerns the four purely rational relations, that none of these differences can be discerned solely by the faculty that informs us of a priori, self-evident, or demonstrable truth. Rationalists may go on to claim that Hume has placed unfair restrictions on what counts as a purely rational relation. Couldn't there be propositions that do not concern the four relations Hume enumerates and yet nonetheless possess the hallmarks of pure rationality? To this question, Hume responds by challenging rationalists to articulate the additional relation such propositions could concern. He writes:

Shou'd it be asserted, that the sense of morality consists in the discovery of some relation, distinct from these, and that our enumeration was not compleat, when we comprehended all demonstrable relations under four general heads: To this I know not what to reply, till some one be so good as to point out to me this new relation. 'Tis impossible to refute a system, which has never yet been explain'd. (THN 3.1.1.20)

According to Hume, no one has ever articulated a purely rational relation distinct from the four he has enumerated. And so, since the four relations he has enumerated cannot fund the content that our moral judgments possess, we have no reason to think that the faculty that informs us of a priori, self-evident, and demonstrable truth produces our moral judgments on its own.

C. Arguments from the Best Explanation of the Moral Phenomena

The third category of Hume's arguments against moral rationalism consists of his own sentimentalist explanations of our substantial moral judgments and other relevant moral phenomena. These explanations imply that sentiment is instrumental in the development of all of our morally significant conduct, judgments, and institutions – that sentiment plays a leading causal role in every aspect of our moral lives. To the extent that these sentimentalist explanations capture the multifarious observable moral phenomena better than the rationalist alternative, they constitute an abductive argument for the claim that what we think of as morality does not originate in reason alone – that what we think of as morality has come into being because we possess certain sentiments.

In "Moral distinctions deriv'd from a moral sense," Hume gestures toward a sentimentalist account of morality but does not do much more than that (THN 3.1.2.1–5). He says that the anti-rationalist arguments of his previous section imply that sentiment plays an essential role in moral judgment, he asserts that the sentiment essential to positive moral judgments is a particular kind of pleasure and the sentiment essential to negative moral judgments is a particular kind of uneasiness, and he briefly answers an objection to which he provides a fuller response later on.[7]

But if we want to dig into the meat of Hume's arguments from the best explanation, we need to go past Part 1 of Book III of the *Treatise* to Parts 2 and 3. It is in Parts 2 and 3 that Hume presents his full-dress sentimentalist explanations of (among other things) justice, property, promising, political allegiance, chastity, admiration of military valor, approval of benevolence, and admiration for physical talents. To assess the success of Hume's attack on moral rationalism, we must examine the details of those explanations. We must ask how well Hume's sentimentalist account fits the tones and contours of our actual conduct, judgments, and institutions. Hume's account purports to explain the observable phenomena. So to determine whether his account is superior to his predecessors', we have to determine whether his explanations capture the phenomena better than theirs. As I read Book III of the *Treatise*, in other words, the weight of Hume's arguments for his particular version of moral sentimentalism falls more on the empirical explanations of Parts 2 and 3 than on the conceptual moves of Part I.

When we emphasize Parts 2 and 3, moreover, Book III of the *Treatise* looks to have much *less* in common with Hutcheson than Part 1 of Book III may have led us to believe. For the explanations of moral phenomena Hume presents in Parts 2 and 3 are incompatible not only with moral rationalism but also with Hutcheson's moral sense theory. Indeed, to the extent that they are successful, Hume's explanations undermine not only the rationalist and moral sense versions of the Positive Answer but also the Calvinist and egoist versions of the Negative Answer, draining the philosophical life blood out of the Human Nature Question as a whole. And reading the *Treatise* this way – with the result that Hume ends up on one side of a crucial philosophical divide and the rationalists and moral sense theorists end up together on the other – elucidates crucial aspects of Hume's account of morality that the division between rationalism and sentimentalism obscures. Or so I try to show in the next three chapters.

Did Hume himself view Book III this way? Did he think that the empirical explanations of Parts 2 and 3 were more important to his theory than the conceptual moves of Part 1? You might not get that idea if you read Part I on its own. Hume packages Part 1 as though the arguments there are a conclusive refutation of moral rationalism and this refutation is of great moment. But Hume's arguments in Part 1 do not advance significantly beyond what Hutcheson had developed in *The Moral Sense*.[8] And while Hume seems to think that Part 1 accomplishes the negative goal of defeating moral rationalism, its two sections leave us with only the barest of positive accounts, little more than the negation of the claim that morality originates in reason alone. The rich positive account of the multifarious observable moral phenomena – the distinctively Humean view of morality – is what Hume spends the eighteen sections of Parts 2 and 3 providing.

There is evidence, furthermore, that Part 1 was a late addition to the *Treatise*, something Hume tacked on in an attempt to appease Hutcheson, who had been dissatisfied with the unpublished version Hume had sent him (a version that Hume had already worked on for a number of years and which he presumably would not have sent to Hutcheson had he not thought it in nearly finished form).[9] If this is the case, then there is even more reason to think that the empirical explanations of Parts 2 and 3 – explanations that undermine Hutcheson's moral sense theory as well as moral rationalism – were more central to Hume's thinking when he wrote the *Treatise* than the arguments of Part 1 that overlap so significantly with Hutcheson's *Moral Sense*.

17

Hume's Associative Moral Sentiments

A. The Positive Answer and a Theological
Conception of Human Nature

In the seventeenth and eighteenth centuries, the Positive Answer to the Human Nature Question was embedded in theological conceptions of human nature. Cudworth, for instance, held that human rationality was attuned to the eternal and immutable truths of morality and that human rationality derived directly from the mind of God. And Hutcheson held that all of our senses were originally either benevolent or consistent with benevolence and that all our senses were originally implanted by God.

This combination of the Positive Answer and a theological conception of human nature went hand in hand with a certain view of justification. According to this view, something is justified if it is based on an aspect of human nature that is innate, instinctive, hard-wired, or unchanged by contingent interactions with the empirical world. Human nature, according to this view, was created by God, and God is perfectly moral. So something based on an original feature of human nature – on a feature that is the same now as it was when God first created it – possesses a pristine pedigree, an unimpeachable provenance. Moral sense theorists such as Hutcheson contended that our original moral affections possessed this status. Rationalists such as Cudworth contended that only reason did. But the structure of justification is the same for both of them. They both hold that justifying something involves tracing it back to what is original to human nature. On this view, justification, like legitimacy and a claim to the throne, has everything to do with parentage.[1]

The idea that justification involves tracing things back to what is original was, moreover, central not only to moral philosophy but to a number of other charged subjects as well. The Tories, for instance, tried to justify royalism by showing that the ancient constitution of England was a divine-right monarchy, and the Whigs tried to justify parliamentarianism by showing that the ancient constitution guaranteed the liberties of subjects.[2] Locke argued that a legitimate claim to property is one that can be traced back, in the right way, to original acquisition. And even the Calvinist proponents of the Negative Answer, who were otherwise so different from the moral rationalists and moral sense theorists, agreed that our original constitution was morally perfect and that anything that flowed directly from it was justified. The problem, as the Calvinists saw it, was that sin had corrupted human nature so thoroughly that it was impossible for us to access any of our original principles. The Bible, on the other hand, could be traced directly back to God's dictation, and so its injunctions were perfectly justified.

Hume attacked this view on numerous fronts. In "Of Miracles" he questioned the Calvinists' literalist reading of the Bible, and in the *Natural History of Religion* he suggested that Christianity grew out of pagan polytheisms. In his *History of England*, he drew a picture of the ancient Anglo-Saxons that undermined both Tory and Whig claims about Britain's ancient constitution. In Book I of the *Treatise of Human Nature*, he argued that beliefs that we think are justified because they are based on reason alone actually depend on experience. And in Books II and III of the *Treatise*, he argued that morality is based not solely on principles original to human nature but on features forged by our interaction with the empirical world. It is this last aspect of Hume's attack that will be our focus here.

The key to Hume's attack is the *explanatory symmetry* between his accounts of what is virtuous and what is not. Hume's rationalist and moral sense predecessors held that things that are morally correct or praiseworthy are based on original human principles, on principles that do not admit of any kind of empirical explanation. The only explanation we can give of these principles, according to Hume's predecessors, is that they derive directly from God. Hume's predecessors also thought that things that are morally incorrect or blameworthy are based on features whose existence is best explained by persons' interactions with the empirical world. Hume's predecessors thus asserted an explanatory asymmetry between what is morally correct or praiseworthy and what is not: The former, they held, is based on explanatorily fundamental features of human nature – or features that can be explained only by invoking God – while the latter results from changes empirical interactions have wrought on those fundamental features.

Hume's account implies that this claim of explanatory asymmetry is untenable. According to Hume's account, there is no feature that is part of the best explanation of all immoral traits but not part of the best explanation of any moral traits. Traits that are impeccable and traits that are condemnatory both turn out to be based on dispositions shaped by empirical factors. Nothing that is morally significant has a perfectly pure, non-empirical origin. So if we want to draw distinctions between traits that should be allowed or encouraged and traits that should be eliminated or suppressed, we need to do it in some way other than by trying to determine what is original to human nature and what is not.

In this chapter, we will look at how Hume uses the principles of association to produce explanatorily symmetrical empirical accounts of a number
of morally relevant traits. We will see that Hume's uses of the principles of
association imply that the distinction between what is original to human
nature and what is caused by empirical interaction is not coextensive with
the distinction between what is good and bad or what is praiseworthy and
blameworthy.[3] We will also see that this implication undermines the combination of the Positive Answer and the theological conception of human
nature characteristic of Hume's predecessors.

In Section B, I review how Locke and Hutcheson used the notion of the
association of ideas (this brief section summarizes points made in more
detail in Chapter 14). In C, I explain how Hume uses association in his
account of justice. In D, I explain how Hume uses association in his account
of natural virtue. In E, I examine one of Hume's favorite principles of association, our "addiction to general rules." And in F, I explain how Hume's
uses of association undermine his predecessors' combination of the Positive
Answer and a theological conception of human nature.

B. Locke and Hutcheson's Uses of Association

Locke used the notion of the association of ideas to explain mistakes in reasoning and belief. Associations, Locke maintained, cause people to believe
that one idea follows from another when in fact the two are "loose and independent one of another" (Locke 397). Ideas that "have in Nature nothing
to do one with another" become, as a result of association, confounded in
our minds so that we come to think there is a natural connection between
them when there is none in reality (Locke 398). If, for instance, a child is
made sick by an overdose of honey and so comes to associate sickness with
honey, he may as an adult come to think that honey is harmful, even though
it is actually innocuous (Locke 397). Similarly, if a child's upbringing causes
him to associate "Figure and Shape" with "the *Idea* of God," he may as an
adult come to think that God really does possess those characteristics, even
though He does not (Locke 400).

Hutcheson, like Locke, used the notion of the association of ideas to
explain mistakes. But while Locke focused on errors of reasoning and belief,
Hutcheson explained how association corrupts the affections. He argued,
for instance, that if a person comes to associate a political party with political
correctness, he may approve of and promote the advancement of his party
even when it turns out to conflict with the public good. And if a person, say,
comes to associate the architecture of Catholic churches with the evils of
popery, he may fail to appreciate the real beauty of such buildings.

The crucial point for our purposes here is that Locke and Hutcheson used
association only to explain things that are incorrect or blameworthy. They
also both believed that freeing a line of reasoning or an affective response
from the effects of association would rehabilitate it. If a judgment or passion

has been caused by association – or, more prolixly, if it is based on a principle of our nature whose original shape has been altered by association – there will be something wrong with it. But if it issues directly from an original principle of our constitution, it will be beyond reproach. Anything that flows directly from our original principles is aligned to what is natural, true, and real, while anything that results from association (anything that is the way it is because mental associations have altered an original principle) is unnatural, prejudicial, or fantastick.

As I explained in Chapter 14, Hutcheson's associative explanations of moral error play a crucial role in his defense of the Positive Answer and a theological conception of human nature. Hutcheson wanted to convince us that humans are naturally good, that humans were created by God, and that God is good. Hutcheson went about this task, first, by equating what is natural to humans with what is original and, second, by attributing what is original to God's creation. He then had to establish, third, that the distinction between what is good and what is bad is coextensive with the distinction between what is original and what is not original. And the key to Hutcheson's attempt to establish this coextensiveness was his arguments purporting to show that all the pre-associative aspects of our constitution are good (or at least consistent with goodness) and that the bad aspects of human conduct all result from associative changes to our constitution. So Hutcheson could maintain his Positive Answer and his theological conception of human nature only if the bad aspects of human nature bear the mark of association and the good aspects do not. But Hume's account implies that this idea is nothing but wishful thinking.

C. Association and the Origins of Justice

Hume uses principles of association far more than Locke or Hutcheson. They are central to his accounts of causality, the passions, and morals. Indeed, Hume wrote in the *Abstract* that "if anything can intitle the author [of the *Treatise*] to so glorious a name as that of an *inventor*, 'tis the use he makes of the principle of the association of ideas, which enters into most of his philosophy" (THN Abstract 35).[4]

Hume's associative account of justice begins with the denial of one of Hutcheson's most fundamental claims: that love of humanity is pre-associative and original, while hatred is associative and unoriginal. Hume's rejection of an explanatory asymmetry between love and hatred relies to a large extent on the psychology he develops in Book II of the *Treatise*. There Hume argues that love and hatred are caused by the qualities individual persons possess, not by their simple humanity itself (THN 2.2.1). I feel love for someone, Hume tells us, because she is associated in my mind with a quality that causes me pleasure, just as I feel hatred for someone because he is associated in my mind with a quality that causes me pain. Both people are humans, but that fact merely enables the association of impressions

and ideas to work in my mind. Their humanity is merely an associative conductor of impressions and ideas, not a quality that itself can arouse either
love or hatred. As Hume puts it when attacking a conception of justice that
resembles Hutcheson's:

[M]an in general, or human nature, is nothing but the object both of love and
hatred, and requires some other cause, which by a double relation of impressions
and ideas, may excite these passions. In vain wou'd we endeavour to elude this
hypothesis. There are no phenomena that point out any such kind affection to men,
independent of their merit, and every other circumstance. (THN 3.2.1.12)[5]

There is no such thing as the love of humanity merely as such, and all
of our particular loves are just as associative in origin as our hatreds. So
if we condemn hatred because it is associative and unoriginal, we have to
condemn love as well. But, of course, we do not want to condemn love. And
this implies that we must reject Hutcheson's view that everything associative
is condemnable.

But although Hume thinks love and hatred have associative origins, he
does not think all our passions do. Some passions, he tells us, are "implanted
in human nature" and cannot be explained by principles of association
(THN 3.2.1.12). It is these implanted or original passions that fill the
explanatory role, within Hume's philosophy, of Hutcheson's natural senses.
They are the points at which empirical explanations must end, the unexplained explainers. Observation cannot discover anything behind them.[6]

But Hume does not find as many pre-associative original passions as
Hutcheson does. Instead he finds these three: the "natural appetite betwixt
the sexes,"[7] "the natural affection, which [parents] bear their children," and
"*selfishness*" (THN 3.2.2.4–5). Hume goes on to argue, moreover, that these
passions alone would originally have combined to form in us an "unequal
affection" or the tendency to promote the welfare of ourselves and our families even if it means harming humanity in general (THN 3.2.2.8).[8] As Hume
sees it, the constitution of our original pre-associative passions is character-
ized by "partiality," not by a Hutchesonian concern for the human species
as a whole (THN 3.2.2.8). Hume writes:

In vain shou'd we expect to find, in *uncultivated nature*, a remedy to this inconvenience; or hope for any inartificial principle of the human mind, which might
controul those partial affections, and make us overcome the temptations arising
from our circumstances.... [O]ur natural uncultivated ideas of morality, instead of
providing a remedy for the partiality of our affections, do rather conform themselves
to that partiality, and give it an additional force and influence. (THN 3.2.2.8)

We should not fail to see in these statements a criticism of Hutcheson, who
believed that humans' original passions would have led them to live together
in perfect harmony.[9]

Hume himself argues that justice originates in rules or conventions that
alter or restrict the "partial and contradictory motions" of the original

implanted human passions.[10] As he puts it, "The remedy, then, is not deriv'd from nature, but from *artifice;* or more properly speaking, nature provides a remedy in the judgment and understanding, for what is irregular and incommodious in the affections" (THN 3.2.2.9). So while Hutcheson thinks that any redirection of our original passions brought about by convention pulls us away from morality, Hume thinks it is only as a result of convention that justice ever comes into being. "And thus justice establishes itself by a kind of convention or agreement. . . . Without such a convention, no one wou'd ever have dream'd, that there was such a virtue as justice, or have been induc'd to conform his actions to it" (THN 3.2.2.22).[11]

In Chapter 18, we examine in more detail the convention that brings about the institution of justice by altering our original sentiments; and in Section E of this chapter, we examine how the virtue of justice comes into being. But even at this stage, we can see that the picture of our original constitution that is the starting point for Hume's account of justice is incompatible with Hutcheson's fundamental conception of human nature. For that original constitution, if left unchanged, lacks the impartiality essential to justice on both Hume's and Hutcheson's account.

D. Association and the Origins of Natural Virtue

Hume's account of natural virtue might initially seem to share many features with Hutcheson's.[12] But although Hume and Hutcheson reject moral rationalism for similar reasons, the differences between their positive views on the approvals that define natural virtue are no less significant than their differences on justice. For while Hutcheson holds that the approvals that define correct moral judgment originate in non-associative senses, Hume attempts to show that those approvals owe their existence to the operation of associative principles.

The key to Hume's explanation of our approvals is sympathy, which is, as he puts it, the "chief source of moral distinctions" (THN 3.3.6.1). Now Humean sympathy is not a passion itself but rather the process whereby passions are communicated from one person to another. And what is crucial for our purposes is that this process, just like that which produces love and hatred, is associative. Indeed, Hume points out that all three principles of association can play a role in the sympathetic communication of passions.

> For besides the relation of cause and effect, by which we are convinc'd of the reality of the passion, with which we sympathize; besides this, I say, we must be assisted by the relations of resemblance and contiguity, in order to feel the sympathy in its full perfection. (THN 2.1.11.8)

On Hume's account, passions that are sympathetically communicated are not original in the sense of being non-associative.[13] They are, rather, two or three times removed from original pre-associative dispositions.

So for Hume, none of our approvals – correct or incorrect – occupy the ultimate explanatory position Hutcheson claimed for them. They all result from the associative process of sympathy. To the extent that Hume's sympathy-based explanation of approval is successful, therefore, Hutcheson's project of trying to read the content of morality off of our pre-associative constitution must be counted a failure. For if Hume is right, the origins of the passions that ground all moral evaluations are ineluctably associative.

Now Hume is like Hutcheson in holding that correct moral judgments are those that are based not on every actual or occurrent approval but only on certain privileged ones. Hutcheson holds that correct moral judgments are those in accord with approvals that flow from our original pre-associative moral sense, and Hume holds that correct moral judgments are those in accord with approvals we feel (or would feel) from general points of view (I will discuss these general points of view in more detail in Chapter 19). But Hume does not think the approvals we experience from general points of view are privileged because they are more original or less associative than other approvals. Hume argues, rather, that these general points of view are privileged because they correct for the contradictory nature of many of our actual approvals.[14] As Hume explains, we tend to sympathize more "[w]ith our countrymen, than with foreigners" and so must "fix on some steady and *general* points of view" in order to "prevent those continual *contradictions*" that the variability of our moral sentiments would otherwise precipitate (THN 3.3.1.15).

So both Hutcheson and Hume emphasize the fact that correct moral judgments are made from a privileged point of view. But where Hume's account of that point of view involves the associative process of sympathy, approvals that are typically contradictory, and a learned shift of perspective, Hutcheson's account relies on an explanatorily fundamental moral sense.

Hume realizes, however, that his sympathy-based explanation of approval and his account of the general points of view still do not adequately explain all the moral judgments we make. For Humean sympathy alone would cause us to approve of only that which *actually* benefits people. It seems, that is, that Hume must say that the favorable sentiments that give rise in us to approval will be sympathetically communicated to us only if someone else actually experiences them. But we sometimes approve of character traits that produce no benefit. Some of our approvals seem unconnected to any other favorable sentiments. The socially useful traits of a person stranded in the desert, for instance, help no one and yet we approve of them nonetheless. "Virtue in rags is still virtue." As Hume puts the objection:

Sympathy interests us in the good of mankind; and if sympathy were the source of our esteem for virtue, that sentiment of approbation cou'd only take place, where the virtue actually attain'd its end, and was beneficial to mankind. Where it fails of its end, 'tis only an imperfect means; and therefore can never acquire any merit from that end. (THN 3.3.1.19)

Hume responds to this objection by deploying one of his favorite principles of association: the addiction to general rules. Since the ways in which Hume uses this principle throughout the *Treatise* illustrate well the larger issues under consideration here, let us turn to a fuller discussion of them now.

E. Our Addiction to General Rules

As we saw in the *Abstract,* Hume was quite proud of his use of the principles of association. But I think he was especially pleased with his discovery of "our addiction to general rules." At several points in the *Treatise* he goes out of his way to underscore the novelty and explanatory power of this principle. In one passage, for instance, he writes, "It may not be amiss to observe on this occasion, that the influence of general rules and maxims on the passions very much contributes to facilitate the effects of all the principles, which we shall explain in the progress of this treatise" (THN 2.1.6.9). And Hume frequently italicizes the term "general rules," as though he were using it to denote a specific, well-defined piece of his technical apparatus.[15]

Hume offers a particularly clear description of his conception of our addiction to general rules in his discussion of the "measures of allegiance" (THN 3.2.9). There he argues that our feeling of obligation to obey government originates in the benefits the government provides. He acknowledges, however, that some people feel the obligation to obey even after their government has become so tyrannical that it does not benefit them at all. This would seem to constitute a counterexample to Hume's account, since he claims that the benefit causes the feeling of obligation, but in such a case the feeling of obligation exists even though the benefit does not. In response Hume writes:

[W]e may observe, that the maxim wou'd here be false, that *when the cause ceases, the effect must cease also.* For there is a principle of human nature, which we have frequently taken notice of, that men are mightily addicted to *general rules,* and that we often carry our maxims beyond those reasons, which first induc'd us to establish them. Where cases are similar in many circumstances, we are apt to put them on the same footing, without considering, that they differ in the most material circumstances, and that the resemblance is more apparent than real.... [G]eneral rules commonly extend beyond the principles, on which they are founded.... (THN 3.2.9.3)

Whatever it is we believe or feel in many cases of one kind of phenomenon, Hume tells us, we will also tend to believe or feel in resembling but crucially different cases. "[W]e transfer our experience in past instances to objects which are resembling, but are not exactly the same with those concerning which we have had experience" (THN 1.3.13.8). Our addiction to general rules is something like the associative tendency to *over*generalize. As Hume puts it:

When an object is found by experience to be always accompany'd with another; whenever the first object appears, tho' changed in very material circumstances; we naturally fly to the conception of the second, and form an idea of it in as lively and strong a manner, as if we had infer'd its existence by the justest and most authentic conclusion of our understanding. (THN 2.2.8.5; cf. 2.1.6.8–9)[16]

It is this tendency to overgeneralize that explains why some individuals feel obligated to obey tyrannical governments: Although the original cause of this feeling of obligation was the coincidence of obedience and self-interest, such people eventually come to associate (or sentimentally con-fuse) the feeling directly with obedience itself and so feel obligated to obey even when obedience and self-interest no longer coincide.[17]

For our current purposes, what is so interesting about Hume's addictive general rules is that they are startlingly similar to Hutcheson's fantastick associations of ideas. Hume's account of obedience to tyrants and Hutcheson's account of political factionalism both turn on the same psychological principle. In both cases, the explanations rely at crucial junctures on the claim that humans have the tendency to develop associative habits that nourish sentiments to such an extent that they eventually outgrow their original causes.

Do Hume and Hutcheson use this associative principle to explain the same types of things? Do they share the same attitude toward our tendency to overgeneralize? Well, as we've seen, Hutcheson uses fantastick associations to explain error. Such associations, as he sees it, lead us away from what is true and right and are therefore condemnable. And Hume sometimes uses general rules for a similar purpose, namely, to explain why people make the mistakes they do. The feeling of obligation some have toward obedience to tyrants is a good example. Hume thinks we ought to resist tyrants, not obey them. But the people he is discussing at THN 3.2.9.3 fail to realize that they ought to resist because their addiction to general rules has led them to associate obligation directly with obedience. Racial prejudice is another mistake we make because of our addiction to general rules. If we develop the habit of thinking that "an *Irishman* cannot have wit, and a *Frenchman* cannot have solidity," we might very well continue to think this even after we have met a witty Irishman or a judicious Frenchman (THN 1.3.13.7). We may get into the habit, that is, of transferring our experience of past Irishmen and Frenchmen to our experience of the Irishman or Frenchman in front of us right now, even though the two cases might differ in the most material circumstances. Hume also maintains that the "notions of modesty" to which women must conform are caused by men's addiction to general rules (THN 3.2.12.7). And although Hume does not overtly condemn these notions, we might suppose that he harbored some private misgivings (cf. THN 2.1.9.13).

But unlike Hutcheson's fantastick associations, Hume's addictive general rules do not mark a consistent boundary between the unreal or vicious, on the one hand, and the real or virtuous, on the other. For Hume invokes addictive general rules to explain not only judgments and traits we ought to avoid but judgments and traits we ought to embrace as well.[18] Hume argues, for instance, that our addiction to general rules enables us to distinguish emotionally charged fiction from cold-blooded fact (THN 1.3.10.10–12) and to prefer 1001 pounds to 1000 (THN 1.3.12.24). It also causes us to feel compassion for a "person of merit" who "is not dejected by misfortunes" (THN 2.2.7.5) and grief for children murdered in their sleep (THN 2.2.7.4–6). But all of these are, I take it, aspects of a sensible and perhaps even admirable character.

Moreover, it is only because we are addicted to general rules that we come to approve of virtue in rags. We approve of the ineffectual qualities of someone stranded in a desert only because his qualities resemble qualities of others that are of actual benefit.

Where a character is, in every respect, fitted to be beneficial to society, the imagination passes easily from the cause to the effect, without considering that there are still some circumstances wanting to render the cause a compleat one. *General rules* create a species of probability, which sometimes influences the judgment, and always the imagination. (THN 3.3.1.20)

But Hume gives us no reason to think that we are wrong to judge as virtuous the deserted person who would benefit others were he in society. The fact that this judgment has its origins in a passionate overgeneralization does not undermine it.

Hume's discussion of racial prejudice adds even more force to the impression that his general rules do not mark a consistent boundary between the mistaken or condemnable, on the one hand, and the correct or praiseworthy, on the other. For while Hume claims that our addiction to general rules gives rise to prejudice, he goes on to argue that the tendencies that enable us to combat prejudice are also born of general rules.[19] People who manage to free themselves from racial prejudice, Hume argues, often do so by recalling all the times in the past that their rash initial judgments led to destructive mistakes. But transferring those past events to the present is yet another example of the addiction to general rules.

Thus our general rules are in a manner set in opposition to each other. Sometimes the one, sometimes the other prevails, according to the disposition and character of the person. The following of general rules is a very unphilosophical species of probability; and yet 'tis only by following them that we can correct this, and all other unphilosophical probabilities. (THN 1.3.13.12)

Perhaps, though, Hume's most important use of general rules to explain characteristics that ought to be cultivated is his account of how we come to disapprove of our own self-interested acts of injustice. The pressure on Hume to explain this phenomenon is especially great given that his account of justice starts from the claim that "our natural uncultivated ideas of morality, instead of providing a remedy for the partiality of our affections, do rather conform themselves to that partiality, and give it an additional force and influence" (THN 3.2.2.8). Hume claims that the original "uncultivated" human constitution is such that people would not disapprove of unjust actions that promote their own interests. So how does Hume bridge the explanatory gap between this original partiality and the "cultivated" impartiality of our disapproval of acts that benefit us? He does so, first, by pointing out that unjust acts generally cause more harm than good. This fact, he continues, coupled with our sympathetically grounded disposition to disapprove of that which harms others, leads us to disapprove of unjust acts that do not affect our own interests. But if we have represented to us enough harmful acts of injustice that do not affect our own interests, and if (as we must) we feel disapproval in most of these cases, we will eventually develop the associative habit of conjoining disapproval and injustice. And once this habit develops, we will tend to feel disapproval toward all unjust acts, even those that benefit us. Our tendency to overgeneralize, in other words, causes our disapproval of the injustice of others to become connected in our minds (or sentimentally con-fused) to the injustice we commit ourselves.

And tho' this [disapproval of injustice], in the present case, be deriv'd only from contemplating the actions of others, yet we fail not to extend it even to our own actions. The *general rule* reaches beyond those instances, from which it arose. (THN 3.2.2.24)

F. Association, Theology, and Human Nature

According to Hume, then, the addiction to general rules grounds aspects of human life that ought to be encouraged, such as our moral obligation to justice, as well as aspects that ought to be discouraged, such as racial prejudice.[20] But as we've seen, Hutcheson's combination of the Positive Answer and a theological conception of human nature requires that correct judgments and admirable traits have different origins from incorrect judgments and despicable traits. Hutcheson's view demands an explanatory asymmetry between the praiseworthy and the condemnable: The latter must admit of an empirical explanation that the former do not. Hume's explanatorily symmetrical accounts thus constitute a rejection of Hutcheson's method of justification and of the Positive Answer and the theological conception of human nature out of which it grew. To the extent that his explanations are successful, Hume establishes that Hutcheson was wrong to privilege what is original to our nature, and in so doing he fatally undermines the theologically sanctioned project of trying to trace justificatory borders along explanatory fault lines.

Hume's explanatorily symmetrical explanations are equally damaging, moreover, to the views of the other British moralists who subscribed to the Positive Answer and a theological conception of human nature. The rationalists, for instance, like Hutcheson, believed that correct judgment and virtuous conduct originated in an aspect of human nature that did not admit of any empirical explanation. Like Hutcheson, the rationalists believed that morality is based on a principle that is part of every human's original, God-given constitution. The rationalists thought this internal principle was reason, while Hutcheson thought it was the moral sense. But Hume's associative explanations – which imply that moral judgment and conduct depend on non-rational, non-original sentiments – are an attack on both positions.

But do Humean accounts damage theological conceptions of human nature in general or only those of his immediate predecessors? Even if some type of Humean explanation turns out to be correct, might it not still be possible to maintain that the changes to our original constitution that lead to correct judgment and virtuous conduct derive directly from God, while the factors that lead to incorrect judgment and vicious conduct do not? Couldn't one hold that God's design is manifest in the mental mechanisms that lead to morality, and that the factors that lead to immorality are a corruption of that design?

While Humean accounts might not prevent one from holding such a position on the theological origin of human nature, the symmetry of Hume's explanations drains it of substance. For Hume argues that the associative principles that lead to moral traits also lead to immoral traits, and that our original or explanatorily fundamental principles (i.e., self interest, sexual attraction, and concern for one's children) also play a role in the development of both moral and immoral traits. So if a Humean account is right, the distinction between what is derived from God and what is not will not correspond to any explanatory difference. The distinction between what is derived from God and what is not will, rather, be parasitic on the distinction between what we judge to be moral and what we judge to be immoral. "Derived from God" will turn out to be an explanatorily irrelevant label we bestow on things after we have already determined that they are worthy of praise. If this is a theological conception of human nature, it is so in name alone.[21]

18

Hume's Progressive View of Human Nature

The Calvinists thought that people were rotten through and through. But most people believe that humanity manifests both goodness and badness. Most people believe that some individuals are morally superb, that some are morally loathsome, and that most are morally good sometimes and in certain respects and morally bad at other times and in other respects.

Proponents of the Positive Answer are in the majority in thinking that humanity manifests both goodness and badness. Their distinctive claim is that the good aspects of humanity are natural and the bad aspects unnatural. If this claim is to have any substance, however, proponents of the Positive Answer have to draw a distinction between the natural and the unnatural that is conceptually independent of the distinction between the morally good and the morally bad. And if this claim is to be true, the distinction between the natural and the unnatural must track the conceptually independent distinction between the morally good and the morally bad.

Hume argued that proponents of the Positive Answer could not fulfill both of these requirements. But Hume's rejection of the Positive Answer should not lead us to conclude that he was a proponent of the Negative Answer. In fact, Hume thought the Negative Answer was just as misconceived as the Positive. And by rejecting the dichotomy the Human Nature Question posed, Hume was able to adopt insights from both sides and combine them into a new and improved position, one that effected a real advance in the "science of man" (THN Introduction 7).

In this chapter, I examine an aspect of Hume's thought that distinguishes him from proponents of both the Positive and the Negative Answers and that, I think, truly does advance our understanding of human nature and the origin of morality. This aspect – which I will call Hume's "progressive view of human nature" – stands out most clearly when Hume's account of the virtue of justice is placed against the backdrop of a dispute between proponents of the Negative and Positive Answers on the origin of human sociability.

In Section A, I outline the dispute on the origin of human sociability as it occurred between Mandeville, on the one hand, and Shaftesbury and Hutcheson, on the other. In B, I show that there are significant respects in which Hume's account of justice is in agreement with Mandeville and in disagreement with Shaftesbury and Hutcheson. In C, I show that there are other significant respects in which Hume's account is in agreement with Shaftesbury and Hutcheson and in disagreement with Mandeville. And in D, I explain how Hume's combination of these two different aspects resulted in a new and improved view of human nature, one that is dynamic or progressive where that of his predecessors was static.[1]

A. Hutcheson and Shaftesbury versus Mandeville

Human beings are sociable. They seek out company, live together "in Multitudes" (Mandeville I 41), undertake large cooperative endeavors, and act in ways that benefit others. They are not solitary creatures engaged in perpetual warfare. On this point proponents of the Positive Answer, such as Shaftesbury and Hutcheson, and proponents of the Negative Answer, such as Mandeville, all agree. What Mandeville disagrees with Shaftesbury and Hutcheson about is the origin of human sociability: while Shaftesbury and Hutcheson believe that human sociability originates in natural benevolence, Mandeville believes that it originates in self-interest.

Shaftesbury points to our friendships and our morals as compelling evidence of our natural benevolence. We all prefer "Company" to "Solitude," he says, and "almost all our Pleasures" are built upon "mutual Converse" and "Society" (Virtue or Merit 59). The aspect of friendship that gives us the most pleasure of all, moreover, is being benevolent or "doing good" for our friends (Moralists 135). But to be virtuous is to be benevolent or to "do good" for the human species as a whole, which is just to be a "*Friend of Mankind*" (Moralists 136). This is why being virtuous provides us with such pleasure – because it, like friendship, is the expression of our natural benevolence. Indeed, benevolence is so deeply engrained in us that we even take pleasure simply in witnessing a "*generous Action*" (Moralists 135; cf. Virtue or Merit 17–18, 25). And given that this benevolence is so universal and trenchant, we can only conclude that it is "*Innate*," or an "*Instinct*" in every human being, originating not in "*Art, Culture*, or *Discipline*" but in "*mere Nature*" (Moralists 229–30).

Hutcheson offers a similarly benevolent view of human nature. Hutcheson argues, in particular, that every human possesses both a public and a moral sense. The public sense is a "Determination to be pleased with the *Happiness* of others, and to be uneasy at their *Misery*" (Passions and Affections 5), and the moral sense is that which approves of virtue, which tends to the "Publick Advantage," and disapproves of vice, which tends to the Publick "Detriment" (Passions and Affections 7). Hutcheson takes great pains to establish that these two senses are entirely distinct from self-interest – that self-interest could never give rise to all of our motives to benefit others nor lead us to approve of all the benevolent actions of which we do in fact approve. Hutcheson also takes great pains to establish that these two benevolent senses are "*fix'd*, and *real* and *natural*" to all humans (Beauty and Virtue 82), "instincts" that do not result from custom, education, or habit but have been "*implanted in our* Nature" (Beauty and Virtue 216).

Mandeville paints a very different picture, one in which humans are motivated not by "Love to others" but almost entirely by "selfishness" (Mandeville II 178). As he puts it in his attack on "Mr. *Hutcheson*," "it is not the Care of others, but the Care of itself, which Nature has trusted and charged every individual Creature with" (Mandeville II 346). And it is this self-regard, according to Mandeville, not any putative "Love of our Species," that is the cause of the "Sociableness of Man" (Mandeville II 182; cf. I 4, 325, 344, 346, 364).

In support of his claim that sociability originates in selfishness, Mandeville tells a long story about how humans moved, over a period of thousands of years, from their initial savage state to the complex societies we find ourselves in today. There were three stages to this development. At the first stage, early humans banded together into small groups to protect themselves from the predation of "wild Beasts" (Mandeville II 230). At the second stage, small groups formed into larger groups to protect themselves from the aggressive advances of other humans, maintaining a mutual defense against "the Danger Men are in from one another" (Mandeville II 266). At neither of these two stages did love for others play any role. Self-preservation alone did all the work.

The large groups formed at the second stage were unstable, however. This is because the members of the groups were liable to attack and steal from each other, as well as to betray the agreements of mutual protection that brought them together in the first place. What were needed, then, were "Antidotes, to prevent the ill Consequences" of these selfish tendencies that are "inseparable from our Nature; which yet in themselves, without Management or Restraint, are obstructive and pernicious to Society" (Mandeville II 283). The development of a written language filled this role. For once we had "Letters," we could write down our "Laws." And written laws were the means by which we could hold people to their agreements, which was the condition for the creation of groups that were large and tolerably stable. "Therefore the third and last Step to Society is the Invention of Letters" (Mandeville II 269).

Mandeville then describes how society, once established, grows and prospers. He argues that what powers society – what generates sociable interaction and improves everyone's standard of living – is the development of commerce and standards of politeness, honor, and shame. But commerce and the standards of politeness, honor, and shame originate not in benevolence but in conventions built by and upon nothing other than self-interest (see Mandeville I 42ff. and II 341ff.).

So while Mandeville acknowledges that people do perform acts that are sociable and benefit others, he denies that humans possess any natural sentiments of sociability and benevolence. Our tendency toward sociable and benevolent action is, rather, the by-product of an artifice others invented for their own self-interest and we promote for ours. As Mandeville puts it in a passage that could sum up his attack on Shaftesbury and Hutcheson, "What you call Natural, is evidently Artificial, and belongs to Education" (Mandeville II 270). Or as he puts it elsewhere, "My Business is to demonstrate to you, that the good Qualities Men compliment our Nature and the whole Species with, are the Result of Art and Education" (Mandeville II 306).

B. Ways in Which Hume Agrees with Mandeville

With whom does Hume side in this dispute when he is writing the *Treatise*? Certainly, Hume is no egoist, and so at least in one important respect he is much closer to Shaftesbury and Hutcheson than he is to Mandeville. Hume also believes that humans possess "natural" virtues, many of which are inherently sociable, and this too seems to place him with Shaftesbury and Hutcheson (THN 3.3.1).[2]

At the beginning of his account of justice, however, Hume seems to side squarely with Mandeville and against Shaftesbury and Hutcheson. For the title of the first section of Hume's discussion is "Justice, whether a natural or artificial virtue?", which can be taken to be an indication of his intention to enter into the dispute between Mandeville, Shaftesbury, and Hutcheson (THN 3.2.1). And Hume says flat out that his view is that justice is "not natural" but the result of "artifice," which looks to be an unambiguously Mandevillean answer (THN 3.2.1.1).

The "short, and, I hope, convincing argument" Hume presents for the artificiality of justice seems to confirm his Mandevilleanism (THN 3.2.1.1).[3] Hume begins the argument by claiming that to be virtuous is to have a certain kind of motive. Hume next maintains that a virtue is natural only if the motive of which it consists is one that humans possessed in their precivilized or "rude and more *natural* condition, if you are pleas'd to call such a condition natural" (THN 3.2.1.9). If, in contrast, the virtue consists of a characteristic possessed only by "civiliz'd" individuals as a result of their having been "train'd up according to a certain discipline and education," it is an artificial virtue (THN 3.2.1.9). Hume then canvasses all the possible motives people could have for performing actions we think of as just and contends that none of these is both equivalent to the virtue of justice and present in precivilized humans.

The first possible motive that Hume examines is a "regard to justice, and abhorrence of villainy and knavery" (THN 3.2.1.9). Hume acknowledges – in a passage that will be very important to our later discussion – that people do possess this "regard to justice." But he contends that only "civiliz'd" humans possess it, and that humans in their "rude and more *natural* condition" did not (THN 3.2.1.9). Hume's argument here rests on the idea that a virtue consists of the possession of a certain kind of motive (THN 3.2.1.2). But a regard to justice is simply the motive to perform the actions that would be performed by someone who possesses the virtue of justice. The person who possesses the virtue of justice, therefore, must *first* possess some motive other than the regard to justice before anyone else can *later* develop the (derivative) regard to justice. Another way to put this point is to say that a simple regard to justice on its own has no content; it is a de dicto motive, or the motive to-perform-just-actions. A simple regard to justice can arise, therefore, only *after* a person knows what the content of justice is. Thus the simple regard to justice cannot be the origin of the content-ful idea of justice, since the content-ful idea must predate the simple regard.[4]

The second motive for justice that Hume examines is "self-love" or "a concern for our private interest or reputation" (THN 3.2.1.10). This motive, unlike the simple regard to justice, has existed in all humans at all times, civilized or not. But self-love is obviously not the motive that constitutes the virtue of justice. For just conduct is not always in one's self-interest, so someone motivated exclusively by self-love will at least sometimes be guilty of injustice. And to the extent that self-love remains in its precivilized or "*uncultivated*" condition, the divergence between it and justice will be very great indeed (THN 3.2.2.8).

The third candidate for the motive of justice that Hume considers is "the *regard to publick interest*" or "public benevolence," a desire to benefit humanity as a whole (THN 3.2.1.11). Hume's view of this candidate is particularly important for our purposes, since Mandeville disagrees with Shaftesbury and Hutcheson precisely on the question of whether or not humans possess the motive of benevolence toward humankind. And thus Hume's rejection of this motive seems to leave little room for doubt as to which side he takes in the dispute between his three predecessors.

Hume offers three "considerations" for denying that the virtue of justice consists of a "regard to the publick interest." The first reason is that someone motivated solely by the desire to benefit humanity as a whole would at least sometimes commit injustice, since a "single act of justice" may actually harm the "public interest," as for instance when "a man of merit ... restores a great fortune to a miser, or a seditious bigot" (THN 3.2.2.22). Hume acknowledges that most acts of justice do benefit the public and that even the "single act" of restoring a great fortune to a miser or bigot can have the beneficial effect of serving as an example to those who would otherwise be tempted to commit harmful injustice. But this connection between the public interest and the example of the single act (which is harmful when considered in isolation but beneficial when considered as an example) is not natural since it will hold only within civilized societies, in which the rules of justice are already established and well known.

Hume's second "consideration," furthermore, consists of a counterexample that shows that even within a civil society with established rules of justice, the connection between the public interest and single acts of justice will not always hold. He points out, specifically, that the conditions of a loan to a miser or seditious bigot might include that the repayment of it be made in secret, "as when the lender wou'd conceal his riches," in which case the repayment could not achieve even the beneficial goal of serving as an example to others (THN 3.2.1.11). But although in such a case there is not even an artificial convention that creates a connection between justice and the public interest, "there is no moralist, who will affirm, that the duty and the obligation ceases" (THN 3.2.1.11). There is, then, no chance that the duty or obligation is the same thing as the motive to benefit the public.

Hume's third "consideration" for rejecting "public benevolence" as the origin of justice cuts even deeper than the first two. He begins by pointing out that it is simply an undeniable fact that people do not have "the public interest" in mind when they "pay their creditors, perform their promises, and abstain from theft, and robbery" (THN 3.2.1.11). "That is a motive," he says, "too remote and too sublime to affect the generality of mankind, and operate with any force in actions so contrary to private interest as are frequently those of justice and common honesty" (THN 3.2.1.11).

Hume goes on, moreover, to argue that the public interest could *never* be the motive behind acts of "justice and common honesty" because the motive of public interest – upon which Shaftesbury and Hutcheson build their entire theory of human nature – does not exist in any human, "rude" or "civiliz'd." As he puts it, "In general, it may be affirm'd, that there is no such passion in human minds, as the love of mankind, merely as such, independent of personal qualities, or services, or of relation to ourself" (THN 3.2.1.12).

Hume's denial of the existence of a love for mankind merely as such is grounded in the psychology he develops in Book II of the *Treatise*, where he argues that love and hate are caused by the qualities individual persons possess, not by their simple humanity itself (THN 2.2.1). As we discussed in Chapter 17, Hume holds that I feel love for someone because she is associated in my mind with a quality that causes me pleasure, just as I feel hatred for someone because he is associated in my mind with a quality that causes me pain. Both people are humans, of course, but that fact merely enables the association of impressions and ideas to work in my mind. Their humanity is merely an associative conductor of impressions and ideas, not a quality that itself can arouse either love or hatred.[5]

Hume acknowledges that humans prefer being with others to being alone. But like Mandeville, he denies the Shaftesburean claim that this preference for company reveals a benevolent concern for humanity. Just as Mandeville says that most people engage in friendly leisure activity simply for their own enjoyment (Mandeville I 336–44, II 183), so too Hume maintains that we "love company in general; but 'tis as we love any other amusement" (THN 3.2.1.12).

Hume also acknowledges that we have the capacity to feel friendship or love for any other individual under certain circumstances. But he denies that this capacity constitutes evidence that we have the quite different capacity to feel love or friendship for all humans under any circumstances. He writes:

> An *Englishman* in *Italy* is a friend: A *European* in *China*; and perhaps a man wou'd be belov'd as such, were we to meet him in the moon. But this proceeds only from the relation to ourselves; which in these cases gathers force by being confined to a few persons. (THN 3.2.1.12)

Hume's examples in this passage are particularly revealing, for they are clear echoes of the following passage from *The Fable of the Bees* in which Mandeville is explicitly attacking Shaftesbury's benevolent view of human nature:

> Two *Londoners*, whose Business oblige them not to have any Commerce together, may know, see, and pass by one another every Day upon the *Exchange*, with not much greater Civility than Bulls would: Let them meet at *Bristol* they'll pull off their Hats, and on the least Opportunity enter into Conversation, and be glad of one another's Company. When *French*, *English* and *Dutch* meet in *China* or any other Pagan Country, being all *Europeans*, they look upon one another as Country-men, and if no Passion interferes they will feel a natural Propensity to love one another. . . . These things by superficial Judges are attributed to Man's Sociableness, his natural Propensity to Friendship and love of Company; but whoever will duly examine things and look into Man more narrowly, will find that on all these Occasions we only endeavor to strengthen our Interest, and are moved by the Causes already alleg'd. (Mandeville I 343)

Our capacity to feel friendship for other particular individuals, Mandeville says here, has misled "superficial Judges" such as Shaftesbury into attributing to humans a public benevolence, while in fact this phenomenon is better explained by other "Causes." But this is the same point we have just seen Hume advance in his denial of the existence of public benevolence. We find, then, that when criticizing Shaftesbury and Hutcheson's publicly benevolent conception of human nature, Hume and Mandeville speak in the same voice.

The final candidate for the original motive of justice that Hume considers is the motive of "*private benevolence, or a regard to the interests of the party concern'd*" (THN 3.2.1.13). But Hume quickly dismisses this candidate on the grounds that we might hate the person toward whom we have an obligation of justice, and indeed, the person may actually deserve the hatred of all humankind, but our obligation to the person does not diminish nonetheless. Hume also points out that the person toward whom we have an obligation of justice may be a "miser" who "can make no use of what I wou'd deprive him of" or a "profligate debauchee" who "wou'd rather receive harm than benefit" from my giving him what he's owed (THN 3.2.1.13). Once again, however, our obligation to give the person what he's owed would remain the same, even though our giving it to him will not benefit him at all. So our desire to benefit a particular person, or "private benevolence," cannot be the origin of the virtue of justice.

So according to Hume, if our sense of justice is natural, it will have at its foundation a natural sentiment. There is, however, no such natural sentiment to be found. All the possible sentimental candidates are either non-existent (public benevolence), non-natural (a regard to the virtue of justice), or incompatible with some instances of our obligation to justice (self-love and private benevolence [as well as public benevolence, if it did exist]). Hume concludes, therefore, that "the sense of justice and injustice is not deriv'd from nature, but arises artificially" (THN 3.2.1.17) – a result that is conspicuously Mandevillean.

Hume's positive, constructive account of the development of society and the artifice of justice is also basically Mandevillean in that it too is grounded almost entirely in self-interest.[6] Hume begins his account by noting the relative helplessness of individual humans to meet their needs and satisfy their desires.[7] As he explains:

Of all the animals, with which this globe is peopled, there is none towards whom nature seems, at first sight, to have excercis'd more cruelty than towards man, in the numberless wants and necessities, with which she has loaded him, and in the slender means, which she affords to the relieving these necessities.... In man alone, this unnatural conjunction of infirmity, and of necessity, may be observ'd in its greatest perfection. (THN 3.2.2.2)

Mandeville is impressed by the same point, maintaining that humans are uniquely "curs'd" by "Obstacles" and that "[a]ll the Element are our Enemies" (Mandeville I 344–5; cf. Mandeville I 205).

Hume and Mandeville both then go on to argue that humans develop societies because it is the only way for them to overcome their relative helplessness. As Mandeville puts it, "The Love Man has for his Ease and Security, and his perpetual Desire of meliorating his Condition, must be sufficient Motives to make him fond of Society; considering the necessitous and helpless Condition of his Nature" (Mandeville II 180; cf. Mandeville I 344). And as Hume has it:

'Tis by society alone he is able to supply his defects.... By society all his infirmities are compensated; and tho' in that situation his wants multiply every moment upon him, yet his abilities are still more augmented, and leave him in every respect more satisfied and happy, than 'tis possible for him, in his savage and solitary condition, ever to become. (THN 3.2.2.3)

Here Hume attributes "the origin of society" to "self-interest." As he explains, "There is no passion ... capable of controlling the interested affection, but the very affection itself, by an alteration of its direction" (THN 3.2.2.13). And we must take the antecedent of this view to be Mandeville, not Shaftesbury or Hutcheson.

Clearly Mandevillean as well is Hume's story of how justice originates in conventions grounded in "*selfishness* and *limited generosity*" (THN 3.2.2.16). Everyone wants to secure his or her "goods," Hume tells us. But certain of those goods – namely, "possessions . . . we have acquir'd by our industry and good fortune" – are inherently insecure, since other people both can "ravish" them and have a motive to do so (THN 3.2.2.7). Humans come to realize, however, that they will stand to benefit if they enter into a stabilizing "artifice" or "convention" whereby each person leaves every other person "in the peaceable enjoyment of what he may acquire by his fortune and industry" (THN 3.2.2.9).

I observe, that it will be for my interest to leave another in the possession of his goods, *provided* he will act in the same manner with regard to me. He is sensible of a like interest in the regulation of his conduct. When this common sense of interest is mutually express'd, and is known to both, it produces a suitable resolution and behaviour. (THN 3.2.2.10)

Hume's account of this mutual agreement to refrain from taking each other's goods is fascinating and compelling. Hume argues that this agreement is one that does not rely on "the interposition of a promise" but "arises gradually, and acquires force by a slow progression, and by our repeated experience of the inconveniences of transgressing it" (THN 3.2.2.10). And it is as a result of this gradual agreement that there "arise the ideas of justice and injustice" (THN 3.2.2.11). This progressive agreement, in other words, is the very origin of justice.

Now for our purposes here, what is most crucial about this story is that in it Hume very clearly attributes the artifice that is the origin of justice to "the love of gain" and not to natural benevolence (THN 3.2.2.3). The artifice, Hume says, is grounded entirely in a "sense of interest" (THN 3.2.2.10). Indeed, a few pages after his story of the development of the artifice of justice, Hume explicitly claims that justice would never have come into existence if, instead of being selfish, "every man had a tender regard for another" (THN 3.2.2.16). "Encrease to a sufficient degree the benevolence of man," Hume maintains, "and you render justice useless" (THN 3.2.2.16). The very purpose of justice is to restrain the "selfishness of man," and it is thus the selfishness of man in which justice originates.

I should not overemphasize the similarity between Mandeville and Hume on the origins of society and justice. Hume clearly thinks that even in their "rude" and "uncultivated" state people are not as exclusively self-interested as Mandeville does (THN 3.2.2.5).[8] But Hume does insist that societies and the conventions of justice develop as a result of the redirection of self-interest, and this is an unmistakably Mandevillean position. As Hume explains, it is "*only from the selfishness and confin'd generosity of men, along with the scanty provision nature has made for his wants, that justice derives its origin*" (THN 3.2.2.18).

C. Ways in Which Hume Agrees with Shaftesbury and Hutcheson

Within Hume's account of justice, however, there is also one very conspicuous point at which he appears to side with Shaftesbury and Hutcheson and against Mandeville. This point concerns the sincerity of persons' commitment to the virtue of justice.

Mandeville insists that the vast majority of people who pretend to be virtuous are in fact hypocrites. Indeed, one of the most characteristic features of Mandeville's writings as a whole is the view that most of what passes in society for virtue is really just a counterfeit – that although we all claim to occupy a moral high ground, our overriding motives are actually almost entirely selfish and thus possess no moral worth. As Mandeville puts it, "There is not a quarter of the Wisdom, solid Knowledge, or intrinsick Worth, in the World, that Men talk of, and compliment one another with; and of Virtue or Religion there is not an hundredth Part in Reality of what there is in Appearance" (Mandeville II 340; cf. I 254, I 331).

One of the most characteristic features of the writings of both Shaftesbury and Hutcheson, in contrast, is the view that many people at least some of the time do really and truly care about what is virtuous. Central to Shaftesbury and Hutcheson's arguments for this more positive view of human nature is the contention that people such as Hobbes and Mandeville fail miserably in their attempts to find selfishness at the heart of all human behavior.

Does Hume think people really and truly care about the virtue of justice and are not simply hypocritical moral counterfeiters? He clearly does. Does he think the virtue of justice is distinct from self-interest? He clearly thinks that as well. And this would seem to place him with proponents of the Positive Answer, despite the Mandevillean account of justice we discussed in the previous section.

We have seen that Hume believes that "in his rude and more *natural* condition," a human would reject "as perfectly unintelligible" the idea of repaying a loan simply out of a regard to justice (THN 3.2.1.9). But Hume also believes that this idea is entirely intelligible to people within society, and that in fact a regard to justice does play a role in the conduct of "civiliz'd" people. As he puts it:

I ask, *What reason or motive have I to restore the money?* It will, perhaps, be said, that my regard to justice, and abhorrence of villainy and knavery, are sufficient reasons for me, if I have the least grain of honesty, or sense of duty and obligation. And this answer, no doubt, is just and satisfactory to man in his civiliz'd state, and when train'd up according to a certain discipline and education. (THN 3.2.1.9)

We find, then, that at this point in the *Treatise*, in the midst of his Mandev-illean argument for the artificiality of justice, Hume attributes to civilized people the "antipathy to treachery and roguery" that he will later rely upon in the *Second Enquiry* in his much more Hutchesonian account of the reason to be just (Second Enquiry 155–6).

Nor is Hume's reference to a "sense of duty and obligation" an isolated comment. In the next section of the *Treatise*, when addressing the question of why "*we annex the idea of virtue to justice, and of vice to injustice,*" he explains in detail how we acquire this sense of duty, or regard to justice (THN 3.2.2.23). People initially care about justice only because it accords with self-interest he tells us there. But over time, they develop mental associations that lead them to approve of justice even when it does not promote their self-interest, and to disapprove of injustice even when it does promote their self-interest (I discussed this aspect of Hume's account in more detail in Chapter 17, Section C).[9] And these unselfish approvals and disapprovals constitute not a counterfeit concern for the virtue of justice but the real thing. Hume argues, in other words, that as a result of an associative "progress of sentiments" (THN 3.2.2.25), people who originally had only selfish reasons for caring about justice eventually come to possess a commitment to justice that can run "contrary to private interest" (THN 3.2.1.11).

If there is any lingering doubt about where Hume stands in the debate between Shaftesbury, Hutcheson, and Mandeville on the sincerity of per-sons' commitment to the virtue of justice, his discussion of the "artifice of politicians" should dispel it. In that discussion, Hume acknowledges that the commitment to justice has been "forwarded by the artifice of politicians, who, in order to govern men more easily, and preserve peace in human soci-ety, have endeavour'd to produce an esteem for justice, and an abhorrence of injustice" (THN 3.2.2.25). Hume then maintains, however, that this point "has been carry'd too far by certain writers on morals, who seem to have employ'd their utmost efforts to extirpate all sense of virtue from among mankind" (THN 3.2.2.25). The implication here, of course, is that there *is* a sense of virtue among mankind. And this is significant for our purposes because in making this claim Hume is clearly signaling his disagreement with Mandeville and his agreement with Shaftesbury and Hutcheson. We can be sure this is Hume's aim since Mandeville was infamous for claiming that "the Distinction between *Virtue* and *Vice*" was "the Contrivance of Politi-cians" (Mandeville I 50–1), and Hume says in this passage that the "writers on morals" are led astray by their false belief that the artifice of politicians is "the sole cause of the distinction we make betwixt vice and virtue" (THN 3.2.2.25; cf. 3.2.6.11 and 3.3.1.11–12).[10] When attacking Mandeville on this point, moreover, Hume is obviously seconding Hutcheson, who scorned Mandeville's contention that people act virtuously only because they have been manipulated by the "*Statues* and *Panegyricks*" of "cunning Governours" (Beauty and Virtue 130).

D. Hume's Progressive View of Human Nature

So Hume claims, first, that justice is an artificial virtue that originates in self-interest. He also claims, second, that people really do exhibit the non-self-interested virtue of justice. Mandeville would agree with the first claim, Shaftesbury and Hutcheson would agree with the second, but none of them would allow that both could be true. Indeed, all of the seventeenth- and eighteenth-century moralists who preceded Hume would have thought these two claims incompatible. Hume's two-part position on justice is thus something significantly new in British moral philosophy.

What's significantly new in Hume's account will stand out clearly when set against a point on which Mandeville, Shaftesbury, and Hutcheson all agreed. They all believed (1) that if Mandeville was right that human sociability originated in self-interest, then most of what passes for virtue is really just hypocrisy or counterfeit. This is because all three of them believed (2) that if Mandeville was right that human sociability originates in self-interest, then there is no difference between the ultimate motives of the saint and the motives of the knave. They believed that if human sociability originates in self-interest, then the seeming benevolence of the saint will really be just as selfish as the mischief of the knave. Now (1) does follow plausibly enough from (2), for if everyone is equally selfish, then the person who pretends to care about others simply for their own sake will be trading in counterfeit virtue. If no distinction can be drawn between the motives of the saint and the motives of the knave, then there will be a very important sense in which virtue is not real.[11]

But why think that (2) is true? Why think that the claim that humans were originally motivated to become sociable because it served their self-interest implies that self-interest still remains humans' only ultimate motive to sociable behavior?

Shaftesbury, Hutcheson, and Mandeville all believed (2) because of their adherence to an *originalist* or *static view of human nature*. According to this view, humans' original motives always remain their only truly fundamental ones. The basic elements of human motivation are fixed. Experience and socialization can alter the focus or direction of the original human motives, but they cannot create a new kind of motive altogether.[12] The ultimate driving forces of human conduct stay the same. Thus, on the static view, if humans were in the past initially motivated to become sociable because it served their self-interest, then it must be the case that their motivation to continue to be sociable in the present is also self-interested. And if humans in the present are motivated to be sociable for non-selfish reasons, then it must be the case that they were in the past motivated to become sociable for non-selfish reasons. What is impossible, according to this view, is that an original selfish motive to become sociable could be supplemented and even contravened by a non-selfish motive that did not exist before sociability emerged.

This originalist or static view of human nature underlies the thought not only of Shaftesbury, Mandeville, and Hutcheson but also of philosophers otherwise as diverse as Hobbes and Cudworth. Hobbes, for instance, maintained that in the state of nature humans' chief motivation was self-interest – that self-interest was far and away the most predominant original human motive. And it was this self-interest that led humans to form a commonwealth. Now the situation in the commonwealth is very different from the state of nature, and so the focus or direction of self-interest will be different as well. There are rules that are in one's self-interest to follow in the commonwealth that would not be in one's interest to follow in the state of nature. Hobbes even suggested at times that once we are in a commonwealth we ought to reconceive our entire way of thinking about how to promote our self-interest. But self-interest always remains the underlying motivation for Hobbes. For Hobbes, the fundamental human drive in the commonwealth is the same as the fundamental human drive in the state of nature.[13]

Cudworth, of course, adamantly opposed Hobbes' position, holding that humans possess non-selfish motives to perform actions that accord with the immutable and eternal principles of morality. What is important for our purposes here, however, is that Cudworth took great pains to establish that these moral motives are based on principles that are innate to human nature – that they have not developed over time but have always been fully present in the mind of every human who has ever lived. Indeed, Cudworth believed that we can be moral agents only if our moral motives are based on innate principles. And he believed this because he thought that truly moral motives could never be generated from non-moral ingredients. If we did not originally possess truly moral motives, according to Cudworth, we never would. If a certain kind of motive is not innate to human nature, then it will not be able to exist in human nature at all.[14]

Hume's predecessors believed, then, that we were stuck with our original motives, and that we could change human behavior only by changing the circumstances in which those original motives operated. They thought that if people possessed a sincere, non-selfish concern for justice at the present time, then humans must always have possessed a sincere, non-selfish concern for justice; and that if people in the past did not possess a sincere, non-selfish concern for justice, then people could not possess such a concern at the present time.

In contrast to this originalist or static view of human nature, Hume holds what we can call a *dynamic* or *progressive* view, one that allows that original concerns can evolve into other concerns of different kinds.[15] Hume believes we can develop new motives, ones that were not part of our original endowment. And what he reveals in his account of the virtue of justice is how – as a result of "a progress of sentiments" – a new motive can develop.[16] He shows how there can evolve a commitment to justice that is not original but is nonetheless entirely sincere – how a real commitment to the impartiality of justice can grow out of our originally partial nature.[17]

Attention to the word "original" and its cognates may help bring what is importantly new about Hume's position into sharper focus. In the decades prior to the publication of the *Treatise*, many moralists addressed the question of the "origin of morals," and their answers often involved claims about what was and what was not an original principle of human nature.[18] But what did they mean by "original"? We can separate out two different senses of originality: a chronological one and a foundational one.

When we ask about the origin of morals in the chronological sense, we are asking about the genealogical history or earliest causes of morality. This question is analogous to the question of, say, the origin of the game of chess, an answer to which would involve a discussion of other, earlier games with different rules and how they evolved into the game of chess we know today.

When we ask about the origin of morals in the foundational sense, in contrast, we are asking about the normative source of, or underlying justification for, our moral judgments. This question is analogous to the question of, say, the origin of the authority of our elected officials, an answer to which might cite the moral values underlying our democratic system of government.

In the dispute between Mandeville, Shaftesbury, and Hutcheson, the chronological and foundational senses were conflated. This is because the three of them implicitly assumed that the chronological origins of human sociability would also be the normative foundation of, or underlying justification for, our current sociability. Indeed, virtually all of the British moralists who preceded Hume conflated the chronological and foundational origins of morality. Virtually all of them assumed that the chronologically earliest cause of human morality would also be the normative foundation of, or the underlying justification for, our current moral judgments.[19]

But Hume is plainly aware of the difference between chronology and normative foundations. And nowhere is this more apparent than in his account of justice, in which he explicitly distinguishes the historical causes of the institution of justice from the reasons people currently have for their regard to justice. As he puts it, *"Thus self-interest is the original motive to the* establishment *of justice; but a* sympathy *with public interest is the source of the* moral approbation *which attends that virtue"* (THN 3.2.2.24; cf. 3.2.6.10–11 and 3.2.1.9–12). To arrive at this statement would have been impossible for Hume's predecessors because from their originalist or static perspective they could not see the difference between the motive to establish justice and the basis of our feeling morally obligated to be just. But from Hume's progressive view of human nature, the difference is clear.[20]

In the introduction to the *Treatise*, Hume maintains that scientific advance will come only through an accurate and comprehensive conception of human nature. He praises "some late philosophers in *England*, who have begun to put the science of man on a new footing" and declares his intention to build upon their work (THN Introduction 7). As I noted in Chapter 15, this list of philosophers includes Shaftesbury, Hutcheson, *and* Mandeville.

These predecessors of Hume made astute observations of persons' actual conduct, observations that afforded real insights. Hume truly was indebted to their broadly empirical approach to the study of human nature and morality. He also used some of their more specific ideas: from Locke and Hutcheson, he took the mind's tendency to associate; from Mandeville, he took the idea of a non-contractual and yet still basically self-interested explanation of the temporal origin of justice; from Shaftesbury and Hutcheson, he took a set of powerful arguments against egoism.

But Hume's science of man was not beholden to the Human Nature Question. He didn't take on the burden of trying to shoehorn all the phenomena into either a Positive or Negative Answer. As a result, he was free to use various explanatory tools to develop an account of morality and human nature that was more accurate and comprehensive than those that had come before. In Chapter 17, I discussed how he used principles of association to develop part of that account. In this chapter, I've discussed how he used a progressive view of human nature. In Chapter 19, I'll discuss how he used comparison.

Let me close this chapter, however, by noting that while Hume has consistently been given credit for the cleverness of specific arguments he made in support of isolated theses, he has at times been found lacking in the ability to produce a plausible, profound, large-scale philosophical view. One of the things I've hoped to reveal in this and the preceding chapter is that the opposite assessment is closer to the truth. The details of many of his arguments can be found in other philosophers. What's really impressive about Hume is his big picture.

19

Comparison and Contingency in Hume's Account of Morality

Moral sentimentalists hold that our moral judgments are contingent on our sentiments. If we had different sentiments, according to moral sentimentalists, we would make different moral judgments, and if we had no sentiments, we would make no moral judgments at all.

Moral rationalists of the seventeenth and eighteenth centuries thought this sentimental contingency was unacceptable. According to the rationalists, when we make moral judgments, we attempt to represent truths that are independent of our sentiments. So if we come to believe that our moral judgments are contingent in the way sentimentalism implies, we will not be able to maintain confidence in them. Call this the "contingency objection" to moral sentimentalism.

Hutcheson and Hume were aware of this objection, and they gave the same official answer to it. But while that official answer reflects accurately Hutcheson's moral sense theory, it obscures at least as much of Hume's sentimentalism as it reveals.

In Section A, I briefly describe some examples of the contingency objection and Hutcheson and Hume's official answer to it. In B, I discuss the role comparison plays in Hume's account of several kinds of non-moral judgments. In C, I examine the role comparison plays in Hume's account of moral judgment. In D, I elaborate on the conflict between Hume's account and the official answer to the contingency objection. And in E, I show how Hume uses comparison to mount a final, decisive attack on the Human Nature Question.

A. The Contingency Objection and the Hutchesonian Analogy

The charge that moral sentimentalism fails because of the contingency it imputes to morality can be found in many early modern moral rationalists.[1] Cudworth, for instance, contends in the first chapter of *Eternal and Immutable Morality* that his goal is to show that if morality exists at all, it must exist *necessarily* – that morality will be real if and only if it is as "eternal and immutable" as logic and mathematics (EIM 16). Samuel Clarke says that a proper account of morality must show that it is as necessary as "geometry and arithmetic" (Raphael 1991, 192). John Balguy argues that Hutcheson's moral sense theory fails because it cannot show that our moral ideas possess "the same *Necessity of Nature* that makes the Three Angles of a Triangle equal to Two Right ones; or that fixes a certain Proportion between a Cone and a Cylinder of the same Base and Height" (Balguy 1976, II 6; cf. I 9). Richard Price maintains that Hutcheson and Hume go wrong because they do not accommodate the "indisputable" fact that "we express necessary truth, when we say of some actions, they are right; and of others, they are wrong" (Price 47; cf. 50, 85). And in his epistolary exchange with Hutcheson, Burnet argues that "moral good and evil must be immutably fixed" (Burnet vs. Hutcheson 201). If we are to have confidence in our moral judgments, according to Burnet, our moral ideas must be grounded in truths that are "self-evident," "certainly demonstrable," or impossible to doubt, truths that "we cannot but acquiesce in," truths about which we have "as much certainty as we are capable of" (Burnet vs. Hutcheson 223).

Hutcheson responds to the contingency objection in *The Moral Sense*. He writes:

> The *Perception of Approbation or Disapprobation* aris[es] in the Observer, according as the *Affections of the Agent* are apprehended *kind* in their *just Degree*, or *deficient*, or *malicious*. This *Approbation* cannot be supposed an *Image of any thing external*, more than the *Pleasure of Harmony, of Taste, of Smell*. But let none imagine, that calling the *Ideas of Virtue* and *Vice* Perceptions of a *Sense*, upon apprehending the *Actions* and *Affections* of another does diminish their *Reality*, more than the like *Assertions* concerning all *Pleasure* and *Pain, Happiness* or *Misery*. (Moral Sense 283; cf. 236–8; Burnet vs. Hutcheson 229–30; Beauty and Virtue 14–15, 47)

According to Hutcheson, our moral judgments are analogous to our judgments of secondary qualities such as harmony, taste, smell, and color. Our judgment that a thing is harmonious, tasty, smelly, or colored depends upon our sensory apparatus. If we had different sensory apparatus, we would make different judgments about sounds, tastes, smells, and colors, and if we had no sensory apparatus, we would make no judgments about sounds, tastes, smells, and colors at all. But the sensory contingency of our judgments of secondary qualities does not undermine them or diminish their importance. Even after I come to realize that I would like the taste of different things if I had different taste buds, I will still care just as much about eating things that taste good to me. Even after I come to realize that I would enjoy different sounds if my ears were constructed differently, I will still care just as much about the music I find beautiful. But our moral judgments are no more contingent than – are contingent in just the same way as – our judgments of secondary qualities. And since the contingency of the latter does not undermine them or diminish their importance, the contingency of the former should not undermine them or diminish their importance either.

So Hutcheson's response to the contingency objection relies on there being a very close similarity between the moral sense and the external senses. His response consists of drawing a very tight analogy between moral judgments and judgments of secondary qualities. Call this response the "Hutchesonian analogy."[2]

Chapters 13 and 14 should have made it clear that this analogy is, for Hutcheson, not casual, offhand, or peripheral. For central to Hutcheson's thought is the idea that moral judgments originate in an internal principle that is both original to the human constitution and distinct from reason. And the external senses on which our judgments of color are based model this idea perfectly.

The Hutchesonian analogy constitutes the sentimentalists' official answer to the contingency objection. Here is Hume offering the same response:

Vice and virtue, therefore, may be compared to sound, colours, heat, and cold, which, according to modern philosophy, are not qualities in objects, but perceptions in the mind: and this discovery in morals, like that other in physics, is to be regarded as a considerable advancement of the speculative sciences; though, like that too, it has little or no influence on practice. Nothing can be more real, or concern us more, than our own sentiments of pleasure and uneasiness; and if these be favourable to virtue, and unfavourable to vice, no more can be requisite to the regulation of our conduct and behaviour. (THN 3.1.1.26; cf. Essays 166, Letters 39–40)

The similarity between this passage and the passage quoted from Hutcheson's *Moral Sense* is striking. Moreover, Hume's goal in this part of the *Treatise* – to show that moral distinctions originate not in reason alone but also in a moral sense – is as Hutchesonian as it could be. And many of the specific arguments Hume makes here have clear antecedents in Hutcheson's *Moral Sense*.[3]

But this similarity is superficial, or at least atypical. Hutcheson and Hume both maintain that moral distinctions originate not in reason alone but at least partly in sentiment, but they give very different accounts of the sentiments that play an essential role in moral judgment. And while Hutcheson's account of those sentiments coheres with the analogy to secondary qualities, Hume's account does not.[4] For the sentiments on which Humean moral judgment is based are more contingent – are subject to other dimensions of contingency, are contingent on more factors – than the perceptions that are the basis for judgments of secondary qualities. In the previous two chapters, we've examined Hume's use of principles of association and his progressive view of human nature, both of which imputed an additional contingency to the moral sentiments. In this chapter, we'll examine how Hume's use of *comparison* imputes to moral sentiments a kind of contingency that the Hutchesonian moral sense and secondary qualities do not possess.

B. Comparison and Nonmoral Sentiments

Comparison plays a role in Hume's explanation of a number of important sentimental phenomena, such as pride and humility, envy and malice, allegiance to government, and natural virtue.[5] At several points, Hume goes out of his way to highlight the importance of comparison to human judgment, maintaining that we "judge more of objects by comparison, than by their intrinsic worth and value" (THN 3.3.2.4).[6]

Hume provides a clear example of the importance of comparison in his discussion of pride and humility. The things I feel proud of are associated in my mind with my idea of self and cause pleasure, and the things I feel humiliated by are associated in my mind with my idea of self and cause pain. But not all things closely related to me that cause pleasure make me feel proud, and not all things closely related to me that cause pain make me feel humiliated. To give rise to pride or humility, something must be "peculiar" to me, or special to me and only "a few persons" (THN 2.1.6.4). Something closely related to me that gives me pleasure will not make me proud if it is shared by many other people. It will make me proud only if it causes me to stand out in comparison to others.

We . . . judge of objects more from comparison than from their real and intrinsic merit; and where we cannot by some contrast enhance their value, we are apt to overlook even what is essentially good in them. . . . [G]oods, which are common to all mankind, and have become familiar to us by custom, give us little satisfaction; tho' perhaps of a more excellent kind, than those on which, for their singularity, we set a much higher value. (THN 2.1.6.4)

To feel proud about something, I must think that it makes me *better* than most other people. Pride has an ineluctably *comparative* aspect. That is why something such as health, which is enjoyed by "vast numbers," does not make me feel proud even though it affords me a "very sensible satisfaction" (THN 2.1.6.4).

Comparison infects Humean pride with a contingency secondary qualities are free of.[7] So long as I continue to think that an object will cause a perception of redness under normal lighting conditions, I will continue to think it is red. But my thinking that something is a cause of pride is contingent not only on my thinking that the thing will cause its possessor to feel pleasure under normal conditions. My thinking that the thing is a cause of pride is *also* contingent on my thinking that it is peculiar or rare. So even if I continue to think that the thing will cause its possessor to feel pleasure under normal conditions, I will not think it is a cause of pride if I come to think it is common. I may, for instance, be proud of owning a "fine scritoire" and "handsome chairs and table" (THN 2.1.4.5). But if the same furniture were to become common to every house in the neighborhood, it would not make me proud, even though it would be just as pleasing to look at and just as comfortable to use.[8] What is unusual and extraordinary at one time could be usual and ordinary at another, and so something that in one situation makes me feel proud can in another situation make me feel humiliated, even though the direct sensations the thing causes in me remain the same.

The additional contingency that distinguishes pride from color is particularly evident in the case of riches, which is one of Hume's leading examples of the causes of pride (THN 2.1.10, 2.1.1.18). What counts as riches is an inherently comparative matter. It depends not merely on how much money one has but also on how much other people have. Imagine that two people possess the same buying power; both of them can purchase the same items. But one of them is living in a community in which she has more money than most, while the other is living in a community in which he has less money than most. Although the money and what it will buy are the same in both cases, the first person will feel pride in her wealth, while the second person will not.

Comparison also plays a crucial role in Hume's account of aesthetic judgment. We judge a work to be beautiful, Hume argues in the "Standard of Taste," only when it stands out favorably in comparison to other works we've seen. Our aesthetic judgment of a work of art varies in relation to our experience of other works. As Hume explains:

> It is impossible to continue in the practice of contemplating any order of beauty, without being frequently obliged to form *comparison* between the several species and degrees of excellence, and estimating their proportion to each other.... By comparison alone we fix the epithets of praise or blame, and learn how to assign the due degree of each. (Taste 238)

Our judgments of aesthetic merit cannot be fully explained by the relationship between a work's intrinsic properties and our direct perception of them. For we judge a work to have aesthetic merit only if we think it possesses certain qualities to a greater extent than most other works. Our judgment of the merit of a work of art is contingent not merely on its properties and our perception of them but also on the properties of other works we've seen.

This comparative aspect pulls Humean aesthetic judgment away from an analogy with secondary qualities, just as the comparative aspect of Humean pride pulls it away from the same analogy. Our judgment that an object is red is not contingent on how many other red things we have happened to encounter.[9] In worlds that differ from ours only in that there are more or fewer red things, the apple that we judge to be red here we would still judge to be red. But Hume's use of comparison implies that our aesthetic judgments are afflicted by an additional kind of contingency. In a world with nothing but the "coarsest daubings," what we now consider to be a merely competent painted likeness we would judge to be beautiful, of the highest aesthetic merit. And in a world in which artworks such as those of the Sistine

Chapel were commonplace, some things we judge to be masterpieces in this world we would judge to be of little or no aesthetic merit.

Indeed, Hume claims not merely that our aesthetic *judgments* have an inherently comparative aspect but also that the sentimental responses on which those judgments are based are themselves sensitive to comparison. Whether perceiving a work is pleasurable or unpleasurable, Hume argues, depends in part on the comparisons we draw. As Hume explains:

> The coarsest daubing contains a certain lustre of colours and exactness of imitation, which are so far beauties, and would affect the mind of a peasant of Indian with the highest admiration. The most vulgar ballads are not entirely destitute of harmony or nature; and none but a person, familiarized to superior beauties, would pronounce their numbers harsh, or narration uninteresting. A great inferiority of beauty gives pain to a person conversant in the highest excellence of the kind, and is for that reason pronounced a deformity: As the most finished object, with which we are acquainted, is naturally supposed to have reached the pinnacle of perfection, and to be entitled to the highest applause. (Taste 238)

When a "peasant or Indian" looks at a "coarse daubing" or hears a "vulgar ballad," he will experience pleasure. But when someone who has seen many great paintings and heard many great symphonies looks at the same daubing or hears the same ballad, he will not experience pleasure. The same object arouses different feelings in different people, and that's because different people compare the object (perhaps usually unconsciously) to different things. It is not as though everyone gains the same pleasure from the same works of art, and that people with greater experience are merely more qualified to judge which of the various pleasures is greater (i.e, Hume is not making the kind of competent judgments argument found in chapter two of Mill's *Utilitarianism* and book nine of Plato's *Republic*). A person whose experience has saddled her with one comparison class will really gain pleasure from a work that will really cause displeasure to a person whose experience has bestowed upon him a different comparison class.[10]

In the *Treatise*, Hume provides a number of similar illustrations of comparison's influence on the sentiments in the *Treatise*. He notes, for instance, that the same object will arouse a feeling of admiration when compared to something smaller and a feeling of indifference when compared to something bigger, that comparison with an ugly object will make the perception of a beautiful one more pleasant, and that comparison with a beautiful object will make the perception of an ugly one more painful (THN 2.2.8.8–11). Hume also points out that because of comparison's influence on sentiments, consideration of the same amount of wealth will be pleasant to a peasant but unpleasant to a gentleman (THN 2.1.11.18).

Hume's belief that comparison affects not only our judgments but our sentimental responses themselves helps explain the distinction he draws between "intrinsic" and "comparative" sentimental judgments (THN

2.1.6.4–6, 2.1.8.7–8, 3.3.2.4–5). Intrinsic sentimental judgments are based on sentimental responses that can be disengaged from comparison, while comparative sentimental judgments are based on sentimental responses that are inherently comparative. The impression of the color of a coat, for instance, can be disengaged from comparison, while the impression of largeness of a Clydesdale cannot. It is, consequently, possible to make an "intrinsic" judgment about the color of a coat, but it is not possible to make an intrinsic judgment about the size of a Clydesdale. The judgment that a Clydesdale is large is inherently comparative (THN 2.2.8.16). At the same time, there's another kind of judgment about the coat that is also inherently comparative, namely, whether it is worthy of pride. We can, that is, make an intrinsic judgment about a coat (it is red) and a comparative one (it is something to take pride in). So when Hume says that we judge "more" by comparison than by intrinsic worth, he must have in mind our judgments of objects (such as coats) that can be judged both intrinsically and comparatively, and he must be pointing out that we are often animated more by the comparative judgments we make about them than by the intrinsic ones.

The crucial point for our purposes is that Hume believes that certain kinds of judgments, such as those concerning largeness, pride, and aesthetic merit, are inherently comparative. And this is because comparison plays an essential role in the production of the perceptions on which these judgments are based. A horse will produce in us the impression that is the origin of judgments of largeness only if its size compares favorably to the size of other horses we've seen. A possession will produce in us the pleasurable feeling that is the origin of judgments of pride only if it compares favorably to the possessions of others of which we're aware. A work of art will produce in us the pleasurable feeling that is the origin of our judgments of aesthetic merit only if it compares favorably to other works of art we've observed. The impressions that are the origins of our ideas of largeness, pride, and aesthetic merit depend on – are contingent on – the comparisons we happen to draw.

C. Comparison and Moral Sentiments

But what of Humean moral judgments? Are they inherently comparative, like judgments of largeness, pride, and aesthetic merit? Are the sentiments on which Humean moral judgments are based contingent on comparisons we draw? Or are Humean moral judgments, like the judgment that a coat is red, judgments of intrinsic properties? Can the impressions of approval and disapproval be disengaged from comparison?

The answer to this question bears directly on whether Hume can legitimately use the Hutchesonian analogy in response to the contingency objection. The objection, recall, was that sentimentalism implies that our moral judgments are too contingent for us to have confidence in. Hutcheson replied to this objection by contending that on his view moral judgments are no more contingent than judgments of secondary qualities, and that since we have full confidence in our judgments of secondary qualities, there is no reason to think that sentimentalism is incompatible with confidence in our judgments of morality. If Humean moral judgments are non-comparative or intrinsic, then Hume may be able to use the analogy in the same way. But if Humean moral judgments are inherently comparative, they will have an additional kind of contingency – a kind of contingency judgments of secondary qualities do not share – and this will vitiate the attempt to use the Hutchesonian analogy to respond to the contingency objection.

Hume's account of aesthetic judgment gives us at least a prima facie reason for thinking that Humean moral judgments do possess the kind of comparative contingency that would preclude Hume from using the Hutchesonian analogy. For as we've seen, Hume contends that judgments of artistic merit are inherently comparative, and there are at least prima facie grounds for thinking that Hume's account of moral judgment parallels his account of aesthetic judgment.[11]

Additional evidence for thinking that Humean moral judgments are inherently comparative comes from the essay "Of the Dignity or Meanness of Human Nature," which Hume wrote shortly after completing the *Treatise*.[12] There Hume places comparison at the heart of the judgment that a person is virtuous. He writes:

It is also usual to *compare* one man with another; and finding very few whom we can call *wise* or *virtuous*, we are apt to entertain a contemptible notion of our species in general. That we may be sensible of the fallacy of this way of reasoning, we may observe, that the honourable appellations of wise and virtuous, are not annexed to any particular degree of those qualities of *wisdom* and *virtue*, but arise altogether from the comparison we make between one man and another. When we find a man, who arrives at such a pitch of wisdom as is very uncommon, we pronounce him a wise man: So that to say, there are few wise men in the world, is really to say nothing: since it is only by their scarcity, that they merit that appellation. (Dignity or Meanness 83)

To call someone wise is to say that he's smarter than most other people. Our judgment that someone is wise is contingent on how smart other people we've observed have been. And, Hume implies, the same is true of the judgment that someone is virtuous. To say that someone is virtuous is to say that her character compares favorably with that of most other people. But if this is so, our judgment that a person is virtuous does not originate simply in the qualities of her character and the original physiological and psychological mechanisms that cause us to feel direct pleasurable passions. Contingent facts of the other characters we've happened to observe will also play an essential role.

Hume's account of the causes of pride also seems to imply that moral judgments are inherently comparative. To cause pride, according to Hume, something must be "peculiar" to me, or special to me and only "a few persons." It must make me stand out favorably in comparison to most other people. But Hume maintains that virtue and vice "are the most obvious causes of" pride and humility (THN 2.1.7.2; cf. 2.2.2.8–9). Indeed, he says that producing pride and humility "is, perhaps, the most considerable effect that virtue and vice have upon the human mind" (THN 3.1.2.5). It seems to follow, then, that I will judge that I possess virtue only when I think that I possess a certain pleasant quality to a greater extent than most.

But let us now turn to Book III of the *Treatise*, where Hume gives his full-dress account of virtue and vice. Does comparison play an essential role there?

In Book III, Hume distinguishes between artificial virtue, or the virtues related to justice, and natural virtue. Most of his account of artificial virtue does not involve comparison.[13] To possess the artificial virtue of justice is to obey the laws of the land, and whether someone has obeyed the law is generally an all-or-nothing, non-comparative matter. The judgment that a person has or has not broken a law is, or at least usually can be, independent of thoughts about how other people have acted in relation to the law.

But that most of Hume's account of artificial virtue does not involve comparison does not give us reason for thinking that he can legitimately adopt the Hutchesonian analogy to establish confidence in our judgments of justice. For the Hutchesonian analogy holds that judgments of secondary qualities and of virtue share the same kind of innocuous contingency. On Hume's account, however, our judgments of the artificial virtues are contingent on a number of factors that play no role in our judgments of secondary qualities. They depend, for instance, on "outward circumstances," such as there being a relative scarcity, and on our developing associations, and on our sentiments "progressing" in a certain way (THN 3.2.2). I have discussed these additional contingencies – and how they sharply distinguish Humean justice from Hutchesonian virtue – in the previous two chapters. I hope that was enough to show that Hume's account of the artificial virtues is not going to fit well with the Hutchesonian analogy.

A more promising place to try to situate the analogy, it might seem, is Hume's account of natural virtue, which is at least nominally more similar to Hutcheson's view than is his account of artificial virtue. Humean natural virtues fall into three categories: the virtues of "greatness of mind," the virtues of "goodness and benevolence," and virtuous "natural abilities." Let us look at the virtues of greatness of mind and natural abilities first. We will then examine in more detail the virtues of goodness and benevolence.[14]

We judge people to possess "greatness" when we attribute to them "those great actions and sentiments, which have become the admiration of mankind" (THN 3.3.2.12). Such people possess "heroic virtue" or "courage, intrepidity, ambition, love of glory, magnanimity, and all the other shining virtues of that kind." The prime example of this sort of virtue is Alexander the Great.

It's clear that the "shining virtues" characteristic of the great are necessarily rare. We judge that someone is great or heroic only if we think he possesses certain characteristics to a much greater degree than the normal run of people. Our admiration for the great is inextricably linked to our comparing their outstanding accomplishments to the accomplishments of others. As Hume puts it immediately after an extended discussion of the principle of comparison and how it shapes our sentiments:

> All this is easily apply'd to the present subject. We sink very much in our own eyes, when in the presence of a great man, or one of a superior genius; and this humility makes a considerable ingredient in that *respect*, which we pay our superiors.... Sometimes even envy and hatred arise from the comparison; but in the greatest part of men, it rests at respect and esteem. (THN 3.3.2.6)

Our respect of the great depends on our thinking that they stand out in comparison to most other people. Or as Hume put it in "Of the Dignity or Meanness of Human Nature," the terms of great and heroic virtue are "honourable appellations" that "are not annexed to any particular degree of those qualities ... but arise altogether from the comparison we make between one man and another." Judgments about greatness are inherently comparative.

Hume's comments on how the great should feel about themselves confirm the inherently comparative aspect of judgments of "greatness of mind." A great person, Hume says repeatedly, should feel pride in his character (THN 3.3.2.6–13). But a person should feel pride in something only if it is uncommon, only if it distinguishes him from most other people. That is why we endorse pride in a person who is really distinguished and disparage pride in a person who is average: the pride of the former is warranted, while the pride of the latter is not.[15]

Let us now turn to admirable "natural abilities." Hume discusses a number of these, but he focuses most of his attention on two: "wisdom and good sense" and "wit and eloquence" (THN 3.3.4.8). And he seems to think that our admiration for these two qualities also has an inherently comparative component. When discussing wisdom and good sense, for instance, Hume writes:

> Men are superior to beasts principally by the superiority of their reason; and they are the degrees of the same faculty, which set such an infinite difference betwixt one man and another. All the advantages of art are owing to human reason; and where fortune is not very capricious, the most considerable part of these advantages must fall to the share of the prudent and sagacious. (THN 3.3.4.5)

Hume suggests here that we judge someone to be "prudent and sagacious" if he gets a larger share than most, and this implies that such judgments are inherently comparative. Moreover, in the final paragraph of "Of natural abilities," Hume writes:

Before I leave this subject of *natural abilities*, I must observe, that, perhaps, one source of the esteem and affection, which attends them, is deriv'd from the *importance* and *weight*, which they bestow on the person possess'd of them. He becomes of greater consequence in life. His resolutions and actions affect a greater number of his fellow-creatures. Both his friendship and enmity are of moment. And 'tis easy to observe, that whoever is elevated, after this manner, above the rest of mankind, must excite in us the sentiments of esteem and approbation. (THN 3.3.5.14)

The person who possesses the natural abilities Hume has been discussing is "elevated . . . above the rest of mankind." Such a person possesses qualities that make her stand out in comparison to everyone else. She is *especially* talented in some way. That Hume thinks our admiration of natural abilities is inherently comparative gains even more confirmation from his "farther reflections concerning the natural abilities." For in that section the two examples he gives are "extraordinary [amorous] vigour" and great "fortune" or riches (THN 3.3.5.2), and those two qualities – the first because it is *extra*ordinary, and the second because what counts as riches is necessarily tied to how much wealth others have – are clearly inherently comparative.

That's not to say that Hume thinks we judge most people *deficient* in the natural abilities we have in mind when we speak of wisdom, good sense, wit, and eloquence. We attribute wisdom, good sense, wit, and eloquence to those people who are unusually intelligent, prudent, entertaining in conversation, and effective at public speaking. And we attribute the corresponding unappealing traits to those who are unusually unintelligent, imprudent, humorless, and boring. But to most people – to those who are ordinary – we attribute neither the talents nor the deficiencies. A person of more or less average intelligence is judged to be neither wise nor stupid. A person of more or less average conversational skill is judged to be neither witty nor humorless. And that's because the appellations "wise" and "stupid," "witty" and "humorless" are inherently comparative. Their function is to designate those on the extremes of a bell-shaped curve. But judgments about someone's place on a bell-shaped curve cannot be assimilated to judgments of secondary qualities, at least not in a way that can undergird the claim that the former sorts of judgments are no more contingent than the latter. For judgments about someone's place on a bell-shaped curve possess an additional kind of contingency. If the intelligence or humor of the general population were different, then the standards for our judgments of whether a person is wise or witty would be different as well. But we would still judge the apple to be red regardless of whether there were more or fewer red things.

So Humean judgments of greatness and natural abilities both involve comparative aspects that vitiate the Hutchesonian analogy. But what of the remaining part of Hume's account of the natural virtues? Mightn't judgments of "goodness and benevolence" be non-comparative in a way that makes it legitimate for Hume to rely on the analogy in response to the contingency objection?

Initially, it might seem that this part of Hume's account does fit well with the Hutchesonian analogy. Hume begins his discussion, for instance, by saying that having explained the origin of "every thing we call *great* in human affections," he will "now proceed to give an account of their *goodness*" (THN 3.3.3.1). And we might think that while greatness and natural talent may be analytically limited to the exceptional few, there's nothing in the concept of goodness that limits how many people we can attribute it to. In "Of goodness and benevolence," moreover, Hume never mentions the idea of comparison. He does conclude the section with a brief discussion of the "perfect" character (THN 3.3.3.9), but for the most part he seems to be concerned with qualities we attribute to our friends. And almost everyone is a friend to someone. Perhaps there are kinds of admiration and respect that are reserved for the great, but the affections described in "Of goodness and benevolence" seem to be much more common that that.

When we look closely at Humean judgments of goodness, however, we find that in fact they do share the contingency that characterizes the other, inherently comparative judgments we've already examined. The Hutchesonian analogy doesn't fit any better with Humean judgments of goodness than it does with Humean judgments of greatness or natural abilities.

In Books II and III of the *Treatise*, Hume usually uses "comparison" as a technical term to signify the mental effect of perceiving two things that differ from each other in a single, very pronounced way (e.g., THN 2.2.8.12–13 and 3.3.2.4–5). Hume does not discuss this type of comparison in "Of goodness and benevolence." But Humean judgments of goodness involve another type of comparison that is just as inimical to the Hutchesonian analogy. To see this, we need first to remind ourselves of the point of view from which we make judgments of goodness.

As we've seen, Hume believes that moral distinctions originate in sentiments. But he also points out that our sentiments vary in a way that our moral judgments do not. The sentiments I feel when I consider good deeds done now and in my immediate vicinity will typically be much stronger than the sentiments I feel when I consider good deeds done a thousand years ago or on the other side of the world. But if the distant deeds benefit the same number of people in a similar way as the near deeds, I should make the same moral judgment about them. This is because my judgment of a person's goodness should not be a function solely of how I *actually* feel at the moment when I make my judgment. Rather, my judgment should be based on how I *would* feel if I were to consider the person's conduct from a particular point of view. My moral judgment should be based, specifically, on how I would feel about the person if I were in her immediate vicinity when she acted.

> Our servant, if diligent and faithful, may excite stronger sentiments of love and kindness than *Marcus Brutus*, as represented in history; but we say not upon that account, that the former character is more laudable than the latter. We know, that were we to approach equally near to that renown'd patriot, he wou'd command a much higher degree of affections and admiration. (THN 3.3.1.16)

Our moral judgment of a person is based not on a sentiment we necessarily experience at the moment we are making the judgment but on a sentiment we would experience were we to adopt the point of view of those directly affected by the person's actions. Or as Hume puts it in his discussion of goodness, our moral judgment is based on how we feel when "we consider the tendency of any passion to the advantage or harm of those, who have any immediate connexion or intercourse with the person possess'd of it" (THN 3.3.3.2).

So when we make moral judgments of goodness, we privilege one perspective on the person we are judging over other perspectives. But why is this particular perspective privileged? Hume says that we need to "fix on some *steady* and *general* points of view" in order to prevent "continual *contradictions*" and "converse together on any reasonable terms" (THN 3.3.1.15). But that explains only why we privilege *some* point of view. It doesn't explain why we privilege the particular point of view of those in the person's immediate sphere of influence.[16] If we all judged a person's character based on how her conduct affected only herself – or if we judged a person's character based on how her conduct affected everyone in her country or all of humanity – we would still be able to converse together on reasonable terms. In order to prevent the "contradictions" that would result if moral language reflected only our occurrent feelings, we all need only to privilege one point of view, regardless of what it is.[17] But Hume says that we privilege the point of view of those in direct contact with the character being judged. What's his explanation for this feature of moral judgment?

Hume's answer to this question comes at the very beginning of "of goodness and benevolence." He writes:

> When experience has once given us a competent knowledge of human affairs and has taught us the proportion they bear to human passion, we perceive, that the generosity of men is very limited, and that it seldom extends beyond their friends and family, or, at most, beyond their native country. Being thus acquainted with the nature of man, we expect not any impossibilities from him; but confine our view to that narrow circle, in which any person moves, in order to form a judgment of his moral character. (THN 3.3.3.2)

When we morally judge a person's character, we consider how her conduct affects only that narrow circle in which she moves. And we focus our

considerations in this way because in the past we have observed that generally people care strongly only about those within their narrow circle. We
judge that a person who benefits her narrow circle is good because our past
experience has led us not to expect a more expansive generosity. If our past
experience had been different, our expectations would be different and our
moral judgment would differ accordingly. Imagine, for instance, that you
had lived your life among apparently exceedingly generous people – people
who, you believed, typically tried to create the greatest benefit for humanity
as a whole (perhaps you lived on a different world with different kinds of
people, or on this world among a group of extraordinarily public-spirited
people, or among people who managed to deceive you into thinking that
they were more public-spirited than they really were). You would then expect
a person to try to benefit a great deal of humanity, and so you would not
judge to be good a person who benefited only her narrow circle. Or, alterna-
tively, imagine that you had lived your life among exceedingly selfish people,
people who, you believed, hardly ever did anything to benefit anyone else.
If this were your past experience, you would not expect a person to benefit
anyone else, and so you would not judge to be bad a person who neglected
to benefit those within her narrow circle.

Humean goodness is thus necessarily not extraordinary, and that's
because the point of view that defines goodness has itself been defined by the
bounds of the ordinary.[18] So while Humean judgments of goodness do not
involve comparison in the technical sense of drawing a single sharp contrast
between otherwise similar things, they do involve comparison in that they
are based on a state of mind that essentially involves thoughts about how one
person's conduct measures up to the conduct of others. Most importantly
for our purposes, Humean judgments of goodness, like the other inherently
comparative judgments we've examined, are contingent in a way that judgments of secondary qualities are not. On Hume's account, my judgment
that a person is good is based on a sentimental response of mine that is
contingent on (1) my physiological and psychological constitution, (2) the
qualities the person exhibits, *and* (3) the frequency with which those qualities have been exhibited by other people I've observed. Vary any of these
three things enough and my moral judgment will vary with it. My judgment
that an apple is red, in contrast, is based on a sensory response of mine that
is contingent on (1′) the constitution of my visual apparatus and (2′) the
properties of the apple. There is no (3′). Even if the number of red things
varies, I'll still judge the same apple to be red, so long as (1′) and (2′) stay
the same. The sentimental response that grounds my moral judgment has
an inherently comparative aspect. But the sensory response that grounds
my color judgment does not.[19]

I said earlier that Humean judgments of greatness and the natural abilities of wit and wisdom designate those at one extreme of the bell-shaped
curve. Well, Hume's explanation of the "steady and general points of view"

implies that judgments of goodness are essentially curved as well. It's just that judgments of goodness serve to designate those who fall toward the front of the thicker part of the bell-shape. Greatness is something like an A in a class that is graded on a strict curve, while goodness is something like a B.

D. Humean Moral Contingency

So Hume's account imputes to moral judgment a kind of contingency that pulls away from the Hutchesonian analogy.[20] For central to Hume's account is the idea that there is a necessary connection between our judgments of virtue and the percentage of people we judge to be virtuous. On Hume's account, it is conceptually impossible that we would judge that most people are great, or that most are atrocious, or that extremely few are ever good. But this kind of necessary connection does not hold between our color judgments and the percentage of things we judge to be one color or another. The percentage of things in the world that happen to be red is an open question. And because Hume's account implies that there's a necessary connection between our moral judgments and the percentage of people we judge to be virtuous, it also implies that the connection between our moral judgments and the *content* of that which we judge to be virtuous is contingent on the human conduct we've happened to observe. If we had consistently observed different conduct, what we now judge to be morally neutral we might have judged to be morally good, and what we now judge to be morally bad we might have judged to be morally neutral. So even if we have strong a posteriori grounds for thinking that a certain kind of limited generosity is uniform and constant to all humans, Hume's account will still imply that the content of morality is not only more contingent than mathematics (which was enough to throw the rationalists into high dudgeon) but also more contingent than color (which would have greatly consternated Hutcheson).

One way to express this difference between Hume and his predecessors is to say that Hume's account of moral judgment is more profoundly empiricist – more bound up in experience – than theirs. The rationalists tried to establish the a priori nature of moral properties and moral judgment, which would have insulated those things from contingent experience. Hutcheson held that morality is based not on reason alone but at least partly on sentiment, and this made him a non-rationalist, which is perhaps enough to qualify him as a kind of empiricist. But Hutcheson did not think that the sentiment at the base of moral judgment is necessarily sensitive to experience. The content of Hutchesonian moral judgment is not in principle going to be affected by the experiences moral judges have happened to have. Hutcheson's moral sense is an original, fundamental part of human nature, hard-wired into our makeup. And it's that moral sense that produces the affections on which moral judgments are based. Humean moral judgments,

256 *David Hume*

in contrast, are based on sentiments that are necessarily responsive not only to the immediate object of judgment but also to the kinds of conduct we've happened to observe in the past. Hutcheson bases moral judgment on human tendencies that most contemporary philosophers would call innate. Hume bases moral judgment on responses that are ineluctably shaped by our contingent experiences.

Another way to put this point is to say that Hume draws a tight connection between normative expectations and predictive expectations. When I say "I expect you to do *x*" (or "*X* is what's expected of you") in the normative sense, I'm expressing the judgment that doing *x* is morally right, required, or obligatory. When I say "I expect you'll do *x*" in the predictive sense, I'm merely telling you what I think you'll do, not what I think you ought to do. Now of course, Hume doesn't hold that our normative expectations are identical to our predictive expectations. He acknowledges that we often believe someone will act in a way she ought not to. But Hume's arguments do imply that our normative expectations are leashed to our predictive expectations, that our judgments of what people ought to do are made from a point of view shaped by our beliefs about what people are likely to do. This leashing of the normative to the non-normative distinguishes Hume not only from the rationalists but also from Hutcheson.

Hume's uses of comparison also invite relativistic implications that sharply distinguish him from his predecessors. According to Hume, my judgments of moral goodness are contingent on the fact that many people sometimes benefit those in their narrow circle and hardly ever benefit many beyond their narrow circle. Now one might hold that that fact is just as fixed as the physical features we respond to when we have the perceptions that are the origins of our judgments of color. We can entertain the possibility of people who are much more selfish or much more public-spirited than we are, just as we can entertain the possibility of people who have very different visual apparatus. But, one might hold, just as there's no reason to think that the visual apparatus of most people is actually going to change, so too there's no reason to think that the generosity of most people is actually going to shrink or grow. Limited generosity – the tendency to benefit those in one's narrow circle – is as much a constant of human nature as is the human visual apparatus. And so, one might hold, Hume can claim that on his account, judgments of goodness are just as fixed as judgments of color.

Hume himself suggests this way of fitting the Hutchesonian analogy into his account when he says, "Being thus acquainted with the nature of man, we expect not any impossibilities from him; but confine our view to that narrow circle, in which any person moves, in order to form a judgment of his moral character" (THN 3.3.3.2). Here Hume seems to imply that it would be "impossible" for a person to benefit many people beyond her narrow circle, that the extent of our generosity is firmly fixed. The extent of our generosity is based on psychological mechanisms, while our color perception is based on physical mechanisms. Hume suggests here, however, that the psychological mechanisms are just as invariable as the physical.

But this statement of Hume's overstates the constancy and uniformity of human generosity and conflicts with the most distinctive elements of his account of the moral sentiments. Perhaps no one consistently acts in ways that benefit all of humanity, and perhaps exceedingly few people are entirely selfish. But between those two extremes there is a continuum, and human nature is compatible with a wide swath of it. Some people are more generous than others, and certain groups at certain times and places tend to be more generous than other groups at other times and places. But if this is so, it seems that Hume's account implies that one's judgment of what is morally good will vary in accord with the variations in the generosity of the people one has encountered. A person growing up in a very hardened environment (say, in a war-torn country or in a Dickensian orphanage) may expect behavior that is different from what a person growing up in a very comfortable or compassionate environment may expect. A person with certain past experiences may be powerfully impressed by an action to which a person with different past experiences may not have any particularly strong response. Indeed, Hume himself suggests that individuals' moral judgments might vary as a result of variations in their sentimental dispositions. He writes, "[M]en naturally, without reflection, approve of that character, which is most like their own. The man of mild disposition and tender affections, in forming a notion of the most perfect virtue, mixes in it more of benevolence and humanity, than the man of courage and enterprize, who naturally looks upon a certain elevation of mind as the most accomplish'd character" (THN 3.3.3.4).

Hume's uses of association give us even more reason to think that there will be variations in the sentiments in which moral judgments originate. As we saw in Chapter 17, Hume believes that our moral sentiments owe their existence to associations we form. Were it not for our associations, we would never have the impressions of approval and disapproval on which moral judgments are based. But our associations develop as a result of past experience. And if one person's past experience is different enough from another's, then the two of them may form associations that cause one to approve of something that the other does not.

That is not to say that Hume's account implies that there is no common moral ground. There may very well be features of almost every human life that ensure that there are certain associations and certain comparisons that almost everyone will form. The approval and disapproval of almost everyone may overlap to a large extent. And given that the aim of avoiding "contradiction" is an ingredient in the development of moral judgment, moral harmony, especially among people who live in close proximity, is likely be very common. But contradiction avoidance is not the only ingredient in the development of moral judgment. Contingent empirical experience also plays an essential role. And there are enough differences in the circumstances and accidents of human lives to make it likely both that there will be some traits to which one person will have favorable moral associations while another person will not, and that one person will develop a comparison class that leads her to approve of something that a person who has developed a different comparison class will not.[21]

Of course, Hutcheson and the rationalists also acknowledged variation in moral judgment. They all realized that there are moral differences, and they all provided accounts of how such differences arise. But Hume's predecessors also believed that if a person knew and fully appreciated all the relevant facts, he or she would come into moral agreement with everyone else who knew and fully appreciated all the relevant facts. They believed that if people reflected scrupulously enough, they would all end up arriving at the same moral judgments. This is because Hume's predecessors thought that scrupulous reflection enables us to form moral judgments that reflect an original principle of human nature. The rationalists thought this original principle was reason. Hutcheson thought it was a moral sense. But all of them held that this principle was essential to human nature. They all held that scrupulous reflection could neutralize the effects of variable, contingent experience, scrubbing our moral nature clean of the encrustations of association and comparison.

For Hume, however, the encrustations are the origin of morality. Humean moral reflection – reflection that issues in a moral judgment – cannot bring us back to an original principle of our nature, because our original principles cannot fund moral judgment. What Humean moral reflection produces, rather, are dispositions formed by variable, contingent experience. And if one person's experiences are different enough from another's, then it is entirely possible that after scrupulous reflection the former will judge to be virtuous something the latter will not.[22]

Hutcheson and Hume are both moral sentimentalists. But while Hutcheson is a moral sense theorist, Hume is not. The analogy between the moral sense and the external senses is integral to Hutcheson's thought, suggesting as it does that moral distinctions originate in a non-rational principle that is original to human nature and thus due to God's design. But the bulk of Hume's explanation implies that moral distinctions originate in non-rational principles that are *not* original – in non-rational principles that do not have the kind of provenance demanded by Hutcheson's theological commitments.[23]

E. Comparison and the Human Nature Question

There are certain sects, which secretly form themselves in the learned world, as well as factions in the political; and though sometimes they come not to an open rupture, they give a different turn to the ways of thinking of those who have taken part on either side. The most remarkable of this kind are the sects, founded on the different sentiments with regard to the *dignity of human nature*; which is a point that seems to have divided philosophers and poets, as well as divines, from the beginning of the world to this day. Some exalt our species to the skies, and represent man as a kind of human demigod, who derives his origin from heaven, and retains evident marks of his lineage and descent. Others insist upon the blind sides of human nature, and can discover nothing, except vanity, in which man surpasses the other animals, whom he affects so much to despise. (Dignity or Meanness 80–1)

In the previous two chapters, we've seen how Hume's account of morality undermines various aspects of the Positive and Negative Answers to the Human Nature Question. In the remainder of this chapter, let me explain how Hume's use of comparison drains the last bit of philosophical life blood out of the Question.

According to the Negative Answer of the English Calvinists, human beings on their own are incapable of discerning how they ought to live. In responding to this Negative Answer, the rationalists took seriously the idea that all the moral judgments we make on our own are fundamentally mistaken. Thus, the rationalists thought it imperative to show that each of us has within him- or herself all the resources necessary for arriving at true moral judgments. To show that each of us possesses such internal resources, the rationalists believed, was to establish a substantively important fact about human nature. This fact was the core of the rationalists' Positive Answer.

Hutcheson's moral sense theory, in contrast, defined correct moral judgment in terms of certain affective responses of each person. So Hutcheson did not take as seriously the idea that correct moral judgments could be in principle inaccessible to us, as he thought that the content of morality is defined by our own affective responses. The rationalists' Positive Answer – the supposedly substantive fact that moral correctness is accessible to every human – Hutcheson took to be merely a conceptual truth about the structure of moral judgment. In this, Hutcheson was part of the Copernican Revolution in moral philosophy, which Shaftesbury initiated with his mental enjoyment account. But Hutcheson did take very seriously the idea (propagated by the egoists) that human beings systematically fail to live in accord with the content of morality. He thought it possible that people almost always performed very poorly in relation to the standard of morality that their own moral sense established. Hutcheson set out to show, consequently, that most of the time most people did conduct themselves in accord with morality. To show this, according to Hutcheson, was to establish a substantively important fact about human nature. It was this fact that was the core of Hutcheson's Positive Answer.

Hume, being a moral sentimentalist, agreed with Hutcheson that what the rationalists took to be a crucially important Positive Answer was merely a conceptual truth about the structure of moral judgment. But as we've seen in this chapter, Hume's account also implies that the fact at the core of Hutcheson's Positive Answer is considerably less substantive as well. Hume acknowledges that humans in general are not morally atrocious, that the conduct of most people most of the time fails to elicit from us a negative moral response. But Hume argues that this is because our concept of morally acceptable conduct is necessarily connected to the conduct of most of the people most of the time. Hume can acknowledge that whether a *particular* person is or is not good is not merely a conceptual matter. He can acknowledge that whether a particular person morally measures up is a substantively important fact about that person. But to say that most people most of the time act in morally acceptable ways does not on its own tell us anything substantively important about human nature in general because our concept of moral acceptability is defined by how most people act most of the time. To say that most people most of the time act morally acceptably is merely to reflect the structure of moral judgment.

The rationalists argued that all human beings have within themselves all the resources necessary to make correct moral judgments. Hutcheson agreed with this claim, but his sentimentalist account made it conceptual necessity, empty of substance. Hutcheson then went on to argue that most of the time most humans act in accord with our moral judgments. Hume agrees with this Hutchesonian claim, but his comparison-based explanations make *it* (i.e., the Hutchesonian claim) a conceptual necessity, empty of substance. Hutcheson eviscerates the rationalists' Positive Answer, and Hume eviscerates Hutcheson's.

In "Of the Dignity or Meanness of Human Nature," Hume makes clear how the Human Nature Question collapses in light of the comparative character of our judgments. As he explains in that essay, some thinkers, when addressing the Question, "are apt to make a comparison between men and animals," while other thinkers form "a new and secret comparison between man and beings of the most perfect wisdom" (Dignity or Meanness 82–3). Those who mentally compare humans to animals are likely to give a Positive Answer to the Question. Those who mentally compare humans to God are likely to give a Negative Answer. And it may appear that these two groups disagree. But since their different answers are based on different comparison classes, their disagreement is really "only verbal," not "real" (Dignity or Meanness 81). Since this is the case, the best course of action is "to neglect such disputes as manifest abuses of leisure, the most valuable present that could be made to mortals" (Dignity or Meanness 619).

Hume also argues that thinkers are misled into thinking that the Question is more interesting than it really is because they fail to notice that moral judgments often involve comparison between people. As Hume puts it in a passage we have already seen in part:

It is also usual to *compare* one man with another; and finding very few whom we can call *wise* or *virtuous*, we are apt to entertain a contemptible notion of our species in general. That we may be sensible of the fallacy of this way of reasoning, we may observe, that the honourable appellations of wise and virtuous, are not annexed to any particular degree of those qualities of *wisdom* and *virtue*, but arise altogether from the comparison we make between one man and another. When we find a man, who arrives at such a pitch of wisdom as is very uncommon, we pronounce him a wise man: So that to say, there are few wise men in the world, is really to say nothing; since it is only by their scarcity, that they merit that appellation. Were the lowest of our species as wise as Tully, or lord Bacon, we should still have reason to say, that there are few wise men. For in that case we should exalt our notions of wisdom, and should not pay a singular honour to any one, who was not singularly distinguished by his talents. In like manner, I have heard it observed by thoughtless people, that there are few women possessed of beauty, in comparison of those who want it; not considering, that we bestow the epithet of *beautiful* only on such as possess a degree of beauty, that is common to them with a few. The same degree of beauty in a woman is called deformity, which is treated as real beauty in one of our sex. (Dignity or Meanness 83–4)

Those who give a Negative Answer on the basis of the judgment that most human beings lack wisdom and virtue fail to realize that "wisdom" and "virtue" are inherently comparative honorable appellations that are conceptually reserved for the very few. That most people don't deserve these appellations doesn't tell us any more about human nature in general than only one team's winning last season's league championship tells us about the quality of the league.

In the passage I quoted in the previous paragraph, Hume focuses on "honourable" appellations and how they can mislead people into expounding the Negative Answer. But he could just as easily have focused on dishonorable appellations and how they can mislead people into affirming the Positive Answer. There are few people whom we judge to have unmitigatedly *vicious* characters. Almost everyone seems to have a grain of virtue. And this fact has been offered by some thinkers as evidence of the basic goodness of human nature. But such thinkers, Hume might have argued, fail to realize that we judge someone to have a wholly vicious character only if we think he is extraordinarily bad. That we judge very few people to be wholly vicious doesn't tell us any more about human nature in general than only one team's coming in last place in the league tells us about the quality of the league.

Despite this criticism, Hume does not conclude that we should disregard all discussions of the Human Nature Question. He mocks philosophers for having expended so much energy on the Question, but his mockery is relatively gentle, and he stops short of saying that all the responses to the Question have been worthless. He says, rather, that the Question, despite the conceptual pitfalls it poses, has spurred some thinkers toward profound insights into human nature, from which we can learn many things of great moral importance (Dignity or Meanness 81). With this assessment, I couldn't agree more.[24]

20

What Is a Humean Account, and What Difference Does It Make?

In addition to being the last chapter of the book, this chapter is also the sketchiest. In Section A, I maintain that Hume's explanations of morality and human behavior are superior to Hutcheson's and the rationalists'. In B, I present four features that I think are distinctive of all accounts that are rightly called "Humean" and point to some of the negative and positive implications that set of features has for moral philosophy. In C, I raise the question of whether Humean accounts debunk or undermine morality. And in D, I hold that a fifth distinctive feature of Humean accounts is the belief that Humean explanations do not necessarily debunk or undermine morality and that this belief is eminently plausible. I do not, however, provide anything like a thorough account or defense of these claims. My aim in this chapter is only to give a rough idea of the philosophical territory I think we come to after we have traveled from Whichcote and Cudworth, through Shaftesbury and Hutcheson, to Hume – a territory I point toward but whose exploration would mark the end of this study and the beginning of another.

A. The Superiority of Hume's Explanations

Hume's explanations of morality and human behavior are superior to Hutcheson's. Hume's nuanced views of the complex of concerns underlying justice and the different types of qualities we judge to be virtuous capture what we do and say more accurately than Hutcheson's attempt to account for all the phenomena in terms of benevolence. Hume's explanations accord better with the moral variation that exists between people and for the internal conflict that exists within individuals. And Hume tells a much richer story about the very considerable interpersonal and intrapersonal concord that does exist: while Hutcheson offers no explanation other than that each of us possesses numerous distinct senses that happen to be in natural harmony, Hume explains how our possessing a few basic mental tendencies and living in certain conditions leads us to develop thoughts and motives that generally dovetail with each other. "The minds of men are mirrors to one another" (THN 2.2.5.21), Hume says, and he uses this insight to account more satisfactorily than Hutcheson had done for interpersonal agreement. "One passion will always be mixt and confounded with the other" (THN 2.3.9.12), he says elsewhere, and he uses this insight to account more satisfactorily for intrapersonal agreement.

It is more difficult to assess whether Hume's account is superior to the rationalists'. This is because it is not always clear that Hume and the rationalists are offering competing accounts of the same thing. Hume is trying to explain observable human behavior, while the rationalists are trying to discern eternal and immutable relations. But I believe Hume does do a better job than the rationalists at the explanatory task he sets for himself. The thin logical mental operations the rationalists focus on do not capture the vast array of moral judgments and human behaviors nearly as well as Hume's associative-progressive-comparative account.

B. Four Features of a Humean Account

But of course, Hutcheson and the rationalists were writing hundreds of years ago. Since then, there have been many more sophisticated accounts of morality and human behavior. Is there any reason to still take Hume's views seriously? Do his explanations hold up when compared to recent developments?

Some of the details of Hume's arguments almost certainly do not hold up. But recent accounts that are still basically Humean – even if it they are not exactly Hume's – are still very much a going concern. What do I mean by a Humean account of morality and human behavior? I mean an account of which at least the following four things can be said:

1. God does not play any role in the explanation of morality and human behavior.
2. Sentiment plays an essential and robust role in the explanation of morality and human behavior.
3. Empirical, contingent experience plays an essential and robust role in the explanation of morality and human behavior.
4. There is an explanatory symmetry between accounts of what is morally correct or praiseworthy and accounts of what is morally incorrect or condemnable – an explanatory symmetry that makes it impossible to claim that all virtue is natural and all vice unnatural.

I realize that 1–4 are very vague and that I would need to say much more in order to develop anything like a sharp picture of what makes an account

Humean. But I think even this low-resolution image reveals the incompatibility between Humean accounts and a number of other influential views.

Humean accounts will, for instance, be incompatible with the view that we cannot satisfactorily account for morality and human behavior without acknowledging the existence of God. Humean accounts will be incompatible with the view that morality is – and human behavior may be – based on reason alone. Humean accounts will be incompatible with the view that morality and human behavior are determined almost entirely by innate features of our constitution that are insensitive to empirical, contingent experience. And Humean accounts will be incompatible with the view that there is an important sense in which all natural things are good or virtuous and all unnatural things are bad or vicious. Each of these views, in one form or another, is still with us today, just as it was in the seventeenth and eighteenth centuries.

Such are some of the negative implications of Humean accounts. But what are the positive implications? To answer this question, we need to draw a distinction between the descriptive task of explaining morality and human behavior and the prescriptive task of showing that we ought to structure society and live our lives in certain ways.

Humeans engaged in the descriptive task will, first and foremost, attend to the contingent phenomena of human life. They will "cautiously observe" what humans actually do and say, and the circumstances in which these things are done and said (THN Introduction 6). The well-used philosophical tools of introspection and thought experiment will undoubtedly play important roles in this sort of observation. But it seems to me that Humeanism also bids those engaged in the descriptive task to make use of tools that were not as commonly employed in philosophical inquiry during the twentieth century – that is, the empirical tools of cognitive science, psychology, and sociology.[1]

It is more difficult to say what implications Humeanism will have for the prescriptive task. Certainly if an account tells us that certain things are incompatible with (or necessary to) human nature, then that would give us a conclusive reason not to require (or not to condemn) those things. But Humeanism implies that human nature is quite malleable, and it thus seems that Humeanism won't support many of these kinds of conclusive normative claims. And of course, on Humean accounts, the fact that something is "natural" or "unnatural" will not constitute a reason to embrace or reject it. That is not to say that Humean accounts will be of no help at all in thinking about how to structure society and how to live. Specific Humean accounts might very well reveal that creatures such we are are better suited to certain types of society and ways of life than to others. Specific Humean accounts might very well provide powerful considerations in favor of important normative conclusions. But from the basic general shape of Humeanism – from 1–4 as

I sketched them – it is difficult to see how we can draw any clear implications for specific moral prescriptions.

C. A Debunking or Undermining Explanation?

Some have held, however, that the distinction I've just drawn between the descriptive and the prescriptive misses out on something highly significant – that there is another crucial moral issue that falls between the cracks of explanation and first-order ethics. This is the issue of the justifiability or normativity of morality as a whole. Descriptive accounts explain why morality operates as it in fact does in our lives. Prescriptive accounts tell us what morality requires of us in particular situations. But mightn't we also want to ask whether morality as a whole is something we should place any normative confidence in? When we are addressing the descriptive task, we are not actively morally engaged; we are taking morality simply to comprise phenomena to be explained. When we are addressing the prescriptive task, we are actively morally engaged; we are taking for granted that morality makes legitimate demands on us and are trying to determine what those demands are. But isn't there also a question of whether we ought to become morally engaged at all? Don't we need to ask whether there is any good reason to take up the moral point of view in the first place?

The worry that many people who have asked this question have had is that Humean accounts amount to a *debunking* or *undermining* of morality – that if Humean explanations are correct, we will have to conclude that we do not have good reason to become morally engaged.[2] An influential and admirably clear recent example of this worry can be found in Korsgaard (1996). But the same worry was forcefully advanced in Scotland during Hume's own lifetime.[3]

Indeed, we have already seen, in Chapter 19, one example of this worry: the contingency objection, which holds that sentimentalist moral theories make morality too contingent for us to have confidence in. We also saw that while Hutcheson could respond to this objection by claiming that his theory implied that morality is contingent only on original or natural (what many contemporary philosophers would call "innate") principles of our constitution, Hume's account implies that the contingency of morality is considerably more robust than that. The sentiments at the base of Humean morality are determined not only by our original principles but also by the associations we form and the comparisons we make, and these associations and comparisons are partly determined by the accidental circumstances of our experience. Hume's account implies that it is a robustly contingent fact that we happen to value the things we value. And this robust Humean contingency was enough to lead not only the rationalists but also theological moral sense theorists like Hutcheson to worry about the ramifications Hume's account would have for our commitment to morality.

A way of illustrating why some might think the contingency of Hume's account undermines morality is by revisiting the idea that we ought to act in ways that we ourselves can "own" or "approve." As we saw in Chapter 3, Whichcote maintained that to be truly righteous is to conduct oneself in a manner that gives one "mental Peace, Satisfaction, and Content" (Aphorisms 949). We saw in Chapter 9 that Shaftesbury advanced the same idea when he said that being virtuous will make one's soul "well-compos'd, quiet, easy within itself, and such as can freely bear its own Inspection and Review" (Virtue or Merit 71). Whichcote and Shaftesbury also both emphasized that virtue produces "integrity," that virtuous action creates a unified and harmonious self. Now Hume adopts the same kind of talk when explaining why we should be just. Living justly, Hume contends, gives us "inward peace of mind, consciousness of integrity [and] a satisfactory review of our own conduct" (Second Enquiry 155–6). Like Whichcote and Shaftesbury, Hume tells us that moral conduct will enable us to bear our own survey. But his account of moral sentiments makes Hume's use of this idea very different from what it was in Whichcote and Shaftesbury.[4] When Hume speaks of the importance of being able to bear one's own survey, he's putting new wine in an old bottle. For Whichcote and Shaftesbury could have complete confidence in the results of their own surveys because they believed that the internal surveyor inside each of them was a conduit to the mind of a morally perfect God. They believed their internal survey was aligned to an independent standard of morality. But Hume's internal surveyor can claim no such credentials. According to Hume, that our internal survey issues in a certain verdict does not reflect the design of any other, morally perfect mind; it does not constitute evidence of our being aligned to any independent moral standard. It is simply a fact – a robustly contingent one at that – about us. And some might think that if this fact lies at the base of morality, then morality must be deemed a normative failure.

D. Hume and Morality

I have said before that Hume completes a Copernican Revolution in moral philosophy in that his account implies that we can't hold humanity as a whole up to some independent moral standard because morality is itself an aspect of human nature. Of course, when Galileo completed the first Copernican Revolution, he too came under attack. Galileo was also accused of debunking or undermining the normative foundations of morality and religion. From our perspective, however, the opprobrium directed at Galileo looks to have been misconceived for at least two reasons. First, it misconceived Galileo's role as a scientist. As a scientist, Galileo's rightful aim was to describe the world as accurately as he could. That his results contradicted others' cherished beliefs was no legitimate scientific grounds for criticism of him. Second, it misconceived the normative foundations of morality and religion. Galileo's detractors thought that morality and religion could find no place in a heliocentric universe – that morality and religion could draw breath only within a Ptolemaic cosmology. But this conclusion now looks to be simply mistaken. People before Galileo held different cosmological beliefs from those who came after, but some of the latter have been truly moral and religious nonetheless. It's clear that someone can believe that the Earth revolves around the sun and still be fully committed to morality and religion.

Defenders of Hume might hold that the same two misconceptions underlie the charge that his account debunks or undermines morality. They might hold that insofar as he is trying to advance the "science of man," Hume's aim is to explain the observable phenomena as accurately as possible, and that the effect his explanations have on anyone's normative commitments is simply irrelevant to the success of that endeavor.[5] And they might hold that the claim that Hume's explanations undermine morality involves specious or dispensable views of morality's normative foundation.

This second point can be elaborated through an examination of why some might claim that Hume's account is undermining. Some might claim this because they think that morality will be normative only if it accords with God's will and immorality does not; but Hume denies that we have any grounds for drawing such a conclusion about the will of God. Some might claim this because they think that morality will be normative only if it originates in reason alone; but Hume denies that morality originates in reason alone. Some might claim this because they think that morality will be normative only if living morally is more natural than living immorally; but Hume denies that morality is any more natural than immorality.

But that does not mean that *everyone* will think that Hume's account undermines morality. If a person does not believe that the normativity of morality depends on the truth of something Hume denies, then she may very well continue to think that morality is normative even after coming to believe a Humean account.

Moreover, even those who think that morality's normativity depends on things Hume denies might not give up on morality if they come to believe Hume is right. All the logic of the matter demands is that if these people come to believe a Humean account, they give up either on morality or on their prior view of what needs to be true in order for morality to be normative. Someone who comes to believe a Humean account cannot hold both (1) that morality is normative only if it accords with God's will and immorality does not, or it originates in reason alone, or it is natural to human beings and immorality is unnatural and (2) that morality is normative. But someone who comes to believe a Humean account may be able to give up (1) and hold on to (2) instead of vice versa.[6]

Of course, someone ardently committed to (1) will probably contend that there are decisive or inescapable reasons not to give it up. But Hume would deny that what such a person cites as reasons for (1) are actually as decisive or inescapable as she thinks they are. Indeed, I think it is characteristic of Humeanism in general to hold that the reasons for the meta-ethical claims that constitute versions of (1) are weaker than the reasons to maintain a commitment to morality even if (1) turns out to be false. So let me add to the list of distinguishing features of a Humean account the following:

5. The considerations in favor of maintaining a commitment to morality and giving up the belief that morality is normative only if [it accords with God's will and immorality does not, or it originates in reason alone, or it is natural to human beings and immorality is unnatural] are more compelling than the considerations in favor of abandoning a commitment to morality and holding onto the belief that morality is normative only if [it accords with God's will and immorality does not, or it originates in reason alone, or it is natural to human beings and immorality is unnatural].

To be committed to morality, for Hume, is to care about the happiness and pleasure of our friends and family and of ourselves. And these concerns, at least for most people Hume observed, should override the commitment to a morally engaged God, the commitment to moral rationalism, and the commitment to a Positive Answer.[7]

One might object, however, that 5 is a psychological oversimplification. For 5 implies that some people who come to believe in a Humean account should abandon other commitments in order to maintain their commitment to morality. But can a person really abandon those other commitments just like that? If someone is convinced that morality is worth taking seriously only if, say, it derives from a certain conception of God, then is it plausible to suppose that if she came to believe a Humean account, she could simply give up her prior theological commitment and carry on morally just as before? Mightn't she suffer some kind of crisis that will weaken her commitment to morality?

The answer will depend, I suppose, on the particular person and on how entrenched her theological commitment had been. But I acknowledge that matters will probably be a lot more complicated than simply performing disjunctive syllogism on purely formal symbols. A person who comes to believe that her normative commitments conflict with each other may very well experience significant and protracted cognitive dissonance. And even if she continues to care about morality in a general sense, she may come to think that some of the things she had thought to be right are in fact wrong and vice versa. Giving up a theological conception of morality will probably not leave one's moral character exactly as it was before.

But such transformations do occur. Some people do come to think that commitments they had held are incompatible with confidence in morality and yet nonetheless continue to live morally committed (albeit nontrivially altered) lives. In this study, we've already examined several such cases. Whichcote, Cudworth, and Hutcheson were all raised to believe that morality depended on the existence of a God who was as the voluntarist Calvinists described Him. All three of them came to think that this voluntarist-Calvinist conception of God was fundamentally mistaken. But all three of them remained deeply committed to morality nonetheless (even if they ended up holding moral and religious views that differed in nontrivial ways from those with which they were raised).

And Hume himself went through a similar transformation.[8] Like Whichcote, Cudworth, and Hutcheson, Hume was raised in a religious environment that emphasized the sinfulness of human beings and the utter dependence of all things (morality included) on a voluntarist God. Hume accepted these Calvinist ideas early on, but in his late teens and early twenties he came to reject them – just as Whichcote, Cudworth, and Hutcheson had done.

Was Hume's rejection of his religious upbringing a simple, easy thing for him? Probably not. When he was eighteen and just beginning the philosophical inquiries that would eventually result in the *Treatise of Human Nature*, Hume suffered a rather severe psychological crisis. And while it is not entirely clear what precipitated this crisis, it seems likely that at least part of Hume's problem stemmed from the impossibility of reconciling his new philosophical ideas with some of his prior normative commitments. But when the crisis passed, Hume neither gave up his new ideas nor exhibited a morally dubious character. Many people in eighteenth-century Scotland assumed that the author of the *Treatise* would be a vicious or amoral rogue. But his conduct was far from what would be expected from someone who had come to think that morality had been debunked or undermined. Indeed, virtually every account we have of those who knew Hume well suggests that he was a kind, decent, and conscientious person.

That Hume possessed an admirable moral character is certainly no reason to accept his explanations of morality and human behavior. It may not even show that his opponents were wrong about the normative ground of morality; perhaps there really is a decisive or inescapable reason for thinking that in order to be justified morality requires a theistic or rational or natural foundation, even if Hume himself failed to appreciate it.[9] But Hume's admirable moral character, combined with his writings as a whole, do show how one can be a Humean – how one can deny that morality is any more natural than immorality, deny that there is a purely rational basis for action, and deny that we have any evidence for the existence of a morally engaged God – and still lead a good life and be a good person.

Notes

Introduction

1. For discussion of many of the important works of this period that I do not do justice to, see Norton (1982), Darwall (1995), Beiser (1996), and Schneewind (1998).

2. At least I hope I am charting a path that does actually take us through the historical territory. Once in a while, when I am struck by how many influential figures from the period I have failed to discuss, a different metaphor occurs to me: I worry that I'm merely describing an astrological constellation, picking out an arbitrary group of the myriad stars in one part of the night sky in order to draw a picture that, while perhaps entertaining, does not tell us much if anything about how things out there really are. My more settled view is that the thinkers I discuss are important enough to make an examination of them revealing of the period as a whole. I also think that these thinkers are intrinsically extremely interesting and appealing, and that philosophical time spent with them is well spent.

1. The Negative Answer of English Calvinism

1. Throughout this part of the book, I will be discussing Cudworth and Whichcote's reactions to the English Calvinism propounded by Williams Perkins. It is important to note, however, that Perkins is not simply a conduit for Calvin himself, and the views I call "English Calvinist" should not all be equated to Calvin's own. For a very helpful discussion of Calvin's own views and their bearing on seventeenth-century English religious and moral thought, see Beiser (1996), 20–45.

2. Whichcote and Cudworth's Positive Answer

1. An important recent work on Whichcote is Beiser (1996, 134–83). Schneewind (1998) is also a noteworthy contribution. Beiser (1996), Schneewind (1998), and Darwall (1995) all do an excellent job of explaining the seventeenth-century philosophical context of Whichcote's thought.

2. For excellent discussions of the Cambridge Platonists' relationship to Calvinism, see Cassirer(1953), 65–85, and Beiser (1996), 159–65.
3. See Beiser (1996), 84–133.
4. See Russell (1990), 84–5.
5. Whichcote, Cudworth, Smith, and More did not always speak with one voice. There were differences among them, usually only in tone or emphasis, but sometimes in substance. The similarities, however, predominate. And because their ideas are so similar, it is difficult to say with whom any particular idea originated. Whichcote was older, of course, and initially a tutor when the other three were students. But it seems likely that before too long, the others were exerting as much influence on Whichcote as he was on them. Indeed, Cudworth and More possessed a kind of driving intellectual ambition to construct philosophical systems, something that Whichcote seemed to lack. So while Whichcote's ideas constituted the inspiring starting points, More and Cudworth probably did more of the work of developing the details of the views they all came to hold.
6. For discussion of the neo-Platonist antecedents of the Cambridge Platonists' deiformity claim, see Cassirer (1953), 25–8, and Roberts (1968), 20–41.
7. We should note, however, that the Calvinists thought that man's corruption was due to the Fall. Prior to the Fall, humans had their original God-given shape. So the English Calvinists might have allowed that there is a sense in which human nature is good, but they would then immediately have pointed out that all human beings who currently exist are so corrupt that they are completely unable to achieve righteousness on their own. So the Negative Answer of the English Calvinists amounts to the claim that, since the Fall, all humans tend ineluctably toward sin, that no human has within himself the resources necessary to achieve righteousness, that every human absolutely requires moral assistance from some external source. The Positive Answer of Cudworth and Whichcote can then be taken to be the negation of that version of the Negative Answer; that is, their Positive Answer can be taken to be the claim that every human's natural tendencies are toward virtue, that all humans have within themselves all the resources necessary to achieve righteousness, that no human absolutely requires moral assistance from an external source.
8. Culverwell is sometimes called a Cambridge Platonist. For reasons that should be clear from my discussion of his reading of Psalms 20:27, I don't classify him as such.
9. For discussion of the historical importance of Whichcote's anti-voluntarism and his belief in the rationality of religion, see Beiser (1996), 135–83, and Schneewind (1996).
10. See also Whichcote I 39, 230; II 107–8, 126–7, 195; III 216–17, 227, 232, 335–7, 354–9.
11. As Whichcote puts it, "They, that are *Reconciled* unto God, in the Frame and Temper of their Minds; that Live according to the Law of Heaven (the everlasting and immutable Rule of Goodness, Righteousness and Truth;) may truly be said to have begun *Heaven*, while they are upon the earth: But They, who confound the Difference of good and evil; and who Care not to Approve themselves to God; but act without Difference of Distinction; *These* are Partakers of the *Devilish* Nature, and are in the Hellish State" (Aphorisms 282).

12. The definitive work on ethical internalism in early modern British moral philosophy is Darwall (1995).

3. Whichcote and Cudworth on Religious Liberty

1. For an account of the relevant events of Whichcote's life, see Roberts (1968), 1–16.
2. For discussion of the Cambridge Platonists' influence on the Latitudinarian movement in particular and on the Church of England in general, see Powicke (1926/1970), Roberts(1968), Griffin (1992), and Spellman (1993).
3. See Chapter 6 for discussion of the relationship between Locke and Cudworth's daughter.

4. Rationalism, Sentimentalism, and Ralph Cudworth

1. The claim that morality originates in reason alone is multiply ambiguous, suggesting a cluster of positions that can be separated from each other. One of these positions is metaphysical: the view that morality is constituted by reason alone. Another of these positions is epistemological: the view that we discern morality through the use of reason alone. A third of these positions is what we can call practical: the view that moral conduct is motivated by reason alone. Cudworth held all three of these positions, and he (along with most of the other ethical rationalists of the seventeenth and early eighteenth centuries) did not clearly distinguish between them. In Section B of this chapter, when I discuss the necessity of morals thesis, I try to explain how Cudworth brought together the metaphysical and epistemological versions of moral rationalism. But it's not clear to me that he was consciously concerned to distinguish between these two versions.
2. Passmore (1951), 51–78, has argued that we should not think of Cudworth as a moral rationalist. Proper attention to all of Cudworth's writings, Passmore maintains, reveals that his position is in important respects much closer to that of sentimentalists such as Hutcheson and Hume than it is to that of rationalists such as Clarke and Balguy. As I will explain later in this chapter, I believe that Passmore rightly points to non-rationalist elements of Cudworth's thought (which are particularly prominent in the 1647 sermons), but I also think he goes too far in denying the rationalist elements that are also present (particularly in EIM).
3. That Cudworth aimed at such a target is easy to understand given that scholasticism still had a strong hold over much of Cambridge University in the 1640s, and that he had been exposed at Emmanuel College to some of the strongest criticisms of it.
4. This makes Cudworth's sermons an ancestor of Hutcheson's anti-rationalist arguments based on ultimate ends (which I discuss in Chapter 12) and Hume's anti-rationalist motivational arguments (which I discuss in Chapter 16).
5. I do not mean to imply that Cudworth's rejection of scholasticism is equivalent to, or in and of itself implies, the rejection of moral rationalism. Many moral rationalists rejected scholasticism, and Cudworth continued to reject it even while writing his most rationalist works. My point is that in the sermons

Cudworth used his attacks on scholasticism as a launching pad for a more general dismissal of the importance of propositional thought as a whole. Perhaps this shows that when Cudworth was delivering the sermons, he hadn't yet fully realized that the syllogistic reasoning he associated with the scholastics was not the only conception of reason one could have.

6. In Chapter 5, I discuss further Cudworth's Pelagian tendencies, which are present not only in the 1647 sermons but also in EIM, where Cudworth apotheosizes reason within every individual.

7. John Smith, another of the Cambridge Platonists, makes similar proto-sentimentalist claims in his "True Way or Method of attaining to Divine Knowledge," an essay that bears a striking resemblance to Cudworth's "Sermon preached before the House of Commons." See Patrides (1970), 128–9. For discussion of Smith, see Schneewind (1998), 199–202.

8. See Beiser (1996), 179–83, for a penetrating analysis of the Cambridge Platonists' philosophical engagement with religious mystery. For further discussion of Cudworth's view of the mystery of the Trinity in his *True Intellectual System*, see Popkin (1992), 340–1. See also John Smith's "True Way" (Patrides 1970, 133 and 141–2).

9. I discuss the role of the necessity of morals thesis in Balguy, Price, and Kant in Gill (1998) and briefly in Chapter 19.

10. I am discussing *Cudworth's* conceptions of voluntarism and Hobbesianism. It's important to note, however, that Cudworth may not have had the most accurate understanding of these views. When he is attacking voluntarism, Cudworth often seems to have in mind the English Calvinist variety of William Perkins (see, for instance, EIM 22); Cudworth's arguments might not apply as readily to the views of someone like Pufendorf, whose view is more sophisticated and amenable to the use of human reason than that of Perkins. See Schneewind (1996) and (1998), 8–9, 21–36, 119–40 for a very helpful discussion that provides a fuller view of seventeenth-century voluntarism than Cudworth himself provides. When he is attacking Hobbesianism, Cudworth doesn't seem to consider the possibility that Hobbes's laws of nature might themselves be eternal and immutable, or that the decisions of a Hobbesian sovereign might be controlled by moral considerations. For rich discussion of these issues in Hobbes interpretation, see Gauthier (2001) and Sewell (2001). But even if Cudworth's conceptions of voluntarism and Hobbesian are oversimplified, I believe that there remains a crucially important core difference between Cudworth's view of morality in EIM and that of the voluntarists and Hobbesians. In EIM, Cudworth maintains that our grasp of right and wrong can be the same as God's or the sovereign's; reason enables us to learn about right and wrong in the same way that God and the sovereign do. Voluntarists and Hobbesians, in contrast, hold that there is a lawgiver (God or the sovereign) whose relationship to right and wrong differs in a significant way from ours. Right and wrong, for voluntarists and Hobbesians, depend on a lawgiver in a way that they do not depend on each of us; but, for Cudworth, there is no fundamental difference between our relationship to right and wrong and the relationship between God or sovereign and right and wrong.

11. See EIM 80, 118–20, 124, 129, 139, 142.

12. For an excellent discussion of the seventeenth-century view that we can in certain subjects gain a certainty equivalent to that of God, see Craig (1987), 13–68. Craig traces this idea through Galileo's *Dialogue Concerning the Two Chief World Systems*, Descartes's *Meditations*, and Leibniz's *Discourse on Metaphysics* (although Craig also points out that he neglects "one exception which Leibniz makes: existential propositions [apart from 'God exists'] are not analytic, even to God" [Craig 1987, 61]).

13. My reading of EIM conflicts in some respects with Darwall's interpretation (Darwall 1995, 119–47). What Darwall claims is that Cudworth is an "autonomist internalist," which means that Cudworth believes that moral obligation consists of "the motives of a self-determining agent" (Darwall 1995, 109). As Darwall puts it, "In fact, however, Cudworth made a fundamental distinction between purely speculative intellect and *practical* mind, and asserted that ethical propositions are made true or false by the nature of the latter. This is only implicit in the sole work Cudworth published during his lifetime, the massive tome *The True Intellectual System of the Universe*. But it is explicit in the *Treatise*, even if it is not directly relevant to that work's main aims" (Darwall 1995, 114).

I believe Darwall's internalist autonomist reading of EIM runs into several problems. First of all, it seems to me that Darwall misconstrues Cudworth's claim that immutable entities exist entirely within mind (Darwall 1995, 123–4). For while Cudworth does say this, Darwall underplays the extent to which Cudworth argues that the mind in which the immutable entities exist must be the *mind of God*. The immutable entities, mind-dependent though they are, necessarily have an existence independent of *human* minds. This seems to me to imply that morality, which consists of immutable entities, cannot be constituted by the motives of human agents, since it necessarily has an existence independent of human minds.

The particular kind of conspicuous anti-voluntarism in EIM also seems to me to be a problem for Darwall's autonomist internalist reading, as this kind of anti-voluntarism seems to imply that morality cannot consist of the motives of any agent (not even God). Darwall acknowledges that EIM's anti-voluntarism seems to conflict with his reading, but he says that there are passages in EIM that nonetheless show that Cudworth was an autonomist internalist (Darwall 1995, 113–14). I'm not sure, however, how Darwall explains away the numerous anti-voluntarist passages of EIM. It seems to me that these passages remain problems for his interpretation. I'm also not sure how Darwall explains away the numerous passages that argue that morality consists of claims that have the same kind of necessity as geometric propositions. These also seem to me to remain problems for Darwall's interpretation. And given that these anti-voluntarist and geometric-like passages constitute the bulk of the book, I think there is some reason to question Darwall's interpretative strategy of reading Cudworth as an autonomist internalist on the basis of the four passages he cites (I.ii.4, I.ii.6, IV.vi.4, and IV.vi.13).

That is not to say that it is impossible to coherently combine anti-voluntarism, moral rationalism, and the view that morality depends on motives that beings capable of moral action must be able to have. Kant, for one, makes plausible the possibility of such a combination. My claim in this chapter is that *Cudworth's*

arguments (as well as the arguments of the other seventeenth-century rationalists) do not constitute a coherent combination of this sort. And that is because
Cudworth's arguments against voluntarism (unlike Kant's) imply that morality
consists of principles that are independent of anyone's motives. Cudworth (as
well as the other seventeenth-century rationalists) seemed to think that this very
strong kind of anti-voluntarism was required in order to give substance to God's
goodness and to affirm the essential goodness of human nature. Kant seemed
not to think that such a strong anti-voluntarism was required, and Kant generally did not require theological commitments that were as robust as Cudworth
and the other seventeenth-century rationalists required. But then again, Kant's
view was deeply informed by Hutcheson and Hume's attacks on the very strong
motive-independence view of moral rationalists such as Cudworth. The general
problem I am attributing to Darwall's reading is that it imports back into the
seventeenth-century rationalists such as Cudworth a view of the relationship
between morality and the motives of moral agents that developed only after
Hume had completed what I am calling the Copernican Revolution in moral
philosophy. I think Darwall's reading fails to appreciate fully that Kant's view
of the relationship between morality and the motives of moral agents is post-
Humean, while Cudworth's is pre-Humean.

But let me now turn to an examination of the four passages Darwall cites.
The first two – I.ii.4 and I.ii.6 – appear in a chapter that opens with some of
the strongest anti-voluntarist claims in all of Cudworth's writings. Cudworth
starts this chapter, that is, by arguing that morality has an existence entirely
independent of all will, that the essential character of everything (moral as
well as non-moral) is eternally and immutably fixed by nature, not by any will
whatsoever. After making these anti-voluntarist claims, however, Cudworth is
compelled to address the following question: how can a person be obligated to
obey just civil authorities when they prescribe laws that are not eternally and
immutably just (e.g., why are we obligated to drive on the right side of the
road, given the fact that there is nothing in the eternal and immutable essential nature of driving on the left that is unjust?)? How, that is, can something
that is in itself morally indifferent become, through the command of a lawgiver,
morally obligatory? The sentences Darwall emphasizes are part of Cudworth's
response to this question (Darwall 1995, 119–21). And what Cudworth says is
that a person is obligated to obey such "positive" laws when he and the lawgiver
are in a relationship of "natural justice and equity," that is, when the lawgiver has
justly and legitimately acquired his position of prescribing laws to the subject,
and not when he has acquired his position simply through brute power (EIM
18–21). So when Cudworth is speaking in this chapter of "obligation," he is not
necessarily speaking of morality in general. He is, rather, speaking specifically
of the obligation to obey civil laws prescribed by a just civil authority. When he
says, that is, that obligation is based on the "intellectual nature of him that is
commanded," he is not necessarily saying that morality in general consists of
the motives of each moral agent, but only that the obligation to obey positive
civil laws is grounded in the fact that there exists between subject and magistrate a relationship that accords with "natural justice and equity." It's true that
Cudworth also says in these passages that we are obliged to do what is "naturally good" by "the intellectual nature" (EIM 20). But the intellectual nature

that obliges us to do what is naturally good does not seem to be *our* intellectual nature, but rather *the* intellectual nature, that is, the nature of reality as it exists eternally and immutably, independent of our particular minds.

The next passage Darwall cites is EIM IV.vi.4, which he takes to be a clear indication that Cudworth drew a distinction between the theoretical and practical aspects of the mind (Darwall 1995, 126–7). Now I am not entirely sure how this distinction is supposed to work, but it seems to me that in this passage Cudworth is *not* distinguishing between geometric and moral propositions – that whatever else is going on in this passage, Cudworth is here adhering to the view (promulgated throughout the rest of EIM) that geometry and morality have the same epistemological and metaphysical status. This is because in this passage Cudworth is summarizing prior arguments that were intended to show that our geometric ideas, because they give us real knowledge, are innate, arising from the active vigor of our minds. Cudworth is saying, in other words, that just as he has shown that our geometric ideas can achieve the status of true knowledge, so too he will show – and in just the same way – that our moral ideas can achieve the status of true knowledge. His point is that we will be able to have confidence in the reality of morality because he will show that morality is just like geometry. That is not to say that Darwall's reading is completely without grounds: Cudworth certainly does say in this passage that "anticipations of morality spring . . . from some . . . inward, and vital principle, in intellectual beings, as such, whereby they have a natural determination in them *to do some things, and to avoid others*, which could not be, if they were mere naked passive things" (italics added). But I think Darwall's reading requires our placing a tremendous amount of interpretative weight on that single sentence, and in a way that does not jibe with the rest of the passage of which it is a part. The reading that fits better with everything else Cudworth says here takes the claim about *doing* certain things to be a claim not about conduct but about the active nature of the mind; it takes it to be a claim that applies equally to doing geometry (judging that certain theorems are true) and distinguishing moral good from moral evil.

The final passage Darwall cites is EIM IV.vi.13 (Darwall 1995, 127–8). Darwall claims to find in this passage evidence of Cudworth's distinguishing between God's relationship to geometry and God's relationship to morality. I must confess that I just don't see the basis for this claim. In the paragraph immediately preceding IV.vi.13, Cudworth seems to be talking about all knowledge, moral and geometric. And in the sentence Darwall quotes, Cudworth says that the mind of God is "the first original and source of all things," which seems to me to suggest that He has the same relationship to all things. And as Darwall himself points out, his reading makes it unclear "why God would have to exist in order for there to be moral truths" (Darwall 1995, 128). Yet Cudworth says in this very passage that "it is not possible that there should be any such thing as morality, unless there be a God" (EIM 150). Because of these interpretative difficulties, I am reluctant to attribute autonomist internalism to Cudworth on the basis of EIM alone.

Darwall goes on to say, however, that the best evidence for his autonomist internalist reading of Cudworth occurs in the manuscripts on free will. I discuss the manuscripts in notes 15 and 16.

14. For an excellent discussion of More's *Enchiridion*, see Schneewind (1998), 202–5.

15. I must acknowledge, however, that in the first twenty-five pages or so of one of Cudworth's unpublished manuscripts (in the British Library, Additional Manuscript 4982) Cudworth does seem to be very hostile to the idea of moral demonstrations. In those pages, he does not sound at all like someone who would construct a system of morality (such as More's *Enchiridion*) modeled on Euclidean geometry. In fact, these passages, with their hostility to speculative reason, seem to me to be remarkably similar to Cudworth's sermons from 1647. I am tempted, consequently, to date them to the 1640s or 1650s, fifteen or twenty years prior to the composition of EIM. But Passmore claims that an analysis of the handwriting establishes that Cudworth wrote these passages toward the end of his life, in the 1680s. So I can only say that if Passmore's claims about Cudworth's handwriting are correct (and while my inspection of the manuscripts didn't convince me that Passmore was correct, it also didn't convince me that he wasn't), then I have to acknowledge that Cudworth was drawn in the 1680s to ideas that conflict with the ideas I attribute to him when he was writing EIM in the 1660s.

   Passmore admits that he has read Cudworth selectively and notes that "there are obvious dangers in a policy of selection; but Cudworth must somehow be rescued from his own wordiness. No doubt other Cudworths could be hewn out of the great mass of his work" (Passmore 1951, vii). I suppose I have also read Cudworth selectively. Perhaps that is inevitable. And maybe the Cudworth I've hewn answers to Cudworth's texts no better than Passmore's or Darwall's. The biggest difference between our interpretations is that I place more weight on the most conspicuous strands of EIM, while they place more weight on certain of the manuscript passages. It's only fair to point out, however, that neither the manuscripts nor EIM were published in Cudworth's lifetime. EIM, no less than the manuscripts, was either a work in progress or a trying out of ideas that Cudworth did not ultimately deem fit for publication.

16. I should point out, however, that the claim that Whichcote's ethical demonstrations and More's *Enchiridion* are the logical extensions of EIM would be denied by both Passmore and Darwall (and probably by Sarah Hutton as well [see EIM xxv and 145]). Passmore and Darwall (and probably Hutton) would reject the claim because they believe that Cudworth's unpublished manuscripts show that he did not think ethics was rational in the geometric, demonstrative way that More's *Enchiridion* and Whichcote's demonstrations imply (Passmore 1951, 51–68; Darwall 1995, 116–17). To Passmore and Darwall's interpretations, let me offer the following two responses.

   First, even if Passmore and Darwall are right in holding that some of the unpublished manuscripts conflict with my claim, that doesn't prove that when Cudworth was writing EIM, he didn't believe that he was paving the way for a system of ethics that consisted of geometric-like theorems and demonstrative proofs. Cudworth wrote a great many things over the course of his philosophical career, and they do not all cohere. Any Cudworth commentator will have to contend with his seemingly contradictory statements, and this is especially true when we take into account all the handwritten unpublished notes Cudworth jotted throughout his lifetime. I have tried to argue that the rhetorical framing, the leading examples, and the deep philosophy of EIM – the skin, flesh, and bones of the work – implies that a system of ethics will consist of geometric-like theorems and demonstrative proofs. If there are manuscripts that conflict with that implication, then I believe we have no choice but to chalk them up to Cudworth's inconsistency. I don't believe that a geometrically rationalist interpretation of EIM can be dismissed simply because there are other writings of Cudworth's that conflict with it.

Second, the manuscripts do not speak as clearly against the geometrically rationalist interpretation as Passmore and Darwall suggest. Passmore, in particular, overstates the sentimentalist character of the manuscripts, ignores some of the obviously innatist parts (compare, for instance, Passmore 1951, 53, with Cudworth ms. 4981, p. 104), and quotes heavily from ms. 4983, which may very well have not been written by Cudworth at all (see Darwall 1995, 146). Moreover, both Passmore and Darwall's interpretations rely to a large extent on Cudworth's statements about human free will, which is the main topic of many of the manuscripts. But there are two big problems in trying to interpret EIM's conception of morality through the prism of Cudworth's statements about human free will.

The first problem is that the manuscript statements on free will are so multifarious and confusing that they strongly suggest that Cudworth himself was never completely satisfied with any single position. Cudworth was greatly vexed by the question of free will. That some of his attempts to answer it seem incompatible with a demonstratively rational ethics should not be taken as evidence that he never thought a demonstratively rational ethics was possible, since he himself was trying out, changing, and abandoning ideas on free will throughout his career.

The second problem is that in the manuscripts Cudworth frequently makes a claim that appears to draw a sharp divide between human free will and EIM's conception of morality. The claim is that God does not have free will. Free will only belongs to imperfect human beings. If we were perfect, as God is, we wouldn't have free will (see, for instance, EIM 185–6 and 177–8; ms. 4979, 20–1, 102/106; and ms. 4982, 130–1). But the entire structure of EIM is built on the idea that God understands all of morality and that we participate with the mind of God when we understand morality. EIM argues, in other words, that there is an isomorphism, or perhaps identity, between our conception of morality and God's conception of morality, that when we recognize morality our minds are in the same kind of state that God's is (cf. ms. 4982, 109). Cudworth makes it clear that the morality that is the subject of EIM *does* belong to God – that God is moral. Indeed, he tells us in EIM that the nature of God is "the first rule and exemplar of morality" (EIM 150). This seems to me to make it very difficult to draw any conclusions about EIM's conception of morality from the manuscripts' statements about uniquely human (emphatically non-God-like) free will. And it also seems to me to make very questionable the claim that the manuscripts on free will constitute the drafts of the sequel to EIM, insofar as God is the exemplar of EIM's conception of morality, while free will is something that does not belong to God. Another way of explaining the difference between EIM and the manuscripts on free will is in terms of the distinction Cudworth explicitly draws between, on the one hand, the "hegemonic of the soul," which is what he identifies as human free will, and, on the other hand, our "necessary understanding" (EIM 180) or the "speculative power of contemplating . . . whatsoever is and is not in nature, and of the truth and falsehood of things universal" (EIM 193–6). The manuscripts on free will are an examination of the hegemonic. But in EIM, Cudworth makes it clear that morality (if it is a real thing at all) is something that we discern through the use of our "speculative power" or "necessary understanding." We should, consequently, expect the sequel to EIM (which will explain the nature of morality) to consist not of an examination of the hegemonic but rather of deliverances of our "necessary understanding" or "speculative power."

Now Darwall argues that the manuscripts make it clear that Cudworth drew a crucial distinction between the speculative understanding and practical reason, and such a distinction seems incompatible with a system of geometric-like moral demonstrations (Darwall 1995, 136). But while Darwall does identify places where Cudworth draws this distinction, there are also passages in the manuscripts that *equate* the speculative and practical (ms 4979, 19–21; ms 4981, 108; ms 4982, 36–7). Moreover, whatever else the speculative–practical distinction is, it's not, for Cudworth of EIM, a distinction between morality (which we typically think of as practical) and geometry (which we typically think of as speculative). For one of the main epistemological points in EIM is that our ideas of both morality *and* geometry are innate, *both* arising from the active vigor of our minds themselves. It seems, in other words, that Cudworth is pulling geometry onto the active side of the mind rather than distinguishing between (practical) morality and (speculative) geometry. And then he is claiming that we should have confidence in the reality of morality because we have already seen that we can have confidence in the reality of geometry.

17. A number of people who read earlier drafts of this chapter have suggested various ways of reconciling EIM and the 1647 sermons. In response, let me note, first, that I do not mean to claim that it is impossible to coherently combine antivoluntarism, moral rationalism, and the view that morality depends on motives that beings capable of moral action must be able to have. As I noted in note 13, my claim in this chapter is that *Cudworth's* arguments do not seem to constitute a coherent combination of this sort, and that this is because Cudworth had certain theological commitments and beliefs about the relationship between morality and human nature that made such a coherent combination very difficult if not impossible to achieve. But let me now consider some of the attempted reconciliations.

One might, first of all, try to explain away the apparent differences between the sermons' mysterious heart and EIM's public reason by arguing that the works are about different things. The sermons are about religion, and EIM is about morality. And religion and morality, so this reconciling line of thinking might go, are distinct from each other, making it perfectly consistent for Cudworth to hold both that the latter is rational and publicly accessible and that the former is emotional and mysterious.

The problem with this attempted reconciliation is that it's clear that Cudworth did *not* draw a sharp distinction between morality and religion, and that as a result we should take EIM and the sermons to be concerned with the same topic. For Cudworth claims in EIM that the nature of God is "the first rule and exemplar of morality" (EIM 150), and this claim is in line with the general intention of all the Cambridge Platonists to oppose those thinkers who separated morality from religion. The seventeenth-century thinkers who separated morality from religion did so at the expense of the former, contending that morality was an unimportant code of conduct, as peripheral in achieving salvation as etiquette or manners. But Cudworth, along with the other Cambridge Platonists, believed that to comprehend moral ideas is to partake of the mind of God (EIM 26, 137, 150), which is also what he takes to be the essence of religion (Commons 377, 383; Lincolnes 26). This explains why Cudworth moves seamlessly between discussion of Christian religion and Greek virtue, speaking as though the two things were one and the same (Commons 375). It's true that the rhetorical setting of the sermons makes it appropriate to emphasize the language of religion, and that the philosophical context of EIM makes it appropriate to emphasize the language of morality. But the underlying topic of the sermons and EIM is the same: righteousness and how it enables us to participate with the mind of God. And I've tried to show that while EIM tells us that we can achieve righteousness and divine participation through rationality alone, the sermons tell us that we can achieve it only through a non-rational passion.

Another way in which one might try to reconcile the sermons and EIM is to hold that EIM intends to show only that the existence of morality requires the existence of eternal and immutable moral natures, and not that the only way for a person to become moral is through knowledge of these natures. According to this reconciling line of thinking, Cudworth thought that a person could be fully moral without possessing demonstrable knowledge of the moral natures, which would mean that the sermons' description of a moral life that does not necessarily involve demonstrable knowledge could be consistent with EIM's description of the demonstrable truth of morality.

Now I acknowledge that Cudworth does make comments that suggest that he sometimes thought that his emphasis on passion in the sermons and on rational necessity in EIM fit together in just this way (see EIM 9, 181; but for a seemingly contrary view, see Lincolnes 5–6). But the central positions for which he argues in the sermons and EIM don't admit of this sort of reconciliation. For in both the sermons and EIM, Cudworth is attempting to describe the highest goal of a human life. In both the sermons and EIM, Cudworth is attempting to describe the greatest good to which human beings can aspire. In both the sermons and EIM, moreover, Cudworth maintains that when human beings achieve that highest goal or greatest good, they become one with God (Commons 377, 383 and Lincolnes 26; EIM 150). In the sermons, he says that achieving the highest good and becoming one with God is an essentially non-rational matter; it's a matter of feeling a certain kind of love, not of possessing any kind of propositional understanding (Commons 375, 380, 387, 389–90; Lincolnes 49). But in EIM, he implies that achieving the highest good and becoming one with God is an essentially rational accomplishment; it's the result of understanding the eternal and immutable truth of certain propositions (EIM 128–32, 137). That's not to say that EIM implies that the highest good we can achieve has nothing to do with conduct and character. When he was writing EIM, Cudworth probably thought that when one understands the eternal and immutable truth of moral propositions, one will inevitably be motivated to act in a morally appropriate way (see EIM 145). But what EIM does imply is that the motive to act in a morally appropriate way can be based entirely on a purely rational understanding of ethical propositions. And the sermons maintain, in contrast, that the God-like motivation to which we should aspire can never arise from rational understanding alone.

A third explanation is that throughout his entire career, Cudworth held that the essence of morality and religion is something that is both a movement of the heart and a self-evident truth. According to this explanation, Cudworth was trying to stake out conceptual ground on which a single principle could be both necessarily motivating in the way that love is and rationally necessary in the way that a logical proof is. If there was any change, it was merely the non-substantive, terminological one of how he used the terms "reason" and "rationality." In 1647, Cudworth seemed to equate reason and rationality with the syllogistic reasoning taught by the scholastics. But by the time he wrote EIM, he was working with a non-syllogistic conception of reason and rationality – a conception that was practical in ways that syllogistic reasoning was not and that, with some non-substantive terminological tweaking, could be coherently situated at the heart of the view of morality and religion of the 1647 sermons.

Now this explanation might very well capture what Cudworth thought he was doing. But even if Cudworth thought that what he said in EIM could be coherently combined with the 1647 sermons, it does not follow that it could be. There might be differences between the works that are not merely non-substantively terminological, whether Cudworth realized it or not. Moreover, I find it unlikely that Cudworth failed to realized that the attitude expressed toward "reason" and "rationality" in EIM differed from the attitude expressed toward what those terms referred to in the 1647 sermons. And it seems to me that a full account of Cudworth's thought should explain why Cudworth thought it necessary to develop a new way of talking about these things, and why he thought the ideas he expressed in the sermons had to be (at the very least) recast.

I suspect that the differences between the sermons and EIM are probably also partly due to the fact that Cudworth's positions were defined as much by what he was opposed to as by what he was in favor of. Cudworth was at times a polemic writer. He often had as his goal the refutation of specific views held by his contemporaries. In his attempt to show that one view was mistaken, he was sometimes inclined to travel quite far in one direction. In his attempt to show that another view was mistaken, he was sometimes inclined to travel quite far in another direction. And the destination he arrived at when attacking one view was sometimes rather different from the destination he arrived at when attacking another. Thus, in the sermons, Cudworth's desire to discredit scholasticism may have generated a philosophical momentum that pushed him toward an emphasis on the passions that left little room for reason. And, in EIM, his goal of defeating the English Calvinist brand of voluntarism may have generated a philosophical momentum that pushed him toward an apotheosis of reason that left little room for the passions. This is worth noting because Cudworth has sometimes been dismissed as an "antiquarian's antiquarian," that is, as nothing but a philosophical excavator who spent his life digging ever deeper into old texts that had little relevance to matters of the day. Nothing could be further from the truth. Cudworth's thought was in intense interaction with the intellectual movements and political events of his time.

18. See also Coward (1994), 460.
19. The possible explanation I have given for the differences between Cudworth's sermons and EIM are (I hope) in line with Beiser's superb account of the seventeenth-century dispute over enthusiasm and its role in the development of rationalism (Beiser 1996, 184–219). Particularly relevant to what I have said about Cudworth is Beiser's illuminating discussion of what he calls the "epistemological argument" against enthusiasm. When deploying this argument, Beiser explains, rationalists establish the requirement that enthusiasts provide some justification for their claim that their spiritual experience is divinely inspired. The rationalists force this requirement on the enthusiasts by pointing "out the notorious fact that there are competing claims to divine inspiration. The Fifth Monarchist, Familist, Anabaptist, Quaker, and Ranter all have their mystical experience, and they all draw conflicting conclusions from them. Not all these conclusions can be true. So which experience can we accept as the true one? There seems to be no escape, then, from the demand to 'test the spirits,' to establish some criteria to distinguish between genuine and spurious inspiration" (Beiser 1996, 210). This testing of the spirits was, however, exceedingly problematic for the enthusiasts, as allowing such a test would inevitably involve their having to admit that their enthusiastic experience had to live up to the standards of rationality. "This is already a significant concession because the mere demand to test the spirits, to find some criteria to distinguish between true and false prophecy, shows that reason has acquired some degree of sovereignty over inspiration. It is not possible for inspiration to be a sufficient rule of faith when it requires the general criteria and universal rules of reason to distinguish between its true and false forms" (Beiser 1996, 211). Beiser concludes his discussion by saying, "In the end, then, the enthusiast had to make a difficult choice: either a nonrational but private religion, or a public but rational one. There is no middle path where he can have public acknowledgement of his experience and avoid the discourse of reason" (Beiser 1996, 213). Beiser is right about this. And I believe that Cudworth came to recognize the inescapability of this choice, and to opt for the public and rational side, sometime after delivering his sermons and before writing EIM.

5. The Emergence of Non-Christian Ethics

1. For a similar discussion of this problem in Whichcote, see Beiser (1996), 164–5, 175–83.
2. Schneewind errs, consequently, in attributing to Whichcote the view that "[m]orality suffices to win salvation" and that the "one part of religion in twenty that comes by institution . . . has . . . merely instrumental value" (Schneewind

1998, 196–7). Cragg encourages this same mistake when he maintains that Whichcote believed that "the moral element in the Gospel [is] supremely important" and that "[b]oth the institutions and the prescriptions of organized religion must ... serve moral ends or they would cease to be religious instruments" (Cragg 1968, 20). That Schneewind and Cragg mischaracterize Whichcote in this regard is clear from the fact that Whichcote explicitly contrasts what he calls the "instrumental part of religion" with both the moral *and instituted* parts. Now it might seem as though this mischaracterization is of minor importance – a reflection simply of the difference between the way in which we today tend to use the word "institution" (to refer to the parts of organized religion that Whichcote calls "instrumental") and Whichcote's semitechnical use of the word (to refer specifically to the acceptance of Jesus Christ). But really the mischaracterization is more serious than that, for it obscures the most central problem of Whichcote's thought – namely, the problem of reconciling rationalism and distinctly Christian commitments.

3. I have taken this point largely from Craig's discussion of what he calls the "Similarity Thesis" or the "Image of God doctrine" (Craig 1987, 13, 19, 21, 29). I should note, though, that it might be thought that I have overstated the similarity between human and divine reason. For, as Beiser puts it, "The human intellect perceives things discursively, going gradually from part to whole, whereas the divine intellect perceives things intuitively, proceeding from the whole to the parts. They both have the same object, but they have different ways of conceiving it. This could be described as a difference in degree, but also in kind" (Beiser, correspondence). In response, I note that Whichcote's suggestions of the actual *identity* of human and divine reason seem to me to warrant attributing to him the view that the particular things humans can know (although they constitute only a proper subset of what God knows) they can know with just the same certainty that God knows them; such suggestions seem to me to warrant attributing to Whichcote the view that while the (discursive) manner in which humans come to know things is not the same as the (intuitive) manner in which God knows them, the "manner of knowing itself" (Craig 1987, 29) is the same in both the human and divine intellect (or, as Schneewind puts it, for Whichcote "our minds and God's are not really separate" [Schneewind 1998, 197]). That Cudworth's epistemology is grounded on an equally strong claim of the similarity of human and divine reason seems to me to constitute additional evidence for interpreting Whichcote in this way.

4. Passmore discusses the relationship between the Christian and secular aspects of Cudworth's moral philosophy in his chapter "Ethics and Religion" (Passmore 1951, 79–89).

5. I should note that at an earlier point in *Freewill* (EIM 181–2; cf. 186) Cudworth also mentions the idea that the weakness of human reason requires us to believe certain things in the gospel of which we cannot develop clear and distinct ideas. But the larger context of the passage makes it clear that Cudworth's main point is that we can and should prevent ourselves from falling into error by assenting only to those things we can clearly and distinctly conceive. The mention of faith in the gospel is an aberration; it doesn't seem to fit at all with the central claims of the chapter in which it occurs.

6. Shaftesbury and the Cambridge Platonists

1. See Hutton (1993) and Frankel (1989).
2. For valuable discussions of Shaftesbury's connections to the Cambridge Platonists, see Passmore (1951), 96–100, Cassirer (1953), 159–202, and Darwall (1995), 176–81.
3. With the startling exception of an addition to the 1711 version of the *Inquiry*, which we will discuss in Chapter 9.
4. For further discussion of Shaftesbury's criticism of Locke, see Cassirer (1953), 189–91, Darwall (1995), 177–8, and Schneewind (1998), 296.
5. For more on this letter, see Voitle (1984), 119.

7. Shaftesbury's *Inquiry*

1. This ambivalent attitude toward humanity riddled Shaftesbury throughout his twenties. It's evident not only in his philosophical writing, but also in his letters, private notebooks, and personal behavior. Shaftesbury was, for instance, deeply conflicted about public service: sometimes powerfully drawn toward political activity, with great aspirations for the improvement of the commonwealth; at other times, deeply hostile toward politics and highly dubious of the possibility of any real national progress. He was equally conflicted about many interpersonal interactions, exhibiting by turns a gregarious love of company and an ornery desire to be left alone. At some points in his twenties, he seems to have wanted to be an integral part of society; at other points, he seems to have wanted to resign from the party of humankind altogether. It seems likely, moreover, that this tension between sociableness and misanthropy mirrors Shaftesbury's own view of himself. In his notebooks from this period, there are statements of supreme confidence and self-approval as well as expressions of disgusted self-loathing that are so prolonged, vehement, and explicit as to be positively disturbing, if not obscene.
2. See Darwall (1995), 183.
3. In defense of Shaftesbury, Darwall has stressed the importance of distinguishing between natural goodness and moral goodness, maintaining that for Shaftesbury it is only moral goodness, and not natural goodness, that depends upon the reflections of the moral sense. But I do not think that this distinction is as sharp in Shaftesbury as Darwall suggests (nor that Shaftesbury intended it to be sharp). As I argue later, Shaftesbury's account of moral goodness is built on, or presupposes, his account of natural goodness. For he distinguishes between properly and improperly functioning moral senses by noting which of the moral senses is in accord with natural goodness. Darwall has also suggested that the problems I raise for Shaftesbury are due to my incorrectly attributing to him too sharp a distinction between non-motivating rational judgments and motivating sentimental judgments. Darwall wonders why we should not attribute to Shaftesbury the idea that an appreciation of something's contributing to the good of the system of which it is a part (which is what makes a thing naturally good) can be motivating and the idea that the assessments of the moral sense may be rational. In response, I would first point to passages that seem to indicate that Shaftesbury

did not think that reason alone could be a cause of motivated action (Virtue or Merit 23–5, 50). And I would then point to passages that seem to indicate that Shaftesbury thought that assessments of whether something contributes to the good of the system of which it is a part are purely rational (Virtue or Merit 8–12). It's true that Shaftesbury thinks that deliverances of the moral sense are "rational affections," but they are still clearly affections nonetheless. They are rational in that only beings with the ability to reflect on their first-order affections can have them; that is, their rationality consists of their being second-order affections, or affections that arise when we reflect on our first-order affections (Virtue or Merit 16–18). But that Shaftesbury thinks the deliverances of the moral sense are rational in this sense does not imply that he thinks that reason alone can give rise to these deliverances. That said, I wholeheartedly agree with Darwall's basic point that the distinction between what we call sentimentalist and rationalist moral theories was not salient to Shaftesbury and Cudworth in the way it would become for Balguy, Hutcheson, Hume, and Price. It's just that while Darwall seems to think that Shaftesbury and Cudworth managed to transcend the distinction, I think they crossed back and forth between both sides of it.

4. See the discussion of the teleological account of the reason to be virtuous in Chapter 9.

5. I suppose Shaftesbury could avoid both horns of the dilemma if he could provide an account of the "public good" that was based entirely on biological-like facts of human nature, that is, if he could provide an account of the public good that was scientifically proven. But I don't think such an account is in the offing.

8. *The Moralists; a Philosophical Rhapsody*

1. Outside of twentieth-century Anglo-American philosophy, however, *The Moralists* had an enormous impact. For discussion of this impact on aesthetics in general and on eighteenth-century German thought in particular, see Cassirer (1953), 166–7 and 195–200.

2. For full discussion of Shaftesbury's use of the dialogue form and its relationship to the philosophical dialogues that came later (such as those of Berkeley and Hume), see Prince (1996), 23–73.

3. For discussion of the practicality of Shaftesbury's writings, see Klein (1999), x–xv.

4. For an excellent discussion of Shaftesbury's anti-voluntarist moral realism, see Schneewind (1998), 303–5.

5. In an unpublished manuscript entitled "The Adept Ladys" Shaftesbury made abundantly clear his contempt for this type of fanatic enthusiast. There Shaftesbury equates fanatical enthusiasts to people who cherish their own urine and excrement.

6. Shaftesbury discusses the distinction between real enthusiasm and false fanaticism in his "Letter concerning Enthusiasm" (Characteristics I 34–5). For a full treatment of Shaftesbury's enthusiasm, see Grean (1967), 19–36. See also Klein (1999), xxx–xxxi.

7. See Moralists 191–239.

8. In a documentary I once saw, a paleontologist was asked why the dinosaurs disappeared. "They didn't disappear," he said. "They turned into birds and flew

into the sky" (camera panning from the paleontologist's face to a flock of birds on the wing). This is similar to the way one could respond to the question of whatever happened to the Cambridge Platonists: "They turned into Shaftesbury and flew into the sky."

9. Hutcheson and Hume were both clearly influenced by Shaftesbury in their comparisons of morality and beauty (although Hutcheson did not draw the comparison as tightly as Shaftesbury or Hume did). For discussion of how Shaftesbury influenced eighteenth- and nineteenth-century German aesthetic thought, see Cassirer (1953), 198–202.

10. For an account of the differences between the early and late editions of the *Inquiry*, see Virtue or Merit [1st ed.], 121–3.

11. See Chapter 6, Section C.

12. Although I have to say that I, for one, find *The Moralists'* narrative elements to be, at best, mildly entertaining and, at worst, annoyingly distracting. *The Moralists'* ventures into the realm of the dramatic almost always strike me as cloying, strained, and overwritten. I find it tiresome to hear about "pompous rural scenes" and mountains whose "brows are adorned with ancient woods" (Moralists 126). I grow impatient with characters who, instead of agreeing to meet tomorrow, tell each other that they should be content to wander together "when the eastern sun with his first beams adorns the front of yonder hill, there" (Moralists 138). And I can't help but roll my eyes at dialogue that includes lines such as "Ye verdant plains, how gladly I salute ye!" (Moralists 193). I'm also bothered by the fact that the character of Theocles never seems to go to sleep. It seems to me that while Shaftesbury was a splendidly talented writer, when he wrote *The Moralists* he overreached. But maybe this says more about my limitations as a reader of early-eighteenth-century literature than about Shaftesbury's limitations as a writer.

13. For a very clear statement of the need to anchor enthusiastic feelings in a rational view of things, see Characteristics I 34–6.

14. As Grean explains, "Leibniz, surprised to find that much of his *Theodicy* (1710) had already been expressed in Shaftesbury's *Moralists* (1705), wrote that 'if I had seen this work before my *Theodicy* was published, I should have profited as I ought and should have borrowed its great passages'" (Grean 1964, xiii).

15. For further discussion of this point, see note 1 in Chapter 7.

16. A large part of the reason Shaftesbury went to the Netherlands was ill health, and financial pressures also played a big role in his closing up of his estate. But I think it's clear from his notebooks that he had more philosophical and emotional reasons as well.

17. I think Shaftesbury resolved this tension in the final years of his life by focusing all of his energies on perfecting both the philosophical and physical presentation of his ideas in the *Characteristics*. Making the book as perfect as possible was a way of benefiting the public without having to deal with any of them. His incredible attention to the physical appearance of the book was also an embodiment of his practical sentimentalism and his conflation of goodness and beauty. For all that, I find his obsession with the physical book (clear throughout many of the letters he wrote in his final years) somewhat depressing.

9. Shaftesbury's Two Reasons to Be Virtuous

1. For excellent discussion of Shaftesbury's conception of our reason to be virtuous, see Darwall (1995), 193–6, and Schneewind (1998), 306–9.
2. See also Characteristics I 69.
3. But recall that in Section C of Chapter 7, I objected that Shaftesbury's conception of what will promote the interests of the system of which a member is a part is something that we cannot give substance to without making some kind of moral judgment ourselves (at least not insofar as the system is the human species).
4. This is what Schneewind has in mind when he says that the moral affection is "special because through it we become aware of an objective order" (Schneewind 1998, 302). David Fate Norton makes the same point in his discussion of Shaftesbury's "cognitive moral sense" (Norton 1982, 41–2). Darwall, too, speaks of Shaftesbury's "*rationalist* theory of moral sense" (Darwall 1995, 187).
5. See also Regimen 53–9.
6. This account of Shaftesbury's is very similar to Mill's view of the higher pleasures (Mill 8–11).
7. See also Characteristics I 108–10.
8. And if you don't remind yourself of your past actions, others will do it for you. As Shaftesbury puts it, "Or shou'd he be of himself unapt; there are others ready to remind him, and refresh his Memory, in this way of Criticism" (Virtue or Merit 68).
9. In "Good and Ill," Shaftesbury notes that the pleasures of friendship can have the same kind of constancy (Regimen 54–5). I believe that in the end the immediate mental enjoyments of benevolence collapse back into the reflective mental enjoyment of being aware of having conducted oneself virtuously.
10. For the fullest discussion of Shaftesbury's stoicism, see Voitle (1984), 111–63.
11. Compare Regimen 112 and 133–9. Winkler (2000) is a trenchant and fascinating analysis of Shaftesbury's view of personal identity. An equally fascinating and important account of Shaftesbury's view of self, and its central role in his moral philosophy, is Darwall (1995), 180–1 and 197–204.
12. See also Characteristics I 75–7 and I 198–200.
13. Grean, Darwall, and Schneewind each present a unified picture of Shaftesbury's view, and thus do not seem to think that what I am calling Shaftesbury's two accounts are distinct in the manner presented here. I believe Darwall (1995, 187, 196) and Schneewind (1998, 304) underestimate the strength of the skeptical hypothesis (as perhaps Shaftesbury did himself), while Grean (1967, 15) simply misinterprets it. Voitle attributes two different positions to Shaftesbury, but they are not the same two that I have in mind here (1984, 160). Prince also argues that Shaftesbury's thought pulled in two different directions, although he too focuses on a tension different from what I am discussing (1996, 23–46).
14. At one point Theocles does say that his position will remain the same even if "[a]ll else may be only dream and shadow," even if "[a]ll which even sense suggests may be deceitful" (Moralists 207). But he says this in the midst of his explanation of his belief in God. And his belief in God is grounded in the

beauty of the world he perceives. So what Theocles seems to think is that his a posteriori argument from design can survive the supposition that all his sense are deceitful. But I don't see how this can be. I don't see how the supposition of the deceitfulness of all the senses can accord with the argument from design-based belief in God that Theocles relies on throughout most of *The Moralists*. That Theocles says this does constitute evidence, however, that Shaftesbury himself believed that the hypothesis of extreme skepticism was compatible with his teleological account. What I am trying to show in this chapter is that this belief of Shaftesbury's was untenable, that Shaftesbury probably held this belief because of his desire to develop an account of morality that had its ontological ground in both the mind-independent structure of reality and the internal constitution of human beings, and that a choice has to be made between these two ontological grounds, whether Shaftesbury realized it or not.

15. See Schneewind (1998), 298–9.
16. For discussion of this point in Hume, see Postema 1988, 23–40.
17. I have mentioned before how intensely self-reflective Shaftesbury was. He was constantly scrutinizing his own psyche, almost as though he were a Calvinist ransacking his soul for sin. Alongside Shaftesbury's intense self-reflectiveness (either as a cause, an effect, or both) was a profound unsettledness about his own identity. Shaftesbury was greatly exercised by worries not only about what sort of person he should be, but also about what it meant for him to be a person or self at all. At one point in his notebooks, for instance, he wrote: "What am I?" And the oversized, darkened letters of his script seem to indicate that the question caused him particularly passionate vexation. At another point, he wrote, "How long is it that thou wilt continue thus to act two different parts and be two different persons? Call to mind what thou art; what thou hast resolved and entered upon; recollect thyself wholly within thyself. Be one entire and self-same man" (Regimen 112; cf. Characteristics I 114–15 and 176–7).

Shaftesbury's biographer, Robert Voitle, has tried to resolve apparently conflicting tendencies in Shaftesbury's work by distinguishing Shaftesbury's real, private character and his fabricated public masks. I believe, however, that there's no basis for thinking that any one of Shaftesbury's personae was more or less real than any other, no basis for thinking that there was a single and unitary Shaftesburean self who consciously used masks to conceal his true features from the rest of the world. The tensions between Shaftesbury's various positions were not merely superficial but reflected his profound unsettledness about himself. Shaftesbury was at least as uncertain about his true self as any of his audience was. From the inside of Shaftesbury's life, there was just as much tension as there appeared to be from the outside.

And perhaps this unsettledness explains the different conceptions of self implied by the teleological and mental enjoyment accounts. For while the teleological account implies that fully becoming one's true self involves achieving some kind of correspondence to a divinely designed model, the mental enjoyment account is compatible with the idea that there is no pre-existing pattern out there to which one's self must correspond. And while Shaftesbury did at times seem to think there was a divine design that he should follow, it seems likely to me that when he was engaged in his most profound self-questioning he felt that he was lost, without a map, wandering alone in the wilderness.

And when he was engaged in this profound self-questioning, it might very well have seemed to him that a self was something that had to be constructed, made up.

Related to these two different conceptions of self are two different ways of viewing artistic creation. I said in Chapter 8 that Shaftesbury had an objective conception of beauty, and that he saw artistic creation as the attempt to unite with beauty in its most objective sense. I also said that this view of creativity was at odds with many contemporary notions, which involve the idea that true artistic creation consists of creating something new, original, a manifestation of one's own idiosyncratic sensibility. Well, I think that this more contemporary notion of artistic creation is not totally absent from Shaftesbury, even if it does conflict with his official view. I think his mental enjoyment account does suggest this more subjectivist notion, and that it reflects the unsettled constructivist aspects of his personality.

18. See Virtue or Merit 43.

10. Early Influences on Francis Hutcheson

1. Throughout my discussion of Hutcheson, I attend almost exclusively to his work from the 1720s: the *Inquiry into the Original of our Ideas of Beauty and Virtue*, first published in 1725 and revised in 1726, and the *Essay on the Nature and Conduct of the Passions and Affections with Illustrations upon the Moral Sense*, first published in 1728. I generally do not discuss his later works, such as the *Short Introduction to Moral Philosophy*, published posthumously in 1747, nor the *System of Moral Philosophy*, published posthumously in 1755. And when I use the fifth edition of the *Inquiry* (published posthumously in 1753), I do so only when what was added there seems to me to be merely a sharper phrasing of arguments that were already present in the first or second edition. My reasons for sticking to the early works are the same as those given by Frankena, who said that he did not discuss Hutcheson's later works "partly because they may represent a different position, and partly because it was his earlier books, not these later ones, that were important for the discussions of the time" (Frankena 1955, 356).

2. The Scottish Confession of Faith can be found at Early English Books Online: http://eebo.chadwyck.com/search.

3. The Westminster Standards can be found at http://www.presbyterian.org.nz/385.0.html.

4. For very helpful discussion of Simson's views and their influence on Hutcheson, see MacIntyre (1988), 260–2, Cameron (1982), and M. Brown (2002), 75–7.

5. See note 17, Chapter 14.

6. The definitive work on Hutcheson's years in Dublin, and how the milieu he entered there influenced his philosophy, is M. Brown (2002).

7. Hutcheson may have read Shaftesbury's *Characteristics* before meeting Molesworth. For discussion of this issue, see M. Brown (2002), 76.

8. I believe that attention to the Positive Answer to the Human Nature Question reveals the deepest affinity between Hutcheson and Shaftesbury. Darwall has argued, however, that Hutcheson's view of moral obligation soon diverged

significantly from Shaftesbury's (Darwall 1995, 218–23). And Darwall is right that in his later works Hutcheson did move away from Shaftesbury toward a view much more similar to Butler's. But, as I've noted, in my discussion of Hutcheson, I will focus on the early works, those from the 1720s, when he was most under Shaftesbury's influence.

11. Hutcheson's Attack on Egoism

1. Hutcheson also addressed the theological form of the egoist threat; that is, he also set out to refute the claim that we act morally only because we desire God's favor in the afterlife. This theologically egoistic position is a version of the Negative Answer Cudworth and Whichcote associated with Calvinism.

2. As Hutcheson put it, "Suppose we reap the same *Advantage* from two Men, one of whom serves us from *Delight* in our Happiness, and *Love* toward us; the other from Views of *Self-Interest*, or by *Constraint*: both are in this Case equally beneficial or *advantageous* to us, and yet we shall have quite different Sentiments of them. We must then certainly have other Perceptions of *moral Actions* than those of *Advantage*. This perhaps will be equally evident from our Ideas of *Evil*, done to us designedly by a *rational Agent*. Our Senses of *natural Good* and *Evil* would make us receive, with equal Serenity and Compose, an *Assault*, a *Buffet*, an *Affront* from a *Neighbour*, a *Cheat* from a *Partner*, or *Trustee*, as we would an equal Damage from the Fall of a *Beam*, a *Tile*, or a *Tempest*; and we should have the same Affections and Sentiments of both. *Villainy, Treachery, Cruelty*, would be as meekly resented as a *Blast*, or *Mildew*, or an *overflowing Stream*. But I fancy every one is very differently affected on these Occasions, tho there may be equal *natural Evil* in both" (Beauty and Virtue 119–20).

3. Like the Cambridge Platonists and Shaftesbury, Hutcheson seemed to think that a Calvinist conception of God was also a morally destructive influence on persons' conduct. See Passions and Affections 176–7.

4. For excellent discussions of the practical purpose of Hutcheson's writings, see Bishop (1996) and Abramson (2001).

5. Hutcheson's strategy of distinguishing the egoistic view of moral judgment (i.e., the view that one judges others' actions as morally good if and only if they promote one's own interests) and the egoistic view of motivation (i.e., that everyone is motivated always and only by self-interest) foreshadow his later distinction between justifying and exciting reasons, and between the public and moral senses, topics I discuss in note 11 in Chapter 13. But in a sense, Hutcheson does not draw as sharp a distinction between the egoistic view of moral judgment and the egoist view of motivation as might initially seem. We can take him to be viewing my judging of another person's actions as itself an action I perform, or at least as something I do. And he is arguing that it is false to say that everything I do (whether it be a physical action or an act of judging) is based on, or motivated by, self-interest. When we take his non-egoistic view of moral judgment and his non-egoistic view of motivation in this way – as two ways of supporting the same overall thesis that not everything I do (whether a physical action or an act of judging) is based on or motivated by self-interest – then the difference between ethical egoism and psychological egoism begins to blur, as the former (at least

if it's construed as the view that I judge actions to be moral if and only if they promote my self-interest, and not as the view that I judge actions to be moral if and only if they promote the interests of the actor) collapses into the latter.

6. For a full treatment of Hutcheson's view of aesthetic judgment, see Kivy (2003).

7. As Hutcheson said, "And further, the Ideas of Beauty and Harmony, like other sensible Ideas, are *necessarily* pleasant to us, as well as immediately so; neither can any Resolution of our own, nor any *Prospect* of Advantage or Disadvantage, vary the beauty or Deformity of an Object: For as in the external Sensations, no View of *Interest* will make an Object grateful, nor View of *Detriment*, distinct from immediate *Pain* in the Perception, make it disagreeable to the Sense. . . . Hence it plainly appears that some Objects are *immediately* the Occasions of this Pleasure of Beauty, and that we have Senses fitted for perceiving it; and that it is distinct from that *Joy* which arises from Self-love" (Beauty and Virtue 12–13).

8. As Hutcheson explained, "If the reader be convinc'd of [a disinterested sense of beauty], it will be no difficult matter to apprehend another *superior Sense natural to Men*, determining them to be pleas'd with *Actions, Characters, Affections*. This is the *moral Sense*" (Beauty and Virtue xvii). Mortensen maintains that Hutcheson "continues the Shaftesbury theme of the unity of the good and the beautiful," and that any interpretation of Hutcheson must address the problem of the nature of the connection between morality and beauty (Mortensen 1995, 157). There is much of great value in Mortensen's essay, and I think he is right to hold that Shaftesbury unifies the good and the beautiful, but I believe that he overstates the connection in Hutcheson. For Hutcheson, the origin of our moral ideas is a sense that is distinct from the sense that is the origin of our ideas of beauty. These two senses turn out to be harmonious, but the perceptions they produce are distinct from each other. Put another way, Hutcheson's accounts of the two senses are completely parallel but unconnected (or, rather, connected only in that both senses were designed by a benevolent God).

9. Laughter is another example Hutcheson gives of a human behavior that is not based exclusively on self-interest. For helpful discussion of Hutcheson on laughter, see Kivy (2003), 91–3, and Telfer (1995).

10. This claim of Hutcheson's seems to have been confirmed by Batson (1991).

11. This argument of Hutcheson's seems to rely on his commitment to an empiricist view of the origin of ideas (where "ideas" is meant to include affections as well as beliefs). Hutcheson seemed to believe that approval had a phenomenological character that is distinct from every other perception, and that by introspecting we can convince ourselves that approval is different (because it *feels* different) from self-interested desire. But a perception that has this unique phenomenological character must have a difference source from our perceptions of self-interest; that is, there must be a distinct sense that is the origin of approvals; our approval cannot originate in manipulated self-interest. Hume seems to make a similar argument at THN 3.2.2.25.

12. For discussion of Hutcheson's relationship to Cumberland, see Darwall (1995), 209–10.

13. Of course, even in the first edition of the *Inquiry*, Hutcheson argued that moral distinctions originate in a moral *sense*, not in reason alone. I do not mean to

suggest that Hutcheson's view as a whole would have been amenable to the reason alone rationalists. But the crucial points Hutcheson was concerned to make when he first presented his moral sense theory were that moral distinctions originate in an internal human principle that leads us to care about virtue in an immediate, nonderivative, non-self-interested way. And these features of his moral sense theory – features that directly imply the negation of the egoist positions of Cumberland and Pufendorf as well as those of Mandeville and Hobbes – were shared by reason alone rationalists such as Cudworth, Clarke, and Balguy. In later editions of the *Inquiry*, however, Hutcheson changed one passage so that it became a criticism not only of egoism but of reason alone rationalism as well. In the first four editions of the *Inquiry*, this passage read: "I know not for what Reason some will not allow that to be *Virtue*, which flows from *Instincts*, or *Passions*; but how do they help themselves? They say, '*Virtue* arises from *Reason*.' What is *Reason* but *that Sagacity we have in prosecuting any End*? The *ultimate End* propos'd by the common *Moralists* is the *Happiness* of the *Agent* himself, and this certainly he is determin'd to pursue from *Instinct*. Now may not another *Instinct* toward the *Publick*, or the *Good* of others, be as proper a Principle of *Virtue*, as the *Instinct* toward *private Happiness*? And is there not the same Occasion for the Exercise of our *Reason* in pursuing the *former*, as the *latter*? This is certain, that whereas we behold the *selfish* Actions of others, with *Indifference* at best, we see something *amiable* in every Action which flows from *kind Affections* or *Passions* toward others; if they be conducted by Prudence, so as any way to attain their End. Our *passionate* Actions, as we shew'd above, are not always *Self-interested*; since our Intention is not to free our selves from the *Uneasiness* of the Passion, but to alter the *State* of the Object" (Beauty and Virtue 192–3). But in the fifth edition, this passage was changed to: "Some will not allow that Virtue can spring from Passions, Instincts, or Affections of any Kind. 'Tis true, kind particular Passions are but a lower kind of Goodness, even when they are not opposite to the general Good. Those calmer Determinations of the Will, whether of greater or less Extent, or sedate strong Affections, or Desires of the Good of others, are more amiable. These may be as much rooted in the Frame of the Soul, or there may be as natural a Disposition to them as to particular Passions. They tell us, That 'Virtue should wholly spring from Reason;' as if Reason or Knowledge of any true Proposition could ever move to Action where there is no End proposed, and no Affection or Desire toward that End. [Those very Authors who deny any Affections or Motions of the Will to be the proper Springs of sublime Virtue, yet, inconsistently with themselves, must allow in men of sublime Virtue, and even in the Deity too, a settled Disposition of Will, or a constant Determination, or Desire to act in Conformity to Reason, or a fixed Affection toward a certain Manner of Conduct. Now an ill natur'd Adversary would call this an Instinct, an Essential or Natural Disposition of Will, an Affectionate Determination toward a very sublime Object presented by the Understanding.] For this see *Treatise* IV.sect. ii and ii. The ultimate End, according to many of our Moralists, is to each one his own Happiness; and yet this he seeks by Instinct. Now may not another Instinct toward the Publick, or the Good of others, be as proper a Principle of Virtue, as the Instinct toward private Happiness? This is certain, that whereas we behold the selfish Actions of others, with Indifference at best, we see something amiable in every Action which flows from Kind Affections or Passions toward others; if they be conducted by Prudence, so as any way to attain their End" (Beauty and Virtue [5th ed.] 198–9).

14. So I agree with Norton's claim that, in crucially important respects, Hutcheson was on the same side as the rationalists, united in opposition to the egoists (Norton 1982, 69) and disagree with Stafford's criticism of Norton, in which Stafford suggests that Hutcheson and the egoists were on the same side of the most fundamental philosophical divide, while the rationalists were on the other (Stafford 1985, 136). That said, it's also true that the rationalists thought that a moral sense theory was almost as destructive to our commitment to morality as egoism. So while Hutcheson and the rationalists agreed on the importance of moral philosophy's practical task, they disagreed about whether Hutcheson's position really did contribute to it.

15. *Illustrations upon the Moral Sense* was published attached to Hutcheson's *Essay on the Nature and Conduct of the Passions and Affections*. There was in the *Essay* plenty of criticism of the egoist position (Passions and Affections 13–26, 67–8, 85, 97–104) but nothing in the way of anti-rationalist arguments. The *Essay* did talk extensively of a "moral sense" being the origin of our moral ideas, so it would be impossible to mistake it for the work of a moral rationalist. But Hutcheson did not spend any time trying to show that the rationalists were wrong. Often, rather, his focus is on disproving egoism and providing instruction on how to lead a happy, virtuous life, goals he might have expected the rationalists to agree with.

12. Hutcheson's Attack on Moral Rationalism

1. This strictly instrumental view of reason is, in any event, what Hutcheson uses when arguing against moral rationalism in *Illustrations upon the Moral Sense*. But as we will see in Chapter 14, in the *Essay*, Hutcheson argues that a certain kind of meditation and reflection can influence and modify our affections. In addition, Darwall argues that in the *Essay*, Hutcheson holds that we have some ends that are based in motives that are not desires at all, and that reflection can give rise to these motives (Darwall 1995, 223–37). Be that as it may, Hutcheson never strays from the fundamental anti-rationalist claim that reason alone (as distinct from any other, non-rational, contingent feature of human psychology) cannot motivate, and that is probably all he needs for the arguments against moral rationalism I am discussing in this chapter.

2. If something looks brown to me under a dim light, I might take it out into the sunlight and find that it now looks green; if something tastes sour to me right after I have swallowed a dose of medicine, I might drink a glass of water and then find that it tastes sweet. Now there's a sense in which my perceptions of greenness and sweetness are more accurate, or correct, than my perceptions of brownness and sourness. But Burnet would argue that even my perceptions of greenness and sweetness fail to achieve the level of certainty and necessity that is essential for real knowledge. By correcting my sense perceptions I may attain a more accurate picture of how things affect me, but that picture is still

contingent nonetheless. Judgments that are based in sense, even after they've been corrected, cannot tell me how things really are in and of themselves. My most accurate sense perceptions still tell me nothing about the essential nature of things. If morality exists, therefore, it must be based on something other than the deliverances of sense. It must be based on reason alone. For it is reason alone that enables us to understand, reason alone that enables us to comprehend a thing's essential nature and not merely how it affects us.

3. Burnet's father, Gilbert Burnet, Sr., knew Cudworth personally and was deeply influenced by Cudworth's thought.

4. Compare Burnet: "Every man of any degree of understanding who has observed himself and others, immediately with one glance of thought perceives it reasonable and fit that the advantage of the whole should be regarded more than a private advantage or the advantage of a part only of that whole" (Burnet vs. Hutcheson 206).

5. Hutcheson also thought that anyone who really, honestly introspects will realize that his or her moral judgment is based on something that does not have the rational necessity that rationalists claim it does: "But when we *approve* a kind beneficent Action, let us consider whether this Feeling, or Action, or Modification of the Soul, more resembles an act of Contemplation, such as this [when strait Lines intersect each other, the vertical Angles are equal;] or that Liking we have to a beautiful Form, an harmonious Composition, a grateful Sound" (Moral sense [2nd ed.] 136).

6. Indeed, Hutcheson thought that it was not rationally necessary to pursue your own happiness, that failing to pursue your own happiness was not necessarily unreasonable: "But I doubt if any Truth can be assigned which *excites* in us either the Desire of *private Happiness* or *publick*" (Moral Sense 226). In making this point, Hutcheson anticipated Hume's famous claim that it is not contrary to reason to prefer "the destruction of the whole world to the scratching of my finger" (THN 2.3.3.6).

7. While Hutcheson had a nonevaluative conception of happiness ("In the following Discourse, *Happiness* denotes pleasant *Sensation* of any kind, or a continued State of such *Sensations*; and *Misery* denotes the contrary *Sensations*" [Moral Sense 205]), Shaftesbury probably had an evaluative (or perhaps eudemonistic) conception of it. That's why it might be correct to attribute some form of proto-Utilitarianism to Hutcheson, but it's probably incorrect to attribute an early form of Utilitarianism to Shaftesbury.

13. A Copernican Positive Answer and an Attenuated Moral Realism

1. For a good example of this rationalist worry, see the excerpts from Balguy's *Foundation of Moral Goodness* in Raphael 389, 392–3, and 395–6.

2. It is with trepidation that I use the term "realism" in connection with Hutcheson's moral theory, as there has been in recent years a spirited and complicated debate on whether Hutcheson was a moral realist and on what that term should even mean. But given that a number of my claims intersect with that debate, it's incumbent upon me to explain my position on the realism issue and how it fits in.

I think we have to start by distinguishing between two types of eighteenth-century realism: Copernican or anti-egoist realism, and Ptolemaic or mind-independence egoism. Someone is a Copernican or anti-egoist realist if he holds that there is a difference between the motives of those people we judge to be virtuous and the motives of those people we judge to be vicious. Someone is a Ptolemaic or mind-independent realist if he holds that moral properties exist independently of the human mind and that our moral judgments represent those properties accurately. In chapter 4, I tried to show that Cudworth used the language of realism in the mind-independent way; in Chapter 9, I tried to show that Shaftesbury used the language of realism in both the mind-independent and anti-egoist ways; and in Chapter 11, I tried to show that Hutcheson used the language of realism in only the anti-egoist way. This is why I believe it's histor-ically accurate to use the terms in the way that I have. (Actually, there's even a third distinct way that Hutcheson uses the language of moral realism; see Beauty and Virtue 269–70 and Passions and Affections viii–ix.)

I contend that Hutcheson is a Copernican or anti-egoist realist. Now I take it that no one disputes that Hutcheson holds that the motives of those people we (typically, correctly) judge to be virtuous differ from the motives of those peo-ple we (typically, correctly) judge to be vicious. Kail, however, objects to calling this position a realist one (Kail 2001, 58). I have tried to show that Hutcheson believed that defeating egoism was equivalent to affirming the reality of our moral distinctions (and in this I am in complete agreement with one aspect of Norton's interpretation of Hutcheson [Norton 1982, 60–1; Norton 1985, 413]). But if Kail or anyone else prefers not to call this a "moral realist" position – if someone wishes to maintain that anti-egoistic realism is not real realism at all – I am willing to give up the label in order to avoid what seems to me to be merely a verbal dispute.

I also hold that Hutcheson is *not* a mind-independent realist. I hold that Hutcheson believes that moral properties depend on human affections and that these moral judgments do not represent anything in the external world. So according to Hutcheson, if no one had a moral sense, moral properties would not exist; and if everyone had a moral sense that approved of, say, malice, then malice would be as moral as benevolence is now.

Evidence of Hutcheson's *not* being a mind-independent realist occurs in his discussion of beauty, which he takes to be parallel to his discussion of morality (Beauty and Virtue xvii). There is, Hutcheson tell us, "no necessary Connection" between "our pleasing Ideas of Beauty" and the things we find beautiful (Beauty and Virtue 47; cf. 103). We could have been constituted to find different things beautiful or to find nothing beautiful at all. But the beautiful is nonetheless just that which gives rise to our pleasing our ideas of beauty. As Hutcheson explains, by beauty "is not understood any Quality suppos'd to be in the Object, which should of itself be beautiful, without relation to any Mind which perceives it: For Beauty, like other Names of sensible Ideas, properly denotes the *Perceptions* of some Mind; so *Cold, Hot, Sweet, Bitter*, denote the Sensations in our Minds, to which perhaps there is no resemblance in the Objects. . . . [W]ere there no Mind with a *Sense* of Beauty to contemplate Objects, I see not how they could be call'd *beautiful*" (Beauty and Virtue 14–15). Hutcheson goes on to say, "And let it be here observ'd, that our Inquiry is only about the *Qualities* which are beautiful to *Men*; or about the Foundation of their Sense of Beauty: for, as was above hinted, Beauty has always relation to the *Sense* of some Mind; and when we afterwards shew how generally the Objects which occur to us, are *beautiful*, we mean that such Objects are agreeable to the Sense of *Men*: for as there are not a few Objects, which seem no way beautiful to Men, so we see a variety of other *Animals* who seem delighted with them; they may have *Senses* otherwise constituted than those of Men, and may have the Ideas of Beauty excited by Objects of a quite different Form" (Beauty and Virtue 16). And again: "All *Beauty* is relative to the Sense of some Mind perceiving it" (Beauty and Virtue 40). These passages seem to me to constitute a very clear rejection of the mind-independent realist position on beauty. And thus, given that Hutcheson consistently holds that morality and beauty have the same kind of origin (both originate, and originate in the same kind of way, in senses), I think we should take him to be rejecting the mind-independent realist position on morality as well. There is, moreover, considerable direct evidence for Hutcheson's rejection of mind-independent realism about morality. The best way of putting forward this evidence is in the context of an important distinction that exists within the category of those who reject mind-independent realism.

Those who reject mind-independent realism can be either "transpersonal subjectivists" or "personal subjectivists" (see Peach 1971, 50).Transpersonal subjectivists hold that morality is determined by the responses of people in general; they also hold that morality is relative to humanity as a whole. Personal subjectivist hold that morality is determined by the responses of each individual person; personal subjectivists hold that morality is relative to each individual. The transpersonal subjectivist takes it to be a necessary truth that morality is the same for all of us. The personal subjectivist might agree that morality is the same for all of us, but takes this to be a contingent fact. It's possible, according to the personal subjectivist, that what is moral for one person is not moral for another.

I take Hutcheson to be a personal subjectivist. According to my reading, he believes that morality for each person is determined by how that person's moral sense responds to things. He believes that it's possible that different people can have moral senses that respond to the same thing in different ways. And so he believes that it's possible that what's moral for one person will not be moral for another. Now Hutcheson also believes that it turns out that what's moral for one person is also moral for all others, but this coincidence is a contingent fact. His moral ontology equates morality-for-A with what is approved by A's own moral sense, and his moral ontology does not imply that necessarily A's moral sense will approve of the same things that B's moral sense will. Thus Hutcheson writes, "[It is] plain we judge of our own *Affections*, or those of others, by our *moral Sense*, by which we approve kind Affections, and disapprove the contrary. But none can apply *moral Attributes* to the very *Faculty* of perceiving *moral Qualities*; or call his *moral Sense morally Good* or *Evil*, any more than he calls the *Power of Tasting, sweet* or *bitter*, or of *Seeing, straight* or *crooked, white* or *black*. Every one judges the *Affections* of others by his own *Sense*; so that it seems not impossible that in these *Senses* men might differ as they do in *Taste*. A *Sense approving Benevolence* would disapprove *that Temper* which a *Sense approving Malice* would delight in. The *former* would judge of the *latter* by his *own Sense,* so would the *latter* of the *former.* Each one would at first view think the *Sense* of the other perverted. But then, is there no difference? Are both Senses equally *good?* No certainly, any *Man* who observed them would think the *Sense* of the *former* more desirable than of the *latter;* but this is, because the *moral Sense* of every Man is constituted in the former manner" (Moral Sense 234–5). It's important to stress the "man" in this last sentence, as Hutcheson goes on to say that there could be beings who had moral senses constituted differently from us or who had "no *moral Sense* at all" (Moral Sense 235). He also writes, "If [one asks] 'How are we sure that what *we* approve, *all others* shall also approve?' Of this we can be sure upon *no Scheme*" (Moral Sense 280). And he explicitly raises the possibility that some humans could have a moral sense that approves of malice (Moral Sense 235, 238).

It's true that Hutcheson says that a benevolence-approving moral sense is "universal" in all humans. But it's clear that he means by that only that there are conclusive a posteriori grounds for concluding that all humans possess moral senses that approve of the same things (and Hutcheson, like other eighteenth-century philosophers, believed that what we learn a posteriori cannot be necessarily true). It's not universal in the sense of its *having* to be the case. Thus, Hutcheson's attempts "to prove, 'That there is a *universal Determination* to *Benevolence* in *Mankind*" consisting of empirical observations of how people actually conduct themselves (Beauty and Virtue 216; cf. 196). He offers as evidence observations of "the Sentiments of *Children,* upon hearing the Storys with which they are commonly entertain'd as soon as they understand Language" (Beauty and Virtue 214). And he takes as possible (but ultimately not credible) counterexamples to the "*Universality of this* [moral] *Sense . . .* some Storys of Travellers, concerning *strange Crueltys* practis'd toward the *Aged,* or *Children,* in certain countrys" (Beauty and Virtue 202). Or as he says in a section entitled "Of the Universality of the Sense of Beauty among Men": "But as to the *universal Agreement* of Mankind in their *Sense of Beauty* from *Uniformity amidst Variety,* we must consult Experience" (Beauty and Virtue 75). A personal subjectivist interpretation also best explains the following passage: "If one asks, 'how do we know that *our Affections are right when they are kind?*' What does the Word [right] mean? Does it mean *what we approve?* This we know by *Consciousness* of our *Sense.* Again, how do we know that our *Sense* is right, or that we *approve our Approbation?* This can only be answered by another Question, *viz.* 'How do we know we are pleased when we are pleased?'" (Moral Sense 279). It seems to me that here Hutcheson is taking each individual's approbation to be definitive of what is right for that person, a personal subjectivist position. And his personal subjectivism seems to me to be equally clear when he says that ideas of virtue originate in "the *Perception of Approbation* or *Disapprobation* arising in the Observer, according as the *Affections of the Agent* are apprehended *kind* in their *just Degree,* or *deficient,* or *malicious.* This *Approbation* cannot be supposed an *Image of any thing external,* more than the *Pleasure of Harmony, of Taste, of Smell*" (Moral Sense 283).

I think there is also a good deal of evidence for the personal subjectivist interpretation in the *Essay,* where (as I try to show at length in Chapter 14) Hutcheson explains how each individual can correct his judgments by experiencing his own natural affections. In the *Essay*, in other words, Hutcheson implies that correct judgment for a person is defined by that very person's natural affections. Determining how my own natural affections would respond to something is the paradigmatic way for me to determine what the correct judgment for me to make is. I think it's pretty clear that Hutcheson doesn't believe that when I am determining what is a correct judgment I am essentially involved in determining what other people in general think (see Kail 2001, 72). Indeed, it seems that the combination of his Positive Answer to the Human Nature Question and his moral sense theory commits Hutcheson to personal subjectivism, for the Positive Answer implies that everyone has within herself all the resources necessary to fully realize morality, and the moral sense theory implies that realizing morality essentially involves affections.

The preceding paragraph points to yet another distinction, one that can be drawn within the category of personal subjectivism. The distinction is between cognitivist and non-cognitivist personal subjectivism. Cognitivist personal subjectivists hold that a person's moral judgments can be correct or incorrect. Non-cognitivist personal subjectivists hold that a person's moral judgments are not the kinds of things that are either correct or incorrect. I take Hutcheson to be a cognitivist personal subjectivist. This is because (as I try to show in Chapter 14) what is a correct moral judgment for an individual is determined by the moral affections the individual would feel if her affections were in their original (or natural) state, and that if an individual's moral judgment does not accord with her original moral affections her moral judgment is incorrect. Hutcheson also holds (as, once again, I try to show in Chapter 14) that a method for ensuring that our affections are in their original state is to engage in meditation and reflection on the matter at hand and on our own reaction to it. So a Hutchesonian moral judgment is correct if and only if it accords with how the judge would respond if she had engaged in the appropriate kind of meditation and reflection. This reading of Hutcheson takes him to be a *dispositional* cognitivist personal subjectivist, which is to say that it takes him to hold that morality for each person is determined by the affections she *would* experience under certain circumstances (even if when she makes her moral judgment she is not under those particular circumstances); this distinguishes Hutcheson from an *occurrent* personal subjectivist, who would hold that morality for each person is determined by the affections she is *actually* experiencing when she makes her moral judgment. I thus agree with Kail that Hutcheson has an "is good/seems good" distinction within his theory (Kail 2001, 59). Does this mean Hutcheson believes that moral judgment represent mind-independent, external moral properties? No, it does not. On my reading of Hutcheson, rather, our moral judgments try to describe accurately our natural affective reactions, just as our color judgments try to describe accurately the color reactions we'd have under optimal visual conditions.

I said previously that I think Hutcheson is a cognitivist in that he believes that some moral judgments are correct and some are incorrect. But is he a cognitivist in the sense that he thinks some moral judgments are *true* while others are *false*? I believe Hutcheson would say Yes, he is a cognitivist in that sense. But his rationalist opponents would have said No, he's not a cognitivist if what that means is producing a theory that allows for some moral judgments to be true. That's because his rationalist opponents were mind-independent realists: a judgment had to represent accurately a mind-independent moral standard in order to qualify as true. But Hutcheson thought a moral judgment could be true simply if it accorded with one's natural affective reactions.

That I say that Hutcheson is a cognitivist would seem to place me at odds with Stafford, who says that we should take Hutcheson to be a non-cognitivist (Stafford 1985, 134–5). But I don't think we actually disagree. What Stafford calls non-cognitivism is compatible with the cognitivist subjectivism that I am attributing to Hutcheson. But once again, I am willing to give up the label "cognitivist" to avoid what I take to be a verbal dispute. My view is that Hutcheson believes his position contains a distinction between judgments that are correct or true and judgments that are incorrect or false, and that Hutcheson also denies that moral properties exist independently of human affections. Whether we call this position cognitivist or non-cognitivist, realist or anti-realist, is a matter that can (within certain boundaries) be stipulated rather than argued about. The same point applies to Kail. He says that a cognitivist is someone who holds that moral judgments represent accurately a mind-independent moral standard. If this is the definition we are working with, then I grant that Hutcheson is a non-cognitivist, and Kail and I are in substantial agreement.

I am in substantial disagreement, however, with Frankena's non-cognitivist interpretation of Hutcheson (although there are many other aspects of Frankena's interpretations with which I agree). Frankena argues that if Hutcheson were a cognitivist subjectivist, then he would be committed to holding that a person could determine what is moral by using reason alone. This is because a person could use reason to conduct "a statistical investigation into the actual or possible incidence of feelings of pleasure or pain at contemplating the act in question" (Frankena 1955, 371). But, of course, Hutcheson denies that we can make moral judgments through reason alone. So, according to Frankena, Hutcheson cannot be a cognitivist subjectivist. I think this argument of Frankena's gives us reason not to attribute transpersonal subjectivism to Hutcheson, as a person wholly lacking a moral sense could use empirical reasoning to determine how humans in general respond to objects of evaluation. But I do not think it gives us reason not to attribute personal subjectivism to Hutcheson, as the personal subjectivist reading still implies that a person wholly lacking a moral sense could not make moral judgments. It's true that according to cognitivist personal subjectivism, a person can at times make a moral judgment by using reason (namely, by reasoning about how she would feel were her affections in their original state), but she will be using reason to learn something about her own affections, and so there is still a crucially important sense in which her moral judgment is not based on reason alone. Where I think Frankena goes wrong is in holding that Hutcheson believes that moral judgments are essentially based on *occurrent* affections (as I said previously, I believe Hutcheson is a *dispositional* personal subjectivist).

I am also in substantial disagreement with one aspect of Norton's interpretation. I agree with Norton's general historical situating of Hutcheson, and the anti-egoist realism and cognitivism I attribute to Hutcheson accord with much of Norton's reading. But I disagree with the "objectivist" part of Norton's interpretation. Norton claims that Hutcheson thought moral properties exist in the external world, independent of human affections. I think, however, that the textual evidence does not support that claim. Winkler (1985, 1996), Stafford (1985), and Radcliffe (1986, 2001) have all addressed in detail the particular texts from Hutcheson on which Norton's objectivist interpretation turns, and I think they have together shown the untenability of that interpretation.

The Calvinists thought that anyone who did not believe Christ was absolutely necessary for salvation denied the *reality* of religion. The Cambridge Platonists (who didn't believe that Christ was absolutely necessary for salvation) thought that anyone who did not believe that we could access eternal and immutable moral truths in the mind of God denied the *reality* of morals. Hutcheson (who didn't believe that we could access eternal and immutable moral truths in the mind of God) thought that anyone who did not believe that we had natural affections to benefit humanity as a whole denied the *reality* of virtue. Hume didn't believe that we had natural affections to benefit humanity as a whole, but just as the Cambridge Platonists and Hutcheson rejected their predecessors' requirements for moral reality, so too would Hume reject Hutcheson's. The point is that what counted as moral *realism* was itself one of the main points of contention in seventeenth- and eighteenth-century British moral philosophy. To understand the different ways the various philosophers of the period used the term (as opposed to insisting on some nominal categories that appear only in late-twentieth-century meta-ethical discussions) is to understand a central aspect of the progression of moral thinking.

3. As Kivy has put it, "Hutcheson rushed in where Shaftesbury feared to tread" (Kivy 2003, 23).

4. In describing the moral sense, Hutcheson wrote, "This *natural Determination* to approve and admire, or hate and dislike Actions, is no doubt an *occult Quality*. But is it any way more mysterious that the Idea of an Action should raise *Esteem*, or *Contempt*, than that the motion, or tearing of Flesh should give *Pleasure*, or *Pain*; or the Act of Volition should move *Flesh* and *Bones*? In the latter Case, we have got the Brain, and elastic Fibres, and animal Spirits, and elastic Fluids, like the *Indian*'s Elephant, and Tortoise, to bear the Burden of the Difficulty: but go one step further, and you find the whole as difficult as at first, and equally a Mystery with *this Determination* to love and approve, or hate and despise *Actions* and *Agents*, without any Views of *Interest*, as they appear *benevolent*, or the contrary" (Beauty and Virtue 271–2). This is an outstanding statement of the difference between Hutcheson's view of what counts as a satisfactory explanation and the view of rationalists such as Cudworth. For Cudworth, all explanations, if they are to give us knowledge at all, must bottom out in intelligible, necessary truths. An explanation that ends with a contingent or brute fact is not really an explanation at all. So Cudworth would have held that the fact that Hutcheson's explanations end at a brute fact (we just happen to have the kind of moral sense we do; we can't give an intelligible, necessary reason for it) just shows that Hutcheson had not really explained morality at all, and the fact that our explanations of the pains of tearing flesh end at a brute fact (we just happen to have the kind of physiology that leads this to happen; we can't give an intelligible, necessary reason

for it) just shows that we haven't really provided an explanation of such pains either. In other words, Hutcheson and Cudworth would agree that Hutcheson's account of the moral sense is on an explanatory par with our account of why tearing flesh causes pain, but while Hutcheson maintained that this shows that his account is explanatorily acceptable, Cudworth would hold that this shows that Hutcheson's account is an explanatory failure. This issue of what constitutes an acceptable end point of explanation becomes even more interesting and important when we realize that Cudworth and Hutcheson (and virtually every other early modern philosopher before Hume) thought that the ultimate ground of moral *explanation* would also be the ultimate ground of moral *justification*. They thought that the ultimate answer to the "why" of explanation questions would be the same as the ultimate answer to the "why" of justification questions. So just as Cudworth thought that all real explanations had to end in intelligible, necessary truth, so too he thought that all real moral justification had to end in intelligible, necessary reasons. And just as Hutcheson thought that a perfectly legitimate explanation could end in a brute fact, so too he thought that real moral justification could end in a brute fact. (Showing that early modern moral philosophers before Hume conflated the "why" of ultimate explanation with the "why" of ultimate justification, and explaining the deep theological assumptions that account for this conflation, was one of my goals in Gill 1995, 1998.)

5. See Chapter 7, Section A.

6. Hutcheson was accused of being a voluntarist himself, and while that's not entirely fair, there is a sense in which his account of God's goodness is circular. For discussion of the points of similarity and difference between Hutcheson and the voluntarists, see C. Brown (1994), 27, and Herdt (1997), 55.

7. For an excellent discussion of the issue of interpersonal disagreement in Hutcheson, see Carey (2000).

8. For textual evidence of Hutcheson's not being able to rule out moral relativism a priori, see the discussion in note [2] of personal subjectivism and the account in Chapter 14 of what a person can do to correct his or her moral judgments.

9. The central role observation plays in Hutcheson's philosophy is one of the most important ways in which Hutcheson influenced, and did much to pave the way for, Hume, who based his philosophy of human nature on "a cautious observation of human life" (THN Introduction, 10).

10. The definitive discussion of Hutcheson's conception of the senses, and the relationship between the internal and external senses, is Kivy (2003), 23–43.

11. In *The Moral Sense*, Hutcheson drew a sharp distinction between exciting reasons, which motivate us to action, and justifying reasons, which underlie our moral judgments. In what follows, I will skirt discussion of this difference because I do not think it bears directly on the main elements of Hutcheson's Positive Answer to the Human Nature Question. But all the points I make about the possible conflict and actual harmony between the moral sense and self-interest could also be made, mutatis mutandis, about possible conflicts and actual harmony between the public sense and self-interest, between the moral sense and the public sense, between the sense of honor and self-interest, between the sense of honor and the public sense, and between the sense of honor and the moral

sense (see Passions and Affections 144–54). The point is that Hutcheson had no way of logically ruling out conflict between any of his numerous senses, and he had no trans-sensory way of providing a principled adjudication of possible conflicts between the senses. At least he had no way of doing this in his works from the 1720s; in his later works he might have opted for a more Butlerian picture of human nature, according to which certain internal principles have more inherent authority than others. For further discussion of Hutcheson's distinction between exciting reasons and justifying reasons, see Darwall (1995), 218–37, and Purviance (2002).

12. Hutcheson says in the *Essay* that benevolence and self-interest are both equally "calm desires" (Passions or Affections 38), and this makes it very difficult to see how he can claim that one of them is more rational or normative than the other. As Hutcheson put it in his *System of Moral Philosophy*, "We shall find these two grand determinations, one toward our own greatest happiness, the other toward the greatest general good, each independent on the other" (System 50). For discussion of Hutcheson's account in his later works of these "two grand determinations" and the possibility of conflict between them, see Darwall (1995), 223–43.

13. In a very helpful article, Strasser has shown that Hutcheson argued that the pleasures of the "social" senses (i.e., the moral sense, the public sense, and the sense of honor) are "both qualitatively and quantitatively better" than the pleasures of any of the other types of senses (Strasser 1987, 517). But this aspect of Hutcheson's account of the "higher and lower pleasures" does not dispel the worry about non-moral senses' coming into conflict with the moral sense that I am discussing here for two reasons. First, the fact that the social senses are better at producing in me pleasure is a contingent one, something we can discover only through experience and comparison of the various types of pleasure. As Strasser explains, Hutcheson's argument is based on what a "knowledgeable" judge – i.e., someone who has experienced both kinds of pleasure – would prefer (Strasser 1987, 517–18). Before undertaking empirical investigation, Hutcheson has to take the possibility that the non-social pleasures are better at producing in me pleasure just as seriously as the possibility that the social pleasures are better than the non-social. This aspect of Hutcheson's account thus still involves the idea that there is nothing intrinsically more authoritative about the social senses. And second, the superiority of the social senses to the non-social senses does not dispel the worry that the moral sense could come into conflict with one of the *other* social senses. Indeed, Hutcheson himself raises this "truly deplorable" possibility of a "Person" who is "distracted between two noble Principles" (Passions and Affections 145). (Strasser says that in the *System* Hutcheson maintained that "moral pleasures" are superior to "pleasures of the sympathetic kind" [Strasser 1987, 518], but this point does not appear in Hutcheson's earlier works [see, for instance, Passions and Affections 126–7]. As I've mentioned previously, I suspect Hutcheson had developed a more Butlerian view by the time he wrote the *System*.)

14. For an excellent discussion of Hutcheson's attitude toward Locke's rejection of innate ideas, see Carey (2000).

15. See Chapter 6, Section C and Chapter 8, Section C.

14. Explaining Away Vice, or Hutcheson's Defense of a Copernican,
Theistic Positive Answer

1. Hutcheson acknowledged the oddness of, on the one hand, insisting so strenu-
    ously that morality is distinct from self-interest and then, on the other, working
    so hard to show that they coincide. But he explained that the combination of
    his anti-rationalist meta-ethical position and his practical purpose of promoting
    virtue committed him to both of these tasks. "It may perhaps seem strange, that
    when in this *Treatise* Virtue is suppose'd *disinterested*; yet so much Pains is taken,
    by a *Comparison* of our several *Pleasures*, to prove the *Pleasures* of *Virtue* to be the
    greatest of which we are capable of, and that consequently it is our truest *Interest*
    to be *virtuous*. But let it be remember'd here, that tho there can be no *Motives* or
    Arguments suggested which can directly raise any *ultimate Desire*, such as that of
    our *own Happiness*, or *publick Affections* (as we attempt to prove in *Treatise* IV;) yet
    if both are *natural Dispositions* of our Minds, and nothing can stop the Operation
    of *publick Affections* but some *selfish Interest*, the only way to give publick Affections
    their full Force, and to make them prevalent in our Lives, must be to remove
    these *Opinions of opposite Interests*, and to shew a superior Interest on their side.
    If these Considerations be just and sufficiently attended to, a *natural Disposition*
    can scarce fail to exert it self to the full" (Passions and Affections viii–ix). The
    arguments Hutcheson used to show the coincidence of self-interest and moral-
    ity are largely taken from Shaftesbury (compare Passions and Affections 136–65
    and Virtue or Merit 61–87). And Shaftesbury, like Hutcheson, combined these
    arguments for the coincidence (or coextensiveness) of morality and self-interest
    with arguments showing that morality is distinct (or has a different intension)
    from self-interest.
2. See Darwall (1995), 223–33, and Darwall (1997), 83–5, for further discussion
    of this aspect of Hutcheson's thought.
3. This definition of "natural" is only one of three that Hutcheson gives at Passions
    and Affections (198–200). But it's one that he clearly endorsed and, I believe,
    the one that he used most often throughout his *Inquiry* and his *Essay*.
4. I'm tempted to say that Hutcheson's natural affections are innate because I
    believe they fit very well into the category that current philosophy of mind labels
    "innate." But, of course, that word carried a lot of rationalist baggage at the time
    Hutcheson was writing, baggage that Hutcheson wanted to dump. Specifically,
    when someone in the early eighteenth century spoke of innate principles, he
    was referring to propositional knowledge of the mind-independent structure of
    reality, but Hutcheson's natural affections are emphatically *not* bits of proposi-
    tional knowledge of the mind-independent structure of reality (see Locke 67;
    Beauty and Virtue 82, 135). At the same time, Hutcheson's natural affections are
    built-in features of the original structure of the human mind. They are parts of
    our constitution that cannot be explained by the world's effect on us. Contempo-
    rary philosophy of mind tends to call such things "innate." Shaftesbury thought
    "instinctive" was a good word to describe them, as it captured their built-in-ness
    without suggesting that they had anything to do with propositional knowledge.
    Hume generally called them "original." Hutcheson calls them "natural."
5. Hutcheson acknowledged that most of our affections have been altered at least
    somewhat by custom, education, and habit, and that we cannot therefore simply

read our natural constitution off of our present conduct and behavior. To determine what our natural affections are, we have to "abstract" from the effects of custom, education, and habit. Showing that when we perform this task of "abstracting" we find that everyone is "naturally" constituted to be in benevolent and happy harmony with others and with oneself was the overriding goal Hutcheson set for himself in the *Essay*. As he puts it in the Preface, "To define *Virtue* by agreeableness to this moral Sense, or describing it to be *kind Affection*, may appear perhaps too uncertain; considering that the Sense of particular Persons is often depraved by *Custom, Habits*, false Opinions, Company: and that some *particular kind Passions* toward some Persons are really pernicious, and attended with very unkind Affections toward others, or at least with a Neglect of their Interests. We must therefore only assert in general, that 'every one calls that Temper, or those Actions *virtuous*, which are approv'd by his *own Sense*;' and withal, that 'abstracting from particular Habits or Prejudices, every one is so constituted as to approve every *particular kind Affection* toward any one, which argues no *want of Affection* toward others. And constantly to approve that Temper which desires, and those actions which tend to procure the greatest Moment of Good in the Power of the Agent toward the most extensive System to which it can reach;' and consequently, that the Perfection of Virtue consists in 'having the *universal calm Benevolence*, the prevalent Affection of the Mind, so as to limit and counteract not only the *selfish Passions*, but even the *particular kind Affections*'" (Passions and Affections xv–xvii). This passage is strong evidence, I think, that Hutcheson was a personal subjectivist ("every one calls that Temper, or those Actions *virtuous*, which are approv'd by his own sense"), that he believed that nonetheless a person can make incorrect moral judgments ("the Sense of particular Persons is often depraved by *Custom, Habits*, false Opinions"), that he believed that the correct judgment is that which accords with the approvals and disapprovals a person would feel if her affections were in their natural state (we must "abstract from particular Habits or Prejudices"), and that he believed that it was a contingent fact that every person is naturally constituted to approve of benevolence. This makes Hutcheson a cognitivist, dispositional, personal subjectivist, who also holds that we have overwhelming inductive evidence for thinking that whenever a person makes a moral judgment that conflicts with benevolence, she is making a mistake. See Passions and Affections 29, 201–3 and Moral Sense 280–1.

6. As Hutcheson put it in a very Shaftesburean passage that uses the human constitution as a posteriori proof for the existence of God, "It was observed above, how admirably our Affections are contrived for good in the *whole*.... [T]hey all aim at *good*, either private or publick; and by them each particular Agent is made, in a great measure, subservient to the *good of the whole*. Mankind are thus insensibly link'd together, and make one great *System*, by an invisible Union. He who *voluntarily* continues in this Union, and delights in employing his Power for his *Kind*, makes himself happy: He who does not continue this Union freely, but affects to break it, makes himself wretched; nor yet can he break the *Bonds of Nature*. His *publick Sense*, his *Love of Honour*, and the very *Necessities* of his Nature, will continue to make him depend upon his *System*, and engage him to serve it, whether he inclines to it or not. Thus we are formed with a View to a general good *End*..." (Passions and Affections 177–8). See also Passions and Affections 117, 136–65, 200–3.

7. It's important to emphasize that Hutcheson believed that our *natural* or *original* affections are all in interpersonal and intrapersonal accord. He acknowledged that there's interpersonal and intrapersonal conflict but claimed that it always results from alterations to our natural or original constitution. Thus he wrote, "[Our passions] are by Nature ballanced against each other, like the Antagonist Muscles of the Body; either of which separately would have occasioned Distortion and irregular Motion, yet jointly they form a Machine, most accurately subservient to the Necessities, Convenience, and Happiness of a rational System" (Beauty and Virtue 181). And again, "To assert that 'Men have generally arrived to the *Perfection of their Kind* in this Life,' is contrary to Experience. But on the other hand, to suppose 'no Order at all in the *Constitution* of Our Nature, or no *prevalent Evidences* of good Order,' is yet more contrary to Experience, and would lead to a Denial of Providence in the most important Affair which can occur to our Observation. We actually see such Degrees of *good Order*, of *Social Affection*, of *Virtue* and *Honour*, as make the Generality of Mankind continue in a tolerable, nay, an *agreeable* State. However, in some Tempers we see the *selfish Passions* by Habits grown too strong; in others we may observe *Humanity, Compassion*, and *Good-nature* sometimes raised by Habits, as we say, to an Excess. Were we to strike a *Medium* of the several Passions and Affections, as they appear in the whole Species of Mankind, to conclude thence what has been the natural Ballance previously to any Change made by Custom or Habit, which we see casts the Ballance to either side, we should perhaps find the *Medium* of the publick Affections not very far from a sufficient *Counter-ballance* to the *Medium* of the Selfish; and consequently the *Overballance* on either side in particular Characters, is not to be looked upon as the *original Constitution*, but as the *accidental Effect* of Custom, Habit, or Associations of Ideas, or other preternatural Causes: So that an universal *increasing* of the Strength of *either*, might in the whole be of little advantage" (Passions and Affections 200–1).

8. As I mentioned in Chapter 13, Section D, Hutcheson did not restrict his discussion of intrapersonal conflict to conflict between the moral sense and self-interest. He also addressed the possibility of various permutations of intrapersonal conflict between our moral sense, our public sense, our sense of honor, and our external senses. To simplify matters, I'll restrict my discussion to Hutcheson's attempts to show that the moral sense and self-interest naturally coincide and to the (theological) conclusions he draws from that coincidence. But the same things could be said, mutatis mutandis, about the natural coincidence of the other senses as well.

9. In *The Moral Sense*, Hutcheson wrote, "If [one asks], 'Will the doing what our *moral Sense* approves tend to *our Happiness*, and to the avoiding Misery?' 'Tis thus we call a *Taste wrong*, when it makes that *Food* at present *grateful*, which shall occasion *future Pains*, or *Death*. This Question concerning our *Self-Interest* must be answered by such *Reasoning* as was mentioned above, to be well managed by our *Moralists* both ancient and modern" (Moral Sense 280–1). The "*Reasoning*" to which Hutcheson refers in the last sentence consists of the a posteriori arguments of "*Cumberland, Puffendorf, Grotius, Shaftesbury*," which showed that observation of human life reveals that we will be happier if we're virtuous (Moral Sense 277).

10. I believe my interpretation here, and indeed throughout this chapter, is in accord with Herdt's outstanding account of similar aspects of Hutcheson's thought (see Herdt 1997, 56).

11. Hutcheson wrote: "To every Nature there are certain *Tastes* assigned by the great Author of all. To the *human Race* there are assigned a *publick Taste*, a *moral one*, and a *Taste for Honour*. These Senses they cannot extirpate, more than their *external Senses*: They may pervert them, and weaken them by false *Opinions*, and foolish *Associations* of Ideas; but they cannot be happy but by keeping them in their natural State, and gratifying them" (Passions and Affections 130–1).

12. Balguy objected to what he took to be the voluntarist implications of Hutcheson's theory in *The Foundation of Moral Goodness*. See excerpts in Raphael (1991), 390, 395.

13. For further discussion of the role of God in Hutcheson's moral theory, see Rauscher (2003). I believe Rauscher incorrectly attributes to Hutcheson the view that we can infer that our moral affections are non-arbitrary because they were implanted by God. On my reading, Hutcheson held that we can infer things about God (e.g., that He is benevolent) only because of the nature of our moral affections. Rauscher goes on to argue, however, that while in the early works Hutcheson seemed to rule out a priori arguments for claims about God, he ends up advancing a priori arguments in his later *System of Moral Philosophy* (Rauscher 2003,172–7). I think it's very clear that Hutcheson did not use a priori proofs for God in his early works (Beauty and Virtue 134, 218, 303), so if he did use them in his later works, that would constitute evidence of his having changed his mind. But it's also worth noting that his first biographer, William Leechman, claimed that Hutcheson remained steadfast throughout his life in holding that only a posteriori arguments could be give for God's existence. Kivy quotes the relevant passage from Leechman's biography and, as always, provides a very illuminating discussion of the main point (Kivy 2003, 112).

14. Hutcheson also used association in the *Inquiry*, although not quite as much as in the *Essay*. For a very helpful discussion of Hutcheson's use of the association of ideas and his indebtedness to Locke, with a particular emphasis on the *First Inquiry*, see Kivy (2003), 82–7. Hutcheson was also probably influenced by Shaftesbury, whose explanations of moral corruption involve pernicious association of ideas, even if Shaftesbury did not use that term. See Virtue and Merit 25–9, which I discuss in Chapter 7, Section C.

15. I should point out, however, that there are two similar passages, one in the *Inquiry* (Beauty and Virtue 234–7) and one in the *Essay* (Passions and Affections 9–11), where Hutcheson seemed to allow that some aesthetic and moral associations are beneficial or at least not harmful. Hutcheson said in those passages that associations have had the salutary effect of introducing into our culture notions of honor and shame that have discouraged selfishness and encouraged magnificence and obedience to the state. Associations also account for the esteem in which certain types of "*Dress, Equipage, Retinue, Badges of Honour*," and ceremony are held (Beauty and Virtue 235). And although Hutcheson was clear that there is no natural connection between these conventions and the affections they have been taken to represent, he still thought it a mistake to eschew the conventions completely, as evidenced by his criticism of the "*recluse Philosophers*" who pride

themselves on "despising these external Shews" (Beauty and Virtue 235). That Hutcheson thought we ought to heed these conventions, however, should not be taken as an endorsement of associations of ideas. Rather, he thought it is just a fact that most people will retain the associations that give rise to conventions, and that it is consequently necessary to heed the conventions in order to influence humanity for its own benefit. "Nor is it vain," he wrote, "that the wisest and greatest Men regard these things; for however it may concern them to break such Associations in their own Minds, yet, since the bulk of Mankind will retain them, they must comply with their Sentiments and Humours in things innocent, as they expect the *publick Esteem*, which is generally necessary to enable Men to serve the Publick" (Passions and Affections 10). The *"recluse Philosophers"* who refuse to play the game of convention will never be able to serve the public, while the "wisest and greatest," who do play the game, will be able to serve them. That is not to say, however, that the wisest and greatest will sanguinely allow themselves to retain the associations that make the game possible. They may very well try to break them off in their own minds while realizing still that there are natural or non-associative reasons for playing the game. Hutcheson also thought that association is necessary for "all our *Language* and much of our *Memory*... beside many other valuable *Powers* and *Arts*" (Passions and Affections 11). But he suggested that these effects of association are not counterproductive only because (or to the extent that) they do not wrench our passions out of their original shape. We ought to allow such associations, that is, only if we can still "separate Ideas when it may be useful for us to do so" (Passions and Affections 11).

16. Hutcheson often tries to convince us that there is actually very little really despicable vice in the world, contending that when a person acts badly, it is almost always either because she mistakenly believes that what she is doing is for the good of humankind or because she is influenced by false beliefs about what is in her self-interest, which is something to be pitied more than condemned. Even if there are some cases of truly despicable behavior, Hutcheson maintains, they are greatly outnumbered by good-natured action. Thus he writes, "[T]he Vice and Misery in the World are smaller than we sometimes in our melancholy Hours imagine. There are no doubt many furious Starts of Passion, in which Malice may seem to have place in our Constitution; but how seldom, and how short, in comparison of Years spent in fixed kind Pursuits of the Good of a *Family*, a *Party*, a *Country*? How great a Part of human Actions flow directly from *Humanity* and *kind Affection*? How many censurable Actions are owing to the same Spring, only chargeable on *Inadvertence*, or an Attachment to too *narrow a System*? How few owing to any thing worse than *selfish* Passions above their Proportion? Here Men are apt to let their Imaginations run out upon all the *Robberies, Piracies, Murders, Perjuries, Frauds, Massacres, Assassinations*, they have ever either heard of, or read in History; thence concluding all Mankind to be very wicked: as if a *Court of Justice* were the proper Place of making an Estimate of the *Morals* of Mankind, or an *Hospital* of the *Healthfulness* of a Climate. Ought they not to consider, that the Number of honest *Citizens* and *Farmers* far surpasses that of all sorts of Criminals in any State; and that the innocent of kind Actions of even Criminal themselves, surpass their Crimes in Numbers? That 'tis the *Rarity* of Crimes, in comparison of innocent of good Actions, which engages our

Attention to them, and makes them be recorded in History; while incomparably more honest, generous, domestick Actions are overlooked, only because they are so common; as one great *Danger*, or one *Month's Sickness*, shall become a frequently repeated Story, during a long Life of Health and Safety" (Passions and Affections 183–5).

17. Hutcheson did sign The Scottish Confession of Faith – in fact, he signed it twice, in 1719 and 1730. But he was also accused, in 1738, of expounding doctrines that violated the Confession. For helpful discussion of these events, see M. Brown (2002), 18–20, 89, 95, and MacIntyre (1988), 245–6, 261.

18. For excellent discussion of Hutcheson's teaching at Glasgow, see M. Brown (2002), 15–24.

15. David Hume's New "Science of Man"

1. Unless otherwise noted, I intend what I say about Hume to apply to *A Treatise of Hume Nature*, and not necessarily to the *Enquiry concerning the Principle of Morals* or to any other of Hume's later works. For discussion of the relationship between the *Treatise* and Hume's later works, see Herdt (1997), Abramson (2001), and Moore (2002).

2. In "Of the Study of History," which was published a year after Book III of the *Treatise*, Hume makes the same point as he did in the letter to Hutcheson and in the conclusion to Book III. Reading history, Hume says in that essay, "strengthens virtue" (Essays 565). Historians, because they manifest an "approbation of virtue" that is "warm," are "the true friends of virtue" (Essays 567). Philosophers, in contrast, are likely to "bewilder" us by "the subtilty of their speculations," which makes their writings unsuited for the job of instilling virtue. As Hume puts it, "When a philosopher contemplates characters and manners in his closet, the general abstract view of the objects leaves the mind so cold and unmoved, that the sentiments of nature have no room to play, and he scarce feels the difference between vice and virtue" (Essays 568).

I think the most natural conclusion to draw from Hume's letter to Hutcheson, his conclusion to Book III, and "Of the Study of History" is that when he was writing Book III of the *Treatise* Hume thought that the task of explaining our moral judgments and practices was distinct from the task of providing normative reasons for living in accord with morality, and that he took himself to be engaged in the former task but not the latter.

A number of other commentators, however, have held that when Hume was writing the *Treatise* he was attempting to do more than simply explain our moral judgments and practices. Baier and Korsgaard, for instance, argue that Hume advances a general justificatory test that can be applied to all human "faculties" or "mental operations." To show that a faculty of mental operation can pass the test, according to the readings of Baier and Korsgaard, is to show that the activities it grounds are justifiable or normative. It is to show that we ought to go in for these activities, that we ought to live in accord with them.

The tests of normativity that Baier and Korsgaard claim to find in Hume revolve around the concept of reflection or reflexivity. Now "reflection" can mean simply sustained thought or conscious attention, and that sense of the word is relevant here. But to ground normativity, on this view, a faculty or mental operation must also survive reflection of a more focused sort. Specifically, it must survive when turned back on itself, i.e., it must not be destroyed by its own reflection. In slogan form, something is justified if and only if it can bear its own survey. As Korsgaard puts it, "According to this theory a faculty's verdicts are normative if the faculty meets the following test: *when the faculty takes itself and its own operations for its object, it gives a positive verdict*" (Korsgaard 1996, 62). Or as Baier writes, "The whole of the *Treatise* searches for mental operations that can bear their own survey, sorting those that can (causal reasoning in its naturalistic and non-metaphysical employment, virtues and the moral sentiment which discerns them) from those that get into 'manifest contradictions' or self-destructive conflict when turned on themselves" (Baier 1991, 97). In her most succinct statement of the view, Baier writes, "*Successful reflexivity is normativity*" (Baier 1991, 99–100).

Initially, there seems to be quite strong support for this reflexivity reading in the conclusion to Book III of the *Treatise*. For there Hume speaks of the importance of one's being able to bear one's own survey and of the "new force" the "sense of morals" acquires when it "reflect[s] on itself." He writes, "It requires but very little knowledge of human affairs to perceive, that a sense of morals is a principle inherent in the soul, and one of the most powerful that enters into the composition. But this sense must certainly acquire new force, when reflecting on itself, it approves of those principles, from whence it is deriv'd, and finds nothing but what is great and good in its rise and origin" (THN 3.3.6.3). Baier and Korsgaard suggest that these passages warrant attributing to Hume the view that reflexivity is the key to normativity. But the context in which the passages occur suggests otherwise.

The conclusion of Book III has a typographical break in it about a third of the way through (THN 3.3.6.2–3). What comes before the break is written in the tone of someone reviewing what has come before. Hume tells us, in that first third, what it is he thinks Book III has accomplished. It is there that he runs through, in rapid summary fashion, the arguments he has made in the order in which he has made them. The arguments summarized there are all explanatory; they are explanations, that is, of how we come to make the moral judgments we do. He does not give reasons to be moral or refer to any arguments seeking to justify the faculty of mental operation that grounds our moral practices in general.

The comments about reflexivity and bearing one's own survey occur after the break. This in itself is not necessarily damaging to the reflexivity interpretations, since it is possible that Hume reserved that ultimate spot in the *Treatise* for the justificatory conclusion to which his explanatory project had been building.

The problem with that interpretation is that Hume explicitly distances himself and the *Treatise* from the reflexivity comments. After the break and just before the crucial text, Hume writes: "Were it proper in such a subject to bribe the readers assent, or employ any thing but solid argument, we are here abundantly supplied with topics to engage the affections" (THN 3.3.6.3). If any comment should warn us off reading the remarks of a few paragraphs back into the entirety of a very long book, it seems that this one should. Later in the section, too, in the sentence immediately succeeding the one in which "one's own survey" is mentioned, Hume writes, "But I forbear insisting on this subject. Such reflexions require a work a-part, very different from the genius of the present" (THN 3.3.6.6).

There is also external evidence that an appeal to the "peace and inward satisfaction" of being able to bear one's own survey does not function in the general justificatory way the reflexivity reading requires. Hutcheson says in the introduction to his *Inquiry concerning Moral Good and Evil* that he will show that moral motives cannot be reduced to self-interest, i.e., that egoism of any stripe fails as a moral theory. He mentions two broad classes of egoistic theories that he takes to be his opponents'. According to the second of these two egoisms, we are motivated to virtue at least in part because we receive a "secret Sense of Pleasure arising from Reflection upon such of our own Actions as we call *virtuous*, even when we expect no other *Advantage* from them" (Beauty and Virtue 115). Although this theory differs from one in which we are motivated by the promised rewards and punishments of a "superior" being, it is still, on Hutcheson's view, egoistic. For its proponents claim "that we are excited to perform these Actions, even as we pursue, or purchase *Pictures, Statues, Landskips*, from *Self-Interest*, to obtain this Pleasure which arises from Reflection upon the Action, or some other future Advantage" (Beauty and Virtue 116).

I do not believe Hume and Hutcheson share all the same philosophical tendencies, and in general, I think it is unwise to answer questions about Hume's texts by use of the default assumption that he was in agreement with Hutcheson. But in this case the two of them do seem to have the same thing in mind. Indeed, when Hume speaks of one's being able to bear one's own survey in his response to the sensible knave (Second Enquiry 155–6), he seems pretty clearly to be thinking of the self-interested motive that Hutcheson describes as the "sense of pleasure arising from reflection upon such of our actions as we call virtuous." This explains why Hume lists the happy survey of one's own conduct as one of the "advantages" of virtue. Indeed, in the paragraph of the *Second Enquiry* in which the text occurs, Hume seems to be making suggestions about how we might carry out the relatively straightforward task of showing that the advantages of the social virtues outweigh "any advantages of fortune." Or as he puts it in the first sentence of this part of the *Enquiry*, "Having explained the moral *approbation* attending merit or virtue, there remains nothing, but briefly to consider our interested *obligation* to it, and to enquire, whether every man, who has any regard to his own happiness and welfare, will not best find his account in the practice of every moral duty" (Second Enquiry 152). But this task is different from the one undertaken in the *Treatise*. The egoistic nature of the task, furthermore, sharply distinguishes it from the justificatory project the reflexivity reading locates in the concluding section of Book III.

But what I have said here addresses only what Baier says about the final section of the *Treatise*. But Baier does not claim that section as her only support for the reflexivity reading. For a full discussion of Baier's view, see Gill (1996b).

Another reading that takes the *Treatise* to attempt to justify morality as a whole is that of Sayre-McCord (1994). In the introduction to his article, he writes:

Significantly, Hume has two separate but, as it turns out, related ambitions for his moral theory. He attempts, first of all and most explicitly, to give an *explanation* of morality. . . . At the same time, though, he hopes his theory succeeds not just in explaining moral thought but also in *justifying* it. . . . Far from alienating us, reflection on the nature of morality will, Hume thinks, bring it closer to our hearts. In fact, he is convinced, the sense of morals "must certainly acquire new force, when reflecting on itself, it approves of those principles, from when it is deriv'd, and finds nothing but what is great and good in its rise and origin." (Sayre-McCord 1994, 203)

I believe Sayre-McCord's account of Hume's explanatory project is astute, and he does an excellent job of showing that Hume's general point of view should not be conflated with the perspective of an ideal observer. But Sayre-McCord's claim to find in the *Treatise* justificatory ambitions runs into problems similar to those that afflicted Baier and Korsgaard's interpretation.

Note, first of all, that in the passage just quoted, Sayre-McCord refers to the conclusion of Book III, which, as I have explained, does not lend nearly as much support to a justificatory reading as might initially appear. Secondly, Sayre-McCord maintains that Hume set himself the justificatory task because he was concerned to provide "grounds for criticizing . . . the monkish virtues of celibacy, fasting, penance, mortification, self-denial, humility, silence, and solitude that are 'everywhere rejected by men of sense'" (Sayre-McCord 1994, 208). But (as I argue in Gill 1996b) Hume's criticism of the monkish virtues is merely an explanatory one: he argues that his account captures the observable phenomena of moral judgment better than the monkish hypothesis, not that the monks were guilty of some justificatory failure.

But the central claim of Sayre-McCord's justificatory reading is that Hume argued that judgments made from the general point of view – i.e., from the point of view that considers those within the "narrow circle" of an agent's immediate sphere of influence – are justified because the general point of view is superior to any other at doing what we need morality to do. Sayre-McCord argues, specifically, that the general point of view is superior to the point of view of an ideal observer because the former is "mutually accessible," while the latter is not, and that a point of view's being mutual accessible makes it better suited to resolve conflict, which is just what we need morality to do (Sayre-McCord 1994, 217).

The point about accessibility that Sayre-McCord raises is interesting, and may be a good reason to encourage people to make judgments from a general point of view rather than from the point of view of an ideal observer. The crucial thing to note for our purposes, however, is that Hume does not himself make this point. What Hume says is that we judge people based on how they affect their narrow circle because "experience" has taught us "that the generosity of men is very limited, and that it seldom extends beyond their friends and family" (THN 3.3.3.2; I discuss this point in more detail in Chapter 19). And the *because* here is entirely explanatory. Now that explanation of why we judge from the general point of view does bring mutual accessibility in its wake. Because our judgments are tied to sentimental tendencies most people exhibit, and because most of us have those tendencies, most of us will be able to figure out what those tendencies would lead a typical person to do. But nowhere in the *Treatise* does Hume use this feature of the general point of view to try to convince us that we are justified in making the kinds of moral judgments we typically make.

The same thing can be said about Hume's discussion of why we approve of "virtue in rags." If a certain kind of character trait is generally beneficial,

Hume tells us, then we will approve of it in every situation, even in those unusual situations in which it has been prevented from producing the benefits it normally produces. Sayre-McCord says that this feature allows us to "correct for . . . distortions" and thus "recommends" the general point of view to us – i.e., that this feature furthers Hume's goal of justifying the general point of view (Sayre-McCord 1994, 219). But all Hume says in the *Treatise* is that we approve of virtue in rags because of our addiction to general rules or our tendency to overgeneralize (I discuss this point in more detail in Chapter 17). And, once again, the *because* here is entirely explanatory.

That is not to say that Hume would deny that the general point of view serves a crucially important function in our lives. But his task is to explain how this situation developed, not to show that it is justified. Hume's task is akin to that of an evolutionary biologist who is trying to give an account of the specific features of the human eye. Of course, the more we learn about the eye, the more we might marvel at how wonderfully it works. But the evolutionary biologist is not trying to show that a situation in which humans have eyes is more justified than a situation in which humans do not. That humans have eyes is an explanadum, not something the evolutionary biologist is in the business of trying to show us we have good reason to accept. And so, too, that we judge people from a general point of view is Hume's explanadum. Perhaps learning more about the general point of view will lead us to marvel at its usefulness. But eliciting that response is not the purpose of the *Treatise*.

The comparison with evolutionary biology also points to why it is important to be clear about the *Treatise*'s explanatory purpose. Unlike those who believe that we have been created by a perfectly intelligent and benevolent being, an evolutionary biologist does not need to hold that everything that is natural to human beings is perfect or morally good. Her explanations of evolved traits will be compatible with moral criticism of some of those traits or with the judgment that some of our evolved traits can be improved on. She could allow, for instance, that while the eye bestowed tremendous evolutionary advantages, the addition of certain kinds of visual technology can make our lives even better. She can allow that we might be better off combatting some dispositions – such as tribalism and sexual aggression – that may have once been evolutionarily advantageous. Similarly, the *Treatise*'s explanation of the practices that most humans engage in does not commit Hume to endorsing all those practices. By remaining clear about the *Treatise*'s explanatory purpose, we keep sight of the fact that Hume can allow that there is conceptual space to criticize or try to improve on things that may be firmly entrenched in the way most humans live. And this is important because it marks one of the most significant ways in which Hume differs from theological thinkers, such as Hutcheson and Butler (see especially Butler 51–66, where he presents a morally saturated teleology of human nature), who held that if something is natural to humanity it must be good or justified.

Should we judge people from the general point of view, which is to say, from the perspective of how they treat their narrow circle? Or should we – as Peter Singer, Shelly Kagan, and Peter Unger have argued – try to adopt and propagate a broader perspective, one according to which I am obligated to benefit anyone

314 Notes to Pages 203–7

anywhere in the world who is in great need and whom I can help? Or should we privilege a more egoistic perspective, as David Gauthier and Gregory Kavka have proposed? Or should we judge everything based on how well it accords with the ideals of Christian asceticism? Sayre-McCord seems to think that the first perspective – the perspective that underlies our commonsense morality – is the best one. And he may be right. But Hume's account in the *Treatise* does not commit us to that. The reason Hume spends his time on the general point of view is that it underlies the actual moral judgments people most commonly make. Its commonness – not any justificatory credentials – is what makes the general point of view Hume's subject matter.

The recent secondary literature on Hume includes discussions of whether and to what extent Hume was conservative or liberal. And in some of his later writings, Hume argues for positions that are fair fodder for such discussions. But on the first-order moral and political questions about which conservatives and liberals disagree, the explanations of the *Treatise* are neutral. To place those explanations at the service of first-order moral and political positions is perfectly acceptable. But to suggest, as Sayre-McCord does, that doing this was essential to the *Treatise*'s "science of man" is to obscure one of the most significant ways in which Hume's account of human nature differs from – and improves on – those offered by his theologically committed predecessors.

3. Although in the *Leviathan*, after pointing out that a typical person will arm himself when he goes on a journey and lock his doors at night, Hobbes wrote, "Does he not there as much accuse mankind by his actions, as I do by my words? But neither of us accuse man's nature in it. The desires and other passions of man are in themselves no sin" (Hobbes 77). This is a clear precursor to Hume's rejection of the Human Nature Question.

4. Hume insisted that his claim that justice was "artificial" did not imply that justice was arbitrary, unimportant, or optional. He also said that there was a sense in which justice was in fact natural. See THN 3.2.1.19, 3.2.2.28, and 3.3.6.4 and *A Letter from a Gentleman to his friend in Edinburgh*, 30–3.

5. See Norton (1982), 147–8, and C. Brown (1994), 26. Hume's philosophical relationship to Hutcheson has been a particularly fertile ground for commentary. Kemp Smith (1941) has argued that Hume is greatly indebted to Hutcheson. Moore (1994) has argued that Hutcheson had very little influence on Hutcheson. More nuanced – and, to my mind, more accurate – accounts of how Hutcheson did and did not influence Hume can be found in Darwall (1994, 1997), Herdt (1997), Abramson (2001), and Norton (2005). See also A. MacIntyre (1988), 284–325.

6. See Herdt (1997), 39–81.

7. These arguments are an ancestor of Hume's attack on the argument from design in his *Dialogues on Natural Religion*. "An early fragment on evil," which was probably meant to be included in the *Treatise*, is an even clearer attack on Hutcheson and Shaftesbury's design-based argument for the existence of a benevolent God (Stewart 1994). In that fragment, Hume argues that we have no grounds for holding that God possesses "moral Attributes" such as benevolence, because we have no grounds for holding that there is a great deal more "Good" or "Happiness" in the universe than "Evil" or "Misery" (Stewart 1994, 165–6, 168).

16. Hume's Arguments against Moral Rationalism

1. Harrison (1976), Stroud (1977), Mackie (1980), and Norton (1993b) offer helpful discussions of the main lines of debate in interpretation of Hume's anti-rationalist arguments. Other useful discussions include Penelhum (1993), Radcliffe (1994a), Millgram (1995), Garrett (1997), Cohon (1997), Cohon and Owen (1997), Sayre-McCord (1997), Schauber (1999), and Weller (2002).

2. Hume also presents a number of arguments against the moral theory of Wollaston (see THN 3.1.1.15), but I will not discuss those here.

3. C. Brown (1988) raises worries about whether Hume's arguments from motivational skepticism cohere with the account of morals that he gives in later parts of Book III of the *Treatise*. I believe Blackburn's view of morality's motivational force captures Hume's basic insight into this issue, and this view also avoids the problem Brown raises. Blackburn says that while there might be individual cases in which a person makes a moral judgment without having any corresponding motivation, "these cases are necessarily parasitic, and what they are parasitic upon is a background connection between ethics and motivation. They are cases in which things are out of joint, but the fact of a joint being out presupposes a normal or typical state in which it is not out" (Blackburn 1998, 61). For an excellent discussion of this issue, see Abramson (2002).

4. For the view that Hume's skeptical arguments about reason's role in the development of causal beliefs are directed at a specifically seventeenth- and eighteenth-century conception of reason, see Beauchamp and Rosenberg (1979). Baier (1991) also argues that Hume's criticism of rationalist theories should be seen as directed at a seventeenth- and eighteenth-century conception of reason. For critical discussion of these interpretations of Hume's anti-rationalist arguments, see Owen (1999), which is the best account I know of what Hume meant by "reason" in the *Treatise*.

5. See Korsgaard (1986).

6. But in one paragraph (THN 3.1.1.26), Hume also addresses the possibility that morals originate in a posteriori reason. The fullest discussion of Hume's arguments against the view that morals originate in a posteriori reason is Sturgeon (2001).

7. The objection is that Hume's sentimentalist account cannot explain why, even though we might have disagreeable feelings toward an enemy, we might nonetheless judge that he is virtuous (THN 3.1.2.4). Hume treats this question more fully when he discusses the "general points of view" in THN 3.3.1 and 3.3.3. I discuss this issue in Chapters 17 and 19.

8. See Darwall (1997).

9. See Moore (1994).

17. Hume's Associative Moral Sentiments

1. As Lamprecht explains it, "[T]he validity of an idea was settled by appealing to the conditions of its origin in the divine seeds sown in man's nature. . . . The appeal to origins was typical of this age in all field of human interest. A government was a just government which abided by original contracts; a religion was true

which held to the original simple truths antecedent to the corruptions of priests; an idea was true which was part of the native endowment of the mind. That is, legitimacy, primitiveness, or innateness were tests of validity, and were used for apologetic purposes rather than utility, results flowing from a thing, or outcome" (Lamprecht 1926, 571).

2. See Wooten (1994), 296–307, for discussion of this strategy of political justification and how Hume's *History of England* helped to undermine it.

3. Hume's use of comparison is another clear example of how his account implies an explanatory symmetry that demolishes his predecessors' conception of human nature. Comparative judgments admit of empirical explanation. They are not based entirely on principles that are innate, instinctive, or original to our constitution. They are caused in part by contingent experience. Now some of the comparative judgments Hume examines are linked to traits, such as malice and envy, that are morally bad (THN 2.2.8). And if Hume had used comparison to explain only malice and envy, it would have cohered with his predecessors' view of justification. But as we will see in Chapter 19, Hume also used comparison to explain things that seem to be blameless or correct, such as our admiration of great men and our appreciation of natural talent. So if Hume is right, the distinction between traits that do and do not admit of comparison-based empirical explanation does not track the distinction between traits we should eliminate or suppress and traits we should allow or encourage.

4. For discussion of the authorship of the *Abstract*, see Norton (1993a).

5. Hutcheson's theory of justice is developed for the most part in works (such as *A System of Moral Philosophy*) published after Hume wrote the *Treatise*, so we should not suppose that Hume meant to attack Hutcheson's views on justice per se when he wrote this passage (although Hutcheson's discussion of rights in the *Inquiry* contains the seeds of his theory of justice). I think it is clear, however, that Hume's account of justice does constitute an attack on the picture of human nature that Hutcheson's moral theory presupposes (cf. Letters 33). For while Hutcheson maintains that we originally approve of the motive to benefit humanity as a whole, Hume argues that the possibility of such a motive conflicts with human psychology. When we approve of someone's motives, therefore, we must be approving of motives that are not universal or completely impartial. Of course, Hume also believes that we will sympathize with – and so tend to approve of that which benefits – anyone whose plight is "brought near to us, and represented in lively colours" (THN 3.2.1.12). But the fact that we can sympathize with any particular person at a given time does not imply that we can ever sympathize with all people at any time.

6. See McCormick (1993) for a very helpful discussion of Hume's use of the terms "natural" and "original." McCormick says that for Hume three "clearly original principles . . . are selfishness, sympathy, and the propensity to form habits" (McCormick 1993, 109). I agree that the latter two are original for Hume in that they are for him unexplained explainers (as are lust and parental affection, as I noted previously). But for the purposes of elucidating the difference between Hutcheson and Hume, I am calling original only those *passions* that are unexplained explainers, not the associative habitual mechanisms that give rise to unoriginal passions.

7. Although at THN 3.2.2.5 Hume speaks of the "passions of lust and natural affection" as being the "first and original principle of human society," he says earlier that lust is "a natural impulse or instinct" that gives rise to passions (THN 2.3.9.8), suggesting that he might have thought that lust is not a passion itself. It seems, that is, that Hume may not have been entirely clear about how or whether to distinguish sexual impulses from passions (although I'm not sure that even the passage at THN 2.3.9.8 should be taken to imply any meaningful distinction between the two). What is crucial for our purposes, in any event, is only to locate what for Hume is explanatorily fundamental or, as he puts it, "perfectly unaccountable" (THN 2.3.9.8).

8. See also "Of the obligation of promises," where Hume writes, "Men being naturally selfish, or endow'd only with a confin'd generosity, they are not easily induc'd to perform any action for the interest of strangers, except with a view to some reciprocal advantage, which they had no hope of obtaining but by such a performance. Were we, therefore, to follow the natural course of our passions and inclinations, we shou'd perform but few actions for the advantage of others, from disinterested views; because we are naturally very limited in our kindness and affection" (THN 3.2.5.8).

9. Hutcheson, for instance, writes, "Were we to strike a *Medium* of the several Passions and Affections, as they appear in the whole Species of Mankind, to conclude thence what has been the natural Ballance previously to any Change made by Custom and habit, which we see casts the Ballance to either side, we should perhaps find the *Medium* of the publick Affections not very far from a sufficient *Counterballance* to the *Medium* of the Selfish; and consequently the *Overballance* on either side in particular Characters, is not to be looked upon as the *original Constitution,* but as the *accidental Effect* of Custom, Habits, or Associations of Ideas, or other preternatural Causes" (Passions and Affections 201).

10. Actually, our "partiality" or "limited generosity" alone, according to Hume, would still not give rise to justice. There must also obtain certain "outward circumstances" (THN 3.2.2.7). The principal element of these "circumstances" is that there is a scarcity of certain universally desired goods and that these goods can be taken from one person and transferred to another.

11. Hume's account "Of the rules, which determine property" is also interesting in this regard (THN 3.2.3). In that section, Hume provides two parallel explanations of how property rules develop. In the main body of the text he derives these rules from their tendency to benefit society. But in the extensive footnotes to the section (longer than the main body itself) Hume derives the rules from associative tendencies that have no necessary relation to public utility. He writes, "Thus, in the present case, there are, no doubt, motives of public interest for most of the rules, which determine property; but still I suspect, that these rules are principally fix'd by the imagination, or the more frivolous properties of our thought and conception" (THN 3.2.3.4).

12. Especially if we read only the first part of Book III of the *Treatise.* Moore has suggested that Hume wrote this part of the *Treatise* in response to Hutcheson's criticisms of an earlier draft (Moore 1994, 39). This might at least partly explain the Hutchesonian flavor of these sections. Herdt gives a persuasive account of

how a Hutcheson-like moral sense drops out of Hume's *Treatise* account of morals (Herdt 1997, 66). Or as Blackburn puts it, "It is also significant that the phrase 'moral sense' . . . occurs only twice in the whole corpus: once in the title of 3.1.2, and once more in a very glancing fashion in 3.3.1. It is simply not a theoretical term with which Hume *does* anything, and its prominence as a section title is, I think, misleading (it is partly piety to Hutcheson and partly a slogan, a counterpoise to the preceding title, 'Moral distinctions not derived from reason')"(Blackburn 1993, 275).

13. As McCormick (1993) points out, sympathy is for Hume original to human nature. But sympathy cannot fill the justificatory role in Hume's philosophy that the benevolent moral sense does in Hutcheson's. For Humean sympathy can give rise to condemnable passions (e.g., anger, vengeance, the desire to drink to excess) as naturally as it can give rise to praiseworthy ones. Our capacity to sympathize, moreover, varies with our past experience in a way that original Hutchesonian approval of benevolence does not.

14. Judgments in accord with Hume's general point of view differ not only in origin but also in content from judgments in accord with Hutcheson's natural moral sense. For Hutcheson's moral sense leads us to approve of actions intended to promote the happiness of humanity as a whole, but Hume's general point of view leads us to approve of traits beneficial only to those in the more or less immediate vicinity of the bearer of the trait (see THN 3.3.1). And a trait that benefits those in the more or less immediate vicinity could conceivably harm, or at least not help, humanity overall. (For further discussion, see Sayre-McCord 1994.) Hume also maintains, moreover, that we approve not only of traits that are useful to others but also of traits that are useful to the bearer himself, as well as of traits that are immediately agreeable to others or to the bearer. But this four-part taxonomy cannot be reduced to the impartial benevolence that Hutcheson claims characterizes those things we naturally approve of. (For further discussion see Sayre-McCord 1996.) As Hume wrote in a letter to Hutcheson, "Were Benevolence the only Virtue no Characters cou'd be mixt, but wou'd depend entirely on their Degrees of Benevolence" (Letters 34). In another letter he wrote, "I always thought you limited too much your Ideas of Virtue" (Letters 47).

15. See THN 1.3.10.11, 1.3.12.24, 2.1.6.8, 2.1.10.12, 2.2.5.12, 2.2.7.5, 2.2.8.5, 3.2.2.24, 3.2.6.9, 3.2.9.3, 3.3.1.20, 3.3.2.10.

16. See also THN 2.1.6.8

17. Sometimes when Hume speaks of general rules, he is referring not to the associative tendency to overgeneralize (which is what I am concerned with here) but rather to explicit laws or conventions. Hume tends not to italicize "general rules" when he is speaking of these explicit laws or conventions (an exception to this is THN 1.3.9.6 and possibly THN 2.1.9), and it is usually fairly clear from the context whether he is discussing explicit law or the associative tendency to overgeneralize. See, for instance, THN 3.2.6.9, where Hume distinguishes the results of "general and universal rules" from motives born of "*general rules.* "(See also THN 3.2.3.3, 3.2.4.1, 3.2.10.15.)

18. Hume also uses our addiction to general rules to explain tendencies that are not clearly praiseworthy or condemnable, such as our tendency to feel embarrassed for foolish people who do not themselves realize that they are acting foolishly

(THN 2.2.7.5) and our tendency to be initially suspicious of all expressions of pride (THN 3.2.9.1–3).

19. See also THN 3.2.9.3–5, where Hume suggests that resistance to tyrants is born of general rules no less than obedience.

20. See Hearn (1970) and (1976) for valuable discussion of these matters. Hearn rightly distinguishes between "reflective" general rules, which are the main focus of his 1970 article, and those that arise as a result of our unreflective "generalizing propensity" (which I focus on more here). I believe, however, that Hearn does not take adequate notice of the fact that Hume does not condemn *all* the unreflective or "addictive" general rules. The distinction between general rules we ought to live by and those we ought to avoid does not, that is, track the distinction between reflective and unreflective general rules.

21. I opened this chapter by outlining a strategy of justification that was common in the seventeenth and eighteenth centuries. But this justificatory strategy is far from a mere antiquity. Many people today still try to justify certain things by claiming that they are "natural" and to discredit other things by claiming that they are "unnatural." And some of those people also contend that what is natural is in accord with God's design, while what is unnatural is in disaccord with it. I am thinking here of condemnations of things such as homosexuality and genetic manipulation, and affirmations of things such as meat-eating and traditional sex roles. People who advance such positions owe us a distinction between, on the one hand, the natural and the godly, and, on the other hand, the unnatural and the ungodly, and that distinction, if it is to add anything meaningful to the discussion, must be conceptually independent of the distinction between what they think is justified and what they think is not.

Unlike many participants in contemporary moral discussions, and to his credit, Hutcheson did provide a non-question-begging distinction between, on the one hand, what is natural and in accord with God's and, on the other hand, what is unnatural and in disaccord with God's design. The former, Hutcheson contended, are original or explanatorily fundamental, while the latter are not. But Hume showed that the distinction between what is and is not original cannot fill the role Hutcheson intended for it. Thus, if participants in contemporary moral discussions want to continue to say that what they advocate is natural and godly and what they condemn is unnatural and ungodly, they'll have to come up with a way of drawing that distinction that is better than Hutcheson's and better than Hume's. Until they do, there's no reason to take their claims about what is and is not natural, and what is and is not godly, to be anything more than repetitions of moral conclusions arrived at by other means.

18. Hume's Progressive View of Human Nature

1. Much of what I argue for in this chapter overlaps with two excellent articles by Rachel Cohon (1997a, 2001). Cohon also commented on an earlier version of this chapter, and I am indebted to her suggestions.

2. But as we saw in Chapter 17 and will see again in Chapter 19, even Hume's account of the natural virtues, insofar as it relies on the associative principles of the mind and comparison, is more of a departure from Shaftesbury and Hutcheson than it might initially appear.

3. For a clear and convincing account of this argument of Hume's, see Cohon (1997a).

4. Perhaps Hume moves too quickly here in that he doesn't consider the possibility that all humans – civilized or not – are capable of determining the content of justice through the use of reason alone and that therefore a simple regard for justice and an idea of justice's content can arise simultaneously (or even in a sense be the same thing). Mackie is possibly right as well when he contends that in this argument Hume simply denies without much argument the possibility that there was an original instinct to respect property, keep promises, and in general follow the rules of justice (Mackie 1980, 80–1).

5. I discuss this point of Hume's in Chapter 17.

6. Commentators such as Mackie (1980), 83 and Haakonssen (1981), 21, have noted Mandeville's influence on Hume's constructive account of justice, although I think they tend to understate it.

7. Hume's constructive account of justice is a conjectural history. For an excellent account of the Scottish context of this kind of genetic explanation, see Emerson (1984) and Steward (1992), 152–93.

8. Baier (1991), 222, is especially clear on this difference – on how Hume's pre-civil human beings are naturally much nicer than Mandeville's.

9. See also THN 3.3.1.9, where Hume says that the "inventors of [the laws of nations, of modesty, and of good manners] had chiefly in view their own interest. But we carry our approbation of them into the most distant countries and ages, and much beyond our own interest." Because Hume acknowledges that justice can be counter to self-interest, I think Gauthier is wrong to try to turn moral obligation into a kind of self-interested obligation (Gauthier 1979, 26–9). I also think Baier is on questionable ground in claiming that "Hume seems to require that, for something to be a moral obligation, it must first satisfy the test of self-interest which convention imposes" (Baier 1991, 243).

10. Baron (1982) suggests, I think, that we take this passage with a grain of salt and read Hume as in the end advancing the Mandevillean idea that our sense of virtue is created (albeit from fairly benevolent motives) by the noble lie of politicians.

11. I discuss this kind of moral realism in Chapter 13. See Norton (1982), 55–93, for an excellent account of the issues surrounding moral realism in Hutcheson and Hume.

12. As we saw in Chapter 7, one of Shaftesbury's main purposes in his *Inquiry* was to determine how various religious beliefs affect a person's moral sentiments, although he didn't seem to think that new kinds of sentiments altogether can arise. As we saw in Chapter 14, Hutcheson discussed at great length how original human passions can become corrupted, although he didn't seem to think that a new salutary passion can ever be created. In his later works (particularly the Dialogues in Part II of *Fable of the Bees* and *An Enquiry into the Origin of Honour*), Mandeville gave a more subtle, gradualist account of civilizing developments than he might appear to endorse in his earlier works (such as "The Grumbling Hive" and "An Enquiry into the Origin of Moral Virtue"), although he never strayed far from his fundamentally egoistic view. For discussion of this issue in Mandeville, see Kaye's Introduction in Mandeville (I lxiv–lxvi).

13. For an excellent discussion of this issue in Hobbes, see Hampton (1986), 27–57.
14. See EIM 144–5.
15. Emerson, in his discussion of Scottish conjectural histories, tells us, "Development and progress were used synonymously by eighteenth century Scots for whom progress did not usually imply a necessarily better state but only a change" (Emerson 1984, 65). It is interesting to ask whether Hume thought that small communities in which there was no (need for the virtue of) justice were in a better or worse state than larger nations in which there is (the need of the virtue of) justice. I tend to think Hume would not have been terribly interested in this question, focusing instead on how the development occurred and not on whether it was for good or ill. In any event, Emerson's comment is an important reminder that just because Hume held what I call a "progressive" view of human nature, it does not mean that Hume held to the Whiggish view that human nature was necessarily advancing or improving.
16. Baier's title, "A Progress of Sentiments," comes, of course, from this passage in the text, and throughout her book she does an excellent job of explaining Hume's claims about how humans develop various capacities and judgments that were not part of their original uncultivated endowment. Cohon (1997a, 2001) provides excellent accounts of how Humean justice results from the kind of progression of sentiments I also discuss here. Steward (1992) makes similar points throughout his discussion of Hume's "conjectural history," as does Streeter when he speaks of Hume's "account of socialization" and of "the possibility of a progressional moral cultivation in people" (Streeter 1995, 8–11). I believe that Feiser also describes accurately the role of artifice in the development of the motive to act justly, although he overlooks the role artifice also plays in the development of our approval of (even nonbeneficial acts of) justice (Feiser 1997). See also Mackie (1980), 87. Blackburn has many elucidating things to say about the importance of being clear about the difference between a diachronic explanation of a motive or judgment and a synchronic account of its nature or character (Blackburn 1998, 157, 196–9, 202–7). I believe that Stroud misses somewhat the progressive aspect of Hume's view of human nature, which leads him to conclude that Hume fails to account adequately for our sense of justice (Stroud 1977, 204–10). It seems to me that Stroud notes accurately the generally Mandevillean starting point of Hume's account, but doesn't allow that Hume has the progressivist resources to explain how we can move beyond these selfish beginnings.
17. In the main body of the text, I have skated over a problem with Hume's account of justice. The problem is how to square that account with Hume's view that "the ultimate object of our praise and approbation" is "motive" (THN 3.2.1.2). The passages at THN 3.2.2.23–4 explain our moral approval of justice, but it seems that this approval must have as its object some motive. But it is difficult to see what motive Hume can countenance here. It seems that he thinks that self-interest plays a large role in the motivation to be just, but it doesn't seem that self-interest is what we approve of when we approve of justice. He does suggest that the regard to justice is a motive (THN 3.2.1), but he doesn't explain what exactly it is; he spends most of his time, rather, explaining what the regard to justice is *not*. Very worthwhile discussions of this problem can be found in

Mackie (1980), C. Brown (1988), Darwall (1995), and Schneewind (1998). I find particularly convincing Mackie's claim that to make Hume's "view coherent, we must, I think, take him to be relaxing the principle that actions count as virtuous *only* in so far as they are signs of virtuous motives in the case of the artificial virtues" (Mackie 1980, 80) and Darwall's claim that we must attribute to Hume the idea of a "rule obligation," which is distinct from the natural and moral obligations explicitly mentioned in the *Treatise* (Darwall 1995, 315).

Darwall maintains that "[n]o interpretation can dissolve" entirely all of the internal problems in Hume's account of justice (Darwall 1995, 290). And I am inclined to agree with him if what he means to say is that it is impossible to combine all of Hume's explicit statements on justice and virtue into one perfectly coherent whole. At the same time, I think that attention to Hume's progressive view and its relationship to his predecessors mitigates the problems somewhat. For the problems, I think, can be traced back to an originalist or static idea – a piece of excess originalist or static baggage – that makes occasional appearances in Hume's text but is not organic to his deepest philosophical insights.

The offending originalist or static idea is that the shape and function of every human "passion" and "sense" is sharply defined and fixed by our original constitution, unsusceptible to radical alteration, innovation, or supplementation. This idea is particularly conspicuous in Hutcheson, who erects a firewall between, on the one hand, motivating passions that are approved of ("*Motives* or *Desires*" that lead to "*Election*") and, on the other hand, moral "*Approbation*," which does not motivate (Passions and Affections 208–9).

It is entirely reasonable, however, to think that Hume's deepest philosophical insights are incompatible with this originalist idea, as is evident not only in his progressive account of justice but also in his profoundly anti-Hutchesonian associative account of the passions, according to which "one passion will always be mixt and confounded with the other" (THN 2.3.9.12). But once this originalist idea is jettisoned, the way will be cleared for him to hold (what seems eminently plausible to me) that our selfish endorsements of a large subset of a certain type of action can evolve into moral approvals of that type of action in general, and to hold (what, again, seems eminently reasonable to me) that approvals that originally have no motivational force can evolve into motivations. Hume could hold, that is, that a person may first endorse justice because it promotes her own interest, but over time may come to associate her own interest with the interests of others closely enough so that it leads her not merely to endorse justice selfishly but to approve of it morally, and that over still more time she may come to associate this moral approval of justice closely enough with the motives that elicit it that the approval itself acquires some motivational force. This progression could be strengthened by a phenomenon whereby the person is initially motivated to be just for self-interested reasons (fear of punishment, desire for reward) but notes that others approve of her morally when she is just, and so (as a result of sympathetically catching the moral approval others feel for her own justice) comes to associate moral approval with her motive to be just so strongly that the two passions become "mixt and confounded" with each other. (The fact that there are so many associative steps that must be made before someone possess a full-blown regard to justice should probably be seen as a strength of Hume's account rather than a weakness, as the many ways in which such a regard could fail to develop fully explains why some people come to lack such a regard and why the regard is relatively weak [i.e., weaker than many other kinds of concern] in many other people.) Originalist thinking will, of course, resist the possibility of such instances of sentimental evolution. But what I have been trying to show here is that it is just this originalist thinking beyond which Hume is trying to move.

Of course, it is not enough just to clear the way for this type of progressive account. The account itself has to be plausibly developed. Gauthier (1979), Baron (1982), and Haakonssen (1981) all argue that in order to work, Hume's account must include the idea that at some point we commit the "error" of believing that there is a natural motive to justice when in fact there is none. (Baron, as noted earlier, also attributes to Hume the view that politicians and educators must lie to the people in order to cause them to make this error.) My own view is that the key to Hume's explanation of the development of what Darwall calls our "rule obligation" to justice is Hume's concept of our addiction to general rules, which might appear to be a kind of error but is not necessarily so. See also Ainslie (1995), who explores the idea that the problems with Hume's account might be solved by attention to Hume's idea of "national characters."

Some of the things Hume says about justice do look to contradict others. But there are principled reasons for taking certain of Hume's claims to be central to his thought (e.g., that some people do have a sincere, nonselfish, ultimate regard for justice) and for taking others to be more or less dispensable intellectual inheritances (e.g., that we can approve only of motives). And the conflicts between the former and the latter are almost inevitable – cracks that result from pouring new wine into old skins.

18. Mandeville, for instance, writes "An Enquiry into the Origin of Moral Virtue" and Hutcheson writes "An Inquiry into the Original of our Ideas of Beauty and Virtue."

19. Similar ambiguities infect the words "ground," "foundation," "derive," and "principle."

20. No one appreciated Hume's anti-originalist progressive view of human nature more fully than Mill, who develops the same idea in chapter four of *Utilitarianism* when he explains how virtue, money, fame, and the like can come to be desired as ends even though they were not "originally and naturally" so desired. He says, for instance, that "the strongest natural attraction . . . of power and of fame, is the immense aid they give to the attainment of our other wishes; and it is the strong association thus generated between them and all our objects of desire, which gives to the direct desire of them the intensity it often assumes, so as in some characters to surpass in strength all other desires" (Mill 1979, 36). He also says of virtue that there "was no original desire of it, or motive to it, save its conduciveness to pleasure, and especially to protection from pain. But through the association thus formed, it may be felt a good in itself, and desired as such with as great intensity as any other good" (1979, 37). See also Mill's discussion of conscience (1979, 27–8) and moral feelings (1979, 30–2). Another philosopher with a clearly progressivist view of human nature is Rousseau.

324 *Notes to Pages 241–4*

19. Comparison and Contingency in Hume's Account of Morality

1. I discuss this rationalist criticism of sentimentalism in more detail in Gill (1998).

2. For a clear and convincing account of Hutcheson's use of the analogy between moral properties and secondary qualities, see Winkler (1996). Norton (1985) has an opposing view, but the dispute between Winkler and Norton does not actually bear on the question I'm examining here. Even if, as Norton argues, Hutcheson thought that moral properties are more like primary qualities, the difference between Hume and Hutcheson that I focus on would still hold. Indeed, if Hutcheson thought that moral properties are more like primary qualities, then the difference I point to would be even sharper.

3. See Darwall 1997.

4. What I am calling the Hutchesonian analogy is an analogy between, on the one hand, the judgment "*x* is virtuous" and, on the other, "*x* is red," "*x* is salty," and "*x* harmonizes with *y*." I want to distinguish this from what we might call the "aesthetic" analogy, which is between, on the one hand, "*x* is virtuous" and, on the other, "the colors of *x* go well together; they don't clash," "*x* is delicious," and "*x* is a beautiful piece of music." I'm not sure Hutcheson clearly distinguished between what I am calling the aesthetic and Hutchesonian analogies. Hutcheson might not have clearly distinguished between the two analogies because he believed that aesthetic judgments have the same structure as judgments of secondary qualities, and that moral judgments have the same structure again (the only difference being that judgments of secondary qualities are based on external senses, while aesthetic and moral judgments are based on internal or social senses). But, as I will try to show, Hume gives an account of both aesthetic and moral judgments that is crucially disanalogous to judgments of secondary qualities. That is to say, for Hume, aesthetic and moral judgments both fall on one side of a conceptual divide and secondary qualities fall on another. So Hume might accept the aesthetic analogy but, on his understanding of aesthetics, that would not help to answer the contingency objection. (That Hume had in mind the Hutchesonian analogy and not the aesthetic analogy is evident from the passage from "The Skeptic" in which he compares, on the one hand, "tastes and colours, and all other sensible qualities" and, on the other, "beauty and deformity, virtue and vice" [Essays 166]. Note that secondary qualities are on one side of the analogy, while aesthetic and moral properties are together on the other.)

5. Baier has given a very helpful interpretation of Hume's view of the role of comparison in Book II of the *Treatise* (Baier 1991, 146–9), and she illuminates the important connection between the *Treatise*'s discussion of comparison and the discussion of comparison in "Of the Dignity or Meanness of Human Nature" (Baier 1991, 208–9). I believe, however, that her interpretation of Hume's view of the role of comparison in Book III of the *Treatise* is mistaken, as I explain in note 15.

6. Hume makes the same claim at THN 2.1.6.4, 2.1.8.7–8, 2.2.8.2, and 2.2.8.8. In all of these passages, Hume distinguishes between judgments based on the "intrinsic" qualities of an object and judgments based on our comparison of the object with other similar objects. At 2.2.7.2, Hume seems to make the same point, but he does not use the word "comparison" there. At 2.1.8.7–8, Hume says, "Every thing in this world is judg'd of by comparison," and at 3.2.10.5, he says, "We

naturally judge of every thing by comparison." The context of these statements seems to imply that Hume is using "comparison" here in the same way that he uses it at 3.3.2.4–5, 2.1.6.4, and 2.2.8.2; that is, that he is assuming a distinction between judgments based on an object's intrinsic qualities and judgments based on our comparison of the object with other similar objects, and that he is pointing out our very powerful tendency to make not only the former kind of judgment but also the latter. It's possible, however, that at 2.1.8.7–8 and 3.2.10.5, Hume is using "comparison" in a different sense, one that is meant to characterize *all* judgments; that is, it's possible that Hume is referring here to a kind of comparison of ideas that underlies not merely certain judgments (i.e., the non-intrinsic ones) but the process that is essential to the activity of judgment as a whole. But even if Hume is using "comparison" in this more general sense at 2.1.8.7–8 and 3.2.10.5, his discussion of pride and humility and the texts at 2.1.6.4, 2.1.8.7–8, and 3.3.2.4–5 make it clear that he sometimes uses "comparison" in the more narrow sense (i.e., in the sense that allows for a distinction between "comparative" judgments and "intrinsic" judgments) that I focus on in this chapter.

7. In comments on an earlier draft of this chapter, Kenneth Winkler and John Corvino argued that comparison's role in Hume's account of pride (and the other sentimental phenomena discussed in this chapter) does not pull Humean pride away from an analogy with secondary qualities. For, according to Winkler and Corvino, there can be secondary qualities that are comparative. Winkler gave as examples of comparative secondary qualities being darker in color, being higher in pitch, and being saltier in taste. In Winkler's examples, however, comparison has not produced a new impression. "Being darker in color" is not an impression over and above the impression of the lighter color and the impression of the darker one. The judgment that one color is darker than another concerns two and only two impressions (the impression of the lighter color and the impression of the darker color), and both of those impression are due to our original sensory apparatus. But in the case of pride (and the other sentimental phenomena discussed in this chapter), there is a third impression – the feeling of pride – and this third impression is not due to original physiological or psychological mechanisms. The feeling of pride is not like "being darker in color" because the former has a phenomenological content that is distinct from the impressions of the object of pride and from the pleasure the object of pride causes. Comparison, in the case of pride and the other phenomena discussed here, produces a new sentiment, and judgments based on this new sentiment are what are crucially different from judgments about whether something is darker in color than something else.

8. Distinguishing the properties and perceptions that are essential to Humean pride and the properties and perceptions that are not is actually rather complicated. In order to do a complete job, we'd have to draw two different distinctions: the distinction between intrinsic properties of a possession and relational properties of the possession, and the distinction between direct passions caused by the possession and indirect passions caused by the possession. Very roughly, a chair's intrinsic properties are those properties that can be described without reference to other chairs, for example, that the chair is brown, that its seat is two and a half feet high, that it can support 250 pounds. A chair's relational

properties, in contrast, are those properties whose description requires reference to other chairs, for example, that the chair is browner than others, that its seat is higher than others, that it can support more weight than others. Also very roughly, a direct passion arises immediately upon our perception of an object, as a result of an original instinct we possess, while indirect passions arise indirectly, as a result not only of the properties of the object but also of our ideas of other objects and the associations we draw (THN 2.1.1.4, 2.3.9.2). So to say that pride is inherently comparative is to say that pride is an indirect passion, not a direct one, and that it's caused by relational properties, not only by intrinsic ones. Judgments of secondary qualities (and Hutchesonian moral judgments), in sharp contrast, are based on direct passions (or, to be precise, judgments of secondary properties are based on direct original impressions; Hutchesonian moral judgments are based on direct secondary impressions [THN 2.1.1.2]) that are caused by intrinsic properties.

If we want to draw these points into closer connection with the contingency objection, we can express the same ideas in terms of possible worlds. In all possible worlds on which our original instincts remain the same (THN 2.3.9.2) and the intrinsic qualities of an object remain the same (albeit with the caveat offered in note 9), we will judge that the object is the same color. But there are possible worlds on which our original instincts remain the same and the intrinsic qualities of an object remain the same and yet we do not feel pride about an object that we do feel pride about on this world, and that's because on those possible worlds the object's relational properties are different, which difference alters the indirect passions (such as pride) that the object causes in us. All these points about Humean pride also hold, mutandis mutanda, for Humean beauty and Humean virtue.

9. It may be, however, that if the apple that is red on this world were placed on a world in which *everything* is red, we'd no longer judge it to be red. And if this is so, then there's a sense in which even our judgment that this apple is red is contingent on relational properties of the apple. I don't think, however, that this possibility is enough to make the Hutchesonian analogy something that Hume can use to answer the contingency objection. For pride and beauty will still be *much* more sensitive to comparison than redness. If the number of red things were to double or triple or quadruple, it would still produce in us the same perception of redness. But if objects we take to be beautiful or worthy of pride were to become twice or three times or four times as common, they would (according to Hume's view) no longer produce in us the impression that is the origin of our idea of pride.

10. Of course, Hume doesn't think that the judgment that a coarse daubing is beautiful is just as correct as the judgment that a Michelangelo masterpiece is beautiful. The judgment that the Michelangelo is beautiful, Hume believes, is correct, while the judgment that the coarse daubing is beautiful is incorrect. But that doesn't change the fact that Hume's account attributes a contingency to aesthetic judgment that judgments of secondary qualities don't possess. Hume's use of comparison still implies that accurate judges would judge a coarse daubing beautiful if they were on a world in which no one had ever painted anything more refined (maybe such a world is similar to ours in every way except for

the fact that there do not exist high-quality paints and brushes; or maybe it's the same as ours except for the fact that a genetic mutation has prevented a certain kind of painterly dexterity from ever developing), and would not judge the Sistine Chapel beautiful if most people could produce works as refined as those of Michelangelo. I will discuss similar issues concerning how comparison affects what counts as a correct judgment in the next section, where I consider the "steady and general points of view" from which we make moral judgments.

11. The first four pages of "The Standard of Taste" seem, for instance, to draw a close connection between morals and aesthetics (Taste 226–9). I should note, however, that "The Standard of Taste" was first published in 1757 (Essays xiv), which places it well after the other works I discuss here. So I cannot legitimately place a great deal of interpretative weight on "The Standard of Taste."

12. "Of the Dignity of Human Nature" was first published in 1741. Hume changed the title to "Of the Dignity or Meanness of Human Nature" in 1770. See Essays xii–xiii.

13. The one place Hume uses comparison in his account of artificial virtue is THN 3.2.10, where he argues that our judgment of the amount of time it takes for possession to turn into right depends on the comparisons we draw between how much time a particular thing has been possessed and how much time other things of a like nature have been possessed. This makes certain Humean judgments of ownership and governmental legitimacy contingent in a manner similar to the Humean judgments of natural virtue that I discuss in this section.

14. For a very interesting and comprehensive discussion of Hume's accounts of "greatness" and "goodness," and the relationship between the two, see Abramson (2002).

15. My interpretation here of the role of comparison conflicts with Baier's (Baier 1991, 207–9). According to Baier, Hume distinguishes between two kinds of pride: conceit, which is vicious and comparative, and proper pride, which is virtuous and non-comparative. Book II of the *Treatise* is concerned with conceit, but 3.3.2, according to Baier, is concerned with proper pride, which is something we feel for our own admirable qualities regardless of whether those qualities are common or rare.

Now Hume clearly does distinguish between "an over-weaning conceit of our own merit" and having "a value for ourselves, where we really have qualities that are valuable," and he also clearly thinks the former (which we can call "conceit") is "vicious and disagreeable," while the latter (which we can call proper pride) is "laudable" (THN 3.3.2.7–8). But I do not think the text supports Baier's belief that "proper pride" is non-comparative. I think, rather, that the person with proper pride is one who feels pride upon reflecting on a quality of his that really is unusually useful or agreeable, while a person with conceit is one who feels pride upon reflecting on a quality of his that is not unusually useful or agreeable. Imagine two authors, one of whom is truly great, the other of whom is a common hack whose writing is average at best. And imagine that each feels pride reflecting on his own work, and that each of them feels this pride because each of them believes his work to be unusually fine. The great writer has proper pride and the hack has conceit, but comparison plays a crucial role in the prideful feelings of both of them.

The reading of the last paragraph fits, in any event, with the account of pride in Book II, which is clearly comparative. And in 3.3.2 ("Of greatness of mind"), Hume explicitly refers back to his Book II account twice (3.3.2.4, 3.3.2.6) without ever saying that he is now developing a different conception of pride or is working with a new definition. In Book II, moreover, Hume discussed the relationship between pride and virtue (2.1.5., 2.1.7, 2.2.2), and he did not give any indication there that he was drawing a distinction between a non-comparative kind of pride that was properly connected to virtue and a comparative kind of pride that was not properly connected. In Book II, the argument moves seamlessly between discussion of how virtue causes pride to discussion of how things like riches, which are clearly comparative, cause pride (THN 2.2.2), as though the mechanisms are the same in both cases. Hume also mentions virtue's tendency to cause pride in the opening part of Book III (THN 3.1.2.5), in the midst of his argument for moral sentimentalism, and there is no mention of two kinds of pride (one comparative, one non-comparative) there either.

The examples of proper pride that Hume gives in "Of greatness of mind" also seem to be consistent with a comparative reading. He uses as an example, for instance, the pride of Alexander the Great, as evidenced by Alexander's saying to the soldiers who would not follow him to India: "go tell your countrymen, that you left Alexander compleating the conquest of the world" (THN 3.3.2.12). And it seems pretty clear that Alexander thinks that he possesses qualities that are unusually fine that set him apart from most men. Hume also discusses the heroic virtues that we "admire under the character of greatness" (THN 3.2.2.13) and men "of superior genius," and (as I say earlier) judgments of who possesses "greatness" and "superior genius" do seem to be inherently comparative.

As far as I can tell, Baier bases her interpretation on 3.3.2.7 of "Of greatness of mind" and I acknowledge that this paragraph, taken in isolation, can be read as disapproving of pride that is based on comparison and approving of pride that is non-comparative. But the overall context of the section implies that the object of disapproval in this paragraph is not comparative pride per se, but the outward expressions of pride that is based on faulty comparison. Hume is explaining our disapproval of people of average or below-average ability who are constantly trying to build themselves up by pointing out that they are better than someone else. Hume is not saying that the "man of sense and merit" has a kind of non-comparative pride. Hume is saying, rather, that such a man, who really is superior to the average person, does not need to constantly point out to others the ways in which he is superior. Such a man's pride is secure and stable, and so he does not need to work to try to convince himself and others of his superiority by constantly calling attention to the inferiority of someone else. A "fool," in contrast, is always working hard to convince himself and others that he is superior (which is hard to do because in fact he is not superior), and so he will constantly be pointing out the inferiority of someone else. The "foreign considerations" that do not play a role in the pride of the man of sense and merit but are necessary for the fool to keep in "good humour" are not mental comparisons per se but rather explicit statements of one's superiority to this or that particular person.

16. This point has been clearly noted and discussed by Sayre-McCord (1994) and C. Brown (1994).

17. The reading presented by Sayre-McCord (1994) of Hume's explanation of the general point of view is different from mine. According to Sayre-McCord, Hume argues that only the point of view of those in an agent's immediate vicinity can succeed in preventing people from coming into conflict with each other, where such conflict must be conceived of not as "verbal" contradiction but as a (very mild) kind of Hobbesian war. I think, however, that Sayre-McCord is too quick to dismiss the "verbal" reading of THN 3.3.1.15. For Hume stresses in this passage the way people talk to each other, not how they try to coordinate their actions with each other. And at THN 3.3.1.18, Hume stresses that judgments from the general point of view play a larger role in what we say than in how we act. I also think that Sayre-McCord's reason for rejecting the "verbal" reading is anachronistic, a feature of twentieth-century meta-ethics but not of eighteenth-century moral philosophy.

18. That is not to say that the intrinsic quality of tending to benefit those in one's immediate sphere of influence is necessarily not extraordinary. There is nothing in this intrinsic quality that implies that it is impossible that everyone or no one possessed it. What's necessarily not extraordinary – as well as necessarily not entirely ordinary – is the comparative quality of possessing the virtue of goodness. If the tendency to benefit those in one's immediate sphere of influence were possessed by virtually everyone or virtually no one, it would not elicit in us the impression that is the origin of our idea of goodness.

19. Color judgments do involve the privileging of one point of view over others: we privilege certain (normal) lighting conditions and certain (healthy) physical conditions. The impression we experience when we view an object in black light or when we're jaundiced is not supposed to determine our judgment of the object's color. But the point of view we privilege when making color judgments is not comparative in the way the point of view we privilege when making moral judgments is. The former point of view is contingent on certain light conditions being normal and certain physical conditions being healthy, but it's not contingent on certain colors being common or rare.

20. Blackburn maintains that Hume does not place much stake in the Hutchesonian analogy. According to Blackburn, Hume uses the analogy only "to reassure the reader that [morals'] place in the mind does not detract from the 'reality' of the properties, and this reassurance is clearly the main purpose of introducing the [analogy].... [Hume] is not at all saying: 'here is my full dress theory of virtue and vice: they are secondary properties,' but rather, 'you might be worried whether my full dress theory of virtue and vice, which places them in the mind, undermines enterprises of criticism and morality. But it does not do so, any more than the similar discovery about secondary qualities does.' For the purpose of reassuring his readers, he needs only a weak comparison, building on the one point of analogy that virtue and vice are in the mind, just as much as colours and the rest. He is merely using the analogy to make a local point" (Blackburn 1993, 274–5). The claim I make in this chapter is that Hume's use of comparison undermines even the "local point" to which Blackburn thinks Hume tries to put the analogy. But this claim is not incompatible with Blackburn's interpretation of THN 3.1.1.26. I agree that in this passage Hume does seem to be trying to make the local point Blackburn says he is trying to make. My claim is that the later parts of the *Treatise* undermine the point at 3.1.1.26.

Winkler (1996) and Sturgeon (2001) disagree with Blackburn's interpretation, however. They both maintain that the analogy was of considerable importance to Hume. To situate my claim in relation to Winkler and Sturgeon's, I need to distinguish between two aspects of the analogy: the negative and the positive. On the negative side, the analogy is supposed to advance the idea that moral distinctions do not originate in reason alone. On the positive side, the analogy is supposed to advance the idea that moral distinctions will continue to be just as "real" or of just as much "concern" to us even after we have discovered that they do not originate in reason alone.

My claim here is that Hume's use of comparison undermines the positive aspect of the analogy (even if Hume himself seems to want to advance the positive aspect at 3.1.1.26). But that does not imply that Hume could not have used the negative aspect of the analogy. Hume could have legitimately claimed that moral properties are like secondary qualities in that neither can be discovered by reason alone, even if there is also a disanalogy between Humean moral properties and secondary qualities (the former involve comparison in a way that the latter do not) that made it illegitimate for him to claim that since the contingency of colors does not diminish their importance to us, the contingency of moral properties should not diminish their importance to us either. So the main point I want to make about the analogy is not incompatible with much of what Winkler and Sturgeon say about the negative aspects of the analogy, especially as it applies to THN 3.1.1 and 3.1.2.

I do believe, however, that Sturgeon's lack of attention to comparison leads him to misinterpret other parts of the *Treatise*. Sturgeon suggests, for instance, that Hume analogizes beauty and wit to secondary qualities (Sturgeon 2001, 37). But as we saw earlier, Hume holds that our judgments of whether something has aesthetic merit and whether someone is witty are comparative in a way that judgments of secondary qualities are not, and this casts doubt on Sturgeon's suggestion that the analogy is implicit at 2.1.7.7, 2.1.8.2, and 2.1.8.6. Sturgeon also sometimes mistakenly foists the positive aspects of the analogy on Hume's view of morals. Sturgeon attributes to Hume, for instance, the view that "willful murder is vicious precisely because it is exercising the *power* it has, when contemplated, to produce a certain feeling in us" and says that this view is "faithful to [the] Lockean model" of secondary qualities (Sturgeon 2001, 16). But while THN 3.1.1 and 3.1.2 may on their own support such an interpretation, Hume's uses of comparison makes it misleading to say that a trait is virtuous or vicious because, like a Lockean secondary quality, it has the power "when contemplated, to produce a certain feeling in us." This is misleading because it suggests that what we are responding to when we morally judge an object is *only* a power that it has. But Hume's uses of comparison imply that other factors (i.e., the characteristics of other similar objects) also play a significant role – that the responses on which moral properties depend are inherently sensitive not merely to our original constitution and the powers in the object but also to the comparison class our past experiences have landed us with. And the resulting picture of moral judgment does not look to be "faithful to [the] Lockean model" of secondary qualities.

Sturgeon's lack of attention to comparison also leads him to find in Hume a non-skeptical position on moral knowledge that is not as clearly suggested by Hume's moral explanations as Sturgeon suggests. Sturgeon seems to think that we must attribute to Hume either a skeptical, expressivist position or a subjectivist, naturalistic position according to which moral judgments have the same kinds of truth conditions as judgments of secondary properties (Sturgeon 2001, 23). Sturgeon rejects the skeptical, expressivist reading and so opts for the subjectivist, naturalist reading, which is consistent with a non-skeptical view of moral knowledge (see Sturgeon 2001, 18–20, 36). My claim in this chapter implies, however, that even if Hume is not an expressivist, his account of moral judgment will still not be one according to which the truth conditions for moral judgment can be assimilated to the truth conditions for judgments of secondary properties. And the ways in which moral judgments differ from judgments of secondary properties (the latter are sensitive only to the nature of the object being judged and the constitution of the judger's sensory apparatus, while the former are sensitive not only to those two factors but also to the comparison class the judger's experience has landed her with) might make it more difficult to adopt the straightforwardly non-skeptical position on moral knowledge that Sturgeon claims to find in Hume.

21. Norton (1982), 137–44, Cohon (1997a), Abramson (1999), Sayre-McCord (1994), and Davie (1998) all do an excellent job of explaining how Hume's general points of view generally prevent contradictions in our moral judgments. But they do not show that Hume's general points of view prevent any and all such contradictions. I've tried to show that attention to Hume's uses of comparison and association strongly suggest that his account implies that at least some contradictions in moral judgment can continue to occur, even if agreement among people who successfully adopt a general point of view is the most common. For further discussion concerning the extent to which Hume's view might involve moral relativism, see Livingston (1984), 221–6, Siebert (1990), 183–6, and Herdt (1997), 117–67.

22. Hume owns up to the implications his account has for moral variability in "A Dialogue." In that essay, Hume argues that a few fundamental mental tendencies explain exceedingly wide moral variations, that the same general principles underlie very different particular moral judgments (Second Enquiry 191–2) (although a comparison of Second Enquiry 192 and 197–8 with Essays 227–9 suggests that Hume thought that these general principles were less substantive than most believe). He makes it clear, that is, that the same tendencies and principles lead people to make very different moral judgments about particular kinds of conduct. And, crucially, he never gives any indication that all of these differences will be resolved by scrupulous reflection or that there is any principled way of showing, in every case of variation in moral judgment, that one person's moral judgment is correct and another's is incorrect. Hume implies that about some morally significant matters, two very different judgments can both be equally consistent with the general principles underlying all human morality. Some examples of topics on which people could make different moral judgments that are equally consistent with the general moral principles are infanticide, punishment, the morality of how to resolve conflicts between personal liberty and fealty to the state, and the appropriateness of responding violently to verbal insults. Hume makes similar points about moral variation in the essay "Of National Characters." He says there that the value systems of most

people in one country can be quite different from the value systems of most people in another country (Essays 198–202). For an excellent discussion of "A Dialogue," see Abramson (1999).

23. In comments on an earlier draft of this chapter, Winkler made some extremely interesting and perceptive suggestions about why Hutcheson would have resisted using comparison in the account of morality. As Winkler put it, "No such comparativeness or experience-sensitivity figures in Hutcheson's account of moral judgment. It is interesting to ask why, and although I cannot offer a full answer here, I suspect that at least three things are at work: a suspicion of the kind of debunking explanations of moral judgments put forward for example by Mandeville (Hutcheson's worry perhaps being that acknowledging the comparativeness and experience-sensitivity of moral judgments comes uncomfortably close to admitting that they rest in the end on politics, fashion, custom, or education); his belief that benevolence is the whole of virtue (which makes the comparativeness of such alleged virtues as wit, wisdom, and greatness of mind irrelevant to his enterprise); and (a point closely related to the last) his very 'democratic' conviction that ordinary people are no less capable of virtue than great ones. As he says, no one is excluded by circumstances 'from the most heroick Virtue.' The greatest virtue – the greatest ratio of moral good to ability – can be found in anyone."

24. Hume goes on, moreover, to endorse one aspect of Shaftesbury and Hutcheson's Positive Answer, namely, their anti-egoist claim that humans are not ineluctably selfish (Dignity or Meanness 84–6). In early editions of the essay, Hume simply referred to Shaftesbury and Hutcheson's arguments against egoism without bothering to go into any detail (Dignity or Meanness 620). In later editions, he did add a bit more detail, pointing out that because we typically associate selfishness with vice and unselfishness with virtue, there's an important sense in which we can say that humans often manifest virtue or "dignity" – an important sense in which humans are not thoroughly vicious or "mean." But according to the Humean picture as I've described it, that we judge that most people are not thoroughly vicious does not constitute independent confirmation of the basic goodness of human nature. It merely reflects the structure of our moral judgment.

20. What Is a Humean Account, and What Difference Does It Make?

1. For discussion of the relationship between Humean "experiments" and contemporary empirical work in psychology and related disciplines, see Nichols (2004), 3–4.

2. I address the issue of whether Humean accounts debunk or undermine morality in more detail in Gill (1996b) and Gill (1998).

3. In 1744, the chair of moral philosophy at Edinburgh University became vacant. Hume, who had published Book III of his *Treatise* four years earlier, sought the post. But the Edinburgh Town Council, which controlled the professorships at the university, decided that he was unfit for the job. This decision was largely based (officially, at least) on what was said to be the moral perniciousness of the doctrines of the *Treatise* – on the charge that the *Treatise* destroyed the foundations of morality. For discussion of this episode, see Emerson (1984), Abramson (2001), Stewart (2001), M. Brown (2002), 169–73, and Moore (2002).

4. I am speaking here of Shaftesbury's teleological account of the reason to be virtuous. Shaftesbury's mental enjoyment account of the value of bearing one's own survey looks very similar to the Humean one I describe later. See Chapter 9 for discussion of the difference between these two accounts in Shaftesbury.

5. There is, however, one passage in the *Second Enquiry* in which Hume seems to suggest that an explanation of morality, no matter how scientifically accurate, should be silenced if it has the harmful consequence of causing people to lose confidence in morality. He writes, "And though the philosophical truth of any proposition by no means depends on its tendency to promote the interests of society; yet a man has but a bad grace, who delivers a theory, however true, which, he must confess, leads to a practice dangerous and pernicious. Why rake into those corners of nature which spread a nuisance all around? Why dig up the pestilence from the pit in which it is buried? The ingenuity of your researches may be admired, but your systems will be detested, and mankind will agree, if they cannot refute them, to sink them, at least, in eternal silence and oblivion. Truths which are *pernicious* to society, if any such there be, will yield to errors which are salutary and *advantageous*" (Second Enquiry 152–3). One could, I suppose, make heavy weather out of this passage, contending that it is an expression of something very important to Hume's view of moral philosophy. To my ear, however, this passage sounds a bit offhand. I would, in any event, question how seriously Hume took the possibility that there could be some truth that ought to yield to error. I would, that is, want to emphasize the phrase "if any such there be" in the last sentence, and would point to his statement that "the philosophical truth of any proposition by no means depends on its tendency to promote the interests of society." I would question whether any similar passage could be found in the *Treatise* (the most obvious candidate is 3.3.6, which I discuss in note 2 in Chapter 15). I would also say that even if Hume did mean to contend that there was something wrong with an explanation, however accurate, that implied an uncomfortable truth, I still don't think that we should take the possibility that Hume's explanation undermines morality to be an objection to the explanation qua explanation.

6. I think I can make the main point of this paragraph more clear by explaining how a defender of Hume could respond to Korsgaard's objection. Korsgaard's objection is based the following story:

> Now let us consider a slightly more attractive version of Hume's sensible knave. Our knave is the lawyer for a rich client who has recently died, leaving his money to medical research. In going through the client's papers the lawyer discovers a will of more recent date, made without the lawyer's help but in due form, leaving the money instead to the client's worthless nephew, who will spend it all on beer and comic books. The lawyer could easily suppress this new will, and she is tempted to do so. She is also a student of Hume, and believes the theory of the virtues that we find in the *Treatise of Human Nature*. So what does she say to herself? (Korsgaard 1996, 86)

The lawyer realizes that she would disapprove of herself if she suppressed the will since "she hates unjust actions and the people who perform them." But

> she also knows that her distaste for such actions is caused by their general tendency, not their actual effects. As Hume has shown, our moral sentiments are influenced by "general rules." And our lawyer knows that this particular unjust action will have no actual effects

but good ones. It will not bring down the system of justice, and it will bring much needed money to medical research. (Korsgaard 1996, 86–7)

Because of her sympathy with other people, the lawyer disapproves of injustice, since it harms society. Why then does she disapprove of destroying the will, which would only help others? She disapproves, according to Hume's account, because her sentiments are subject to the "general rules" principle of association whereby one tends to feel the same way about all things that resemble each other, even if some of those things are crucially different. In this case, destroying the will resembles all the unjust acts that are actually harmful to society even though the particular act will in fact benefit society. Her disapproval of destroying the will, in other words, results from her mind's tendency to *over*generalize, that is, to lump together cases that bear a surface resemblance but are really disparate.

Once the lawyer comes to believe this explanation of her disapproval, however, the legitimacy of the disapproval will be undermined in her own eyes. It is, Korsgaard says, "almost inconceivable" that Hume's explanation will not cause the lawyer to think that her disapproval is "in this case, poorly grounded, and therefore in a sense irrational" (Kosgaard 1996, 87).

What will the lawyer do now? One of two things. She will either ignore her disapproval and destroy the will, which would be unjust. Or she will find herself compelled to reveal the will's contents because, her belief in Hume's explanation notwithstanding, "she cannot destroy a valid will without intense feelings of humility or self-hatred" (Korsgaard 1996, 88). But even in the second case, in which she ends up performing the just act, "there will have been normative failure" (Korsgaard 1996, 88). For the lawyer will no longer believe that the claims her disapproval makes on her are "well-grounded." The lawyer's disapproval, as Korsgaard sees it, will no longer be normative, because once she understands what its basis is, she will think that it ought to lose its influence over her.

I think, however, that Korsgaard overreaches in telling this story. For it is far from clear that every lawyer who becomes convinced of Hume's account will either destroy the will or come to think that her disapproval of destroying the will is ill-grounded. It seems to me plausible that at least some who become convinced of Hume's account will continue to judge that destroying the will is wrong, and that they will continue to have just as much confidence in that judgment as they did before. A Humean lawyer could give as reasons such things as: destroying the will would be a betrayal of my client; or destroying the will would be a violation of my duties as a lawyer; or I would hate myself if I destroyed the will. And if someone pointed out that all these reasons can be explained by various associative principles of the mind, she might very well respond, "Yes, that's all very interesting, but it doesn't change anything. They are still conclusive reasons for not destroying the will."

I do not mean to suggest that explanations of our responses never do or never should affect our attitude toward those responses. An explanation of why I find something funny, beautiful, or virtuous may result in my deciding that the thing in question is not really funny, beautiful, or virtuous after all. But then again, it might not. Explaining is not always explaining away.

In response, Korsgaard might claim that if the lawyer really is convinced of Hume's account but doesn't feel any differently about her disapproval, then it would have to be the case that she is not engaging in honest philosophical reflection. The lawyer, so this charge might go, must be guilty of a kind of split-personality thinking. Even though she believes Hume's account, she does not attend to it when she is considering what she ought to do. It is as though she thinks with one mind about the Humean account of morality and with another when deciding whether to destroy the will. But for how long and on what basis could Korsgaard insist on this charge? What if the lawyer assured us that she *was* considering both things at once but still thought she ought to expose the will? Would Korsgaard eventually have to maintain that the lawyer was lying? Korsgaard's view of the "reflective structure of human consciousness" implies that such a reaction on the part of the lawyer is "inconceivable." On this point, however, I think a cautious observation of human life gives more support to Hume than to Korsgaard. Some people, it is true, may lose normative confidence in a moral judgment if they come to believe that it is caused by associative principles. But others will not. And if some people who believe the Humean associative account of a moral judgment (or some naturalistic descendant of it) do not lose confidence in that judgment, then Korsgaard's worry about Humean explanations begins to look less like a universal truth about the structure of consciousness and more like a description of one of the many different views of morality some humans have developed.

I acknowledge, however, that if a Humean lawyer became absolutely convinced that the consequences of destroying a will truly would be wholly beneficial, then it is possible (but not necessary) that she might decide that she ought to destroy it. But it's not at all clear to me that this result constitutes a criticism of anything in Hume or even that it's such a bad thing in its own right. Judgments that are overturned in the light of true explanations and perfect knowledge of all relevant future events are probably ones that ought to be overturned. In real-life cases, however, one is never absolutely certain of all the future consequences of one's action. And this inescapable everyday uncertainty will usually bolster a Humean's confidence in moral habits born of general rules, not weaken it.

I also acknowledge that it's possible (but, again, not necessary) that the Humean lawyer will be thrown into a kind of crisis by her discovery of the will, that she will find herself forced to choose between two courses of action without having any confidence that she ought to follow one rather than the other. But this crisis need not cause her to lose confidence in morality as a whole. The decision about what to do with the will, the lawyer may think, is one of those isolated wrenching problems with no satisfactory solution. That there is one insoluble problem, however, does not imply that all problems are insoluble or that all solutions are illusory. Most of the time, the lawyer has found satisfactory solutions. She has been confident about what she ought to do. The judgment that she ought to execute her other clients' last wills, for instance, will not be undermined by her doubts about the will of the one rich client with an unfortunate fondness for a comic-loving, beer-swilling nephew.

7. I think the Humean point of 5 is plausible, at least for many people, because I think the possibility of losing confidence in morality as a whole is rather remote

for many people. I think, that is, that it is reasonable for Humeans to maintain that morality as a whole is much more firmly entrenched in the psyches of many people than is any meta-ethical commitment about what justifies morality as a whole.

The reason some critics might initially think Humeanism is more dangerous to our commitment to morality as a whole is that they might think that losing confidence in morality as a whole is really not that different from losing confidence in a particular moral judgment. We are all familiar with the experience of coming to reject a moral judgment that we once accepted. Losing confidence in morality as a whole, it might then seem, would involve the same kind of thing, albeit on a more global scale. But the loss of confidence in morality as a whole cannot be so easily assimilated to the garden variety loss of confidence in a particular moral judgment. For when we come to reject a particular moral judgment we once accepted, we usually do so because of some other moral judgment that we currently accept. Indeed, the rejection of a particular moral judgment is often best thought of as a particular moral judgment itself. Consider, for instance, Korsgaard's lawyer, who, after learning that her disapproval of destroying a particular will is due only to her tendency to be influenced by general rules, decides that she should destroy the will after all because doing so will benefit many people (Korsgaard 1996, 86–7). In this case, the lawyer's rejection of one moral judgment (she should execute the will) is in fact the affirmation of another moral judgment (she should destroy the will). The lawyer has not lost confidence in morality as a whole; she has not come to think that normativity does not exist. She is still morally and normatively engaged. What has changed is her view about what is moral or normative in this particular case.

Someone suffering the kind of crisis critics of Humeanism fear will, in contrast, have lost confidence in moral judgment in general. She will have come to think that there are no good reasons to act one way rather than any other. She will come to think that all her practical judgments are equally arbitrary. What will such a person look like?

One picture we might have is of someone who has come to view all her moral judgments in a new and disturbing way. Let us say, for instance, that a person used to think that her moral judgments had some particular feature, such as being grounded in rationally necessary truth or being based on an original principle of human nature, whereas after reading Hume she has come to think they do not. Let us also say that she finds the fact that her moral judgments lack this feature highly disturbing and that coming to an awareness of this fact makes her feel as though the rug has been pulled out from under her, as though what she thought was solid ground beneath her feet is really nothing but thin air. Such an experience could signal a shift in this person's view of things, but it should not be seen as a loss of confidence in morality unless it also involves a significant alteration in the way she judges actions and conducts herself. If she gets a panicky feeling every time she reflects on the Humean origins of morality but nonetheless proceeds to make more or less the same judgments and conduct herself in a more or less similar way, then it looks as though she is still morally engaged. It appears that morality is still functioning in the same way in her life. What has changed is her theoretical understanding of her practice of morality;

she has lost confidence in a meta-ethical view she used to hold. But since her judgments and conduct remain pretty much the same, it seems empty to claim that she has lost confidence in the actual practice of morality. In claiming that belief in a Humean account will precipitate a global moral crisis, Hume's critics are committed to holding that belief in a Humean account will cause a significant alteration in the way a person judges actions and conducts herself. Hume's critics cannot rely simply on the panicky feeling that coming to believe in Humeanism may cause in some people.

What would count as a significant alteration in judgments and conduct? What would characterize someone suffering a global moral crisis, the breakdown of normativity as a whole? The answer may be that such a person would cease to engage in a great many activities that she used to think worthwhile and begin to engage in a great many activities that she used to think immoral. Perhaps, for instance, such a person would cease working for all the causes to which she used to devote a great deal of time and begin to lie and steal even though she had never lied or stolen before. It is only such dire consequences that could truly signal a global normative crisis, only such a radical result that would indicate that someone who once had confidence in morality no longer does so. Anything less dire or radical might signal only that the person has now come to make different moral judgments than she did before or that she now accepts a different explanation of her practices, although she nonetheless remains committed to these practices.

But once we realize how extreme a global moral crisis or full-scale normative breakdown is, it seems to me to be very implausible to hold that belief in a Humean account will produce such a thing in every honestly reflective human being. Some people may suffer such a crisis or breakdown, just as some theists have suffered after coming to believe that God does not exist. But other people will not. Other people will be able to accept a Humean account while continuing to be just as morally engaged as they were before. And I don't see any reason for thinking that all of these people are guilty of some kind of split-personality thinking or are confused about what they themselves believe. I cannot give a knockdown argument for this point. All I can do is ask you to consider the typically morally engaged people you know and to ask yourself whether it is plausible to think that their conduct would veer drastically away from what is morally acceptable if they became convinced of a Humean account. If it seems implausible that their conduct would change in this way – or, even more powerfully, if you believe there are some actual people who appear both to believe a Humean account and to act well within the moral ballpark – then we must conclude that worries about Humeanism's undermining morality as a whole in the eyes of many people are implausible as well.

8. For helpful accounts of Hume's life and character, see Mossner (1954), Stewart (2001, 2005), Buchan (2003), and Wright (2003).

9. An issue that I have elided in this chapter is the difference between the question of whether a person *will* lose confidence in morality on coming to believe a Humean account and the question of whether a person *should* lose confidence in morality on coming to believe a Humean account. Some who have raised the undermining or debunking worry might claim that I have focused only on the

first question but that what they are concerned with – what is of real importance –
is the second. Such people may hold that there is a fact as to whether morality
is or is not justifiable or normative on the assumption of the truth of a Humean
account, and that that fact is distinct from how any particular person responds
to morality after coming to believe a Humean account. On this way of thinking,
whether a person will continue to act morally engaged on coming to believe a
Humean account is merely a *predictive* question. But what's really philosophically
important is the *justificatory* question of whether such a person has or does not
have rationally defensible grounds for thinking that morality is normative.

The first thing a Humean could say in response to worries about this so-called
justificatory question is that if this issue really is independent of the question of
what people do or say on coming to believe a Humean account, then it is fair to
wonder whether it is of much importance. Such a question might be in danger
of becoming neither practical nor theoretical but merely academic.

But secondly and more significantly, the justificatory and predictive questions
turn out not to be so separate after all. The worry at issue is whether Humean
accounts turn out to be error theories. Now if an account of morality is an error
theory, then that account must deny something (e.g., that morality has a rational foundation and that that rational foundation is what justifies morality) that
is essential to our conception of morality. But how can we determine whether
something is essential to our conception of morality rather than being simply
something that a lot of us believe about morality but that is not essential to our
conception of it? In order to distinguish between something's being essential
to our conception of morality and something's being merely a common belief
about morality, we must look to how people conduct themselves, or would conduct themselves, on coming to think that that thing is no longer true. If people
abandon or drastically alter their moral commitments and practices on coming
to think that the thing is false, then we are warranted in concluding that the
thing was essential to their conception of morality. But if people do not abandon
or drastically alter their moral commitments and practices on coming to think
the thing is false, then we must conclude that the thing was not essential to their
conception of morality. (When people came to think that supernatural curses
did not exist, they stopped hunting down witches, which gives us grounds for
concluding that casting supernatural curses was an essential part of their conception of witches; but when people came to think that not all swans were white, they
did not change in any significant way how they conducted themselves or spoke
with regard to swans, which gives us grounds for concluding that being white
was not an essential part of their conception of swans.) The *justificatory* question
cannot be disengaged from the *predictive* one. For in order to determine whether
morality is justified, we first have to determine what our conception of morality
consists of. And to determine what our conception of morality consists of, we
have to consider (or predict) how people would act on coming to believe or
disbelieve certain things. The distinctive Humean claim of 5, moreover, is that
many people have not and would not abandon or drastically alter their moral
commitments and practices on coming to believe a Humean account. If this is
true, it gives us grounds for holding that what Humean accounts deny is not an
essential aspect of many people's conception of morality. And we may therefore

conclude that Humean accounts are not error theories. (For wonderfully lucid discussion of these issues, see Blackburn 1985 and Tiberius 2000, 2002.)

That is not to say that Humean accounts wouldn't convict *anyone*'s conception of morality of error. It's entirely possible that some people do hold a conception of morality that is such that if they came to believe a Humean account, they would abandon or drastically alter their moral commitments and practices. For instance, someone (e.g., Dostoyevsky's Raskolnokov) may think that if God does not exist everything is permitted, then come to think that God does not exist, and then change his life in all sorts of exceedingly drastic ways. But what 5 claims is that many people are such that coming to believe a Humean account will not have such a drastic effect on them (even if it might lead them to change some of their judgments and practices in nontrivial ways). Humean accounts may be incompatible with some conceptions of morality, but I do not think all of us hold conceptions of morality with which Humean accounts are incompatible.

Bibliography

Primary Sources

Balguy, John (1976) *The Foundation of Moral Goodness*, facsimile of 1728–9 edition. New York and London: Garland. I refer to this work as "Balguy 1976," with the first (roman) numeral denoting the volume number and the second (arabic) numeral denoting the page number.

Birch, Thomas (1845) "An Account of the Life and Writings of Ralph Cudworth, DD.," in Ralph Cudworth, *The True Intellectual System of the Universe*. London: T. Tegg. I refer to this work as "Birch."

Burnet, Gilbert and Hutcheson, Francis (1971) "Letters between the Late Mr. Gilbert Burent, and Mr. Hutchinson, concerning the true Foundation of Virtue or Moral Goodness," in Bernard, Peach (ed.), *Illustrations on the Moral Sense*. Cambridge, MA: Belknap Press. I refer to this work as "Burnet vs. Hutcheson."

Butler, Joseph (1896) *The Works of Joseph Butler: Volume II: Sermons, etc.* New York: Macmillan. I refer to this work as "Butler."

Cudworth, Ralph (1642) *The Union of the Christ and the Church; in a Shadow*. London: Richard Bishop. I refer to this work as "Union."

Cudworth, Ralph (1664) *A Sermon preached to the Honourable Society of Lincolnes-Inne*. London: J. Flesher. I refer to this work as "Lincolnes."

Cudworth, Ralph (1968) "Sermon Preached before the Honorable House of Commons at Westminster, March 31, 1647" in Gerald R. Cragg (ed.), *The Cambridge Platonists*: 369–407. Oxford: Oxford University Press. I refer to this work as "Commons."

Cudworth, Ralph (1996) *A Treatise concerning Eternal and Immutable Morality with A Treatise of Freewill*. Edited by Sarah Hutton. Cambridge: Cambridge University Press. I refer to this work as "EIM."

Cudworth, Ralph (undated) *Manuscripts on freedom of the will*. British Library, Additional Manuscripts, 4978–82. I refer to these manuscripts as "Cudworth ms," with the page number following.

Hobbes, Thomas (1994) *Leviathan*. Edited by Edwin Curley. Indianapolis: Hackett. I refer to this work as "Hobbes."

Hume, David (1932) *The Letters of David Hume*, Volume 1. Edited by J. Y. T. Greig. Oxford: Oxford University Press. I refer to this work as "Letters."

Hume, David (1967) *A Letter from a Gentleman to his friend in Edinburgh.* Edited by Ernest C. Mossner and John V. Price. Edinburgh: Edinburgh University Press.

Hume, David (1987) *Essays, Moral, Political, and Literary.* Edited by Eugene F. Miller. Indianapolis: Liberty Classics. I refer to this work as "Essays."

Hume, David (1987) "Of the Dignity or Meanness of Human Nature," in Hume's *Essays,* 80–6. I refer to this work as "Dignity or Meanness."

Hume, David (1987) "Of the Standard of Taste," in Hume's *Essays,* 226–49. I refer to this work as "Taste."

Hume, David (1998) *An Enquiry concerning the Principles of Morals.* Edited by Tom L. Beauchamp. Oxford and New York: Oxford University Press. I refer to this work as "Second Enquiry."

Hume, David (2002) *A Treatise of Human Nature.* Edited by David Fate Norton and Mary J. Norton. Oxford: Oxford University Press. I refer to this work as "THN," with the numerals following denoting book, part, section, and paragraph.

Hutcheson, Francis (1725) *An Inquiry into the Original of our Ideas of Beauty and Virtue.* London: J. Darby. I refer to this work as "Beauty and Virtue [1st ed.]."

Hutcheson Francis (1726) *An Inquiry into the Original of our Ideas of Beauty and Virtue,* 2nd ed. London: J. Darby. I refer to this work as "Beauty and Virtue."

Hutcheson, Francis (1728) *An Essay on the Conduct of the Passions and Affections with Illustrations on the Moral Sense.* London: J. Darby. Reprinted in facsimile edition, 1971, by Hildesheim: Georg Olms Verlagsbuchhandlung. I refer to the first part of this work as "Passions and Affections" and to the second part as "Moral Sense."

Hutcheson, Francis (1753) *An Inquiry into the Original of our Ideas of Beauty and Virtue,* 5th ed. London: J. Darby. I refer to this work as "Beauty and Virtue [5th ed.]."

Hutcheson, Francis, (1971) *Illustrations on the Moral Sense,* 2nd ed. Edited by Bernard Peach. Cambridge, MA: Cambridge University Press. I refer to this work as "Moral Sense [2nd ed]."

Locke, John (1975) *An Essay concerning Human Understanding.* Edited by Peter H. Nidditch. Oxford: Oxford University Press.

Mandeville, Bernard (1924) *The Fable of the Bees,* edited by F. B. Kaye in two volumes, originally published Oxford: Clarendon Press. Reissued Indianapolis: Liberty Classics, 1988. I refer to this work as "Mandeville," with the first (roman) numeral following denoting the volume number and the second (arabic) numeral denoting the page number.

Mill, John Stuart (1979) *Utilitarianism.* Edited by George Sher. Indianapolis: Hackett.

More, Henry (1930) *Enchiridion Ethicum, The English Translation of 1690,* translated by Edward Southwell, reproduced from the first edition by the Facsimile Text Society of New York, 1930. I refer to this work as "More." The book is preceded by an "Epistle to his Reader," which has no page numbers.

Perkins, William (1970) *The Work of William Perkins.* Introduced and edited by Ian Breward. Appleford, Abingdon, Berkshire: Sutton Courtenay Press. I refer to this work as "Perkins."

Plato (1992) *The Republic.* Translated by G. M. A. Grube; revised by C. D. C. Reeve. Indianapolis: Hackett. I refer to this work as "Plato."

Price, Richard (1948) *A Review of the Principal Questions in Morals.* Oxford: Oxford University Press. I refer to this work as "Price."

Raphael, D. D. (1991) *British Moralists 1650–1800,* Volume I. Indianapolis: Hackett.

Shaftesbury, Anthony Ashley Cooper, 3rd Earl of (1751) "Preface" in Benjamin Whichcote, *The Works*, Volume III: i–xii. Aberdeen: J. Chalmers. Reprinted New York and London: Garland, 1977. I refer to this work as "Preface."

Shaftesbury, Anthony Ashley Cooper, 3rd Earl of (1900) *The Life, Unpublished Letters, and Philosophical Regimen of Anthony, Earl of Shaftesbury*. Edited by Benjamin Rand. London: Swan Sonnenschein. I refer to this work as "Regimen."

Shaftesbury, Anthony Ashley Cooper, 3rd Earl of (1977) *An Inquiry concerning Virtue, or Merit, with an introduction, a selection of material from Toland's 1699 edition and a bibliography*. Edited by David Walford. Manchester: Manchester University Press. I refer to this work as "Virtue or Merit [1st ed.]."

Shaftesbury, Anthony Ashley Cooper, 3rd Earl of (2001) *Characteristics of Men, Manners, Opinions, Times*. Edited by Douglas Den Uyl. Indianapolis: Liberty Fund. I refer to this work as "Characteristics," with the first (roman) numeral following denoting the volume number and the second (arabic) numeral denoting the page number.

Shaftesbury, Anthony Ashley Cooper, 3rd Earl of (2001) "An Inquiry concerning Virtue or Merit," in Characteristics II 1–100. I refer to this work as "Virtue or Merit."

Shaftesbury, Anthony Ashley Cooper, 3rd Earl of (2001) "The Moralists; a Philosophical Rhapsody," in Characteristics II 101–247. I refer to this work as "Moralists."

Shaftesbury, Anthony Ashley Cooper, 3rd Earl of (2001) "Miscellaneous Reflections on the Said Treatises, and Other Critical Subjects," in Characteristics III 1–209. I refer to this work as "Reflections."

Whichcote, Benjamin (1751) *The Works*. London: J. Chalmers. Reprinted New York: Garland, 1977. I refer to this work as "Whichcote," with the first (roman) numeral denoting the volume number and the second (arabic) numeral denoting the page number.

Whichcote, Benjamin (1930) *Moral and Religious Aphorisms*. Edited with an introduction by W. R. Inge. London: Elkin Mathews & Marrot. I refer to this work as "Aphorisms," with the numeral following denoting the number assigned to the aphorism quoted.

Secondary Sources

Abramson, Kate (1999) "Correcting 'Our' Sentiments about Hume's Moral Point of View," *Southern Journal of Philosophy* 37: 333–61.

Abramson, Kate (2001) "Sympathy and the Project of Hume's Second Enquiry," *Archiv für Geschichte der Philosophie* 83: 45–80.

Abramson, Kate (2002) "Two Portraits of the Humean Moral Agent," *Pacific Philosophical Quarterly* 83: 301–34.

Ainslie, Donald C. (1995) "The Problem of the National Self in Hume's Theory of Justice," *Hume Studies* 21: 289–313.

Baier, Annette (1991) *A Progress of Sentiments: Reflections on Hume's Treatise*. Cambridge, MA: Harvard University Press.

Baron, Marcia (1982) "Hume's Noble Lie: An Account of His Artificial Virtues," *Canadian Journal of Philosophy* 12: 539–55.

Batson, D. (1991) *The Altruism Question*. Hillsdale, NJ: Laurence Erlbaum.

Beauchamp, T. L. and Rosenberg, A. (1981) *Hume and the Problem of Causation*. Oxford: Clarendon Press.

Beiser, Frederick C. (1996) *The Sovereignty of Reason: The Defense of Rationality in the Early English Enlightenment*. Princeton, NJ: Princeton University Press.

Bishop, John D. (1996) "Moral Motivation and the Development of Francis Hutcheson's Philosophy," *Journal of the History of Ideas* 57: 277–95.

Blackburn, Simon (1985) "Errors and the Phenomenology of Value," in Ted Honderich (ed.), *Morality and Objectivity*. London: Routledge and Kegan Paul.

Blackburn, Simon (1993) "Hume on the Mezzanine Level," *Hume Studies* 19: 273–88.

Blackburn, Simon (1998) *Ruling Passions*. Oxford: Oxford University Press.

Brown, Charlotte (1988) "Is Hume an Internalist?" *Journal of the History of Philosophy* 26: 69–87.

Brown, Charlotte (1994) "From Spectator to Agent: Hume's Theory of Obligation," *Hume Studies* 20: 19–36.

Brown, Michael (2002) *Francis Hutcheson in Dublin, 1719–1730*. Dublin: Four Courts Press.

Buchan, James (2003) *Crowded with Genius: The Scottish Enlightenment: Edinburgh's Moment of the Mind*. New York: HarperCollins.

Cameron, James K. (1982) "Theological Controversy: A Factor in the Origins of the Scottish Enlightenment," in R. H. Campbell and Andrew S. Skinner (eds.), *The Origins and Nature of the Scottish Enlightenment*. Edinburgh: John Donald.

Carey, Daniel (1997) "Method, Moral Senses, and the Problem of Diversity: Francis Hutcheson and the Scottish Enlightenment," *British Journal for the History of Philosophy* 5: 275–96.

Carey, Daniel (2000) "Hutcheson's Moral Sense and the Problem of Innateness," *Journal of the History of Philosophy* 38: 103–10.

Cassirer, Ernst (1953) *The Platonic Renaissance in England*. Austin: University of Texas Press.

Cohon, Rachel (1997a) "Hume's Difficulty with the Virtue of Honesty," *Hume Studies* 23: 91–112.

Cohon, Rachel (1997b) "Is Hume a Noncognitivist in the Motivation Argument?" *Philosophical Studies* 85: 251–66.

Cohon, Rachel (2001) "The Shackles of Virtue: Hume on Allegiance to Government," *History of Philosophy Quarterly* 18: 393–413.

Cohon, Rachel and Owen, David (1997) "Hume on Representation, Reason and Motivation, *Manuscrito* 1997: 47–76.

Coward, Barry (1994) *The Stuart Age: England 1603–1714*. London and New York: Longman.

Cragg, G. R. (1968) *The Cambridge Platonists*. Oxford: Oxford University Press.

Craig, Edward J. (1987) *The Mind of God and the Works of Man*. Oxford: Clarendon Press.

Darwall, Stephen (1994) "Hume and the Invention of Utilitarianism," in M. A. Stewart and J. W. Wright (eds.), *Hume and Hume's Connexions*: 58–82. Edinburgh: Edinburgh University Press.

Darwall, Stephen (1995) *The British Moralists and the Internal 'Ought'*. Cambridge: Cambridge University Press.

Darwall, Stephen (1997) "Hutcheson on Practical Reason," *Hume Studies* 23: 73–89.

Davie, William (1998) "Hume's General Point of View," *Hume Studies* 24: 275–94.

Emerson, Roger L. (1984) "Conjectural History and Scottish Philosophers," *Historical Papers 1984*: 63–90. Ottawa: Canadian Historical Association.

Emerson, Roger L. (1994) "The 'Affair' at Endiburgh and the 'Project' at Glasgow: The Politics of Hume's Attempts to Become a Professor," in M. A. Stewart and J. P. Wright (eds), *Hume and Hume's Connexions*: 1–22. Edinburgh: Edinburgh University Press.

Feiser, James (1997) "Hume's Motivational Distinction between Natural and Artificial Virtues," *British Journal of the History of Philosophy* 5: 373–88.

Frankel, Lois (1989) "Damaris Cudworth Masham: A Seventeenth Century Feminist Philosopher," *Hypatia* 4: 80–90.

Frankena, William (1955) "Hutcheson's Moral Sense Theory," *Journal of the History of Ideas* 16: 356–75.

Garrett, Don (1997) *Cognition and Commitment in Hume's Philosophy*. New York: Oxford University Press.

Gauthier, David (1979) "David Hume, Contractarian," *Philosophical Review* 88: 3–38.

Gauthier, David (2001) "Hobbes: The Laws of Nature," *Pacific Philosophical Quarterly* 82: 258–84.

Gill, Michael B. (1995) "Nature and Association in the Moral Theory of Francis Hutcheson," *History of Philosophy Quarterly* 12: 281–301.

Gill, Michael B. (1996a) "Fantastick Associations and Addictive General Rules: A Fundamental Difference between Hutcheson and Hume," *Hume Studies* 22: 23–48.

Gill, Michael B. (1996b) "A Philosopher in his Closet: Reflexivity and Justification in Hume's Moral Theory," *Canadian Journal of Philosophy* 26: 231–56.

Gill, Michael B. (1998) "On the Alleged Incompatability between Sentimentalism and Moral Confidence," *History of Philosophy Quarterly* 15: 411–40.

Gill, Michael B. (1999) "The Religious Rationalism of Benjamin Whichcote," *Journal of the History of Philosophy* 27: 271–300.

Gill, Michael B. (2000a) "Hume's Progressive View of Human Nature," *Hume Studies* 26: 87–108.

Gill, Michael B. (2000b). "Shaftesbury's Two Accounts of the Reason to Be Virtuous," *Journal of the History of Philosophy* 38: 529–48.

Gill, Michael B. (2004) "Rationalism, Sentimentalism, and Ralph Cudworth," *Hume Studies* 30: 149–81.

Grean, Stanley (1964) "Introduction" to Anthony Ashley Cooper, 3rd Earl of Shaftesbury, *Characteristics of Men, Manners, Opinions, Times*. Edited by J. M. Robertson. Indianapolis and New York: Bobbs-Merrill.

Grean, Stanley (1967) *Shaftesbury's Philosophy of Religion and Ethics*. Athens: Ohio University Press.

Griffin, Martin I. J. (1992) *Latitudinarianism in the Seventeenth-Century Church of England*. Leiden and New York: E. J. Brill.

Haakonssen, Knud (1981) *The Science of a Legislator*. Cambridge: Cambridge University Press.

Hampton, Jean (1986) *Hobbes and the Social Contract Tradition*. Cambridge: Cambridge University Press.

Harrison, Jonathan (1976) *Hume's Moral Epistemology*. Oxford: Clarendon Press.

Hearn, Thomas K. (1970) "'General Rules' in Hume's Treatise," *Journal of the History of Philosophy* 8: 405–22.

Hearn, Thomas K. (1976) "General Rules and the Moral Sentiments in Hume's Treatise," *Review of Metaphysics* 30: 57–77.

Herdt, Jennifer (1997) *Religion and Faction in Hume's Moral Philosophy*. Cambridge: Cambridge University Press.

Hill, Christopher (1972) *The World Turned Upside Down*. New York: Viking Press.

Hutton, Sarah (1993) "Damaris Cudworth, Lady Masham: Between Platonism and Enlightenment," *British Journal for the History of Philosophy* 1: 29–54.

Kail, P. J. E. (2001) "Hutcheson's Moral Sense: Skepticism, Realism, and Secondary Qualities," *History of Philosophy Quarterly* 18: 57–77.

Kemp Smith, Norman (1941) *The Philosophy of David Hume*. London: Macmillan.

Kivy, Peter (2003) *The Seventh Sense*. Oxford: Oxford University Press.

Klein, Lawrence E. (1999) "Introduction" to Anthony Ashley Cooper, 3rd Earl of Shaftesbury, *Characteristics of Men, Manners, Opinions, Times*. Edited by Lawrence E. Klein. Cambridge: Cambridge University Press.

Korsgaard, Christine (1986) "Skepticism about Practical Reason," *Journal of Philosophy* 83: 5–25.

Korsgaard, Christine (1996) *The Sources of Normativity*. Cambridge: Cambridge University Press.

Lamprecht, Sterling P. (1926) "Innate Ideas in the Cambridge Platonists," *Philosophical Review* 35: 553–73.

Livingston, Donald W. (1984) *Hume's Philosophy of Common Life*. Chicago: University of Chicago Press.

MacIntyre, Alasdair (1988) *Whose Justice? Which Rationality?* Notre Dame, IN: University of Notre Dame Press.

Mackie, J. L. (1980) *Hume's Moral Theory*. London: Routledge & Kegan Paul.

McCormick, Miriam (1993) "Hume on Natural Belief and Original Principles," *Hume Studies* 19: 103–16.

Millgram, Elijah (1995) "Was Hume a Humean?", *Hume Studies* 21: 75–93.

Moore, James (1990) "The Two Systems of Francis Hutcheson: On the Origins of the Scottish in Enlightenment," in M. A. Stewart (ed.), *Studies in the Philosophy of the Scottish Enlightenment*: 37–59. New York: Oxford University Press.

Moore, James (1994) "Hume and Hutcheson," in M. A. Stewart and J. W. Wright (eds.), *Hume and Hume's Connexions*: 23–57. Edinburgh: Edinburgh University Press.

Moore, James (2002) "Utility and Humanity: The Quest for the Honestum in Cicero, Hutcheson, and Hume," *Utilitas* 14: 365–86.

Mortensen, Preban (1995) "Francis Hutcheson and the Problem of Conspicuous Consumption," *Journal of Aesthetics and Art Criticism* 53: 155–65.

Mossner, Ernest Cambell (1954) *The Life of David Hume*. Edinburgh: Thomas Nelson. (Reissued in a 2nd ed. in 1980 by Oxford: Clarendon Press.)

Nichols, Shaun (2004) *Sentimental Rules*. New York: Oxford University Press.

Norton, David Fate (1982) *David Hume: Common-Sense Moralist, Sceptical Metaphysician*. Princeton, NJ: Princeton University Press.

Norton, David Fate (1985) "Hutcheson's Moral Realism," *Journal of the History of Philosophy* 23: 397–418.

Norton, David Fate (1993a) "More Evidence That Hume Wrote the Abstract," *Hume Studies* 19: 217–22.

Norton, David Fate (1993b) *The Cambridge Companion to Hume.* New York: Cambridge University Press.

Norton, David Fate (2005) "Hume and Hutcheson: The Question of Influence." *Oxford Studies in Early Modern Philosophy* 2: 211–56.

Owen, David (1999) *Hume's Reason.* Oxford: Oxford University Press.

Passmore, John (1951) *Cudworth: An Interpretation.* Cambridge: Cambridge University Press.

Patrides, C. A. (1970) *The Cambridge Platonists.* Cambridge, MA: Harvard University Press.

Peach, Bernard (1971) Editor's Introduction, in Francis Hutcheson, *Illustrations on the Moral Sense.* Edited by Bernard Peach. Cambridge, MA: Harvard University Press.

Penelhum, Terence (1993) "Hume's Moral Psychology" in David Fate Norton (ed.), *The Cambridge Companion to Hume.* 117–47. New York: Cambridge University Press.

Popkin, Richard (1992) *The Third Force in Seventeenth Century Thought.* Leiden: E. J. Brill.

Postema, Gerald J. (1988) "Hume's Reply to the Sensible Knave," *History of Philsophy Quarterly* 5: 23–40.

Powicke, F. J. (1926/1970) *The Cambridge Platonists: A Study.* Westport, CT: Greenwood Press.

Prince, Michael (1996) *Philosophical Dialogue in the British Enlightenment.* Cambridge: Cambridge University Press.

Purviance, Susan M. (2002) "Ethical Externalism and the Moral Sense," *Journal of Philosophical Research* 27: 585–600.

Radcliffe, Elizabeth (1986) "Hutcheson's Perceptual and Moral Subjectivism," *History of Philosophy Quarterly* 3: 407–21.

Radcliffe, Elizabeth (1994a) "Hume on Passion, Reason, and the Reasonableness of Ends," *Southwest Philosophy Review* 10: 1–11.

Radcliffe, Elizabeth (1994b) "Hume on Motivating Sentiments, the General Point of View, and the Inculcation of Morality," *Hume Studies* 20: 37–58.

Radcliffe, Elizabeth (1999) "Hume on the Generation of Motives: Why Beliefs Alone Never Motivate," *Hume Studies* 25: 101–22.

Radcliffe, Elizabeth (2001) "Hutcheson's Moral Sense: Skepticism, Realism, and Secondary Qualities," *History of Philosophy Quarterly* 18: 57–77.

Rauscher, Frederick (2003) "Moral Realism and the Divine Essence in Hutcheson," *History of Philosophy Quarterly* 20: 165–81.

Roberts, James Deontis (1968) *From Puritanism to Platonism in Seventeenth Century England.* The Hague: Martinus Nijhoff.

Russell, Conrad (1990) *The Causes of the English Civil War.* Oxford: Oxford University Press.

Sayre-McCord, Geoffrey (1994) "On Why Hume's 'General Point of View' Isn't Ideal – and Shouldn't Be," *Social Philosophy & Policy* 11: 202–28.

Sayre-McCord, Geoffrey (1996) "Hume and the Bauhaus Theory of Ethics," *Midwest Studies in Philosophy* 20: 280–98.

Sayre-McCord, Geoffrey (1997). "Hume's Representation Argument against Rationalism," *Manuscrito* 20: 77–94.

Schauber, Nancy (1999) "Hume on Moral Motivation: It's Almost Like Being in
Love," *History of Philosophy Quarterly* 1999: 341–66.

Schneewind, J. B. (1996) "Voluntarism and the Foundations of Ethics," *Proceedings
and Addresses of the American Philosophical Association* 70: 25–42.

Schneewind, J. B. (1998) *The Invention of Autonomy.* Cambridge: Cambridge University Press.

Scott, William Robert (1900) *Francis Hutcheson: His Life, Teaching and Position in the
History of Philosophy.* Cambridge: Cambridge University Press.

Selby-Bigge, L. A. (1897/1964) *The British Moralists.* New York: Bobbs-Merrill.

Sewell, Tom (2001). "Hobbes and the Morality Beyond Justice," *Pacific Philosophical
Quarterly* 82: 227–42.

Siebert, Donald T. (1990) *The Moral Animus of David Hume.* Newark: University of
Delaware Press.

Spellman, W. M. (1993) *The Latitudinarians and the Church of England.* Athens: University of Georgia Press.

Stafford. J. M. (1985) "Hutcheson, Hume and the Ontology of Value," *Journal of
Value Inquiry* 19: 133–51.

Steward, John B. (1992) *Opinion and Reform in Hume's Political Philosophy.* Princeton,
NJ: Princeton University Press.

Stewart, M. A. (1994) "An Early Fragment on Evil," in M. A. Stewart and J. W. Wright
(eds.), *Hume and Hume's Connexions*: 160–70. Edinburgh: Edinburgh University
Press.

Stewart, M. A. (2001) *The Kirk and the Infidel.* Lancaster: Lancaster University Press.

Stewart, M. A. (2005) "Hume's Intellectual Development 1711–1752," in M. Frasca-
Spada and P. J. E. Kail (eds.), *Impressions of Hume*: 11–58. Oxford: Clarendon
Press.

Strasser, Mark Philip (1987) "Hutcheson on the Higher and Lower Pleasures." *Journal of the History of Philosophy* 25: 517–31.

Streeter, Ryan (1995) "Hume and the Origins of Justice," *Dialogue* 38: 8–14.

Stroud, Barry (1977) *Hume.* London: Routledge & Kegan Paul.

Sturgeon, Nicholas (2001) "Moral Skepticism and Moral Naturalism in Hume's Treatise," *Hume Studies* 27: 3–83.

Telfer, Elizabeth (1995) "Hutcheson's Reflections upon Laughter," *Journal of Aesthetics and Art Criticism* 53: 359–69.

Tiberius, Valerie (2000) "Humean Heroism: Value Commitments and the Source of
Normativity," *Pacific Philosophical Quarterly* 81: 426–46.

Tiberius, Valerie (2002). "Maintaining Conviction and the Humean Account of Normativity," *Topoi* 21: 165–73.

Voitle, Robert (1984) *The Third Earl of Shaftesbury 1671–1713.* Baton Rouge:
Louisiana University Press.

Weller, Cass (2002) "The Myth of Original Existence," *Hume Studies* 28: 195–230.

Winkler, Kenneth P. (1985) "Hutcheson's Alleged Realism," *Journal of the History of
Philosophy* 23: 170–94.

Winkler, Kenneth P. (1996). "Hume and Hutcheson on the Color of Virtue," *Hume
Studies* 22: 3–22.

Winkler, Kenneth P. (2000) "'All Is Revolution in Us': Personal Identity in Shaftesbury and Hume," *Hume Studies* 26: 3–40.

Wooton, David (1994) "David Hume, 'the Historian,'" in David Fate Norton (ed.),
The Cambridge Companion to Hume. 281–312. Cambridge: Cambridge University
Press.

Wright, John P. (2003) "Dr George Cheyne, Chevalier Ramsay, and Hume's Letter
to a Physician," *Hume Studies* 29: 125–41.

Index